THEORIES OF

PUNISHMENT

THEORIES OF

PUNISHMENT

EDITED BY

Stanley E. Grupp

Indiana University Press

Bloomington / London

Library of Congress catalog card number: 73-165047

ISBN: 0-253-35925-2

Manufactured in the United States of America

CONTENTS

Contents

THEORIES OF

PUNISHMENT

Introduction

"Theory of punishment" as used in this volume refers to the guiding rationale for dealing with the adjudicated criminal as implemented by the state's formal system of criminal justice. Punishment theory considers the various points of view regarding the desirable objectives of punishment and the rationale that should sustain the sentencing and correctional system.

Before considering this at somewhat greater length, it should be noted that there are several areas of punishment with which we are not concerned. We do not consider punishment in the interpersonal, informal, or the intrinsic sense, nor is attention given to the nature of punishment in primitive societies. Interesting and important as these areas are, they deal largely with subjects conceptually distinct from formal punishment theory, and can be handled more adequately if treated independently. An effort to combine these quite disparate areas not only would present insurmountable difficulties but also would result in attenuated content with respect to formal punishment theory.[1]

It is this writer's conviction that we do not give sufficient attention to punishment theory in the development, maintenance, and salesmanship of the machinery for the administration of justice. Although matters concerning punishment theory have a way of becoming abstract and difficult to discuss in ordinary terms, it is imperative that every effort be made on the part of *all* persons, those involved in the actual implementation of justice as well as the average citizen, to reflect on the meaning of punishment within the context of the philosophy of punishment. The punishment of the criminal and the objectives of the punishment are, after all, everyone's concern. Too often we circle around questions that face the issue of the theory of punishment, as we rush on to make changes and to innovate. The importance of the issue is nowhere better stated than in the observation attributed to Winston Churchill: "What is done to the criminal is a very accurate index to the quality of any civilization."

Some years ago, Paul Tappan observed that our "total [punishment] objective remains for the most part inexplicit and confused."[2] It would be less than precise, indeed, overly optimistic, to believe that the situation is very much different today. We are confronted with conflicting punishment ideologies. Too often, however, this conflict is submerged or unrecognized and is not brought to the surface for a healthy airing and open debate.

A parallel and reinforcing aspect of this situation is the existence of a high degree of public and individual ambivalence regarding punishment. Regardless of the position we take on the objectives of punishment we are apt to have strong misgivings. The sustained controversy over the death penalty is one case in point; the circular and erratic enforcement and expectations with respect to vice laws is another.

Still another factor contributing to the confused state of affairs is the sustained existence of public indifference and insensitivity to many phases of the crime problem. Viewed from the perspective of the entire machinery for the administration of justice, the result of this set of circumstances is that difficult, indeed, impossible demands are imposed upon it. In Tappan's words, "The incompatibles remain unreconciled but manage to persist, and thus measures of law and corrections are marked by paradox and inconsistency."[3]

Meanwhile, partly by design, more by default, and in response to pressures on legislators who are expected to initiate action to do something about the crime problem, we continue to pass criminal laws with drunken abandon as if the laws themselves had a sacrosanct or charismatic quality. Further, the passage of laws is too often done without asking whether or not it is reasonable to assume that the behavior can be effectively controlled by the system of criminal justice.

The confused state of affairs notwithstanding, we cannot hope to improve or ameliorate the situation—we cannot hope to make progress in our penal policy—without an open and sustained consideration of the issues and our objectives. The collection of readings in this volume is designed to facilitate this task.

Materials are organized around the classical theories of punishment: retribution, deterrence, rehabilitation, and the integrative theory. The focus of each section is on discussions which argue for, critically examine, or empirically investigate a particular theory. With a few exceptions we present each selection in its entirety so that the continuity of the author's reasoning is retained. While the points of view with respect to any one theory vary to some extent from scholar to scholar, each theory may be generally distinguished from the others in terms of its basic assumptions. Remove this support and the entire framework crumbles.

It should be mentioned at the outset that each theory exists as an ideal, as an aspiration which at most is only approached in real life. A given punishment theory stands as a model which is used as a point of reference for generating and evaluating punishment procedures. Also note that to some extent the several theories overlap, and any attempt to summarize them must of necessity do some damage to the total theme. However, we offer a few generalizing comments at this point as an introduction and as a way of raising questions, not as critiques or detailed statements of the particular theory.

RETRIBUTION

THE RETRIBUTIVIST defends the desirability of a punitive response to the criminal by saying that the punitive reaction is the pain the criminal deserves, and that it is highly desirable to provide for an orderly, collective expression of society's natural feeling of revulsion toward and disapproval of criminal acts. It is argued that this expression vindicates the criminal law and in so doing helps to unify society against crime and criminals. In a very real sense it *is* the retributive response which gives meaning to the label *criminal*, for it is this aspect of our response to the criminal which places him in a lower status than that of law-abiding citizens. Stated another way, *if* it were possible to remove the retributive response from our reaction to the criminal, would we not abandon the meaning that is conventionally attached to the label *criminal?*

Retribution must, however, be viewed within the cultural context. The punitive response and its interpretation are relative to time and place. What is viewed as a punitive response today may be viewed differently at another time and place. Today sustained solitary confinement or complete isolation of the criminal is generally viewed as extreme punishment. In 1800 isolation was seen as a vehicle for rehabilitation and a way for the criminal to repent and make peace with his God.

One need not argue, however, for extreme punitiveness in order to support the retributive position. It should be emphasized that today we seldom hear the argument that penal sanctions should be vengeful, cruel, or a means for giving vent to our purely emotional reactions. While we may reject cruel and extreme forms of punishment, is it not imperative that serious thought be given to how we can best provide for the retributive expression? Morris Cohen has observed:

> An enlightened society will recognize the futility of severely punishing unavoidable retrogression in human dignity. But it is vain to preach to any society that it must suppress its feelings. In all our various social relations—in business, in public life, in our academic institutions, and even in church—people are rewarded for being attractive and therefore penalized for not being so.[4]

Assuming that we should avoid vengeance for vengeance' sake, but that nevertheless the retributive demand needs to be legitimately recognized, there are still many questions to be considered. How do we measure the severity of punishment? A given punishment may have one meaning to one person and a quite different meaning to someone else. This is true for the punished as well as the punishers. Still another crucial question harassing us is the common phenomenon of sustained stigmatization, which is one indication of the demand for retribution. Is sustained stigmatization of the criminal inconsistent with the view that retribution should be tempered with restraint and understanding?

DETERRENCE

THE DETERRENT MODEL developed by the classical school of criminology during the eighteenth and early nineteenth centuries saw the overriding objective of punishment as the achievement of the greatest happiness for the greatest number. Deterrence is seen as *the* way of achieving this condition. Taking its departure from the rational view of man as a pleasure-seeking, pain-avoiding creature, the objective is to deal with the criminal in such a way as to serve notice on potential offenders. To this end the focus is on the assignment of that appropriate penalty, no more, no less, which will deter potential offenders from committing crimes. Emphasis placed on potential offenders is known as secondary deterrence, in contrast to the deterrence of the offender himself or primary deterrence.

It should be remembered that the classical deterrent model arose in response to the extreme individualization and capriciousness of punishment that had developed by the late seventeenth century. With a view to correcting this situation, to providing maximum protection for the individual, and to achieving the greatest happiness for the greatest number, the early defenders of deterrence proposed to deal with the convicted offender in an exacting manner through the application of a definite scale of penalties, a specific penalty for a specific crime. In addition, it is usually suggested that the optimum conditions envisaged under the classical deterrent model require both celerity and certainty in the apprehension of the criminal. All of these conditions are difficult, if not impossible, to achieve in today's society.

Difficulties notwithstanding, advocates of this position argue that while it is apparent all persons are not deterred, the deterrent objective, which in fact helps to support our entire structure of law enforcement, is still desirable. Regardless of the prevailing crime rates, it is assumed that many persons are in fact deterred; were it not for the operation of the deterrent machinery, the crime rates would be still higher. While there are certainly many who disagree with this position, it can be argued that deterrence is the primary purpose of the state's sanctions.

Given our tradition and historical development, if one chooses to cast aside or reject the deterrent theory he does so at some risk. The view of man as a value-oriented, value-choosing creature has deep roots. Surely we cannot deny that man does make choices. If this is true, then it seems reasonable to assume also that to some extent he weighs, correctly or incorrectly, the consequences of his behavior. And would this not then apply to choices to violate or

7

not to violate the law? Although extensive data are not available regarding the operation of the deterrent principle, we can point to some examples of persons who *have* been deterred—the decision to take special care to travel within the speed limit when we know that an aggressive effort is being made to arrest speeders. A somewhat different example is our ability to reduce car thefts by locking cars. It is still possible to steal locked cars, and some persons do; but others do not have the technical skills, and still others do not like the odds.

Many questions and problems relevant to the implementation of the deterrent theory remain and we have hardly scratched the surface in our efforts to investigate and to conduct research in this area. This is similarly true of the retributive theory. Because of certain biases which are inherent in the scientific outlook, social scientists have generally eschewed investigations relevant to deterrence and retribution.

REHABILITATION

DURING THE COURSE OF THE TWENTIETH CENTURY there has been an ascendancy of the rehabilitative theory of punishment. Today it is fair to say that on the verbal level an overriding emphasis is placed on this objective by correctional spokesmen.

The keynote of the approach is, of course, the individualization of punishment—perhaps we should say treatment—and working with the individual in such a way that he will be able to make a satisfactory adjustment, or at least a non-criminal adjustment, once he is released from the authority of the state. Since most offenders do return to society, and some never technically leave it, it makes good sense to work with the offender in such a way that he will not again be a criminal liability.

Defenders of the rehabilitative theory sometimes forget, however, that this objective of punishment is also an ideal. Some persons would have us believe that were it not for certain reactionary elements in our society—those defenders of retribution and deterrence who, it is claimed, block the complete realization of the rehabilitative ideal—we would make great strides in dealing with the problem of criminal behavior. At least for the present, however, we must question whether we in fact do have the knowledge necessary to make significant advances in this direction.

Some persons taking the rehabilitative stance assert that they are "anti-punishment"; they speak of the "crime of punishment" and further contend that the rehabilitative objective is not punishment. Consistent with the definition of punishment as the objective of the state's handling of the adjudicated offender, the "anti-punishment" point of view *is* appropriately considered under the rehabilitative rubric.

INTEGRATIVE

THE INCLUSIVE THEORY argues that it is desirable and possible to articulate a theory of punishment which integrates the several functions of punishment. Retribution, deterrence, and rehabilitation are all seen as objectives of penal programs. Proselytizers for this point of view argue that it is both realistic and reasonable to insist that the machinery for implementing punishment in contemporary society be called upon to achieve several objectives.

Punishment involves working with the offender in such a manner that he can be reassimilated into the community. Simultaneously, society asks that we treat the individual in such a manner as to effectively mitigate, if not completely satiate, the demands for retribution. Further, there is some expectation that the offender be dealt with so that his treatment will serve as an effective deterrent to potential offenders. No one argues, of course, that these demands exist or should exist in a balanced or fixed proportion for all crimes, and indeed they vary from case to case with a given type of crime. This is in part why some scholars refer to punishment as an art.[5]

The reasonableness of a particular theory of punishment depends on (1) the assumptions one makes about the nature of man, (2) the information one accepts as useful knowledge, (3) the kind and extent of knowledge one feels it is possible to achieve, and (4) an assessment of the requirements for implementing the particular theory, and of the probabilities of actually being able to meet these requirements.

Similarly it should be emphasized that specific techniques and procedures for dealing with the adjudicated offender make sense only within the context of punishment theory. Whether one recognizes it or not, the commendation or negative criticism of a particular mode of handling the offender emanates from the assumptions one makes about the objectives of punishment and the understanding he has of these assumptions and objectives.

Is a solution to the punishment dilemma possible? Can we reasonably expect to approach agreement regarding the objectives of punishment? Consensus may not be possible, but it is the responsibility of all citizens to reflect thoughtfully and intelligently on this subject. Someone has said that the meaning of a problem doesn't lie in its solution but in working at it incessantly. It seems well-advised to take a similar position with respect to the problem of determining the objectives of punishment and in deciding how they should be implemented. Punishment of the offender is a dynamic process that involves the continuous and careful assessment of our objectives and of the alternative consequences of a given judgment at any particular point in time. It is hoped that the collection of materials in this volume will facilitate this kind of reflection.

NOTES

1. For a very useful and interesting summary of the ramifications when punishment is viewed in the broader context, the reader should consult Alfred R. Lindesmith, "Punishment," *International Encyclopedia of the Social Sciences*, Vol. 13, David L. Stills, editor, The Macmillan Company and Free Press, New York, 1968, pp. 217–222.

2. Paul W. Tappan, *Crime, Justice and Correction*, McGraw-Hill Book Company, New York, 1960, p. 237.

3. Ibid.

4. Morris Raphael Cohen, *Reason and Law*, Collier Books, New York, 1961, pp. 60–61.

5. See, for example, Robert G. Caldwell, *Criminology*, Ronald Press Company, second edition, New York, 1965, p. 403.

RETRIBUTION

D. J. B. Hawkins

Punishment and Moral Responsibility

OUR NATIONAL RELUCTANCE to discuss abstract principles did comparatively little harm when there was a certain instinctive unanimity about sound fundamentals; in such circumstances a healthy moral instinct yields better results than an inadequate abstract theory. The man who merely knows that chicken is wholesome, as Aristotle remarks, is more likely to restore you to health than the man who knows that light meat is easily digested but does not know what kinds of meat are light. At present, however, when instinctive unanimity has disappeared, it becomes imperative to reflect upon abstract principles if we are not to submit to the casual influence of gusts of emotion. You can muddle through only with the aid of sound instincts; without them you make the muddle but you do not get through.

At present, then, the moral philosopher cannot but be concerned with the growing lack of recognition of moral responsibility and with the effects of this neglect upon the conception of punishment. If moral responsibility is a fact, it is a very important fact for those to consider who deal with the making and administration of the laws. Hence a moralist may be permitted to bring the abstract principles which it is his function to discuss to the attention of those who are concerned with their concrete application.

The plain man, if asked how punishment is justified, would reply that it is deserved, that a guilty act demands punishment. In other words, the theory of punishment which is assumed prior to reflection is a retributive theory. Nevertheless it must be admitted that there are considerable difficulties to be overcome before the

Reprinted from *The Modern Law Review*, Vol. 7 (November 1944), 205-208, with permission of the publishers.

retributive view of punishment justifies itself to reflection. To inflict suffering on an offender seems merely to be adding the evil of suffering to the evil of the offence, unless there be some ground other than the offence itself to make this reasonable. That, as we all know, is why many people have given up trying to find the ethical basis of punishment in its reference to the wrong act which is past, and seek it instead in the future effects of reformation and deterrence. A purely reformative theory, seeming at first sight much kinder than the old retributive view, commends itself easily to a vague moral idealism, and is perhaps now the predominant opinion among those who are halfway between the spontaneous reaction of the plain man and the analytic reflection of the moral philosopher.

Yet it has been clearly pointed out by many writers that the motives of reformation and deterrence are not by themselves sufficient to explain and justify punishment. If to deter possible future evildoers be sufficient reason for the infliction of suffering, this end could often be equally well attained by penalising the innocent, as in the shooting of hostages, or at any rate by punishing an innocent man who is commonly thought to be guilty. The reason why these acts are unjust is obviously because their victims are innocent. It follows that we cannot explain punishment without a reference to the past wrong act, and, if we discover what this link is, we shall have done justice to the retributive factor.

Moreover, a past wrong act is not only a necessary condition of the just infliction of punishment, but the extent of past guilt limits the extent of the punishment which it is right to inflict. If the motive of deterrence were alone taken into account, we should have to punish most heavily those offences which there is considerable temptation to commit and which, as not carrying with them any great moral guilt, people commit fairly easily. Motoring offences provide a familiar example. Few types of offence do more harm at present, yet, since no great moral stigma attaches to them in the public mind, people think little of committing them. A scale of penalties which could be justified on a purely deterrent principle would be generally thought excessive. This is plainly because it would not correspond with the moral guilt involved. A change in the public conscience on the subject would be necessary before the penalties for such offences could be acceptably increased.

When people speak of reformation as the motive of punishment, they usually fail to make the important distinction between reformation procured *through* punishment and reformation procured *in association with* punishment. The latter is not part of the punishment at all; it is the conferment of a benefit, not the infliction of an evil. The ministrations of the prison chaplain, for example, are not, or at least ought not to seem to be, part of the punishment. Reformation procured in association with punishment, while it is an eminently worthy aim, leaves the punishment itself unexplained.

Reformation, however, is really procured through punishment, when the delinquent realises that he has deserved his punishment and ought to amend himself accordingly. This at once obliges us to ask how punishment is deserved. We are brought up once again before the retributive factor.

The vice of regarding punishment entirely from the points of view of reformation and deterrence lies precisely in forgetting that a just punishment is deserved. The punishment of men then ceases to be essentially different from the training of animals, and the way is open for the totalitarian state to undertake the forcible improvement of its citizens without regard to whether their conduct has made them morally liable to social coercion or not. But merit and demerit, reward and punishment, have a different significance as applied to men and as applied to animals. A dog may be called a good dog or a bad dog, but his goodness or badness can be finally explained in terms of heredity and environment. A man, however, is a person, and we instinctively recognise that he has a certain ultimate personal responsibility for at least some of his actions. Hence merit and demerit, reward and punishment, have an irreducible individual significance as applied to men. This is the dignity and the tragedy of the human person.

We cannot, therefore, omit the factor of retribution if we are to account adequately for the punishment of human beings. Among modern ethical thinkers, Kant and Hegel, with their followers, deserve credit for having recognized this clearly, but the insufficiency of their explanations in detail has probably contributed to the neglect of the retributive factor. For Kant it is an evident moral principle requiring no justification outside itself that crime deserves punishment, and a punishment equivalent in kind to the evil done. But is the *lex talionis* thus evident? Although it has a certain plausibility in cases where crime and the customary punishment are similar, as in the requital of murder by capital punishment, it would seem that, if the principle were universal and necessary, we should demand that the mode of execution resemble the method of murder. It would seem to follow, too, that the proper punishment for a theft of five pounds is a fine of five pounds. Since these applications are very far from being evident, we can hardly erect the *lex talionis* into a first principle.

For Hegel the wrong act is a negation of right, and the negation has to be negated by the reaction of society in the punishment of the offender. The English Hegelians gave this formula considerable currency in this country. Bradley says that the criminal has become "the realization and the standing assertion of wrong," and "in denying that assertion, and annihilating, whether wholly or partially, that incarnation by fine, or imprisonment, or even by death, we annihilate the wrong and manifest the right."[1] Bosanquet, in the same way, says that "punishment is the 'negation' of a bad will by the reaction of the social will for good."[2]

This Hegelian theory is really excessively obscure. If you could bring the murdered person back to life by executing the murderer, you could truly be said to negate the evil act, and, if you can reform the criminal, you can truly be said to negate his evil will. But how the infliction of a punishment which neither reverses the evil act nor necessarily reforms the evil will can be said to negate the wrong done is surely beyond the comprehension of any literal-minded person. Such an assertion is the kind of thing which causes philosophy to be regarded as a species of poetry rather than of exact thinking.

If we look to the older tradition of mediaeval scholasticism for something more satisfactory, we are often disappointed. Scholastic writers too frequently content themselves with a vague statement, not unlike the view of Hegel, that, when a man has transgressed the order of justice, it is fitting that justice, or whoever embodies its claims and powers, should react to the disadvantage of the offender. This is a foundation for compensation, where compensation is possible, but compensation is not yet punishment. If I steal your watch and merely have to restore it, I am not thereby being punished. The law itself, in the distinction between civil and criminal proceedings, discriminates cases in which redress is sufficient from cases in which positive punishment is required.

Nevertheless a really adequate principle is to be found in St. Thomas Aquinas. This he expresses by saying that "natural equity seems to entail that a man should be deprived of the good against which he acts; for he thereby renders himself unworthy of it."[3] An unwary interpreter might be tempted to apply this in the sense that, if, for example, a man takes away the life of another, it is immediately evident that he should be deprived of his own life. But his life and the life of another are not in fact the same good. The good against which the wrongdoer acts, and of which he is to be justly deprived, must be his own good. Hence the real force of the principle lies in the consideration that wrongdoing is the misuse for an evil purpose of a power which belongs to man for the attainment of good. It is because a man has misused his powers that he deserves to be deprived of them or restrained in the use of them.

Is this not the genuine sense of retribution? In so far as a man has turned his powers towards evil, it is at once evident that he deserves to be restrained in their exercise until he has learned to use them rightly, or even, if the evil be irremediable, to be deprived of them altogether. It will be recalled that Plato, in his myths of judgment, takes a similar point of view. Imprisonment, in particular, is readily construed as a restraint upon the liberty which a man is misusing. Retribution, then, is not a crude tit for tat but a restraint put upon human activity which has been corrupted by being devoted to evil.

The full measure of reward or punishment due to a man for his deliberate actions and their result upon his character does not, of course, fall within the province of the state; this belongs rather to his Creator. But the state is entitled to take cognisance of the evil wills of its citizens in so far as they conflict with that establishment of justice in social relations which is the primary purpose of the state. Obviously where possible, it is better to reform than merely to repress. Practically, therefore, the reformative aim remains the chief consideration in the treatment of the wrongdoer, but what needs emphasis is that no one would be entitled to undertake the forcible reformation of the wrongdoer unless he were really a wrongdoer, unless he had by the misuse of his powers made himself morally liable to social coercion. Whatever new restraints are put upon him, and some restraint upon liberty is involved in even the mildest of reformative establishments, are penal measures which cannot be justified without regard to his past wrong act and its effects upon himself.

This is not, then, a plea for neglecting the factors of reformation and deterrence or for making punishment harder. It is a plea for the proper understanding of retribution as the primary ground of punishment and as setting the limits within which social coercion can legitimately be exercised for the purposes of reformation and deterrence. On a superficial view it seems kinder to think of reformation alone and to forget about retribution, but in the end this is to forget moral responsibility and to incur the danger of looking upon men in the same light as animals to be trained to any pattern which appears desirable. It is impossible to take a just view of punishment unless we remember that the normal adult has a certain ultimate responsibility for his deliberate actions and, if he acts wrongly, deserves his punishment. This recognition is due to the dignity of the human person.

NOTES

1. F. H. Bradley, *Ethical Studies,* 2nd ed., 1927, pp. 27–8.
2. B. Bosanquet, *Some Suggestions in Ethics,* 2nd ed., 1919, p. 195.
3. St. Thomas Aquinas, *Summa contra Gentiles,* lib. III, cap. 144.

K. G. ARMSTRONG

The Retributivist Hits Back

WHEN KINGSLEY AMIS, in his book *Lucky Jim,* wanted to sum up the intellectual outlook of Professor Welch's wife, whose actions throughout show her to be excessively conservative, stodgy, snobbish, authoritarian, and generally disagreeable, he spoke of "Her opposition to social services because they made people lazy, her attitude to 'so-called freedom in education,' her advocacy of retributive punishment, her fondness for reading what Englishwoman wrote about how Parisians thought and felt." This is interesting, for nowhere else in the book was punishment so much as mentioned. Amis uses advocacy of the Retributive theory purely as a symptom of a rather unpleasant, and certainly outdated, attitude, a symptom which his readers would surely recognize; and I think Amis was right—most of the people who read his book would understand the reference just as he intended it, would regard the theory as something which, if it is not dead already, certainly should be.

C. S. Lewis wrote an article[1] defending retributivism. He is not a man whom one would normally expect to have any difficulty getting material published, yet the article appeared in an Australian periodical because, he said, he could get no hearing for his view in England. He claimed it had become clear during the controversy over the death penalty that his fellow-countrymen almost universally adhered to a combination of the Deterrent and Reformatory theories of punishment. In the British philosophical world the position is apparently similar. J. D. Mabbott says: "In the theory of punishment, retribution has been defended by no philosopher of

Reprinted from *Mind,* Vol. 70 (1961), 471–490, with permission of the author and of the Editor of *Mind.*

note [for over fifty years] except Bradley. Reform and deterrence are the theories accepted in principle and increasingly influential in practice."[2]

"And," it may be said, "This is just as it should be in an age that claims to be enlightened. Retributive punishment is only a polite name for revenge; it is vindictive, inhumane, barbarous, and immoral. Such an infliction of pain-for-pain's-sake harms the person who suffers the pain, the person who inflicts it, and the society which permits it; everybody loses, which brings out its essential pointlessness. The only humane motive, the only possible moral justification for punishment is to reform the criminal and/or to deter others from committing similar crimes. By making the punishment of wrongdoers a moral duty, the Retributive theory removes the possibility of mercy. The only people who today defend the Retributive theory are those who, whether they know it or not, get pleasure and a feeling of virtue from seeing others suffer, or those who have a hidden theological axe to grind. In any case, the theory is not only morally indefensible but completely inadequate in practice to determine what penalty the criminal should suffer in each case. Finally, the theory can be shown to be wrong by such simple facts of language usage as, for instance, that it makes sense to say 'He was punished for something he did not do,' because, *inter alia*, the theory demands that to say a man was punished for a crime logically necessitates that he committed it. Historically, morally, and logically, the theory is discredited."

These, then, are some of the objections that have been urged against the Retributive theory of punishment. In my view they are all mistaken—either because they are based on confusions about what the theory is, or else because they spring from erroneous moral judgments. One charge, that the proponents of the theory are sadists or have a vested religious interest in it, I shall not deal with. For all I know it could even be true, but it seems irrelevant to the present discussion; philosophers, of all people, should surely be above using the ploy of analysing a man's motives instead of meeting his arguments. As for the objection that the theory is out of date, *i.e.* unfashionable, this seems so ludicrous philosophically that I would not have mentioned it at all if it were not for the unfortunate fact that it is the most common objection of all. I shall certainly not bother with it any further, giving the reader credit for being free from what Belloc called "The degrading slavery of being a child of one's times."

My aim is not to present, much less to establish as correct, a full-scale Retributive theory, or set of theories, of punishment. I want firstly to sort out the issues in this confusing and confused area, and secondly to meet some of the attempts to discredit retributivism which are made either by painting it, as I myself did in summary fashion above, as a repulsive doctrine which could only be held by the morally insensitive, or else by reducing it to a harmless platitude which we all accept (so that the conflict between it and other theories of punishment turns out to have been no more than a foolish mistake). Let us start the process of clarification by deciding just what is meant by a 'Theory of Punishment', and what it would be for such a theory to be wrong.

I

It soon becomes clear when one studies the contexts in which the phrase appears that there is not just one type of theory being invariably referred to. Usually a theory sets out to resolve one or more of three main problems, although all too often the reader is not told which of them is being tackled. Indeed, one is often forced to the conclusion that the writers are not clear on the point themselves, which has led to a great deal of confusion and many false oppositions between theories which are not simply different but which are attempting to solve different problems.

Problem 1: *Definition*

The first problem is over the meaning of the word 'punishment', and is thus a definitional or logical issue. We examine the way the word is used in ordinary language, the things to which it is applied, and try to produce some rule which covers all these cases and only these cases. Applying the same technique to many other words we would get a single unequivocal answer on which all users of the language would agree—in short, the definition of the term—

but in the case of 'punishment' there is no such universally accept-able answer, and so we may speak of a 'theory of punishment' in the sense of a claim that a certain definition exactly marks out the correct use of the term.[3] For such a theory to be wrong would be for it to mark out some range of things or activities not in fact ordi-narily referred to by the word 'punishment', or else to include only part of the proper range and/or more than the proper range. In this latter case we would probably say that the definition proposed was 'too narrow' or 'too wide', but the theory itself we would say was *wrong*, because it claims that the proposed definition exactly fits normal usage.

PROBLEM 2: *Moral justification of the practice*

The second problem that a theory of punishment may be try-ing to solve is 'What, if anything, is the moral justification of pun-ishment as such?' Why should it be felt that this particular practice requires moral justification, when in the case of so many other prac-tices—from warning to washing-up—we do not feel that the ques-tion even arises? Clearly because punishment involves the deliberate infliction of pain, *i.e.* distress of some sort, normally against the wishes of the recipient, and this is something to which there is a *prima facie* moral objection, the overriding of which requires justi-fication.

It is important to notice that the moral justification of a prac-tice is not the same thing as its general point or purpose, except in the eyes of those who have travelled so far down the Utilitarian road that they never question the means if the end is desirable. Every human practice that is not utterly random or unconscious has some point, but not all have, and many do not need, a moral justifi-cation. An act or practice may have a very sound point indeed and still lack moral justification, *e.g.* torturing prisoners to get informa-tion, so that to say that the general aim of the practice of punishing criminals is, say, the protection of society is not *eo ipso* to produce a moral justification of the practice, unless we assume that Bentham was right all the way. There is an ambiguity in a phrase like 'The general justifying aim of punishment',[4] between *why* we do it, and why it is morally permissible—if it is—for us to do it.

A theory dealing with the moral justification of punishment as such could be wrong in two ways: firstly the general moral theory on which it is based could be incorrect, and secondly the theory of punishment could be a misapplication of the general moral theory.

PROBLEM 3: *Penalty-fixing*

The third problem is this: which method or system of determining penalties for crimes is best? A theory of punishment dealing with this problem might better be called a theory of punishments, or a theory of penalties. The point of view from which the advocated method is said to be best varies; sometimes it is in the interest of society as a whole, sometimes of the criminal, sometimes of both. One thing these theories have in common is that they are not so much concerned with what is as with what should be the case. To be wrong, such a theory would have to be advocating a method of determining penalties which was actually *not* best, either because it was not best from the point of view considered, or because some other factor which ought, morally, to be primary had been overruled.

Of these three problems, then, one is definitional, one is concerned with ethics, and one is largely practical, but with important moral overtones. The last two are very commonly dealt with as one, but the distinction is important for reasons which will become apparent later in this article. Given this division of the problems of punishment, and the answering theories, into three categories, what of the attacks on retributivism?

II

IT IS GENERALLY CONSIDERED that certain phrases which crop up fairly regularly in ordinary discourse, such as the troublesome "He was punished for something he did not do," create at least a *prima facie* difficulty for Retributive theories, and a number of different solutions have been offered in recent years.[5] Because it seems to me that all these solutions are more or less mistaken, I want to look again at this issue in the light of the above analysis.

In the case of which of the three problems could a fact of language usage help to establish or prove wrong a theory of punishment? For the definitional problem it would clearly be relevant, and

I shall later examine the significance of a typical phrase. But can such a language fact prove anything about a theory which deals with the second or third problem, or, more specifically, can it prove such a theory wrong? I suggest that it can do so only indirectly.

Any attempt to solve the second or third problem must assume that the logically prior problem of defining the word 'punishment' has already been solved. Unless we know what punishment *is*, what it means to impose a penalty for a crime, we cannot even start to talk about what system of fixing penalties is best, no matter from what point of view we may be considering it. Similarly, we cannot decide what it is that morally justifies punishment until we know what it is we are trying to justify. If the definition of 'punishment' that these theories had worked with were shown not to be in line with usage then they would be wrong in the sense that they would have turned out not to be theories of punishment at all, but rather to be theories of something else. Incidentally, at this point we can already see where A. C. Ewing goes astray in his book *The Morality of Punishment*, for he starts with the assumption that, whatever it is, punishment is morally justified, and then rejects some definitions because he cannot agree that what they produce is morally justifiable (*e.g.* on p. 34). Clearly the logical order is first to decide what punishment is, *then* to decide whether this thing is morally justifiable or not.

But if the term 'punishment' *had* been correctly defined, is it still possible for a fact about usage to prove a theory dealing with the second or third problem wrong? I have already mentioned what it would be for such theories to be wrong in themselves; what, then, is the relevance of word usage?

Take the third problem. Settling what system of fixing penalties is best, no matter from whose point of view it may be considered, is essentially an exercise in practical reasoning. It is hard to see how the fact that the word 'punishment' is sometimes used in certain phrases could ever show that, say, the criminal was not in fact better off when his sentence had been fixed on such-and-such principles. Yet this is exactly what is required to demonstrate that a theory of punishment of the third type is wrong.

The position with theories of the second type is somewhat similar. The way ethical terms are used certainly can show that a general moral theory is incorrect, but this is not true of the way that non-ethical terms are used. Now 'punishment' is not in itself an ethical term: 'punishment', like all activity words, can occur in ethical propositions, but such propositions are not made ethical by virtue of *its* presence. Nor, if the general moral theory was correct, and, by hypothesis, the term 'punishment' had been correctly defined, could the theory of punishment be shown to be a misapplication of the general moral theory by some fact about word usage. But to establish the truth of this last assertion we will have to make a short excursion into the field of Ethics.

When it has been settled what it is for an activity to be moral or good (general moral theory), we still have to decide whether each particular activity, in this case the activity of punishing, is a case of a moral or good activity. The method employed to decide this varies with the general moral theory, but it will turn out to be one of the following kinds of procedure:

(i) An appeal to intuition in the broadest sense. To decide whether a particular type of activity is good, a duty, what one ought to do, etc., one has simply to reflect (not ratiocinate) on it and one can just 'see' the answer. (Moore, Ross, in fact the majority of recent theories.)

(ii) A factual calculation of the total amounts of pleasure and pain that the action causes. (Hedonistic Utilitarianism.)

(iii) (*a*) A check on whether God has told us, by Revelation, to do it. (The theory that Good is that which God enjoins.)

　(*b*) A check on whether the majority of the community approves of it. (The theory that Morality is social convention, *i.e.* Social Externalism.)

　(*c*) A simple statement of whether the speaker himself likes or approves of it (Subjectivism) and wants others to do so too (Stevenson, Emotivists generally).

(iv) Settling whether it is in accordance with Human Nature and Man's Final End, both by examining our internal, intuitive attitude to it and by reasoning from what we already know of Man's nature and destiny. (Thomist theory.)

(v) Checking it against a set of specific criteria of various sorts provided by the general theory for determining what is in accordance with the Moral Law (Kant) or what are genuine moral rules (Baier).

Now if we consider all these methods it can be seen that in no case could the theory of punishment (moral justification) produced by their use be upset by facts about the use of the word 'punishment'. Remember that the original data about what it is for an activity to be good, moral, etc., and what punishment *is* are, in each case, correct by hypothesis. In method (i) no further data at all are introduced, so there is no possibility of error through false information. In method (ii) the additional information is scientific, mainly psychological; it is about how men feel, not about how they use words. In method (iii) there is room for error over (*a*) what God *has* commanded, or (*b*) what the majority of the community *does* approve of—it is very doubtful whether one could make an error over (*c*) what oneself approves of or likes—but neither of these could be *shown* to be erroneous by the way the word 'punishment' is used in sentences not about Revelation or approval. In method (iv) an error could only come in through a false notion of Human Nature or mistakes about Man's Final End; but our ideas about Man's Nature and End are in no way dependent on the question of which sentences using the word 'punishment' make sense and which do not. In method (v) the possible sources of error will vary with the criteria put up by the general moral theory for determining whether an activity constitutes a breach of a genuine moral rule. However, the only criterion which could be shown to have been misapplied by our noting that it made sense to use the word 'punishment' in some given non-ethical sentence would be one which specified that this must not be the case, *e.g.* 'An activity, to be moral, must be such that the word signifying it cannot sensibly be used in such-and-such sort of non-ethical sentences'. Now, of course, no general theory of morals which would lead to the use of method (v) has such a criterion, and it is hard to see what reason there could ever be for introducing such a one.

We can see, then, that even if a theory of the moral justification of punishment can be wrong in the sense of being a misapplication of the correct general moral theory, whichever that may be, its wrongness can never be proved by the fact that it makes sense to use the word 'punishment' in some given non-ethical sentence. The stage of appeal to language habits has already been passed.

So far, we have established that while a fact about how the word 'punishment' is used might well show that a theory of punishment in the definitional sense was wrong, such a fact could not show that a theory dealing with the moral-justification or penalty-fixing problems had done so incorrectly, except in the sense that they had dealt with something other than punishment. We must now turn back to definitional theories of punishment, to see what precisely is the effect on them of the fact, if it is a fact, that it makes sense to say, for example, "He was punished for something he did not do".

Irrespective of which problem or problems it sets out to solve, a theory of punishment can usually be put under one of three headings: Retributive, Deterrent, or Reformatory. When the problem is to define punishment these theories provide roughly the following answers:

1. *Retributive:* Punishment is the infliction of pain, by an appropriate authority, on a person because he is guilty of a crime, *i.e.* for a crime that he committed. I do not intend to go into the question of just what constitutes an appropriate authority, because the answer would appear in all three definitions, and it is the *differences* between them, concerning who suffers pain and why, that I wish to stress here. Also, I use the word 'crime' deliberately, as it is ambiguous between an offence against a rule, the law, morality, or someone else's rights.[6]

2. *Deterrent:* Punishment is the infliction of pain on a person in order to deter him from repeating a crime or to deter others from imitating a crime which they believe him to have committed. I am here subscribing to Benn's view that deterrence of the person punished is not reform. Reform means that the man intends to avoid repeating the crime, not from fear of punishment but because he sees that it was wrong.[7]

3. *Reformatory:* Punishment is the infliction of pain on a person in order to reduce his tendency to want to commit crimes or to commit crimes of a particular sort.

I am not urging the acceptance of any one of these three definitions in preference to the others. I have set them out so that we may see what difficulties arise for retributivism in this area from the alleged fact that it makes sense to say "He was punished for something he did not do".

What does it come to to say that X makes sense, where X is some sequence of words? If we take it loosely, in what I shall henceforth call the weak way, it comes to saying that when we hear X we can understand what is being asserted by the speaker, and this does not necessarily imply that he is using all the words contained in X in their exactly proper way, but only that what is said is, so to speak, 'near enough'. Thus, for instance, "They half killed him" makes sense in the weak way, even to someone not familiar with the phrase as an idiom, although killing, strictly speaking, is a deed that allows of no degrees—a man is either killed or he is not. But we can also take 'X makes sense' in a tighter way, which I shall henceforth call the strong way, as indicating that each word has been used quite correctly so that an analytical substitution can be made for any term involved without revealing any contradiction, inconsistency, or other logical impropriety.

If 'He was punished for something he did not do' makes sense in the weak way, how does this affect the Retributive definition? It is fairly easy to see that it is not incompatible with the truth of the theory. The person who used the sentence could simply be asserting that someone who was not in fact the perpetrator of a particular crime had been treated as though he were, either because those in authority held sincerely though mistakenly that he *was* guilty of it or because they had deliberately tried to mislead the public.

If, however, the given sentence made sense in the strong way, it is equally obvious that the Retributive theory (definition) *would* be proved wrong. Since, on the definition it proposes, to say that someone was punished for a crime involves saying that he committed it, the Retributive definition would make "He was punished for something he did not do" a self-contradictory proposition. Thus *either* the sentence does not make sense in this strong way *or* the Retributive theory (definition) must be abandoned.

But any satisfaction which advocates of the Deterrent or Reformatory theories might feel over this incompatibility must be short lived, for if the sentence did make sense in the strong way this would be equally fatal to their own proposed definitions, although for a different reason. Here the difficulty lies not in ". . . that he did not do", but in ". . . *for* something . . . ". It is clear that the 'something' referred to is an act, a crime that somebody committed; but on neither the Deterrent nor the Reformatory theory is a man subjected to pain *for* a crime, but *to* deter him or others from committing crimes in the future or *to* rid him of the tendency to commit crime. The only theory with which the given sentence's making sense in the strong way would be compatible would be one which defined punishment as 'The infliction of pain on a person because a crime has been committed, whether by that person or not'. As far as I know, such a theory is not held by any philosopher in the Western World. That this should be so is, I suggest, strong *prima facie* evidence that the sentence does not in fact make sense in the strong way.

To recapitulate: Only theories of punishment of the definitional type could be affected by a fact of language not involving ethical terms. If it makes sense in the weak way to say "He was punished for something he did not do" then the Retributive theory (definition) is still tenable; if it makes sense in the strong way then not only the Retributive, but also the Deterrent and Reformatory definitions are shown to be wrong. Thus the alleged difficulty is either no difficulty at all, or else it is an insuperable difficulty for all three definitional theories. In neither event are there grounds in word usage for discriminating against retributivism *vis-a-vis* its rivals.

In passing we may note an interesting asymmetry between the sentence we have been discussing and the sentence "He was punished although he was innocent", where this is interpreted to mean not just that the man was innocent of the particular crime for which he was 'punished' but that he was 'punished' although he had not committed any crime at all. If "He was punished although he was innocent", interpreted thus, makes sense in the strong way, then whilst the Retributive theory (definition) is shown to be wrong the Deterrent and Reformatory theories (definition) are still viable.

The treatments of this question given by Flew and Quinton have already been effectively criticized by Baier[8]; but Baier's own analysis differs from the one I have just set out. In his view, the fact that it makes sense to say "He was punished for something he did not do" is *not* incompatible with the Retributive theory, because the theory necessitates as a logical precondition of punishment not that the person who suffers the pain *in fact* committed the crime, but only that he was *'found* guilty' of committing it. This 'finding guilty' can either be informal and implicit (as in the case of a parent punishing a child) or formal and explicit (as in the case of a jury announcing its verdict). But the fault in this solution is that whilst the amended Retributive definition it is based on includes everything that we would call punishment, it also includes things we would *not* call punishment. Merely to go through the moves of the 'game', as he puts it, is not enough to constitute a case of punishment .Take the case of a man who clearly did not commit a crime, and who is obviously not even believed to have committed a crime; if, despite his known innocence, a court went through the formal motions of a trial, including the moves of the jury uttering the word "Guilty" at the appropriate time and the Judge sentencing him, and if he was duly executed—would it be proper to call this a case of punishment? Or consider a schoolmaster regularly beating one of his pupils after saying the words "Bloggs! You were laughing!" (an informal declaration of guilt) although Bloggs never so much as cracks a smile and the teacher's eyesight is good—would we say Bloggs was being *punished* regularly? Would it not be more natural to say that these were cases of something other than punishment—victimization perhaps?

III

EARLIER, I claimed that a lot of contemporary writing on the subject of punishment is confused, much of the trouble springing from a failure to distinguish between the three separate problems involved. I can best support this claim by taking my examples from the two most quoted post-war articles on punishment.[9] Consider first this paragraph written by Flew[10] in criticism of J. D. Mabbott's article "Punishment": "The objection to saying that the *sole* justification for punishing someone is that he has committed an offence is that Mabbott and almost everyone else would allow that a punishment in certain circumstances was overdetermined in its justification—was justified twice over. Certainly: because, though Mabbott claims to 'Reject absolutely all utilitarian considerations from its justification', he is prepared to appeal to these to justify *systems* of punishment. But if a *system* is to be justified even partly on such grounds, some cases within the system must be partly justifiable on the same grounds: the system surely could not have effects which no case within it contributed."

Here Flew is confusing Problems 2 and 3. The point is that justifying *systems* of punishment, *i.e.* which method or system of determining penalties for crimes is best (Problem 3), is quite distinct from justifying, morally, the practice of punishment as such (Problem 2). There is nothing inconsistent in Mabbott's view that, whilst the moral justification of inflicting pain on people who commit crimes lies solely in retributive considerations, one system of fixing *what* penalties are to be inflicted for *what* crimes may be better than another from the point of view of its consequences on a particular society, *i.e.* on 'utilitarian' grounds. Flew has failed to realize that the word 'justification' is used in two quite different ways in the context of discussions of punishment, depending on which problem a theory is trying to solve. When dealing with Problem 3 a *system* is 'justified' precisely by establishing that it *is* most in the interests of some stated person or group that penalties should be fixed on the lines it prescribes. Of course it is always possible that some system of determining penalties which has been 'justified' in this way may be objected to on *moral* grounds if it goes against a principle arising from the solution to Problem 2, *e.g.* if a system of fixing penalties, 'justified' by its deterrent effect alone, resulted in overruling the moral principle (derived from a Retributive solution to Problem 2) that a very minor offence ought not to be punished more severely than a very serious one. But this is not surprising; if I say that punishment has a moral justification, I do not thereby resign my right to apply moral criticism to any system of fixing penalties. I might, for instance, hold that the practice of punishing is morally justifiable, yet at the same time say that the Nazi system of partly determining penalties according to the race of the criminal was immoral.

In his article "On Punishment" Quinton recognizes that theories of punishment may deal either with what punishment *is* or with the problem of morally justifying it as a practice (Problems 1 and 2). However, when he proceeds further he confuses the issue by misunderstanding retributivism in two ways. Firstly, he says that it is a logical and not a moral doctrine: "It does not provide a moral justification of the infliction of punishment but an elucidation of the use of the word" (p. 134). We have seen that this is true of the Retributive theory, as it is also true of the Deterrent and Reformatory theories, *but only when the theory deals with Problem 1*. If a particular Retributive theory deals with Problem 2, as it well may, then it *is* a moral doctrine, albeit one that Quinton does not agree with, *e.g.* "The moral justification of punishment is simply that the infliction of pain on those who have inflicted pain on others is a Good-in-itself, since it is a species of justice" would be a possible, though perhaps poor, Retributive theory dealing with Problem 2. Of course it is true that Retributive theories are very often concerned only with definition, but they can be, and sometimes are, concerned with moral justification or systems of penalty-fixing, *e.g.* C. S. Lewis's article "The Humanitarian Theory of Punishment" argues for a Retributive theory of penalty-fixing, and A. C. Ewing argues against such a theory, thus recognizing its existence.[11] Secondly, Quinton misunderstands retributivism when he says that it regards punishment as trying to bring about "A state of affairs in which it is as if the wrongful act had never happened" (p. 135). He criticizes this doctrine as only applicable to a restricted class of cases: "Theft and fraud can be compensated, but not murder." Here he is confusing *retribution* with *restitution*. If we recover stolen property, or if a confidence man repays the money he got by fraud, then although restitution has been made the retributivist would say that punishment was still due, *i.e.* the *loss* has been annulled but the *crime* has not. Only physically are things as they were before the crime. In the case of murder, restitution is clearly impossible—we cannot get back the life that was taken—but Retributive punishment is still possible. Further, the *lex talionis* is not an *extension* of retributivism, as Quinton claims, but a particular Retributive theory dealing with Problem 3 (penalty-fixing), and in my view a poor Retributive theory, as I shall explain later.

IV

WHAT OF THE OTHER CHARGES against retributivism? Is it, as is so often said, inhumane? This charge, if correct, would count as a moral objection against a Retributive theory of penalty-fixing (Problem 3). In the area of this problem it seems to me that Retributive theories stand up very well to comparison with purely Deterrent or Reformatory theories. If we penalize the criminal according to what he has done, we at least treat him like a man, like a responsible moral agent. If we fix the penalty on a Deterrent principle (*i.e.* What penalty given to this criminal, or class of criminal, will effectively deter others from imitating his crime?) we are using him as a mere means to somebody else's end, and surely Kant was right when he objected to that! And why stop at the minimum, why not be on the safe side and penalize him in some pretty spectacular way —wouldn't that be more likely to deter others? Let him be whipped to death, publicly of course, for a parking offence; that would certainly deter *me* from parking on the spot reserved for the Vice-Chancellor! And of course a deterrent will deter as long as the person on whom the pain is inflicted is *believed* to be guilty by those we wish to deter. It really wouldn't matter, if deterrence is our aim in fixing penalties, whether he was in fact guilty or not; as long as we kept his innocence a secret we could make a very effective example of him. This conclusion has been acted on by more than one government in our own times.

If, on the other hand, our aim in fixing penalties is the reform of the criminal—his *cure*, some might say—then the logical pattern of penalties will be for each criminal to be given reformatory treatment until he is sufficiently changed for the experts to certify him as reformed. On this theory, every sentence ought to be indeterminate—'To be detained at the Psychologist's pleasure', perhaps—for there is no longer any basis for the principle of a definite limit to punishment. "You stole a loaf of bread? Well, we'll have to reform you, even if it takes the rest of your life." From the moment he is found guilty the criminal loses his rights as a human being quite as definitely as if he had been declared insane. This is not a form of humanitarianism I care for. Nor does it become any more humane if we drop the word 'punishment'—it is still just as compulsory. C. S. Lewis wrote a sentence on this point that is worth quoting, even if only as a masterly piece of propaganda: "To be taken without consent from my home and friends, to lose my liberty, to undergo all those assaults on my personality which modern psychotherapy knows how to deliver, to be remade after some pattern of 'normality' hatched in a Viennese laboratory to which I never professed allegiance, to know that this process will never end until either my captors have succeeded or I have grown wise enough to cheat them with apparent success—who cares whether this is called punishment or not."[12] And, since prevention is better than cure, why wait until he commits a crime? On the Reformatory theory of penalty-fixing, it is the *tendency* to commit crimes that we want to eliminate, so if a man has the tendency let him be penalized before

33

the damage is done. Let him be penalized for what he is, not for what he does, and let him be made over into what the authorities (or their experts) want him to be.

The usual riposte to the sort of charges I have been making against Deterrent and Reformatory theories of punishment (penalty-fixing) is to refer back to a Retributive *definition* of punishment and rule out the charges as logically inadmissible.[13] "The short answer to the critics of Utilitarian theories of punishment," writes C. K. Benn, "is that they are theories of *punishment*, not of any sort of technique involving suffering."[14] But to say, to those who ask why we shouldn't punish the innocent when it would be socially useful, that "The infliction of pain on a person is only properly described as punishment if that person is guilty"[15] is to give an answer which is technically correct (for those who subscribe to a Retributive definition of punishment) but which misses the point behind the question.

Suppose the questioner comes back as follows: "All right then, if you want to quibble about terminological niceties when I'm trying to make a serious moral and practical enquiry, I'll rephrase my question. Why shouldn't we do to the innocent that which, when it's done to the guilty, is known as punishment?" At this point those theorists who offer a Utilitarian moral justification for the practice of punishing (*i.e.* a Deterrent and/or Reformatory theory on Problem 2) are in a difficult position; for on their view what morally licenses us to inflict pain on a man is not that he is guilty—that is merely what gives us a *logical* license to use the word 'punishment' to refer to the infliction of pain—but that there will be a socially useful result in terms of his reform and/or the deterrence of others, or, to put it more generally and in Mr. Benn's terminology, that the decrease in mischief to the public will be greater than the increase in mischief to those who are subjected to the pain. The only objection these theorists could raise would be that inflicting pain on the innocent is not in fact an effective deterrent. This empirical hypothesis is of very doubtful validity—it is not hard to think of cases where a very great mischief to the public might be avoided by condemning and executing an innocent man under guise of punishing him, *e.g.* who knows but that Klaus Fuchs might have been deterred from passing information on the A-bomb to the Russians if the Government had previously 'framed' some innocent scientist on an espionage charge and executed him in a blaze of publicity? In any case, most people feel that there is more against 'punishing' the innocent than that it wouldn't effectively reduce crime. Nor does our sense of outrage arise solely from the lying imputation of guilt, as Quinton claims, although this is undoubtedly a partial explanation. Surely our principal objection is to the deliberate infliction of *undeserved* pain, to the *injustice* of it, and this moral objection to taking Deterrent and Reformatory theories of penalty-fixing (Problem 3) to their logical conclusion can only be accounted for on a *Retributive* theory of the moral justification of punishment as such (Problem 2), as I shall show in a moment.

But before we leave the question of penalty-fixing it is worth asking why it should be so often thought that Retributive theories in this area are necessarily barbarous. The charge springs from the misconception, which I mentioned before, that there is only one such theory—the *lex talionis*. In fact, all that a Retributive theory of penalty-fixing needs to say to deserve the name is that there should be a proportion between the severity of the crime and the severity of the punishment. It sets an upper limit to the punishment, suggests what is *due*. But the 'repayment' (so to speak) need not be in kind; indeed in some cases it *could not* be. What would the *lex talionis* prescribe for a blind man who blinded someone else? Even in those cases where repayment in kind of violent crime is possible there is no reason why we should not substitute a more civilized equivalent punishment; the scale of equivalent punishments will, of course, vary from society to society. There is also no reason, having got some idea of the permissible limits of a man's punishment from Retributive considerations, why we should not be guided in our choice of the form of the penalty by Deterrent and Reformatory considerations.

In the area of the moral justification of the practice (Problem 2) a Retributive theory is essential, because it is the only theory which connects punishment with desert, and so with justice, for only as a punishment is deserved or undeserved can it be just or unjust. What would a just *deterrent* be? The only sense we could give to it would be a punishment which was just from the Retributive point of view and which also, as a matter of fact, deterred other people. "But," it may be objected, "You are only talking about *retributive* justice." To this I can only reply: What other sort of justice is there?

A vital point here is that justice gives the appropriate authority the *right* to punish offenders up to some limit, but one is not necessarily and invariably *obliged* to punish to the limit of justice. Similarly, if I lend a man money I have a right, in justice, to have it returned; but if I choose not to take it back I have not done anything unjust. I cannot claim more than is owed to me but I am free to claim less, or even to claim nothing. For a variety of reasons (amongst them the hope of reforming the criminal) the appropriate authority may choose to punish a man less than it is entitled to, but it is never just to punish a man more than he deserves. It is a mistake to argue—as Ewing, for example, does in Chapter II of *The Morality of Punishment*—that, on the Retributive theory, to punish a man less than the exact amount due is an injustice similar to punishing an innocent man. The Retributive theory is not, therefore, incompatible with mercy. Quite the reverse is the case—it is only the Retributive idea that makes mercy *possible*, because to be merciful is to let someone off all or part of a penalty which he is recognized as having deserved.

Retributive punishment is not revenge, although both are species of justice. Revenge is private and personal, it requires no authority of one person or institution over another; punishment requires a whole system of authorities given a right to secure justice. As members of the State, we surrender the right to secure justice ourselves to the authorities that the State appoints (though retaining, for example, our right to punish our own children). It is these State-appointed authorities, not ourselves, who must both punish malefactors and recover for us, by force where necessary, what a reluctant debtor owes us.

Finally, it is a distortion of the Retributive theory to say that it involves the infliction of pain-for-pain's-sake. On my understanding of the theory, pain (which the appropriate authority is morally licensed to inflict because it is deserved) is inflicted for the sake of all or any of a number of different ends. Amongst these are the protection of society, the reform of the criminal—which punishment *may* achieve simply by making the criminal realize the full gravity of what he has done, as a child realizes how serious his offence has been when he sees how angry it makes his father—and the deterrence of others. All these ends are in themselves both morally and socially desirable; where the infliction of pain is justified by desert, pain may be a morally permissible *means* to achieving them.

V

I DO NOT CLAIM to have demonstrated in this article that Retributive theories are the correct solutions to each of the problems of punishment. My aim has been to make clear the distinction and interconnection between those problems and to show that, if we are to reject Retributive theories, objections more powerful than those currently advanced and accepted will have to be found, since the current objections rest on confusions, or mis-statements of the problem, or mere prejudice.

Where the problem is to define punishment (Problem 1), some sort of Retributive theory now seems to be fairly generally accepted, although whether the offence for which punishment is inflicted is against the Law, some other set of explicit rules, or just the accepted moral standards of a community is still debated. Most of those who have examined the difficulty raised by the currency of the phrase 'He was punished for something he did not do' rightly conclude that the Retributive definition is more or less immune, even if their reasons for so concluding are faulty. That able philosophers should accept such unsatisfactory solutions to the apparent problem bears witness to the strength of their conviction that a Retributive definition is the right one.

The moral justification for the practice of punishment as such (Problem 2) is today sought almost invariably in Reformatory or Deterrent terms. For those who subscribe to simple Utilitarian theories of morals of the total-pain-and-pleasure-to-society type, this is of course automatic, and short of refuting their moral theory as a whole one cannot hope to shift their position on punishment. But most of those philosophers for whom retributivism is not ruled out *a priori* by their general moral theory—*i.e.* most of that great majority who do not subscribe to Hedonistic Utilitarianism—also reject or, more commonly, ignore the Retributive theory of the moral justification of punishment; and this despite the unique ability of that theory to connect punishment with the notions of desert and justice and, indeed, with the deep-seated general conviction we all have that to strike back and to strike first are two very different things, morally speaking, irrespective of the results they may produce or be intended to produce. This is surprising; for though I have not demonstrated that these considerations in favour of a Retributive theory could never be outweighed by any conceivable arguments for Deterrent and/or Reformatory moral justification, I hope I *have* shown that they are too important to be altogether overlooked, or even to be summarily dismissed. It may be possible not to be moved by them, but they must at least be faced. I have referred to three factors which tend to account for the cavalier treatment of retributivism in the area of Problem 2. First, there is the mistaken belief that a Retributive moral justification of punishment would make the infliction of pain on the guilty a positive, inescapable obligation, instead of merely creating a right to inflict pain which, like other rights, it may in some circumstances be foolish or mean to exercise. Second, there is the failure to distinguish between the moral justification of a practice on the one hand, and its 'general justifying aim' on the other. And third, there is the notion that if one concedes the definitional field to retributivism, there is no further area in which Deterrent and Reformatory theories can have a Retributive rival, that one can 'dissolve' the traditional conflict between the theories by declaring that 'Retributivism is not a moral but a logical doctrine'.

When the problem is to find the best system of penalty-fixing there is no doubt that a purely Retributive theory would have serious weaknesses, both practically, because it may be very difficult to decide which of two crimes is the more serious and thus deserving of severer punishment, and morally, because if Deterrent and Reformatory considerations are altogether ignored when the list of penalties is drawn up a great social good might be sacrificed in order to achieve a small improvement in the accuracy of a punishment from the Retributive standpoint. But, on the other hand, I have pointed out that the charge that Retributive theories of penalty-fixing are barbarous is based on the mistaken assumption that the only such theory is the *lex talionis*, and that a modified Retributive theory is perfectly possible, one which only uses Retributive considerations to fix some sort of upper limit to penalties and then looks to other factors to decide how much and what sort of pain shall be inflicted. Purely Reformatory or Deterrent theories of penalty-fixing, which lack that limit, run the risk of becoming far more inhumane than even a purely Retributive theory.

Finally, I have been concerned to show that only if one subscribes to a Retributive theory of the moral justification of punishment (Problem 2) has one grounds on which to object to taking the Deterrent and Reformatory theories of penalty-fixing (Problem 3) to their logical conclusion, *i.e.* to inflicting pain on the innocent as a deterrent to others and as a means to removing suspected criminal tendencies before they can be manifested in actual offences. Those who object that such action would not (logically) be punishment are not objecting to the action taking place but only to its being given a certain name. Yet surely most people feel that there is more difference between inflicting pain on the guilty and inflicting pain on the innocent than that one can and the other cannot be called punishment?

NOTES

---

1. C. S. Lewis, "The Humanitarian Theory of Punishment," *Twentieth Century* (Aust.), March 1949.*

2. J. D. Mabbott, *Contemporary British Philosophy* (ed. H. D. Lewis), p. 289.

3. The claimed definition that has attracted most attention in recent years is that given by A. G. N. Flew in his article "The Justification of Punishment," *Philosophy*, October 1954.

4. This is a key phrase in H. L. A. Hart's article* referred to below. [n. 13]

5. See especially A. M. Quinton, "On Punishment," *Analysis*, June 1954, reprinted in P. Laslett (Ed.), *Philosophy, Politics, and Society*; A. G. N. Flew, "The Justification of Punishment," *Philosophy*, October 1954; K. Baier, "Is Punishment Retributive?" *Analysis*, December 1955; and C. K. Benn, "An Approach to the Problems of Punishment," *Philosophy*, October 1958.

6. For discussions of what the offence is against, see J. D. Mabbott,*

* Also reprinted in this volume.

Mind, April 1939 and *Philosophy*, July 1955, and C. H. Whiteley, *Philosophy*, April 1956.

7. Benn, "An Approach to the Problems of Punishment."

8. Baier, "Is Punishment Retributive?"

9. Flew, "The Justification of Punishment," and Quinton, "On Punishment."

10. Flew, "Justification of Punishment," p. 301. Mabbott's article* appeared in *Mind*, April 1939.

11. A. C. Ewing, *The Morality of Punishment*. In a note published after this article was written, A. S. Kaufman points out that F. H. Bradley, at least, was a retributivist who was not only concerned with the definition of 'punishment', but had a Retributive view on the moral issue. "Anthony Quinton on Punishment," *Analysis*, October 1959.)

12. C. S. Lewis, "The Humanitarian Theory of Punishment."*

13. In an important and constructive paper, which did not appear until after this article was written, H. L. A. Hart has coined the name 'Definitional stop' for this sort of riposte. ("Prolegomenon to the Principles of Punishment,"* The Presidential Address to the Aristotelian Society, 1959–60, p. 5.)

14. Benn, "An Approach to the Problems of Punishment," p. 332.

15. Quinton, "On Punishment," p. 137.

* Also reprinted in this volume.

J. D. Mabbott

Punishment

I propose in this paper to defend a retributive theory of punishment and to reject absolutely all utilitarian considerations from its justification. I feel sure that this enterprise must arouse deep suspicion and hostility both among philosophers (who must have felt that the retributive view is the only moral theory except perhaps psychological hedonism which has been definitely destroyed by criticism) and among practical men (who have welcomed its steady decline in our penal practice).

The question I am asking is this. Under what circumstances is the punishment of some particular person justified and why? The theories of reform and deterrence which are usually considered to be the only alternatives to retribution involve well-known difficulties. These are considered fully and fairly in Dr. Ewing's book, *The Morality of Punishment*, and I need not spend long over them. The central difficulty is that both would on occasion justify the punishment of an innocent man, the deterrent theory if he were believed to have been guilty by those likely to commit the crime in future, and the reformatory theory if he were a bad man though not a criminal. To this may be added the point against the deterrent theory that it is the threat of punishment and not punishment itself which deters, and that when deterrence seems to depend on actual punishment, to implement the threat, it really depends on publication and may be achieved if men believe that punishment has occurred even if in fact it has not. As Bentham saw, for a Utilitarian apparent justice is everything, real justice is irrelevant.

Reprinted from *Mind*, Vol. 49 (1939), 152–167, with permission of the author and of the Editor of *Mind*.

Dr. Ewing and other moralists would be inclined to compromise with retribution in the face of the above difficulties. They would admit that one fact and one fact only can justify the punishment of this man, and that is a *past* fact, that he has committed a crime. To this extent reform and deterrence theories, which look only to the consequences, are wrong. But they would add that retribution can determine only *that* a man should be punished. It cannot determine how or how much, and here reform and deterrence may come in. Even Bradley, the fiercest retributionist of modern times, says "Having once the right to punish we may modify the punishment according to the useful and the pleasant, but these are external to the matter; they cannot give us a right to punish and nothing can do that but criminal desert." Dr. Ewing would maintain that the whole estimate of the amount and nature of a punishment may be effected by considerations of reform and deterrence. It seems to me that this is a surrender which the upholders of retribution dare not make. As I said above, it is publicity and not punishment which deters, and the publicity though often spoken of as "part of a man's punishment" is no more part of it than his arrest or his detention prior to trial, though both these may be also unpleasant and bring him into disrepute. A judge sentences a man to three years' imprisonment not to three years *plus* three columns in the press. Similarly with reform. The visit of the prison chaplain is not part of a man's punishment nor is the visit of Miss Fields or Mickey Mouse.

The truth is that while punishing a man and punishing him justly, it is possible to deter others, and also to attempt to reform him, and if these additional goods are achieved the total state of affairs is better than it would be with the just punishment alone. But reform and deterrence are not modifications of the punishment, still less reasons for it. A parallel may be found in the case of tact and truth. If you have to tell a friend an unpleasant truth you may do all you can to put him at his ease and spare his feelings as much as possible, while still making sure that he understands your meaning. In such a case no one would say that your offer of a cigarette beforehand or your apology afterwards are modifications of the truth still less reasons for telling it. You do not tell the truth in order to spare his feelings, but having to tell the truth you also spare his feelings. So Bradley was right when he said that reform and deterrence were "external to the matter," but therefore wrong when he said that they may "modify the punishment." Reporters are admitted to our trials so that punishments may become public and help to deter others. But the punishment would be no less just were reporters excluded and deterrence not achieved. Prison authorities may make it possible that a convict may become physically or morally better. They cannot ensure either result; and the punishment would still be just if the criminal took no advantage of their arrangements and their efforts failed. Some moralists see this and exclude these "extra" arrangements for deterrence and reform. They say that it must be the punishment *itself* which reforms and deters. But it is just my point that the punishment *itself* seldom reforms the criminal and never deters others. It is only "extra" arrangements which have any chance of achieving either result. As this is the central point of my paper, at the cost of laboured repetition I would ask the upholders of reform and deterrence two questions. Suppose it could be shown that a particular criminal had not been improved by a punishment and also that no other would-be criminal had been deterred by it, would that prove that the punishment was unjust? Suppose it were discovered that a particular criminal had lived a much better life after his release and that many would-be criminals believing him to have been guilty were influenced by his fate, but yet that the "criminal" was punished for something he had never done, would these excellent results prove the punishment just?

It will be observed that I have throughout treated punishment as a purely legal matter. A "criminal" means a man who has broken a law, not a bad man; an "innocent" man is a man who has not broken the law in connection with which he is being punished, though he may be a bad man and have broken other laws. Here I dissent from most upholders of the retributive theory—from Hegel, from Bradley, and from Dr. Ross. They maintain that the essential connection is one between punishment and moral or social wrongdoing.

My fundamental difficulty with their theory is the question of *status*. It takes two to make a punishment, and for a moral or social wrong I can find no punisher. We may be tempted to say when we hear of some brutal action "that ought to be punished"; but I cannot see how there can be duties which are nobody's duties. If I see a man ill-treating a horse in a country where cruelty to animals is not a legal offence, and I say to him "I shall now punish you," he will reply, rightly, "What has it to do with you? Who made you a judge and a ruler over me?" I may have a duty to try to stop him and one way of stopping him may be to hit him, but another way may be to buy the horse. Neither the blow nor the price is a punishment. For a moral offence, God alone has the *status* necessary to punish the offender; and the theologians are becoming more and more doubtful whether even God has a duty to punish wrong-doing.

Dr. Ross would hold that not all wrong-doing is punishable, but only invasion of the rights of others; and in such a case it might be thought that the injured party had a right to punish. His right, however, is rather a right to reparation, and should not be confused with punishment proper.

This connection, on which I insist, between punishment and crime, not between punishment and moral or social wrong, alone accounts for some of our beliefs about punishment, and also meets many objections to the retributive theory as stated in its ordinary form. The first point on which it helps us is with regard to retrospective legislation. Our objection to this practice is unaccountable on reform and deterrence theories. For a man who commits a wrong before the date on which a law against it is passed, is as much in need of reform as a man who commits it afterwards; nor is deterrence likely to suffer because of additional punishments for the same offence. But the orthodox retributive theory is equally at a loss here, for if punishment is given for moral wrong-doing or for invasion of the rights of others, that immorality or invasion existed as certainly before the passing of the law as after it.

My theory also explains, where it seems to me all others do not, the case of punishment imposed by an authority who believes the law in question is a bad law. I was myself for some time disciplinary officer of a college whose rules included a rule compelling attendance at chapel. Many of those who broke this rule broke it on principle. I punished them. I certainly did not want to reform them; I respected their characters and their views. I certainly did not want to drive others into chapel through fear of penalties. Nor did I think there had been a wrong done which merited retribution. I wished I could have believed that I would have done the same myself. My position was clear. They had broken a rule; they knew it and I knew it. Nothing more was necessary to make punishment proper.

I know that the usual answer to this is that the judge enforces a bad law because otherwise law in general would suffer and good laws would be broken. The effect of punishing good men for breaking bad laws is that fewer bad men break good laws.

[*Excursus on Indirect Utilitarianism.* The above argument is a particular instance of a general utilitarian solution of all similar problems. When I am in funds and consider whether I should pay my debts or give the same amount to charity, I must choose the former because repayment not only benefits my creditor (for the benefit to him might be less than the good done through charity) but also upholds the general credit system. I tell the truth when a lie might do more good to the parties directly concerned, because I thus increase general trust and confidence. I keep a promise when it might do more immediate good to break it, because indirectly I bring it about that promises will be more readily made in the future and this will outweigh the immediate loss involved. Dr. Ross has pointed out that the effect on the credit system of my refusal to pay a debt is greatly exaggerated. But I have a more serious objection of principle. It is that in all these cases the indirect effects do not result from my wrong action—my lie or defalcation or bad faith—but from the publication of these actions. If in any instance the breaking of the rule were to remain unknown then I could consider only the direct or immediate consequences. Thus in my "compulsory chapel" case I could have considered which of my culprits were law-abiding men generally and unlikely to break any other college rule. Then I could have sent for each of these separately and said "I shall let you off if you will tell no one I have done so." By these means the general keeping of rules would not have suffered. Would this course have been correct? It must be remembered that the proceedings need not deceive everybody. So long as they deceive would-be law-breakers the good is achieved.

As this point is of crucial importance and as it has an interest beyond the immediate issue, and gives a clue to what I regard as the true general nature of law and punishment, I may be excused for expanding and illustrating it by an example or two from other fields. Dr. Ross says that two men dying on a desert island would have duties to keep promises to each other even though their breaking them would not affect the future general confidence in promises at all. Here is certainly the same point. But as I find that desert-island morality always rouses suspicion among ordinary men I should like to quote two instances from my own experience which also illustrate the problem.

(i) A man alone with his father at his death promises him a private and quiet funeral. He finds later that both directly and indirectly the keeping of this promise will cause pain and misunderstanding. He can see no particular positive good that the quiet funeral will achieve. No one yet knows that he has made the promise nor need anyone ever know. Should he therefore act as though it had never been made?

(ii) A college has a fund given to it for the encouragement of a subject which is now expiring. Other expanding subjects are in great need of endowment. Should the authorities divert the money? Those who oppose the diversion have previously stood on the past, the promise. But one day one of them discovers the "real reason" for this slavery to a dead donor. He says "We must consider not only the value of this money for these purposes, since on all direct consequences it should be diverted at once. We must remember the effect of this diversion on the general system of benefactions. We know that benefactors like to endow special objects, and this act of ours would discourage such benefactors in future and leave learning worse off." Here again is the indirect utilitarian reason for choosing the alternative which direct utilitarianism would reject. But the immediate answer to this from the most ingenious member of the opposition was crushing and final. He said, "Divert the money but keep it dark." This is obviously correct. It is not the act of diversion which would diminish the stream of benefactions but the news of it reaching the ears of benefactors. Provided that no possible benefactor got to hear of it no indirect loss would result. But the justification of our action would depend entirely on the success of the measures for "keeping it dark." I remember how I felt and how others felt that whatever answer was right this result was certainly wrong. But it follows that indirect utilitarianism is wrong in all such cases. For its argument can always be met by "Keep it dark."]

The view, then, that a judge upholds a bad law in order that law in general should not suffer is indefensible. He upholds it simply because he has no right to dispense from punishment.

The connection of punishment with law-breaking and not with wrong-doing also escapes moral objections to the retributive theory as held by Kant and Hegel or by Bradley and Ross. It is asked how we can measure moral wrong or balance it with pain, and how pain can wipe out moral wrong. Retributivists have been pushed into holding that pain *ipso facto* represses the worse self and frees the better, when this is contrary to the vast majority of observed cases. But if punishment is not intended to measure or balance or negate moral wrong then all this is beside the mark. There is the further difficulty of reconciling punishment with repentance and with forgiveness. Repentance is the reaction morally appropriate to moral wrong and punishment added to remorse is an unnecessary evil. But if punishment is associated with law-breaking and not with moral evil the punisher is not entitled to consider whether the criminal is penitent any more than he may consider whether the law is good. So, too, with forgiveness. Forgiveness is not appropriate to law-breaking. (It is noteworthy that when, in divorce cases, the law has to recognize forgiveness it calls it "condonation," which is symptomatic of the difference of attitude.) Nor is forgiveness appropriate to moral evil. It is appropriate to personal injury. No one has any right to forgive me except the person I have injured. No judge or jury can do so. But the person I have injured has no right to punish me. Therefore there is no clash between punishment and forgiveness since these two duties do not fall on the same person nor in connection with the same characteristic of my act. (It is the weakness of vendetta that it tends to confuse this clear line, though even there it is only by personifying the family that the injured party and the avenger are identified. Similarly we must guard against the plausible fallacy of personifying society and regarding the criminal as "injuring society," for then once more the old dilemma about forgiveness would be insoluble.) A clergyman friend of mine catching a burglar red-handed was puzzled about his duty. In the end he ensured the man's punishment by information and evidence, and at the same time showed his own forgiveness by visiting the man in prison and employing him when he came out. I believe any "good Christian" would accept this as representing his duty. But obviously if the

47

punishment is thought of as imposed *by* the victim or *for* the injury or immorality then the contradiction with forgiveness is hopeless.

So far as the question of the actual punishment of any individual is concerned this paper could stop here. No punishment is morally retributive or reformative or deterrent. Any criminal punished for any one of these reasons is certainly unjustly punished. The only justification for punishing any man is that he has broken a law.

In a book which has already left its mark on prison administration I have found a criminal himself confirming these views. *Walls Have Mouths*, by W. F. R. Macartney, is prefaced, and provided with appendices to each chapter, by Compton Mackenzie. It is interesting to notice how the novelist maintains that the proper object of penal servitude should be reformation (p. 97), whereas the prisoner himself accepts the view I have set out above. Macartney says "To punish a man is to treat him as an equal. To be punished *for an offence against rules* is a sane man's right" (p. 165, my italics). It is striking also that he never uses "injustice" to describe the brutality or provocation which he experienced. He makes it clear that there were only two types of prisoner who were *unjustly* imprisoned, those who were insane and not responsible for the acts for which they were punished (pp. 165–166) and those who were innocent and had broken no law (p. 298). It is irrelevant, as he rightly observes, that some of these innocent men were, like Steinie Morrison, dangerous and violent characters, who on utilitarian grounds might well have been restrained. That made their punishment no whit less unjust (p. 301). To these general types may be added two specific instances of injustice. First, the sentences on the Dartmoor mutineers. "The Penal Servitude Act . . . lays down specific punishments for mutiny and incitement to mutiny, which include flogging. . . . Yet on the occasion of the only big mutiny in an English prison, men are not dealt with by the Act specially passed to meet mutiny in prison, but are taken out of gaol and tried under an Act expressly passed to curb and curtail the Chartists—a revolutionary movement" (p. 255). Here again the injustice does not lie in the actual effect the sentences are likely to have on the prisoners (though Macartney has some searching suggestions about that also) but in condemning men for breaking a law they did not break and not for breaking the law they did break. The second specific instance is that of Coulton, who served his twenty years and then was brought back to prison to do another eight years and to die. This is due to the "unjust order that no lifer shall be released unless he has either relations or a job to whom he can go: and it is actually suggested that this is really for the lifer's own good. Just fancy, you admit that the man in doing years upon years in prison had expiated his crime: but, instead of releasing him, you keep him a further time—perhaps another three years—because you say he has nowhere to go. Better a ditch and hedge than prison! True, there are abnormal cases who want to stay in prison; but Lawrence wanted to be a private soldier, and men go into monasteries. Because occasionally a man wants to stay in prison, must every lifer who has lost his family during his sentence (I was doing only ten years and I lost all my family) be kept indefinitely in gaol after he has paid his debt?" (p. 400). Why is it unjust? Because he has paid his debt. When that is over it is for the man himself to decide what is for his own good. Once again the reform and utilitarian arguments are summarily swept aside. Injustice lies not in bad treatment or treatment which is not in the man's own interest, but in restriction which, according to the law, he has not merited.

It is true that Macartney writes, in one place, a paragraph of general reflection on punishment in which he confuses, as does Compton Mackenzie, retribution with revenge and in which he seems to hold that the retributive theory has some peculiar connection with private property. "Indeed it is difficult to see how, in society as it is to-day constituted, a humane prison system could function. All property is sacred, although the proceeds of property may well be reprehensible, therefore any offence against property is sacrilege and must be punished. Till a system eventuates which is based not on exploitation of man by man and class by class, prisons must be dreadful places, but at least there might be an effort to ameliorate the more savage side of the retaliation, and this could be done very easily" (p. 166, 167). The alternative system of which no doubt he is thinking is the Russian system described in his quotations from *A Physician's Tour in Soviet Russia*, by Sir James Purves-Stewart, the system of "correctional colonies" providing curative "treatment" for the different types of criminal (p. 229). There are two confusions here, to one of which we shall return later. First, Macartney confuses the retributive system with the punishment of one particular type of crime, offences against property, when he must have known that the majority of offenders against property do not find themselves in Dartmoor or even in Wandsworth. After all his own offence was not one against property—it was traffic with a foreign Power—and it was one for which in the classless society of Russia the punishment is death. It is surely clear that a retributive system may be adopted for any class of crime. Secondly, Macartney confuses injustice within a penal system with the wrongfulness of a penal system. When he pleads for "humane prisons" as if the essence of the prison should be humanity, or when Compton Mackenzie says the object of penal servitude should be reform, both of them are giving up punishment altogether, not altering it. A Russian "correctional colony," if its real object is curative treatment, is no more a "prison" than is an isolation hospital or a lunatic asylum. To this distinction between abolishing injustice in punishment and abolishing punishment altogether we must now turn.

It will be objected that my original question "Why ought X to be punished?" is an illegitimate isolation of the issue. I have treated the whole set of circumstances as determined. X is a citizen of a state. About his citizenship, whether willing or unwilling, I have asked no questions. About the government, whether it is good or bad, I do not enquire. X has broken a law. Concerning the law, whether it is well-devised or not, I have not asked. Yet all these questions are surely relevant before it can be decided whether a particular punishment is just. It is the essence of my position that none of these questions is relevant. Punishment is a corollary of law-breaking by a member of the society whose law is broken. This is a static and an abstract view but I see no escape from it. Considerations of utility come in on two quite different issues. Should there be laws, and what laws should there be? As a legislator I may ask what general types of action would benefit the community, and, among these, which can be "standardized" without loss, or should be standardized to achieve their full value. This, however, is not the primary question since particular laws may be altered or repealed. The choice which is the essential *prius* of punishment is the choice that there should be laws. This choice is not Hobson's. Other methods may be considered. A government might attempt to standardize certain modes of action by means of advice. It might proclaim its view and say "Citizens are requested" to follow this or that procedure. Or again it might decide to deal with each case as it arose in the manner most effective for the common welfare. Anarchists have wavered between these two alternatives and a third—that of doing nothing to enforce a standard of behaviour but merely giving arbitrational decisions between conflicting parties, decisions binding only by consent.

I think it can be seen without detailed examination of particular laws that the method of law-making has its own advantages. Its orders are explicit and general. It makes behaviour reliable and predictable. Its threat of punishment may be so effective as to make punishment unnecessary. It promises to the good citizen a certain security in his life. When I have talked to business men about some inequity in the law of liability they have usually said "Better a bad law than no law, for then we know where we are."

Someone may say I am drawing an impossible line. I deny that punishment is utilitarian; yet now I say that punishment is a corollary of law and we decide whether to have laws and which laws to have on utilitarian grounds. And surely it is only this corollary which distinguishes law from good advice or exhortation. This is a misunderstanding. Punishment is a corollary not of law but of lawbreaking. Legislators do not *choose* to punish. They hope no punishment will be needed. Their laws would succeed even if no punishment occurred. The criminal makes the essential choice; he "brings it on himself." Other men obey the law because they see its order is reasonable, because of inertia, because of fear. In this whole area, and it may be the major part of the state, law achieves its ends without punishment. Clearly, then, punishment is not a corollary of law.

We may return for a moment to the question of amount and nature of punishment. It may be thought that this also is automatic. The law will include its own penalties and the judge will have no option. This, however, is again an initial choice of principle. If the laws do include their own penalties then the judge has no option. But the legislature might adopt a system which left complete or partial freedom to the judge, as we do except in the case of murder. Once again, what are the merits (regardless of particular laws, still more of particular cases) of fixed penalties and variable penalties? At first sight it would seem that all the advantages are with the variable penalties; for men who have broken the same law differ widely in degree of wickedness and responsibility. When, however, we remember that punishment is not an attempt to balance moral guilt this advantage is diminished. But there are still degrees of responsibility; I do not mean degrees of freedom of will but, for instance, degrees of complicity in a crime. The danger of allowing complete freedom to the judicature in fixing penalties is not merely that it lays too heavy a tax on human nature but that it would lead to the judge expressing in his penalty the degree of his own moral aversion to the crime. Or he might tend on deterrent grounds to punish more heavily a crime which was spreading and for which temptation and opportunity were frequent. Or again on deterrent grounds he might "make examples" by punishing ten times as heavily those criminals who are detected in cases in which nine out of ten evade detection. Yet we should revolt from all such punishments if they involved punishing theft more heavily than blackmail or negligence more heavily than premeditated assault. The death penalty for sheep-stealing might have been defended on such deterrent grounds. But we should dislike equating sheep-stealing with murder. Fixed penalties enable us to draw these distinctions between crimes. It is not that we can say how much imprisonment is right for a sheep-stealer. But we can grade crimes in a rough scale and penalties in a rough scale, and keep our heaviest penalties for what are socially the most serious wrongs regardless of whether these penalties will reform the criminal or whether they are exactly what deterrence would require. The compromise of laying down maximum penalties and allowing judges freedom below these limits allows for the arguments on both sides.

To return to the main issue, the position I am defending is that it is essential to a legal system that the infliction of a particular punishment should *not* be determined by the good *that particular punishment* will do either to the criminal or to "society." In exactly the same way it is essential to a credit system that the repayment of a particular debt should not be determined by the good that particular payment will do. One may consider the merits of a legal system or of a credit system, but the acceptance of either involves the surrender of utilitarian considerations in particular cases as they arise. This is in effect admitted by Ewing in one place where he says "It is the penal system as a whole which deters and not the punishment of any individual offender."[1]

To show that the choice between a legal system and its alternatives is one we do and must make, I may quote an early work of Lenin in which he was defending the Marxist tenet that the state is bound to "wither away" with the establishment of a classless society. He considers the possible objection that some wrongs by man against man are not economic and therefore that the abolition of classes would not *ipso facto* eliminate crime. But he sticks to the thesis that these surviving crimes should not be dealt with by law and judicature. "We are not Utopians and do not in the least deny the possibility and inevitability of excesses by *individual persons*, and equally the need to suppress such excesses. But for this no special machine, no special instrument of repression is needed. This will be done by the armed nation itself as simply and as readily as any crowd of civilized people even in modern society parts a pair of combatants or does not allow a woman to be outraged."[2] This alternative to law and punishment has obvious demerits. Any injury not committed in the presence of the crowd, any wrong which required skill to detect or pertinacity to bring home would go untouched. The lynching mob, which is Lenin's instrument of justice, is liable to error and easily deflected from its purpose or driven to extremes. It must be a mob, for there is to be no "machine." I do not say that no alternative machine to ours could be devised but it does seem certain that the absence of all "machines" would be intolerable. An alternative machine might be based on the view that "society" is responsible for all criminality, and a curative and protective system developed. This is the system of Butler's "Erewhon" and something like it seems to be growing up in Russia except for cases of "sedition."

We choose, then, or we acquiesce in and adopt the choice of others of, a legal system as one of our instruments for the establishment of the conditions of a good life. This choice is logically prior to and independent of the actual punishment of any particular persons or the passing of any particular laws. The legislators choose particular laws within the framework of this predetermined system. Once again a small society may illustrate the reality of these choices and the distinction between them. A Headmaster launching a new school must explicitly make both decisions. First, shall he have any rules at all? Second, what rules shall he have? The first decision is a genuine one and one of great importance. Would it not be better to have an "honour" system, by which public opinion in each house or form dealt with any offence? (This is the Lenin method.) Or would complete freedom be better? Or should he issue appeals and advice? Or should he personally deal with each malefactor individually, as the case arises, in the way most likely to improve his conduct? I can well imagine an idealistic Headmaster attempting to run a school with one of these methods or with a combination of several of them and therefore without punishment. I can even imagine that with a small school of, say, twenty pupils all open to direct personal psychological pressure from authority and from each other, these methods involving no "rules" would work. The pupils would of course grow up without two very useful habits, the habit of having some regular habits and the habit of obeying rules. But I suspect that most Headmasters, especially those of large schools, would either decide at once, or quickly be driven, to realize that some rules were necessary. This decision would be "utilitarian" in the sense that it would be determined by consideration of consequences. The question "what rules?" would then arise and again the issue is utilitarian. What action must be regularized for the school to work efficiently? The hours of arrival and departure, for instance, in a day school. But the one choice which is now no longer open to the Headmaster is whether he shall punish those who break the rules. For if he were to try to avoid this he would in fact simply be returning to the discarded method of appeals and good advice. Yet the Headmaster does not decide to punish. The pupils make the decision there. He decides actually to have rules and to threaten, but only hypothetically, to punish. The one essential condition which makes actual punishment just is a condition he *cannot* fulfil—namely that a rule should be broken.

I shall add a final word of consolation to the practical reformer. Nothing that I have said is meant to counter any movement for "penal reform" but only to insist that none of these reforms have anything to do with punishment. The only type of reformer who can claim to be reforming the system of punishment is a follower of Lenin or of Samuel Butler who is genuinely attacking the *system* and who believes there should be no laws and no punishments. But our great British reformers have been concerned not with punishment but with its accessories. When a man is sentenced to imprisonment he is not sentenced also to partial starvation, to physical brutality, to pneumonia from damp cells and so on. And any movement which makes his food sufficient to sustain health, which counters the permanent tendency to brutality on the part of his warders, which gives him a dry or even a light and well-aired cell, is pure gain and does not touch the theory of punishment. Reformatory influences and prisoners' aid arrangements are also entirely unaffected by what I have said. I believe myself that it would be best if all such arrangements were made optional for the prisoner, so as to leave him in these cases a freedom of choice which would make it clear that they are not part of his punishment. If it is said that every such reform lessens a man's punishment, I think that is simply muddled thinking which, if it were clear, would be mere brutality. For instance, a prisoners' aid society is said to lighten his punishment, because otherwse he would suffer not merely imprisonment but also unemployment on release. But he was sentenced to imprisonment, not imprisonment *plus* unemployment. If I promise to help a friend and through special circumstances I find that keeping my promise will involve upsetting my day's work, I do not say that I really promised to help him and to ruin my day's work. And if another friend carries on my work for me I do not regard him as carrying out part of my promise, nor as stopping me from carrying it out myself. He merely removes an indirect and regrettable consequence of my keeping my promise. So with punishment. The Prisoners' Aid Society does not alter a man's punishment nor diminish it, but merely removes an indirect and regrettable consequence of it. And anyone who thinks that a criminal cannot make this distinction and will regard all the inconvenience that comes to him as punishment, need only talk to a prisoner or two to find how sharply they resent these wanton additions to a punishment which by itself they will accept as just. Macartney's chapter on "Food" in the book quoted above is a good illustration of this point, as are also his comments on Clayton's administration. "To keep a man in prison for many years at considerable expense and then to free him charged to the eyes with uncontrollable venom and hatred generated by the treatment he has received in gaol, does not appear to be sensible." Clayton "endeavoured to send a man out of prison in a reasonable state of mind. 'Well, I've done my time. They were not too bad to me. Prison is prison and not a bed of roses. Still they didn't rub it in . . .'" (p. 152). This, "reasonable state of mind" is one in which a prisoner on release feels he has been punished but not *additionally* insulted or ill-treated. I feel convinced that penal reformers would meet with even more support if they were clear that they were *not* attempting to alter the system of punishment but to give its victims "fair play." We have no more right to starve a convict than to starve an animal. We have no more right to keep a convict in a Dartmoor cell "down which the water trickles night and day" (p. 258) than we have to keep a child in such a place. If our reformers really want to alter the system of punishment, let them come out clearly with their alternative and preach, for instance, that no human being is responsible for any wrong-doing, that all the blame is on society, that curative or protective measures should be adopted, forcibly if necessary, as they are with infection or insanity. Short of this let them admit that the essence of prison is deprivation of liberty for the breaking of law, and that deprivation of food or of health or of books is unjust. And if our sentimentalists cry "coddling of prisoners," let us ask them also to come out clearly into the open and incorporate whatever starvation and disease and brutality they think necessary *into the sentences they propose.*[3] If it is said that some prisoners will prefer such reformed prisons, with adequate food and aired cells, to the outer world, we may retort that their numbers are probably not greater than those of the masochists who like to be flogged. Yet we do not hear the same "coddling" critics suggest abolition of the lash on the grounds that some criminals may like it. Even if the abolition from our prisons of all maltreatment other than that imposed by law results in a few down-and-outs breaking a window (as O. Henry's hero did) to get a night's lodging, the country will lose less than she does by her present method of sending out her discharged convicts "charged with venom and hatred" because of the additional and uncovenanted "rubbing it in" which they have received.

I hope I have established both the theoretical importance and the practical value of distinguishing between penal reform as we know and approve it—that reform which alters the accompaniments of punishment without touching its essence—and those attacks on punishment itself which are made not only by reformers who regard criminals as irresponsible and in need of treatment, but also by every judge who announces that he is punishing a man to deter others or to protect society, and by every juryman who is moved to his decision by the moral baseness of the accused rather than by his legal guilt.

J. D. Mabbott

NOTES

1. A. C. Ewing, *The Morality of Punishment*, p. 66.
2. Lenin, *The State and Revolution* (Eng. Trans.), p. 93. Original italics.
3. "One of the minor curiosities of jail life was that they quickly provided you with a hundred worries which left you no time or energy for worrying about your sentence, long or short. . . . Rather as if you were thrown into a fire with spikes in it, and the spikes hurt you so badly that you forget about the fire. But then your punishment would *be* the spikes not the fire. Why did they pretend it was only the fire, when they knew very well about the spikes?" (From *Lifer*, by Jim Phelan, p. 40.)

C. W. K. MUNDLE

Punishment and Desert

MY AIM IS TO TRY to do justice to the so-called retributive theory of punishment, and to discuss en route the original features of the accounts of punishment advanced by Dr. A. C. Ewing[1] and Mr. J. D. Mabbott.[2] In section I, I shall examine Ewing's attempt to provide a compromise between retributive and utilitarian principles. In section II, I shall give my own analysis of what I take to be the essentials of the traditional retributive theory, and shall unfold the implications of this analysis by showing how it renders irrelevant various criticisms which have been considered decisive. In Section III, I shall examine what seems to me the most formidable objection to the traditional retributive theory, the difficulty of applying it to punishment by the State, and, after rejecting Mabbott's conclusions, I shall try to solve this problem. In the last section, I shall offer some reasons for accepting my version of the retributive theory.

I

EWING PRESENTS his own theory after examining in turn each of the traditional theories of punishment—Retributive, Deterrent and Reformatory—and dismissing the claim of each to provide an adequate solution. His own theory, developed in chapter IV, is based on what he calls the 'educative function' of punishment, meaning by this its effectiveness in promoting the moral education of the community. This theory fills a gap between the reformatory and deterrent theo-

Reprinted from *Philosophical Quarterly*, Vol. 4, No. 16 (1954), 216–228, with permission of the author and of the publishers.

ries, as these are usually conceived and as they are defined by Ewing; for 'reformatory' is used to refer to the effects of punishment in promoting the moral education of the person(s) punished; 'deterrent' to refer to effects on other members of the community. Ewing's distinction between the deterrent and educative functions is that punishment is deterrent insofar as it makes people refrain from wrong actions through fear of punishment, and is educative insofar as it makes them refrain from such actions because they are thought wrong. In support of his view that a penal system has an educative influence, he argues that people tend to divide the actions they believe to be wrong into two classes— 'wrong' and 'very wrong indeed'; and that if a certain kind of wrong action is made punishable by law, this fact tends to make people put it into the latter class and regard it as something which 'simply must not be done'. Ewing attaches great importance to this function of punishment. He writes: 'The moral education of the community is a very important object indeed, and if it is desirable for the attainment of this object that crimes should be "annulled" by punishment, then surely we have found a fresh purpose to justify the latter' (p. 102). He even speaks of such moral improvement as being the 'special function' of punishment, and says: 'The moral object of punishment as such is to make people think of a certain kind of act as very bad' (p. 104). But although, in Ewing's view, the educative function is of primary importance, he finds a place in his theory for the claims of each of the traditional theories. 'The "educative" function of punishment must not be treated as the only one, but requires to be supplemented by the ordinary reformatory and deterrent views' (p. 120). Ewing's method of coming to terms with the retributive theory is probably the most original part of his theory. He rejects the retributive principle that it is fitting that a person guilty of a moral offence should suffer for it, that an offender *deserves* to suffer for his offence. In place of this principle he substitutes the following propositions—(*a*) that it is fitting that we should disapprove of moral badness, and (*b*) that the infliction of pain is 'a suitable way of expressing' our disapproval. Ewing maintains that the ideal state of affairs would be one in which the good effects normally produced by punishment could be produced by expressing disapproval without inflicting pain; and this ideal, he points out, may be progressively approached in practice, for the more sensitive we become to the disapproval of others, the less the pain which need be inflicted to produce the desired effects.

Ewing considers that this solution incorporates what is true and important in the retributive theory. 'But,' he says, 'our view still differs from the retributive theory, as usually interpreted, for

(1) It holds the valuable element in punishment to be not the pain inflicted in proportion to desert but rather the moral disapproval implied thereby. . . .

(2) Without denying the intrinsic value of this attitude of disapproval or even of its expression in punishment, it justifies punishment rather as a means to good than as an end-in-itself. Punishment is valuable not chiefly because it expresses a right attitude of moral disapproval but because it has good consequences' (p. 109–110).

One obvious criticism of Ewing's solution is that he is exaggerating the importance of the educative function of punishment. It is understandable that he should lay stress on this function, since it had not usually been emphasised by philosophers of the utilitarian school. I can, however, see no reason for describing it as 'the moral object' or 'special function' of punishment. We may agree that the moral education of the community is a very important object, but it seems debatable whether it is more important than those stressed in the deterrent theory—protecting the life, liberty and property of law-abiding people, or maintaining law and order. The achievement of these objects is after all necessary for the existence of a civilised society. Moreover, the efficacy of a penal system in promoting the moral education of the community seems much more uncertain than its efficacy in deterring anti-social behaviour through fear of penalties. I do not wish to dispute the contention (made previously by Rashdall[3]) that a penal system has a considerable influence on conventional estimates of the relative wrongness of different kinds of actions; but I do not understand why people should be said to be 'morally improved' if they come to regard an action as morally worse *solely* because it is made punishable by law, or because the penalty is increased. Presumably the purposes of moral education are to convey the reasons why certain actions are wrong and to strengthen the moral motive. The promulgation of a new penal law may further the first purpose *if* it is accompanied by an explanation of the harm caused by the prohibited behaviour. But in that case it is the explanation, not the threat of penalties, which performs the educative function. Concerning the second purpose of moral education, Ewing concedes that 'men commit crimes as a rule not because they do not know they are wrong, but because the consciousness of their wrongness is lacking in the power to influence action' (p. 100). Can we then have any confidence that the threat of punishment strengthens the moral motive and does not merely provide a non-moral motive for avoiding the proscribed actions? It is, I imagine, on account of such difficulties that utilitarian philosophers have not usually stressed the 'educative' function of punishment, or distinguished it sharply from the deterrent function.

I do not propose to spend more time discussing the relative importance of the reformatory, deterrent and educative effects of punishment. We can readily understand the fact that practical people are often preoccupied with one or other of these functions (e.g. administrators with the prevention of crime, social workers with reform of wayward individuals) and are consequently inclined to justify punishments solely or primarily in terms of one such function. But, from a philosophical standpoint, reformatory, deterrent and educative theories of punishment are merely variations on the utilitarian theme. On utilitarian principles, the question whether a particular punishment, or system of punishments, is justified would depend on the *net* value of *all* its consequences. (And, incidentally, a penal system has consequences of social importance which are not usually taken into account by utilitarian philosophers, e.g. its economic effects on the level of employment, wages, etc.). The basic controversy is between those who maintain that punishment is to be justified by the value of its effects and the defenders of the retributive theory who deny this. Here Ewing attempts to compromise, by saying that punishment is justified partly because it expresses a right attitude of disapproval, but chiefly because it has good consequences.

Now we must keep in mind the reason why moralists have felt that punishment requires to be justified, namely the fact that punishment may be said to involve the 'deliberate infliction of pain'. This phrase suggests pictures of floggings or thumbscrews, so it is important to remember that the pain in question may, and usually does, consist mainly in the frustration of a person's desires, resulting from unwelcome restrictions on his liberty. In most contexts one could substitute 'constraint' or 'curtailment of rights or privileges' for 'infliction of pain' or 'making (a person) suffer'. Such a substitution would be inappropriate in cases of corporal punishment or the death-penalty, but the question whether penalties of these kinds are justifiable is independent of the question whether we should accept a utilitarian or a retributive theory of punishment. Now we would all, I think, admit that we have a duty not to inflict pain deliberately on another person; but we should also agree that this is not an unconditioned duty, since some other duty may provide a good or sufficient reason for inflicting pain. No one would deny that a sufficient reason for inflicting pain on a person may be provided by the fact that it is necessary for his own welfare or for that of others. Consider the things dentists do in the interests of the patient, or the unpleasant quarantine restrictions that are imposed on infectious people in the interests of others. The controversial question is whether the fact that a person has committed a moral offence constitutes a sufficient reason for inflicting pain on him. Though Ewing does not raise this question in this form, it seems clear from what he does say that he would answer this question in the negative. This is, I think, the main point of disagreement between Ewing and defenders of the retributive theory. Ewing attempts to conciliate the retributionists by conceding that punishment is justified *partly* on retributive (though chiefly on utilitarian) grounds. I am very doubtful, however, whether his modification of the retributive theory leaves this compromise open to him.

As we have seen, Ewing rejects the principle that it is fitting (i.e. morally fitting or right) that a person who commits a moral offence should be made to suffer solely on that account. He replaces this with the claims (*a*) that it is fitting that we should disapprove of moral badness, and (*b*) that the infliction of pain is a suitable way of expressing our disapproval. Ewing clearly intends (*a*) to be an ethical proposition, 'fitting' meaning morally fitting or right. The retributionist would have no complaint if (*b*) were also to be interpreted as an ethical proposition, namely, that it is morally fitting that we should express disapproval by the infliction of pain. In that case (*a*) and (*b*) would together imply the proposition they were introduced to replace. Ewing, however, intends (*b*) to describe a natural phenomenon—the fact that all or most human beings have a propensity to express disapproval by inflicting pain. This seems clear from his statement 'all my view presupposes is that in a given society a certain amount of pain is a suitable way of expressing a certain degree of disapproval, *just as one tone of voice may be a more suitable way of expressing it than another*' (p. 105, *my italics*). But on this interpretation the conjunction of (*a*) and (*b*) does not imply that punishment is morally justifiable. Given that we ought to disapprove of wrong-doing, and that we have a *natural inclination* to express our disapproval by inflicting pain, this does not warrant the conclusion that this way of expressing disapproval is morally permissible. For all that Ewing has said, the inclination in question might be one that we ought to inhibit, unless utilitarian considerations justify its expression. In view of this, Ewing ought surely to conclude that punishment is justifiable *solely* on utilitarian grounds.

Ewing makes another apparent concession to the retributive theory when he says that 'punishment implies guilt and must be retrospective, insofar as it is inflicted because of a past offence' (p. 44). He does not, however, treat this statement as a tautology, as I think it is. He says, for example: 'If the pain of punishment is educative, why not inflict it on the innocent? The answer is: because it is educative only for the guilty' (p. 91); and he proceeds to give arguments in support of this last contention. But surely such arguments are superfluous. All one need say in answer to his question is that to speak of 'punishing the innocent' is a contradiction in terms, *unless* it means 'inflicting pain on people because they are mistakenly believed to have committed an offence, or on the pretext that they have done so'. In that case the word 'punishing' is being used to mean 'intending (or pretending) to punish'. This view is confirmed by the fact that the O.E.D. defines 'punish' as 'to cause (an offender) to suffer for an offence'. Someone might protest that this definition is too narrow on the grounds that people often speak of punishing animals and infants, which are not deemed to be morally or legally accountable. I doubt, however, whether people who use 'punish' in such contexts intend to depart from the O.E.D. definition. Parents and animal-lovers often display a surprising confidence regarding the knowledge of their charges—'he knows', they will say, 'that he ought not to play with the poker (bring bones into the dining-room)'. If such people were persuaded to regard the chastising of infants or animals merely as a mechanism for inculcating socially desirable habits, merely as a process of 'conditioning', they would, I think, agree that their use of 'punish' was inappropriate, or at any rate metaphorical. Utilitarian philosophers are of course at liberty to recommend that we redefine 'punishment', e.g. as 'infliction of pain in order to inculcate socially desirable habits' or as 'infliction of pain in order to promote happiness'. But it is not difficult to show that such definitions do not correspond to current usage. The former definition is disposed of by the fact that we describe as a punishment the imprisonment of a hardened criminal, and even if no one believes that the sentence will improve his habits, we regard such punishment as justifiable; the latter by the fact that we do not regard the pain inflicted by a dentist as a punishment.

If the statement that punishment must be inflicted for a past offence is warranted on purely linguistic grounds, it contributes nothing to settling our ethical problem, concerning the *justification* of punishment. A utilitarian may accept the O.E.D. definition and still maintain that punishment can only be justified by the value of its after-effects. On the other hand, the meaning of 'punishment' may change; a time may come when its root meaning is, e.g., 'infliction of pain to inculcate desirable habits'. This eventuality would render it improper to call the retributive theory 'a theory of *punishment*', but the moral principles on which this theory is based would not thereby be invalidated.

II

I SHALL NOW OFFER an analysis of the retributive theory. It is doubtless true that some of its defenders have meant more by 'retribution' than is involved in my analysis, but I feel sure that none of them have meant less. If anyone considers that my analysis omits any essential element of the traditional theory, I should be happy to call my own account 'a moral desert theory'. The theory to be discussed involves three elements, two ethical claims and a verbal recommendation:

Claim 1, that the fact that a person has committed a moral offence provides a sufficient reason for his being made to suffer;

Claim 2 (or 'the principle of proportion') that if (or when) people are made to suffer for their offences, the suffering imposed ought to be proportionate to the moral gravity of their offences;

and *the verbal recommendation* that 'punishment' should be applied only to cases in which a person is made to suffer because (for the reason that) he deserves it on account of a moral offence.

My reasons for formulating the retributive theory in this way will, I hope, become clear in the ensuing discussion. The first points to notice are:

(i) that claims 1 and 2 are not analytic propositions, since they can be denied without contradiction, and the question whether they ought to be accepted cannot be settled simply by studying linguistic usage;

(ii) that although claims 1 and 2 are not usually clearly distinguished, they ought to be distinguished in ethical discussions, since to accept either claim does not commit us to accepting the other;

(iii) that claims 1 and 2 together provide an explication of the concept of *moral desert*;

(iv) that even if claims 1 and 2 are accepted, there are the further questions whether 'punishment' is *in fact* applied only to cases where a person is made to suffer on the ground that he deserves it, or, if not, whether its meaning *should* be restricted in this way. Defenders of the retributive theory must wish to answer at least one of these questions in the affirmative, since they call their view 'a theory of *punishment*'. Now concerning actual usage, I have found that some people are somewhat undecided regarding the kind of reason for which an action must be performed in order to be called 'punishment'. I think it best, therefore, to avoid controversy about 'ordinary language' by interpreting the retributive theory as making a verbal recommendation. This, like any such recommendation, would be in one sense arbitrary; but, if the ethical claims are accepted, the recommendation would be a reasonable one; for it would involve using 'punishment' to mark a distinction which needs to be marked—between cases where people are made to suffer on the ground that they deserve it, and cases where they are made to suffer for other reasons.

The above analysis might, however, be said to be incomplete, on the grounds that claims 1 and 2 do not provide a complete explication of the concept of moral desert, and that for this purpose we need to add a further principle to the effect that for any particular offence there is a determinate kind and/or amount of suffering which is *the* just penalty ('claim 3'). Whereas claim 2 implies only that the worse the offence, the greater should be the penalty, claim 3 involves the notion of an absolute and precise equation between offence and penalty. Claim 3 seems to be implicit not only in formulae like 'an eye for an eye', but also, for example, in the view mentioned by Hegel when he says 'Reason cannot determine . . . any principle whose application could decide whether justice requires for an offence (i) a corporal punishment of forty lashes or thirty-nine, or (ii) a fine of five dollars or four dollars ninety-three, four, etc., cents. . . . And yet injustice is done at once if there is one lash too many, or one dollar or one cent . . . too many or too few'.[4]

I am not certain whether, or to what extent, claim 3 is implicit in the popular conception of moral desert, but I submit that whereas claim 2 is acceptable, claim 3 is not. In order to apply the principle of proportion, all that is necessary is that we should be able (*a*) to compare different offences in respect of their *relative* moral gravity, and (*b*) to compare different penalties in respect of their *relative* unpleasantness—and surely we can make such comparisons in many, if not all, cases. In order to apply the principle of claim 3, we should need to be able to discern an alleged equivalence between the moral gravity of each offence and some specific penalty—and in order to do this we should presumably have to assess, on an *absolute* scale, both the moral gravity of offences and the unpleasantness of penalties. The contention that it is meaningless to speak of such an equivalence, because, e.g., the terms of the equation are not commensurable, provides one of the commonest criticisms of the retributive theory. For example, the objection which Professor W. G. Maclagan[5] treats as decisive in refuting the retributive theory—'the notion [of an equivalence between guilt and penalty] is, in fact, meaningless. . . . Thus there can be no meaning in saying that we ought to act retributively'—is based on treating claim 3 as an essential element in the retributive theory. An unusual variation of this sort of criticism is given by Ewing, purporting to show that punishment by the State cannot be justified on a retributive theory (pp. 39–40). Ewing argues that the State will almost invariably fail to impose *the precise* penalty which an offender deserves; that 'every excess over the just amount must be in the same ethical position as punishment of "the innocent", an injustice which seems much worse than non-punishment of the guilty', and that too light a penalty is equally an injustice; and, he concludes, 'to do an injustice seems worse than to do nothing at all'. Ewing's argument presupposes that the retributive theory involves not only claim 3, but also (and this is indeed gratuitous) the principle that all penalties which deviate at all from *the* just penalty are equally unjust!

It might be said that by rejecting claim 3 we render the retributive theory incomplete, since this implies that the answer to the question—what is *the* just penalty for a given offence—is not in principle determinate. If this *is* an objection, it surely applies with equal force against a utilitarian theory of punishment. A utilitarian who argues[6] that punishment could never be justified on retributive principles, because we cannot *know* the precise degree of the offenders' guilt, etc., is exposed to the reply that punishment could no more be justified on utilitarian principles. If we reject the retributive theory on the ground that God alone knows the extent of our moral guilt, we ought equally to reject a utilitarian theory on the ground that God alone knows what constitutes and conduces to our long-run welfare. We mortals can only have more or less confident beliefs concerning the welfare of others, and as to whether, and if so how, we can best promote this. In practice, it would appear that people responsible for imposing punishments can often be more confident in estimating what penalty is deserved, than they could be in solving the formidable problem of assessing the 'net welfare-productivity' of alternative penalties.

Now let us consider the implications of claim 1. To accept claim 1 does not imply, as Ewing seems to think (pp. 13–14), that we should say that punishment is 'an end-in-itself' or that it has 'intrinsic value'. Ewing assumes that we must say this if we reject the utilitarian view. I suggest that the dichotomy—'good-in-itself' or 'good-as-a-means'—is not applicable here. To say that punishment has intrinsic value would imply that the committing of an offence has instrumental value, but surely no-one would embrace this paradox! We may say that the purpose of punishment is to avoid the *dis*-value of injustice, or that the state of affairs in which an offender is punished is less evil than that in which he goes unpunished.

To accept claim 1 does not imply Ewing's conclusion that 'infliction of pain for pain's sake is what the retributive theory enjoins' (pp. 26, 29). The retributionist would say 'for the sake of justice', not 'for pain's sake'. It may be argued that the psycho-analysts have explained the disposition to accept claim 1, have shown it to be a 'rationalisation' of sadistic (and/or masochistic) impulses. The retributionists may however retort that it is not difficult to find a psychological explanation of the disposition to reject what is really a principle of justice, since most of us would like to avoid the suffering we deserve! The issue can scarcely be settled by speculations about the unconscious motives of opponents.

To accept claim 1 does not imply that people responsible for administering punishments should, when so doing, consider *only* retributive principles. Presumably everyone ought, in all his transactions, to consider, and, so far as his other duties permit, to promote the welfare of others. Judges, parents and teachers are not relieved of this duty on the occasions when they incur the duty to punish (which is, on the present view, the duty to impose deserved suffering). To grant that decisions concerning the nature of a penalty should be made in the light of its probable effects on the welfare of the offender and others, is perfectly compatible with claim 1. It does not follow that one reason for making a person suffer is not independently sufficient, simply because other reasons may also warrant such an action. Admittedly, utilitarian considerations sometimes conflict with retributive considerations and may warrant the remission (or an increase) of a deserved penalty. But I see no problem here. Claim 1 does not imply that the duty to punish is an unconditional duty, which could never be outweighed by the duties stressed in reformatory or deterrent theories. Moreover, the acceptance of claim 1 is compatible with widely different views concerning the relative importance of retributive justice and the goals stressed by utilitarians.

III

THERE REMAINS, HOWEVER, a formidable objection to the retributive theory. If the State had a duty to punish *moral* offences as such, the State ought to punish everyone, for which of us is without sin? Only moral offences which have been legislated against are punishable by the State, and, as Ewing puts it, 'it is obviously impracticable for the State to inflict pain . . . on everyone in accordance with their faults' (p. 43). This difficulty seems to warrant Ewing's conclusion that, so far as the retributive theory is concerned, the State ought not to punish at all. Now this is really the same difficulty as that which Mr. Mabbott considers fatal to the retributive theory, as traditionally interpreted. He presents it as follows—'It takes two to make a punishment, and for a moral or social wrong I can find no punisher. We may be tempted to say, when we hear of some brutal action, "that ought to be punished"; but I cannot see how there can be duties which are nobody's duties. If I see a man ill-treating a horse in a country where cruelty to animals is not a legal offence, and I say to him: "I shall now punish you", he will reply, rightly, "What has it to do with you? Who made you a judge and ruler over me?"' (p. 154*). The difficulty is that the facts seem to be incompatible with claim 1. We may want to insist that a man who commits what is a moral, but not a legal, offence deserves to suffer on that account, but if we treat this as implying that his offence is a sufficient reason for his being made to suffer, the question arises—by whom? By God perhaps; but neither the State nor any private citizen is thought to have a duty or a right to punish *an adult* for a moral offence *as such*. It looks as if the most that could be claimed for the retributive theory is that it applies to punishments inflicted by parents and teachers and by God.

Let us consider how Mabbott reacts to the above difficulty. He will have no truck with utilitarian considerations. 'The truth is that while punishing a man and punishing him justly, it is possible to deter others, and also to attempt to reform him, and if these additional goods are achieved the total state of affairs is better than it would be with just punishment alone. But reform and deterrence are not modifications of the punishment, still less reasons for it' (p. 153†). So far, so good; but Mabbott proceeds to treat punishment as a purely legal matter. He holds that the breaking of a law constitutes the only sufficient reason for an act of punishment. Mabbott sums up his position by saying 'No punishment is *morally retributive* or reformative or deterrent. Any criminal punished for any one of these reasons is certainly unjustly punished. The only justification for punishing any man is that he has broken a law' (p. 158†† *my italics*). Mabbott is, in effect, amending claim 1 by substituting 'legal offence' for 'moral offence'. Mabbott, however, claims to be defend-

* P. 44 this volume.   † P. 42 this volume.   †† P. 48 this volume.

ing a retributive theory of punishment. Thus Ewing and Mabbott meet the same difficulty in very different ways; Ewing by saying that punishment by the State cannot be justified on a retributive theory, Mabbott by adopting a position implying that only punishment by the State is justified, and that such punishment is retributive.

Obviously Mabbott is using 'retributive' in an unusual sense. (He is, I think, using it as equivalent to 'non-utilitarian'.) Neither of the claims which I have taken the retributive theory to be making is involved in Mabbott's theory. Since Mabbott's version of this theory is not based on moral principles, on what, we may ask, is it based? If it were defended as a tautology, on the grounds that 'punishment' *means* 'infliction of pain for a legal offence', its weakness would be transparent; for it is very common indeed for parents, teachers, clergymen, etc., to describe as 'punishment' the infliction of pain for moral offences which are not legal offences. Even if Mabbott were willing to extend his theory to cover breaches of rules promulgated by authorities other than the State, e.g. college authorities—and his examples on pages 155 and 164 suggest this*— his theory would still be unsatisfactory. It would, for example, imply that it is always incorrect to describe a punishment as unjust, provided that the person punished has broken a law and that the penalty falls within the limits prescribed by the law. But this is to ignore something of fundamental importance. Surely a punishment which is legally correct may still be unjust, for example:

(i) where punishment is inflicted for actions which were morally and legally permissible when performed, but are later made punishable by retrospective legislation;[7]

(ii) where punishment is inflicted for breach of a law or order which prescribes a morally wrong action. The sort of case that requires Mabbott's attention is, e.g., that in which an army officer is punished for disobeying an order to kill or torture civilians;

(iii) where the statutory penalty for a legal offence is excessively severe in relation to the moral gravity of the offence, e.g. death for a starving man who steals a loaf.

It seems to me that even if the implications of Mabbott's position might satisfy a practising lawyer, they provide no answer to

* Pp. 44 and 53 this volume.

the questions concerning punishment which have exercised moralists. His position seems tantamount to a refusal to discuss questions concerning the *moral* justification of punishment; for it can, I think, be fairly described as being limited to the claim that punishment for a legal offence and only such punishment is *legally* justifiable.[8] Admittedly this claim cannot be denied without contradiction, but surely the same is true of the claim that punishment for a moral offence, and only such punishment, is *morally* justifiable. To ask if a punishment is legally justified and to ask if it is morally justified is surely to ask two different questions.

We have now called attention to what is cogent in Ewing's criticism of the retributive theory, and what is unsatisfactory in Mabbott's statement of it. The position we have reached is this: the retributive theory breaks down if it is based solely on ethical principles involved in the concept of moral desert; yet if we divorce the theory from these principles we are left with a barren remnant which is of little or no interest to moralists. In view of these findings, is there any escape from the conclusion that punishment, if it *is* justifiable, must be justified on utilitarian grounds? I suggest that there is, provided that we combine the moral and the legalistic versions of claim 1 instead of regarding them as exclusive alternatives. As a *first* step we may replace claim 1, as originally formulated, by the following—'if a person breaks a law, and if his action in so doing constitutes a moral offence, this is a sufficient reason for his being made to suffer'.

To prevent misunderstanding of this formula let me hasten to add that I do not mean by it that, to be justly punishable, an action must be intrinsically wrong, i.e. wrong independently of its being forbidden by law. I am assuming that citizens have a moral obligation to obey the laws of their State, an obligation which derives from the fact that regulation of their behaviour by law is a necessary condition of civilised life. The actions proscribed by law need not, of course, be intrinsically wrong, provided that there is some good reason for proscribing them. However—and this is the point which Mabbott's account ignores—the duty to obey one's State is not an unconditional duty. No problem arises in cases where the State proscribes intrinsically wrong actions, or enforces actions which, as such, are ethically neutral, e.g. the rules of the road. But if the State (or a duly appointed State official) commands one to perform an intrinsically wrong action, one is faced with a conflict of duties, and one's obligation to obey the State *may* be outweighed by one's obligation not to perform actions of the kind in question. In that case, if one disobeys the State one is not committing a *moral* offence, and although the State is *legally* justified in punishing one's disobedience, it would not be *morally* justified in so doing. I am not suggesting, however, that the opinion of a law-breaker, as to whether it was right for him to break the law, is to be accepted as final! Opinions may differ as to whether a particular act of law-breaking was morally justified. My revised claim 1 involves no reference to the question who is to judge whether an act of law-breaking constitutes a moral offence. If such reference *is* to be included in claim 1, it should read 'if a person A breaks a law, and if A's action in so doing is judged by B to be a moral offence, there will, in B's view, be a sufficient reason for A being made to suffer'. Here B is a variable which may refer to any individual, including A, or to any group of people, e.g. the Government or 'the general public'.

My amended version of the retributive theory implies that punishment of a person by the State is morally justifiable, if and only if he has done something which is both a legal and a moral offence, and only if the penalty is proportionate to the moral gravity of his offence. This seems to me to be satisfactory as far as it goes, but it does not go far enough. We must now extend our solution to make it applicable to punishment in the sphere of education. We can do this by expressing claim 1 in more general terms, i.e. instead of speaking of a *legal* offence or of breaking a *law*, we may speak of disobedience to, or breaking a rule laid down by, persons in authority. This is not an arbitrary step, for surely punishment by a parent or teacher is only justifiable if imposed for an action which is both a moral offence and the breach of a rule or command. Assuming that a child has a duty to obey its parents' commands, yet a breach of this duty would not, I think, be held to justify punishment, if the action commanded were morally wrong and the child disobeyed for this reason. Equally, punishment of a child for a morally wrong action would surely not be justified unless the child had previously been told that such actions were forbidden. If one chastised a child for doing something it had not been forbidden to do, the infliction of pain might be justified as a means of inculcating a desired habit, but, in that case, it should not, I think, be called 'a punishment'. Such a chastisement would no more be a just punishment than a case where the State penalised a past action on the strength of retrospective legislation. Furthermore, my proposed solution seems compatible with the concept of Divine Retribution. If, in this connection, theologians do not think it necessary to interpret claim 1 as specifying two distinct conditions (committing a moral offence *and* breaking a rule or law), this would presumably be because they identify our moral duties with laws or commands made by God.

IV

WHAT I HAVE TRIED TO DO, in the preceding sections, is so to formulate the retributive theory that it provides a consistent and comprehensive account of punishment which can be defended against the stock arguments of its critics. While I do not think that the ethical claims of the theory can be established by argument, I think I must say something about the acceptability of these claims.

The principle of proportion seems to me to be acceptable, to be a basic principle of justice and, moreover, to be incapable, as it is normally understood, of being derived from utilitarian principles. My reasons for this last statement are, briefly, as follows. (i) If the purpose of punishment were the reform of the offender, correlation between the painfulness of the cure and gravity of the offence would be accidental. The most effective cure for poaching or drunkenness might be more painful than that for murder or treason. (ii) It is sometimes said that, on a deterrent theory, the severest penalties would be justified for minor offences. This, however, ignores Bentham's maxim[9] that we should be 'frugal' in inflicting penalties, since pain is an evil. But this is not to say that the principle of proportion, as it is normally understood, can be derived from a deterrent theory. If some people perform a prohibited action with calculated deliberation and others perform the same action on impulse or in passion, we regard the former as morally worse and as deserving a heavier penalty. The deterrent aim would require, however, that offences of the latter kind should be punished the more severely, since such offences could only be prevented (if at all) by a penalty greater than is needed to prevent deliberate offences. Such implications surely offend our sense of justice.

If one accepts the views given in the preceding paragraph, one cannot adopt an exclusively utilitarian account of punishment; but one might still adopt a predominantly utilitarian account, if one rejected claim 1. Many people nowadays would, apparently, reject claim 1, but I suspect that their attitude to this claim might be due to misunderstanding its implications. The retributive theory, as I have interpreted it, does not imply that any punishment, which is justified because it is deserved, is not also justifiable on account of the value of its after-effects. I doubt if we can point to any cases of *deserved* punishment which have no valuable effects of any kind for the persons punished or for others. This being so, it may appear to be a matter of indifference whether we adopt a retributive theory, or conclude that punishments are multiply justifiable, meaning by this that retributive considerations and utilitarian considerations *each* provide a sufficient reason for the actions which (when not speaking metaphorically) we call 'punishments'. A solution on similar lines has been suggested by Mr. A. G. N. Flew,[10] and it seems to me to be a tenable view, so far as it goes. But, for the following reason, I do not think it goes to the root of the matter. Unless the utilitarian is prepared to adopt the kind of deterrent theory on which punishment is treated as a kind of arbitrary coercion, as a device for making others conform to one's will irrespective of their own preferences or principles, the good effects of punishment to which the utilitarian appeals depend upon the punishments being regarded by the offenders and by others as just, i.e. as deserved for morally wrong actions. This being so, there is an important sense in which retributive considerations are fundamental and utilitarian considerations derivative.

NOTES

---

1. A. C. Ewing, *The Morality of Punishment*, 1929.
2. J. D. Mabbott, "Punishment," in *Mind*, April 1939.*
3. Rashdall, *The Theory of Good and Evil* (Oxford, 1907), Vol. 1, pp. 296-7.

* Also reprinted in this volume.

4. Hegel, *Philosophy of Right*, tr. T. M. Knox, p. 137.

5. W. G. Maclagan, "Punishment and Retribution," *Philosophy*, July 1939, pp. 290–2.

6. Ewing, *The Morality of Punishment*, pp. 37–8.

7. Mabbott discusses retrospective legislation on p. 155 [p. 44 this volume], but he considers only the situation in which the actions later made punishable were morally wrong when performed.

8. If Mabbott claimed that punishment for a legal offence is alone and is always *morally* justifiable, I could not agree, since, apart from its arbitrary restriction of the meaning of 'punishment,' this view implies that the law of the land is our only criterion, or at any rate our ultimate criterion, of moral justice.

9. Bentham, *Principles of Morals and Legislation*, ch. xv, section xi.

10. A. G. N. Flew, at a symposium of the Scots Philosophical Club at Aberdeen on 16 May 1953.

Herbert Morris

Persons and Punishment

They acted and looked ... at us, and around in our house, in a way that had about it the feeling—at least for me—that we were not people. In their eyesight we were just things, that was all.

[Malcolm X]

We have no right to treat a man like a dog.

[Governor Maddox *of Georgia*]

Alfredo traps in Durrenmatt's tale discovers that he has brought off, all by himself, a murder involving considerable ingenuity. The mock prosecutor in the tale demands the death penalty "as reward for a crime that merits admiration, astonishment, and respect." Traps is deeply moved; indeed, he is exhilarated, and the whole of his life becomes more heroic, and ironically, more precious. His defense attorney proceeds to argue that Traps was not only innocent but incapable of guilt, "a victim of the age." This defense Trap disavows with indignation and anger. He makes claim to the murder as his and demands the prescribed punishment—death.

The themes to be found in this macabre tale do not often find their way into philosophical discussions of punishment. These discussions deal with large and significant questions of whether or not we ever have the right to punish, and if we do, under what condi-

Reprinted from *The Monist*, Vol. 52, No. 4 (October 1968), 475-501, with permission of the publishers.

This essay was presented in its initial form at the Conference on Human Rights at Tuskegee Institute March 2-5, 1967, sponsored by the Council for Philosophical Studies and directed by R. Wasserstrom.

tions, to what degree, and in what manner. There is a tradition, of course, not notable for its present vitality, that is closely linked with motifs in Durrenmatt's tale of crime and punishment. Its adherents have urged that justice requires a person be punished if he is guilty. Sometimes—though rarely—these philosophers have expressed themselves in terms of the criminal's *right to be punished*. Reaction to the claim that there is such a right has been astonishment combined, perhaps, with a touch of contempt for the perversity of the suggestion. A strange right that no one would ever wish to claim! With that flourish the subject is buried and the right disposed of. In this paper the subject is resurrected.

My aim is to argue for four propositions concerning rights that will certainly strike some as not only false but preposterous: first, that we have a right to punishment; second, that this right derives from a fundamental human right to be treated as a person; third, that this fundamental right is a natural, inalienable, and absolute right; and, fourth, that the denial of this right implies the denial of all moral rights and duties. Showing the truth of one, let alone all, of these large and questionable claims, is a tall order. The attempt or, more properly speaking, the first steps in an attempt, follow.

1. When someone claims that there is a right to be free, we can easily imagine situations in which the right is infringed and easily imagine situations in which there is a point to asserting or claiming the right. With the right to be punished, matters are otherwise. The immediate reaction to the claim that there is such a right is puzzlement. And the reasons for this are apparent. People do not normally value pain and suffering. Punishment is associated with pain and suffering. When we think about punishment we naturally think of the strong desire most persons have to avoid it, to accept, for example, acquittal of a criminal charge with relief and eagerly, if convicted, to hope for pardon or probation. Adding, of course, to the paradoxical character of the claim of such a right is difficulty in imagining circumstances in which it would be denied one. When would one rightly demand punishment and meet with any threat of the claim being denied?

So our first task is to see when the claim of such a right would have a point. I want to approach this task by setting out two complex types of institutions both of which are designed to maintain some degree of social control. In the one a central concept is punishment for wrongdoing and in the other the central concepts are control of dangerous individuals and treatment of disease.

Let us first turn attention to the institutions in which punishment is involved. The institutions I describe will resemble those we ordinarily think of as institutions of punishment; they will have, however, addtional features we associate with a system of just punishment.

Let us suppose that men are constituted roughly as they now are, with a rough equivalence in strength and abilities, a capacity to be injured by each other and to make judgments that such injury is undesirable, a limited strength of will, and a capacity to reason and to conform conduct to rules. Applying to the conduct of these men are a group of rules, ones I shall label 'primary', which closely resemble the core rules of our criminal law, rules that prohibit violence and deception and compliance with which provides benefits for all persons. These benefits consist in noninterference by others with what each person values, such matters as continuance of life and bodily security. The rules define a sphere for each person, then, which is immune from interference by others. Making possible this mutual benefit is the assumption by individuals of a burden. The burden consists in the exercise of self-restraint by individuals over inclinations that would, if satisfied, directly interfere or create a substantial risk of interference with others in proscribed ways. If a person fails to exercise self-restraint even though he might have and gives in to such inclinations, he renounces a burden which others have voluntarily assumed and thus gains an advantage which others, who have restrained themselves, do not possess. This system, then, is one in which the rules establish a mutuality of benefit and burden and in which the benefits of noninterference are conditional upon the assumption of burdens.

Connecting punishment with the violation of these primary rules, and making public the provision for punishment, is both reasonable and just. First, it is only reasonable that those who voluntarily comply with the rules be provided some assurance that they will not be assuming burdens which others are unprepared to assume. Their disposition to comply voluntarily will diminish as they learn that others are with impunity renouncing burdens they are assuming. Second, fairness dictates that a system in which benefits and burdens are equally distributed have a mechanism designed to prevent a maldistribution in the benefits and burdens. Thus, sanctions are attached to noncompliance with the primary rules so as to induce compliance with the primary rules among those who may be disinclined to obey. In this way the likelihood of an unfair distribution is diminished.

Third, it is just to punish those who have violated the rules and caused the unfair distribution of benefits and burdens. A person who violates the rules has something others have—the benefits of the system—but by renouncing what others have assumed, the burdens of self-restraint, he has acquired an unfair advantage. Matters are not even until this advantage is in some way erased. Another way of putting it is that he owes something to others, for he has something that does not rightfully belong to him. Justice—that is punishing such individuals—restores the equilibrium of benefits and burdens by taking from the individual what he owes, that is, exacting the debt. It is important to see that the equilibrium may be restored in another way. Forgiveness—with its legal analogue of a pardon—while not the righting of an unfair distribution by making one pay his debt is, nevertheless, a restoring of the equilibrium by forgiving the debt. Forgiveness may be viewed, at least in some types of cases, as a gift after the fact, erasing a debt, which had the gift been given before the fact, would not have created a debt. But the practice of pardoning has to proceed sensitively, for it may endanger in a way the practice of justice does not, the maintenance of an equilibrium of benefits and burdens. If all are indiscriminately pardoned less incentive is provided individuals to restrain their inclinations, thus increasing the incidence of persons taking what they do not deserve.

There are also in this system we are considering a variety of operative principles compliance with which provides some guarantee that the system of punishment does not itself promote an unfair distribution of benefits and burdens. For one thing, provision is made for a variety of defenses, each one of which can be said to have as its object diminishing the chances of forcibly depriving a person of benefits others have if that person has not derived an unfair advantage. A person has not derived an unfair advantage if he could not have restrained himself or if it is unreasonable to expect him to behave otherwise than he did. Sometimes the rules preclude punishment of classes of persons such as children. Sometimes they provide a defense if on a particular occasion a person lacked the capacity to conform his conduct to the rules. Thus, someone who in an epileptic seizure strikes another is excused. Punishment in these cases would be punishment of the innocent, punishment of those who do not voluntarily renounce a burden others have assumed. Punishment in such cases, then, would not equalize but rather cause an unfair distribution in benefits and burdens.

Along with principles providing defenses there are requirements that the rules be prospective and relatively clear so that persons have a fair opportunity to comply with the rules. There are, also, rules governing, among other matters, the burden of proof, who shall bear it and what it shall be, the prohibition on double jeopardy, and the privilege against self-incrimination. Justice requires conviction of the guilty, and requires their punishment, but in setting out to fulfill the demands of justice we may, of course, because we are not omniscient, cause injustice by convicting and punishing the innocent. The resolution arrived at in the system I am describing consists in weighing as the greater evil the punishment of the innocent. The primary function of the system of rules was to provide individuals with a sphere of interest immune from interference. Given this goal, it is determined to be a greater evil for society to interfere unjustifiably with an individual by depriving him of good than for the society to fail to punish those that have unjustifiably interfered.

Finally, because the primary rules are designed to benefit all and because the punishments prescribed for their violation are publicized and the defenses respected, there is some plausibility in the exaggerated claim that in choosing to do an act violative of the rules an individual has chosen to be punished. This way of putting matters brings to our attention the extent to which, when the system is as I have described it, the criminal "has brought the punishment upon himself" in contrast to those cases where it would be misleading to say "he has brought it upon himself," cases, for example, where one does not know the rules or is punished in the absence of fault.

To summarize, then: first, there is a group of rules guiding the behavior of individuals in the community which establish spheres of interest immune from interference by others; second, provision is made for what is generally regarded as a deprivation of some thing of value if the rules are violated; third, the deprivations visited upon any person are justified by that person's having violated the rules; fourth, the deprivation, in this just system of punishment, is linked to rules that fairly distribute benefits and burdens and to procedures that strike some balance between not punishing the guilty and punishing the innocent, a class defined as those who have not voluntarily done acts violative of the law, in which it is evident that the evil of punishing the innocent is regarded as greater than the nonpunishment of the guilty.

At the core of many actual legal systems one finds, of course, rules and procedures of the kind I have sketched. It is obvious, though, that any ongoing legal system differs in significant respects from what I have presented here, containing 'pockets of injustice'.

I want now to sketch an extreme version of a set of institutions of a fundamentally different kind, institutions proceeding on a conception of man which appears to be basically at odds with that operative within a system of punishment.

Rules are promulgated in this system that prohibit certain types of injuries and harms.

In this world we are now to imagine when an individual harms another his conduct is to be regarded as a symptom of some pathological condition in the way a running nose is a symptom of a cold. Actions diverging from some conception of the normal are viewed as manifestations of a disease in the way in which we might today regard the arm and leg movements of an epileptic during a seizure. Actions conforming to what is normal are assimilated to the normal and healthy functioning of bodily organs. What a person does, then, is assimilated, on this conception, to what we believe today, or at least most of us believe today, a person undergoes. We draw a distinction between the operation of the kidney and raising an arm on request. This distinction between mere events or happenings and human actions is erased in our imagined system.[1]

There is, however, bound to be something strange in this erasing of a recognized distinction, for, as with metaphysical suggestions generally, and I take this to be one, the distinction may be reintroduced but given a different description, for example, 'happenings with X type of causes' and 'happenings with Y type of causes'. Responses of different kinds, today legitimated by our distinction between happenings and actions may be legitimated by this new manner of description. And so there may be isomorphism between a system recognizing the distinction and one erasing it. Still, when this distinction is erased certain tendencies of thought and responses might naturally arise that would tend to affect unfavorably values respected by a system of punishment.

Let us elaborate on this assimilation of conduct of a certain kind to symptoms of a disease. First, there is something abnormal in both the case of conduct, such as killing another, and a symptom of a disease such as an irregular heart beat. Second, there are causes for this abnormality in action such that once we know of them we can explain the abnormality as we now can explain the symptoms of many physical diseases. The abnormality is looked upon as a happening with a causal explanation rather than an action for which there were reasons. Third, the causes that account for the abnormality interfere with the normal functioning of the body, or, in the case of killing with what is regarded as a normal functioning of an individual. Fourth, the abnormality is in some way a part of the individual, necessarily involving his body. A well going dry might satisfy our three foregoing conditions of disease symptoms, but it is hardly a disease or the symptom of one. Finally, and most obscure, the abnormality arises in some way from within the individual. If Jones is hit with a mallet by Smith, Jones may reel about and fall on James who may be injured. But this abnormal conduct of Jones is not regarded as a symptom of disease. Smith, not Jones, is suffering from some pathological condition.

With this view of man the institutions of social control respond, not with punishment, but with either preventive detention, in case of 'carriers', or therapy in the case of those manifesting pathological symptoms. The logic of sickness implies the logic of therapy. And therapy and punishment differ widely in their implications. In bringing out some of these differences I want again to draw attention to the important fact that while the distinctions we now draw are erased in the therapy world, they may, in fact, be reintroduced but under different descriptions. To the extent they are, we really have a punishment system combined with a therapy system. I am concerned now, however, with what the implications would be were the world indeed one of therapy and not a disguised world of punishment and therapy, for I want to suggest tendencies of thought that arise when one is immersed in the ideology of disease and therapy.

First, punishment is the imposition upon a person who is believed to be at fault of something commonly believed to be a deprivation where that deprivation is justified by the person's guilty behavior. It is associated with resentment, for the guilty are those who have done what they had no right to do by failing to exercise restraint when they might have and where others have. Therapy is not a response to a person who is at fault. We respond to an individual, not because of what he has done, but because of some condition from which he is suffering. If he is no longer suffering from the condition, treatment no longer has a point. Punishment, then, focuses on the past; therapy on the present. Therapy is normally associated with compassion for what one undergoes, not resentment for what one has illegitimately done.

Second, with therapy, unlike punishment, we do not seek to deprive the person of something acknowledged as a good, but seek rather to help and to benefit the individual who is suffering by ministering to his illness in the hope that the person can be cured. The good we attempt to do is not a reward for desert. The individual suffering has not merited by his disease the good we seek to bestow upon him but has, because he is a creature that has the capacity to feel pain, a claim upon our sympathies and help.

Third, we saw with punishment that its justification was related to maintaining and restoring a fair distribution of benefits and burdens. Infliction of the prescribed punishment carries the implication, then, that one has 'paid one's debt' to society, for the punishment is the taking from the person of something commonly recognized as valuable. It is this conception of 'a debt owed' that may permit, as I suggested earlier, under certain conditions, the nonpunishment of the guilty, for operative within a system of punishment may be a concept analogous to forgiveness, namely pardoning. Who it is that we may pardon and under what conditions—contrition with its elements of self-punishment no doubt plays a role—I shall not go into though it is clearly a matter of the greatest practical and theoretical interest. What is clear is that the conceptions of 'paying a debt' or 'having a debt forgiven' or pardoning have no place in a system of therapy.

Fourth, with punishment there is an attempt at some equivalence between the advantage gained by the wrongdoer—partly based upon the seriousness of the interest invaded, partly on the state of mind with which the wrongful act was performed—and the punishment meted out. Thus, we can understand a prohibition on 'cruel and unusual punishments' so that disproportionate pain and suffering are avoided. With therapy attempts at proportionality make no sense. It is perfectly plausible giving someone who kills a pill and treating for a lifetime within an institution one who has broken a dish and manifested accident proneness. We have the concept of 'painful treatment'. We do not have the concept of 'cruel treatment'. Because treatment is regarded as a benefit, though it may involve pain, it is natural that less restraint is exercised in bestowing it, than in inflicting punishment. Further, protests with respect to treatment are likely to be assimilated to the complaints of one whose leg must be amputated in order for him to live, and, thus, largely disregarded. To be sure, there is operative in the therapy world some conception of the "cure being worse than the disease," but if the disease is manifested in conduct harmful to others, and if being a normal operating human being is valued highly, there will naturally be considerable pressure to find the cure acceptable.

Fifth, the rules in our system of punishment governing conduct of individuals were rules violation of which involved either direct interference with others or the creation of a substantial risk of such interference. One could imagine adding to this system of primary rules other rules proscribing preparation to do acts violative of the primary rules and even rules proscribing thoughts. Objection to such suggestions would have many sources but a principal one would consist in its involving the infliction of punishment on too great a number of persons who would not, because of a change of mind, have violated the primary rules. Though we are interested in diminishing violations of the primary rules, we are not prepared to punish too many individuals who would never have violated the rules in order to achieve this aim. In a system motivated solely by a preventive and curative ideology there would be less reason to wait until symptoms manifest themselves in socially harmful conduct. It is understandable that we should wish at the earliest possible stage to arrest the development of the disease. In the punishment system, because we are dealing with deprivations, it is understandable that we should forbear from imposing them until we are quite sure of guilt. In the therapy system, dealing as it does with benefits, there is less reason for forbearance from treatment at an early stage.

Sixth, a variety of procedural safeguards we associate with punishment have less significance in a therapy system. To the degree objections to double jeopardy and self-incrimination are based on a wish to decrease the chances of the innocent being convicted and punished, a therapy system, unconcerned with this problem, would disregard such safeguards. When one is out to help people there is also little sense in urging that the burden of proof be on those providing the help. And there is less point to imposing the burden of proving that the conduct was pathological beyond a reasonable doubt. Further, a jury system which, within a system of justice, serves to make accommodations to the individual situation and to introduce a human element, would play no role or a minor one in a world where expertise is required in making determinations of disease and treatment.

In our system of punishment an attempt was made to maximize each individual's freedom of choice by first of all delimiting by rules certain spheres of conduct immune from interference by others. The punishment associated with these primary rules paid deference to an individual's free choice by connecting punishment to a freely chosen act violative of the rules, thus giving some plausibility to the claim, as we saw, that what a person received by way of punishment he himself had chosen. With the world of disease and therapy all this changes and the individual's free choice ceases to be a determinative factor in how others respond to him. All those principles of our own legal system that minimize the chances of punishment of those who have not chosen to do acts violative of the rules tend to lose their point in the therapy system, for how we respond in a therapy system to a person is not conditioned upon what he has chosen but rather on what symptoms he has manifested or may manifest and what the best therapy for the disease is that is suggested by the symptoms.

Now, it is clear I think, that were we confronted with the alternatives I have sketched, between a system of just punishment and a thoroughgoing system of treatment, a system, that is, that did not reintroduce concepts appropriate to punishment, we could see the point in claiming that a person has a right to be punished, meaning by this that a person had a right to all those institutions and practices linked to punishment. For these would provide him with, among other things, a far greater ability to predict what would happen to him on the occurrence of certain events than the therapy system. There is the inestimable value to each of us of having the responses of others to us determined over a wide range of our lives by what we choose rather than what they choose. A person has a right to institutions that respect his choices. Our punishment system does; our therapy system does not.

Apart from those aspects of our therapy model which would relate to serious limitations on personal liberty, there are clearly objections of a more profound kind to the mode of thinking I have associated with the therapy model.

First, human beings pride themselves in having capacities that animals do not. A common way, for example, of arousing shame in a child is to compare the child's conduct to that of an animal. In a system where all actions are assimilated to happenings we are assimilated to creatures—indeed, it is more extreme than this—whom we have always thought possessed of less than we. Fundamental to our practice of praise and order of attainment is that one who can do more—one who is capable of more and one who does more is more worthy of respect and admiration. And we have thought of ourselves as capable where animals are not of making, of creating, among other things, ourselves. The conception of man I have outlined would provide us with a status that today, when our conduct is assimilated to it in moral criticism, we consider properly evocative of shame.

Second, if all human conduct is viewed as something men undergo, thrown into question would be the appropriateness of that extensive range of peculiarly human satisfactions that derive from a sense of achievement. For these satisfactions we shall have to substitute those mild satisfactions attendant upon a healthy well-functioning body. Contentment is our lot if we are fortunate; intense satisfaction at achievement is entirely inappropriate.

Third, in the therapy world nothing is earned and what we receive comes to us through compassion, or through a desire to control us. Resentment is out of place. We can take credit for nothing but must always regard ourselves—if there are selves left to regard once actions disappear—as fortunate recipients of benefits or unfortunate carriers of disease who must be controlled. We know that within our own world human beings who have been so regarded and who come to accept this view of themselves come to look upon themselves as worthless. When what we do is met with resentment, we are indirectly paid something of a compliment.

Fourth, attention should also be drawn to a peculiar evil that may be attendant upon regarding a man's actions as symptoms of disease. The logic of cure will push us toward forms of therapy that inevitably involve changes in the person made against his will. The evil in this would be most apparent in those cases where the agent, whose action is determined to be a manifestation of some disease, does not regard his action in this way. He believes that what he has done is, in fact, 'right' but his conception of 'normality' is not the therapeutically accepted one. When we treat an illness we normally treat a condition that the person is not responsible for. He is 'suffering' from some disease and we treat the condition, relieving the person of something preventing his normal functioning. When we begin treating persons for actions that have been chosen, we do not lift from the person something that is interfering with his normal functioning but we change the person so that he functions in a way regarded as normal by the current therapeutic community. We have to change him and his judgments of value. In doing this we display a lack of respect for the moral status of individuals, that is, a lack of respect for the reasoning and choices of individuals. They are but animals who must be conditioned. I think we can understand and, indeed, sympathize with a man's preferring death to being forcibly turned into what he is not.

Finally, perhaps most frightening of all would be the derogation in status of all protests to treatment. If someone believes that he has done something right, and if he protests being treated and changed, the protest will itself be regarded as a sign of some pathological condition, for who would not wish to be cured of an affliction? What this leads to are questions of an important kind about the effect of this conception of man upon what we now understand by reasoning. Here what a person takes to be a reasoned defense of an act is treated, as the action was, on the model of a happening of a pathological kind. Not just a person's acts are taken from him but also his attempt at a reasoned justification for the acts. In a system of punishment a person who has committed a crime may argue that what he did was right. We make him pay the price and we respect his right to retain the judgment he has made. A conception of pathology precludes this form of respect.

It might be objected to the foregoing that all I have shown— if that—is that if the only alternatives open to us are a *just* system of punishment or the mad world of being treated like sick or healthy animals, we do in fact have a right to a system of punishment of this kind. But this hardly shows that we have a right *simpliciter* to punishment as we do, say, to be free. Indeed, it does not even show a right to a just system of punishment, for surely we can, without too much difficulty, imagine situations in which the alternatives to punishment are not this mad world but a world in which we are still treated as persons and there is, for example, not the pain and suffering attendant upon punishment. One such world is one in which there are rules but responses to their violation is not the deprivation of some good but forgiveness. Still another type of world would be one in which violation of the rules were responded to by merely comparing the conduct of the person to something commonly regarded as low or filthy, and thus, producing by this mode of moral criticism, feelings of shame rather than feelings of guilt.

I am prepared to allow that these objections have a point. While granting force to the above objections I want to offer a few additional comments with respect to each of them. First, any existent legal system permits the punishment of individuals under circumstances where the conditions I have set forth for a just system have not been satisfied. A glaring example of this would be criminal strict liability which is to be found in our own legal system. Nevertheless, I think it would be difficult to present any system we should regard as a system of punishment that would not still have a great advantage over our imagined therapy system. The system of punishment we imagine may more and more approximate a system of sheer terror in which human beings are treated as animals to be intimidated and prodded. To the degree that the system is of this character it is, in my judgment, not simply an unjust system but one that diverges from what we normally understand by a system of punishment. At least some deference to the choice of individuals is built into the idea of punishment. So there would be some truth in saying we have a right to any system of punishment if the only alternative to it was therapy.

Second, people may imagine systems in which there are rules and in which the response to their violation is not punishment but pardoning, the legal analogue of forgiveness. Surely this is a system to which we would claim a right as against one in which we are made to suffer for violating the rules. There are several comments that need to be made about this. It may be, of course, that a high incidence of pardoning would increase the incidence of rule violations. Further, the difficulty with suggesting pardoning as a general response is that pardoning presupposes the very responses that it is suggested it supplant. A system of deprivations, or a practice of deprivations on the happening of certain actions, underlies the practice of pardoning and forgiving, for it is only where we possess the idea of a wrong to be made up or of a debt owed to others, ideas we acquire within a world in which there have been deprivations for wrong acts, that we have the idea of pardoning for the wrong or forgiving the debt.

Finally, if we look at the responses I suggested would give rise to feelings of shame, we may rightly be troubled with the appropriateness of this response in any community in which each person assumes burdens so that each may derive benefits. In such situations might it not be that individuals have a right to a system of punishment so that each person could be assured that inequities in the distribution of benefits and burdens are unlikely to occur and if they do, procedures exist for correcting them? Further, it may well be that, everything considered, we should prefer the pain and suffering of a system of punishment to a world in which we only experience shame on the doing of wrong acts, for with guilt there are relatively simple ways of ridding ourselves of the feeling we have, that is, gaining forgiveness or taking the punishment, but with shame we have to bear it until we no longer are the person who has behaved in the shameful way. Thus, I suggest that we have, wherever there is a distribution of benefits and burdens of the kind I have described, a right to a system of punishment.

I want also to make clear in concluding this section that I have argued, though very indirectly, not just for a right to a system of punishment, but for a right to be punished once there is in existence such a system. Thus, a man has the right to be punished rather than treated if he is guilty of some offense. And, indeed, one can imagine a case in which, even in the face of an offer of a pardon, a man claims and ought to have acknowledged his right to be punished.

2. The primary reason for preferring the system of punishment as against the system of therapy might have been expressed in terms of the one system treating one as a person and the other not. In invoking the right to be punished, one justifies one's claim by reference to a more fundamental right. I want now to turn attention to this fundamental right and attempt to shed light—it will have to be little, for the topic is immense—on what is meant by 'treating an individual as a person'.

When we talk of not treating a human being as a person or 'showing no respect for one as a person' what we imply by our words is a contrast between the manner in which one acceptably responds to human beings and the manner in which one acceptably responds to animals and inanimate objects. When we treat a human being merely as an animal or some inanimate object our responses to the human being are determined, not by his choices, but ours in disregard of or with indifference to his. And when we 'look upon' a person as less than a person or not a person, we consider the person as incapable of rational choice. In cases of not treating a human being as a person we interfere with a person in such a way that what is done, even if the person is involved in the doing, is done not by the person but by the user of the person. In extreme cases there may even be an elision of a causal chain so that we might say that X killed Z even though Y's hand was the hand that held the weapon, for Y's hand may have been entirely in X's control. The one agent is in some way treating the other as a mere link in a causal chain. There is, of course, a wide range of cases in which a person is used to accomplish the aim of another and in which the person used is less than fully free. A person may be grabbed against his will and used as a shield. A person may be drugged or hypnotized and then employed for certain ends. A person may be deceived into doing other than he intends doing. A person may be ordered to do something and threatened with harm if he does not and coerced into doing what he does not want to. There is still another range of cases in which individuals are not used, but in which decisions by others are made that affect them in circumstances where they have the capacity for choice and where they are not being treated as persons.

But it is particularly important to look at coercion, for I have claimed that a just system of punishment treats human beings as persons; and it is not immediately apparent how ordering someone to do something and threatening harm differs essentially from having rules supported by threats of harm in case of noncompliance.

There are affinities between coercion and other cases of not treating someone as a person, for it is not the coerced person's choices but the coercer's that are responsible for what is done. But unlike other indisputable cases of not treating one as a person, for example using someone as a shield, there is some choice involved in coercion. And if this is so, why does the coercer stand in any different relation to the coerced person than the criminal law stands to individuals in society?

Suppose the person who is threatened disregards the order and gets the threatened harm. Now suppose he is told, "Well, you did after all bring it upon yourself." There is clearly something strange in this. It is the person doing the threatening and not the person threatened who is responsible. But our reaction to punishment, at least in a system that resembles the one I have described, is precisely that the person violating the rules brought it upon himself. What lies behind these different reactions?

There exist situations in the law, of course, which resemble coercion situations. There are occasions when in the law a person might justifiably say "I am not being treated as a person but being used" and where he might properly react to the punishment as something "he was hardly responsible for." But it is possible to have a system in which it would be misleading to say, over a wide range of cases of punishment for noncompliance, that we are using persons. The clearest case in which it would be inappropriate to so regard punishment would be one in which there were explicit agreement in advance that punishment should follow on the voluntary doing of certain acts. Even if one does not have such conditions satisfied, and obviously such explicit agreements are not characteristic, one can see significant differences between our system of just punishment and a coercion situation.

First, unlike the case with one person coercing another 'to do his will', the rules in our system apply to all, with the benefits and burdens equally distributed. About such a system it cannot be said that some are being subordinated to others or are being used by others or gotten to do things by others. To the extent that the rules are thought to be the advantage of only some or to the extent there is a maldistribution of benefits and burdens, the difference between coercion and law disappears.

Second, it might be argued that at least any person inclined to act in a manner violative of the rules stands to all others as the person coerced stands to his coercer, and that he, at least, is a person disadvantaged as others are not. It is important here, I think, that he is part of a system in which it is commonly agreed that forbearance from the acts proscribed by the rules provides advantages for all. This system is the accepted setting; it is the norm. Thus, in any coercive situation, it is the coercer who deviates from the norm, with the responsibility of the person he is attempting to coerce, defeated. In a just punishment situation, it is the person deviating from the norm, indeed he might be a coercer, who is responsible, for it is the norm to restrain oneself from acts of that kind. A voluntary agent diverging in his conduct from what is expected or what the norm is, on general causal principles, is regarded as the cause of what results from his conduct.

There is, then, some plausibility in the claim that, in a system of punishment of the kind I have sketched, a person chooses the punishment that is meted out to him. If, then, we can say in such a system that the rules provide none with advantages that others do not have, and further, that what happens to a person is conditioned by that person's choice and not that of others, then we can say that it is a system responding to one as a person.

We treat a human being as a person provided: first, we permit the person to make the choices that will determine what happens to him and second, when our responses to the person are responses respecting the person's choices. When we respond to a person's illness by treating the illness it is neither a case of treating or not treating the individual as a person. When we give a person a gift we are neither treating or not treating him as a person, unless, of course, he does not wish it, chooses not to have it, but we compel him to accept it.

3. This right to be treated as a person is a fundamental human right belonging to all human beings by virtue of their being human. It is also a natural, inalienable, and absolute right. I want now to de-

fend these claims so reminiscent of an era of philosophical thinking about rights that many consider to have been seriously confused.

If the right is one that we possess by virtue of being human beings, we are immediately confronted with an apparent dilemma. If, to treat another as a person requires that we provide him with reasons for acting and avoid force or deception, how can we justify the force and deception we exercise with respect to children and the mentally ill? If they, too, have a right to be treated as persons are we not constantly infringing their rights? One way out of this is simply to restrict the right to those who satisfy the conditions of being a person. Infants and the insane, it might be argued, do not meet these conditions, and they would not then have the right. Another approach would be to describe the right they possess as a prima facie right to be treated as a person. This right might then be outweighed by other considerations. This approach generally seems to me, as I shall later argue, inadequate.

I prefer this tack. Children possess the right to be treated as persons but they possess this right as an individual might be said in the law of property to possess a future interest. There are advantages in talking of individuals as having a right though complete enjoyment of it is postponed. Brought to our attention, if we ascribe to them the right, is the legitimacy of their complaint if they are not provided with opportunities and conditions assuring their full enjoyment of the right when they acquire the characteristics of persons. More than this, all persons are charged with the sensitive task of not denying them the right to be a person and to be treated as a person by failing to provide the conditions for their becoming individuals who are able freely and in an informed way to choose and who are prepared themselves to assume responsibility for their choices. There is an obligation imposed upon us all, unlike that we have with respect to animals, to respond to children in such a way as to maximize the chances of their becoming persons. This may well impose upon us the obligation to treat them as persons from a very early age, that is, to respect their choices and to place upon them the responsibility for the choices to be made. There is no need to say that there is a close connection between how we respond to them and what they become. It also imposes upon us all the duty to display constantly the qualities of a person, for what they become they will largely become because of what they learn from us is acceptable behavior.

In claiming that the right is a right that human beings have by virtue of being human, there are several other features of the right, that should be noted, perhaps better conveyed by labelling them 'natural'. First, it is a right we have apart from any voluntary agreement into which we have entered. Second, it is not a right that derives from some defined position or status. Third, it is equally apparent that one has the right regardless of the society or community of which one is a member. Finally, it is a right linked to certain features of a class of beings. Were we fundamentally different than we now are, we would not have it. But it is more than that, for the right is linked to a feature of human beings which, were that feature absent—the capacity to reason and to choose on the basis of reasons—, profound conceptual changes would be involved in the thought about human beings. It is a right, then, connected with a feature of men that sets men apart from other natural phenomena.

The right to be treated as a person is inalienable. To say of a right that it is inalienable draws attention not to limitations placed on what others may do with respect to the possessor of the right but rather to limitations placed on the dispositive capacities of the possessor of the right. Something is to be gained in keeping the issues of alienability and absoluteness separate.

There are a variety of locutions qualifying what possessors of rights may and may not do. For example, on this issue of alienability, it would be worthwhile to look at, among other things, what is involved in abandoning, abdicating, conveying, giving up, granting, relinquishing, surrendering, transferring, and waiving one's rights. And with respect to each of these concepts we should also have to be sensitive to the variety of uses of the term 'rights'. What it is, for example, to waive a Hohfeldian 'right' in his strict sense will differ from what it is to waive a right in his 'privilege' sense.

Let us look at only two concepts very briefly, those of transferring and waiving rights. The clearest case of transferring rights is that of transferring rights with respect to specific objects. I own a watch and owning it I have a complicated relationship, captured in this area rather well I think by Hohfeld's four basic legal relationships, to all persons in the world with respect to the watch. We crudely capture these complex relationships by talking of my 'property rights' in or with respect to the watch. If I sell the watch, thus exercising a capacity provided by the rules of property, I have transferred rights in or with respect to the watch to someone else, the buyer, and the buyer now stands, as I formerly did, to all persons in the world in a series of complex relationships with respect to the watch.

While still the owner, I may have given to another permission to use it for several days. Had there not been the permission and had the person taken the watch, we should have spoken of interfering with or violating or, possibly, infringing my property rights. Or, to take a situation in which transferring rights is inappropriate, I may say to another "go ahead and slap me—you have my permission." In these types of situations philosophers and others have spoken of 'surrendering' rights or, alternatively and, I believe, less strangely, of 'waiving one's rights'. And recently, of course, the whole topic of 'waiving one's right to remain silent' in the context of police interrogation of suspects has been a subject of extensive litigation and discussion.

I confess to feeling that matters are not entirely perspicuous with respect to what is involved in 'waiving' or 'surrendering' rights. In conveying to another permission to take a watch or slap one, one makes legally permissible what otherwise would not have been. But in saying those words that constitute permission to take one's watch one is, of course, exercising precisely one of those capacities that leads us to say he has, while others have not, property rights with respect to the watch. Has one then waived his right in Hohfeld's strict sense in which the correlative is a duty to forebear on the part of others?

We may wish to distinguish here waiving the right to have others forebear to which there is a corresponding duty on their part to forebear, from placing oneself in a position where one has no legitimate right to complain. If I say the magic words "take the watch for a couple of days" or "go ahead and slap me," have I waived my right not to have my property taken or a right not to be struck or have I, rather, in saying what I have, simply stepped into a relation in which the rights no longer apply with respect to a specified other person? These observations find support in the following considerations. The right is that which gives rise, when infringed, to a legitimate claim against another person. What this suggests is that the right is that sphere interference with which entitles us to complain or gives us a right to complain. From this it seems to follow that a right to bodily security should be more precisely described as 'a right that others not interfere without permission'. And there is the corresponding duty not to interfere unless provided permission. Thus when we talk of waiving our rights or 'giving up our rights' in such cases we are not waiving or giving up our right to property nor our right to bodily security, for we still, of course, possess the right not to have our watch taken without permission. We have rather placed ourselves in a position where we do not possess the capacity, sometimes called a right, to complain if the person takes the watch or slaps us.

There is another type of situation in which we may speak of waiving our rights. If someone without permission slaps me, there is an infringement of my right to bodily security. If I now acquiesce or go further and say "forget it" or "you are forgiven," we might say that I had waived my right to complain. But here, too, I feel uncomfortable about what is involved. For I do have the right to complain (a right without a corresponding duty) in the event I am slapped and I have that right whether I wish it or not. If I say to another after the slap, "you are forgiven" what I do is not waive the right to complain but rather make illegitimate my subsequent exercise of that right.

Now, if we turn to the right to be treated as a person, the claim that I made was that it was inalienable, and what I meant to convey by that word of respectable age is that (a) it is a right that cannot be transferred to another in the way one's right with respect to objects can be transferred and (b) that it cannot be waived in the ways in which people talk of waiving rights to property or waiving, within certain limitations, one's right to bodily security.

While the rules of the law of property are such that persons may, satisfying certain procedures, transfer rights, the right to be treated as a person logically cannot be transferred anymore than one person can transfer to another his right to life or privacy. What, indeed, would it be like for another to have our right to be treated as a person? We can understand transferring a right with respect to certain objects. The new owner stands where the old owner stood. But with a right to be treated as a person what could this mean? My having the right meant that my choices were respected. Now if I transfer it to another will this mean that he will possess the right that my choices be respected? This is nonsense. It is only each person himself that can have his choices respected. It is no more possible to transfer this right than it is to transfer one's right to life.

Nor can the right be waived. It cannot be waived because any agreement to being treated as an animal or an instrument does not provide others with the moral permission to so treat us. One can volunteer to be a shield, but then it is one's choice on a particular occasion to be a shield. If without our permission, without our choosing it, someone used us as a shield, we may, I should suppose, forgive the person for treating us as an object. But we do not thereby waive our right to be treated as a person, for that is a right that has been infringed and what we have at most done is put ourselves in a position where it is inappropriate any longer to exercise the right to complain.

This is the sort of right, then, such that the moral rules defining relationships among persons preclude anyone from morally giving others legitimate permissions or rights with respect to one by doing or saying certain things. One stands, then, with respect to one's person as the nonowner of goods stands to those goods. The non-owner cannot, given the rule-defined relationships, convey to others rights and privileges that only the owner possesses. Just as there are agreements nonenforceable because void is contrary to public policy, so there are permissions our moral outlook regards as without moral force. With respect to being treated as a person, one is 'disabled' from modifying relations of others to one.

The right is absolute. This claim is bound to raise eyebrows. I have an innocuous point in mind in making this claim.

In discussing alienability we focused on incapacities with respect to disposing of rights. Here what I want to bring out is a sense in which a right exists despite considerations for refusing to accord the person his rights. As with the topic of alienability there are a host of concepts that deserve a close look in this area. Among them are according, acknowledging, annulling, asserting, claiming, denying, destroying, exercising, infringing, insisting upon, interfering with, possessing, recognizing and violating.

The claim that rights are absolute has been construed to mean that 'assertions of rights cannot, for any reason under any circumstances be denied'. When there are considerations which warrant refusing to accord persons their rights, there are two prevalent views as to how this should be described: there is, first, the view that the person does not have the right, and second, the view that he has rights but of a prima facie kind and that these have been outweighed or overcome by the other considerations. "We can conceive times when such rights must give way, and, therefore, they are only prima facie and not absolute rights." (Brandt)

Perhaps there are cases in which a person claims a right to do a certain thing, say with his property, and argues that his property rights are absolute, meaning by this he has a right to do whatever he wishes with his property. Here, no doubt, it has to be explained to the person that the right he claims he has, he does not in fact possess. In such a case the person does not have and never did have, given a certain description of the right, a right that was prima facie or otherwise, to do what he claimed he had the right to do. If the assertion that a right is absolute implies that we have a right to do whatever we wish to do, it is an absurd claim and as such should not really ever have been attributed to political theorists arguing for absolute rights. But, of course, the claim that we have a prima facie right to do whatever we wish to do is equally absurd. The right is not prima facie either, for who would claim, thinking of the right to be free, that one has a prima facie right to kill others, if one wishes, unless there are moral considerations weighing against it?

There are, however, other situations in which it is accepted by all that a person possesses rights of a certain kind, and the difficulty we face is that of according the person the right he is claiming when this will promote more evil than good. The just act is to give the man his due and giving a man what it is his right to have is giving him his due. But it is a mistake to suppose that justice is the only dimension of morality. It may be justifiable not to accord to a man his rights. But it is no less a wrong to him, no less an infringement. It is seriously misleading to turn all justifiable infringements into noninfringements by saying that the right is only prima facie, as if we have, in concluding that we should not accord a man his rights, made out a case that he had none. To use the language of 'prima facie rights' misleads, for it suggests that a presumption of the existence of a right has been overcome in these cases where all that can be said is that the presumption in favor of according a man his rights has been overcome. If we begin to think the right itself is prima facie, we shall, in cases in which we are justified in not according it, fail sufficiently to bring out that we have interfered where justice says we should not. Our moral framework is unnecessarily and undesirably impoverished by the theory that there are such rights.

When I claim, then, that the right to be treated as a person is absolute what I claim is that given that one is a person, one always has the right so to be treated, and that while there may possibly be occasions morally requiring not according a person this right, this fact makes it no less true that the right exists and would be infringed if the person were not accorded it.

4. Having said something about the nature of this fundamental right I want now, in conclusion, to suggest that the denial of this right entails the denial of all moral rights and duties. This requires bringing out what is purely intuitively clear that any framework of rights and duties presupposes individuals that have the capacity to choose on the basis of reasons presented to them, and that what makes legitimate actions within such a system are the free choices of individuals. There is, in other words, a distribution of benefits and burdens in accord with a respect for the freedom of choice and freedom of action of all. I think that the best way to make this point may be to sketch some of the features of a world in which rights and duties are possessed.

First, rights exist only when there is some conception of some things valued and others not. Secondly, and implied in the first point, is the fact that there are dispositions to defend the valued commodities. Third, the valued commodities may be interfered with by others in this world. A group of animals might be said to satisfy these first three conditions. Fourth, rights exist when there are recognized rules establishing the legitimacy of some acts and ruling out others. Mistakes in the claim of right are possible. Rights imply the concepts of interference and infringement, concepts the elucidation of which requires the concept of a rule applying to the conduct of persons. Fifth, to possess a right is to possess something that constitutes a legitimate restraint on the freedom of action of others. It is clear, for example, that if individuals were incapable of controlling their actions we would have no notion of a legitimate claim that they do so. If, for example, we were all disposed to object or disposed to complain, as the elephant seal is disposed to object when his territory is invaded, then the objection would operate in a causal way, or approximating a causal way, in getting the behavior of non-interference. In a system of rights, on the other hand, there is a point to appealing to the rules in legitimating one's complaint. Implied, then, in any conception of rights are the existence of individuals capable of choosing and capable of choosing on the basis of considerations with respect to rules. The distribution of freedom throughout such a system is determined by the free choice of individuals. Thus any denial of the right to be treated as a person would be a denial undercutting the whole system, for the system rests on the assumption that spheres of legitimate and illegitimate conduct are to be delimited with regard to the choices made by persons.

This conclusion stimulates one final reflection on the therapy world we imagined.

The denial of this fundamental right will also carry with it, ironically, the denial of the right to treatment to those who are ill. In the world as we now understand it, there are those who do wrong and who have a right to be responded to as persons who have done wrong. And there are those who have not done wrong but who are suffering from illnesses that in a variety of ways interfere with their capacity to live their lives as complete persons. These persons who are ill have a claim upon our compassion. But more than this they have, as animals do not, a right to be treated as persons. When an individual is ill he is entitled to that assistance which will make it possible for him to resume his functioning as a person. If it is an injustice to punish an innocent person, it is no less an injustice, and a far more significant one in our day, to fail to promote as best we can through adequate facilities and medical care the treatment of those who are ill. Those human beings who fill our mental institutions are entitled to more than they do in fact receive; they should be viewed as possessing the right to be treated as a person so that our responses to them may increase the likelihood that they will enjoy fully the right to be so treated. Like the child the mentally ill person has a future interest we cannot rightly deny him. Society is today sensitive to the infringement of justice in punishing the innocent; elaborate rules exist to avoid this evil. Society should be no less sensitive to the injustice of failing to bring back to the community of persons those whom it is possible to bring back.

NOTES

1. "When a man is suffering from an infectious disease, he is a danger to the community, and it is necessary to restrict his liberty of movement. But no one associates any idea of guilt with such a situation. On the contrary, he is an object of commiseration to his friends. Such steps as science recommends are taken to cure him of his disease, and he submits as a rule without reluctance to the curtailment of liberty involved meanwhile. The same method in spirit ought to be shown in the treatment of what is called 'crime.' "

Bertrand Russell, *Roads to Freedom* (London: George Allen and Unwin Ltd., 1918), p. 135.

"We do not hold people responsible for their reflexes—for example, for coughing in church. We hold them responsible for their operant behavior—for example, for whispering in church or remaining in church while coughing. But there are variables which are responsible for whispering as well as coughing, and these may be just as inexorable. When we recognize this, we are likely to drop the notion of responsibility altogether and with it the doctrine of free will as an inner causal agent."

B. F. Skinner, *Science and Human Behavior* (1953), pp. 115-6.

"Basically, criminality is but a symptom of insanity, using the term in its widest generic sense to express unacceptable social behavior based on unconscious motivation flowing from a disturbed instinctive and emotional life, whether this appears in frank psychoses, or in less obvious form in neuroses and unrecognized psychoses. . . . If criminals are products of early environmental influences in the same sense that psychotics and neurotics are, then it should be possible to reach them psychotherapeutically."

Benjamin Karpman, "Criminal Psychodynamics," *Journal of Criminal Law and Criminology*, 47 (1956), p. 9.

"We, the agents of society, must move to end the game of tit-for-tat and blow-for-blow in which the offender has foolishly and futilely engaged himself and us. We are not driven, as he is, to wild and impulsive actions. With knowledge comes power, and with power there is no need for the frightened vengeance of the old penology. In its place should go a quiet, dignified, therapeutic program for the rehabilitation of the disorganized one, if possible, the protection of society during the treatment period, and his guided return to useful citizenship, as soon as this can be effected."

Karl Menninger, "Therapy, Not Punishment," *Harper's Magazine* (August 1959), pp. 63–64.

JACKSON TOBY

Is Punishment Necessary?

OF 11 CONTEMPORARY TEXTBOOKS in criminology written by sociologists, ten have one or more chapters devoted to the punishment of
offenders.[1] All ten include a history of methods of punishment in
Western society and, more specifically, a discussion of capital punishment. Seven discuss punishment in pre-literate societies. Seven
include theoretical or philosophical discussions of the "justification"
of punishment—usually in terms of "retribution," "deterrence," and
"reformation." These theoretical analyses are at least as much indebted to law and philosophy as to sociology. Thus, in considering
the basis for punishment, three textbooks refer both to Jeremy
Bentham and to Emile Durkheim; three textbooks refer to Bentham
but not to Durkheim; and one textbook refers to Durkheim but not
to Bentham. Several textbook writers express their opposition to
punishment, especially to cruel punishment. This opposition is alleged to be based on an incompatibility of punishment with scientific considerations. The following quotation is a case in point:

> We still punish primarily for vengeance, or to deter, or in the inter-
> est of a 'just' balance of accounts between 'deliberate' evildoers on
> the one hand and an injured and enraged society on the other. We do
> not yet generally punish or treat as scientific criminology would

Reprinted with permission of the author and by special permission of the
Journal of Criminal Law, Criminology and Police Science, Copyright © 1964 by
the Northwestern University School of Law, Vol. 55, No. 3, pp. 332–337.

This article is a revised version of a paper presented to the 1959 meeting of
the Eastern Sociological Society.

imply, namely, in order to change antisocial attitudes into social attitudes.[2]

Most of the textbook writers note with satisfaction that "the trend in modern countries has been toward humanizing punishment and toward the reduction of brutalities."[3] They point to the decreased use of capital punishment, the introduction of amenities into the modern prison by enlightened penology, and the increasing emphasis on nonpunitive and individualized methods of dealing with offenders, e.g., probation, parole, psychotherapy. In short, students reading these textbooks might infer that punishment is a vestigial carry-over of a barbaric past and will disappear as humanitarianism and rationality spread. Let us examine this inference in terms of the motives underlying punishment and the necessities of social control.

The Urge to Punish

Many crimes have identifiable victims. In the case of crimes against the person, physical or psychic injuries have been visited upon the victim. In the case of crimes against property, someone's property has been stolen or destroyed. In pressing charges against the offender, the victim may express hostility against the person who injured him in a socially acceptable way. Those who identify with the victim—not only his friends and family but those who can imagine the same injury being done to them—may join with him in clamoring for the punishment of the offender. If, as has been argued, the norm of reciprocity is fundamental to human interaction, this hostility of the victim constituency toward offenders is an obstacle to the elimination of punishment from social life.[4] Of course, the size of the group constituted by victims and those who identify with victims may be small. Empirical study would probably show that it varies by offense. Thus, it is possible that nearly everyone identifies with the victim of a murderer but relatively few people with the victim of a blackmailer. The greater the size of the victim constituency, the greater the opposition to a non-punitive reaction to the offender.

It would be interesting indeed to measure the size and the composition of the victim constituencies for various crimes. Take rape as an illustration. Since the victims of rape are females, we might hypothesize that *women* would express greater punitiveness toward rapists than *men* and that degrees of hostility would correspond to real or imaginary exposure to rape. Thus, pretty young girls might express more punitiveness toward rapists than homely women. Among males, we might predict that greater punitiveness would be expressed by those with more reason to identify with the victims. Thus, males having sisters or daughters in the late teens or early twenties might express more punitiveness toward rapists than males lacking vulnerable "hostages to fortune."

Such a study might throw considerable light on the wellsprings of punitive motivation, particularly if victimization reactions were distinguished from other reasons for punitiveness. One way to explore such motivation would be to ask the same respondents to express their punitive predispositions toward offenses which do not involve victims at all, e.g., gambling, or which involve victims of a quite different kind. Thus, rape might be balanced by an offense the victims of which are largely male. Survey research of this type is capable of ascertaining the opposition to milder penalties for various offenses. It would incidentally throw light on the comparatively gentle societal reaction to white-collar crime. Perhaps the explanation lies in the difficulty of identifying with the victims of patent infringement or watered hams.[5]

THE SOCIAL CONTROL FUNCTIONS OF PUNISHMENT

CONFORMISTS WHO IDENTIFY with the *victim* are motivated to punish the offender out of some combination of rage and fear. Conformists who identify with the *offender*, albeit unconsciously, may wish to punish him for quite different reasons. Whatever the basis for the motivation to punish, the existence of punitive reactions to deviance is an obstacle to the abolition to punishment. However, it is by no means the sole obstacle. Even though a negligible segment of society felt punitive toward offenders, it might still not be feasible to eliminate punishment if the social control of deviance depended on it. Let us consider, therefore, the consequences of punishing offenders for (a) preventing crime, (b) sustaining the morale of conformists, and (c) rehabilitating offenders.

Punishment as a Means of Crime Prevention

Durkheim defined punishment as an act of vengeance. "What we avenge, what the criminal expiates, is the outrage to morality."[6] But why is vengeance necessary? Not because of the need to deter the bulk of the population from doing likewise. The socialization process prevents most deviant behavior. Those who have introjected the moral norms of their society cannot commit crimes because their self-concepts will not permit them to do so. Only the unsocialized (and therefore amoral) individual fits the model of classical criminology and is deterred from expressing deviant impulses by a nice calculation of pleasures and punishments.[7] Other things being equal, the anticipation of punishment would seem to have more deterrent value for inadequately socialized members of the group. It is difficult to investigate this proposition empirically because other motivationally relevant factors are usually varying simultaneously, e.g., the situational temptations confronting various individuals, their optimism about the chances of escaping detection, and the differential impact of the same punishment on individuals of different status.[8] Clearly, though, the deterrent effect of anticipated punishments is a complex empirical problem, and Durkheim was not interested in it. Feeling as he did that *some* crime is normal in every society, he apparently decided that the crime prevention function of punishment is not crucial. He pointed out that minute gradation in punishment would not be necessary if punishment were simply a means of deterring the potential offender (crime prevention). "Robbers are as strongly inclined to rob as murderers are to murder; the resistance offered by the former is not less than that of the latter, and consequently, to control it, we would have recourse to the same means."[9] Durkheim was factually correct; the offenses punished most severely are not necessarily the ones which present the greatest problem of social defense. Thus, quantitatively speaking, murder is an unimportant cause of death; in the United States it claims only half as many lives annually as does suicide and only one-fifth the toll of automobile accidents. Furthermore, criminologists have been unable to demonstrate a relationship between the murder rate of a community and its use or lack of use of capital punishment.

Most contemporary sociologists would agree with Durkheim that the anticipation of punishment is not the first line of defense against crime. The socialization process keeps most people law abiding, not the police—if for no other reason than the police are not able to catch every offender. This does not mean, however, that the police could be disbanded. During World War II, the Nazis deported all of Denmark's police force, thus providing a natural experiment testing the deterrent efficacy of formal sanctions.[10] Crime increased greatly. Even though punishment is uncertain, especially under contemporary urban conditions, the possibility of punishment keeps some conformists law-abiding. The empirical question is: *How many* conformists would become deviants if they did not fear punishment?

Punishment as a Means of Sustaining the Morale of Conformists

Durkheim considered punishment indispensable as a means of containing the demoralizing consequences of the crimes that could not be prevented. Punishment was not for Durkheim mere vindictiveness. Without punishment Durkheim anticipated the demoralization of "upright people" in the face of defiance of the collective conscience. He believed that unpunished deviance tends to demoralize the conformist and therefore he talked about punishment as a means of repairing "the wounds made upon collective sentiments."[11] Durkheim was not entirely clear; he expressed his ideas in metaphorical language. Nonetheless, we can identify the hypothesis that the punishment of offenders promotes the solidarity of conformists.

Durkheim anticipated psychoanalytic thinking as the following reformulation of his argument shows: One who resists the temptation to do what the group prohibits, to drive his car at 80 miles per hour, to beat up an enemy, to take what he wants without paying for it, would like to feel that these self-imposed abnegations have some meaning. When he sees others defy rules without untoward consequences, he needs some reassurance that his sacrifices were made in a good cause. If "the good die young and the wicked flourish as the green bay tree," the moral scruples which enable conformists to restrain their own deviant inclinations lack social validation. The social significance of punishing offenders is that deviance is thereby defined as unsuccessful in the eyes of conformists, thus making the inhibition or repression of their own deviant impulses seem worthwhile. Righteous indignation is collectively sanctioned reaction formation. The law-abiding person who unconsciously resents restraining his desire to steal and murder has an opportunity, by identifying with the police and the courts, to affect the precarious balance within his own personality between internal controls and the temptation to deviate. A bizarre example of this psychological mechanism is the man who seeks out homosexuals and beats them up mercilessly. Such pathological hostility toward homosexuals is due to the sadist's anxiety over his own sex-role identification. By "punishing" the homosexual, he denies the latent homosexuality in his own psyche. No doubt, some of the persons involved in the administration of punishment are sadistically motivated. But Durkheim hypothesized that the psychic equilibrium of the *ordinary* member of the group may be threatened by violation of norms; Durkheim was not concerned about psychological punitiveness.

Whatever the practical difficulties, Durkheim's hypothesis is, in principle, testable. It should be possible to estimate the demoralizing impact of nonconformity on conformists. Clearly, though, this is no simple matter. The extent of demoralization resulting from the failure to punish may vary with type of crime. The unpunished traffic violator may cause more demoralization than the unpunished exhibitionist—depending on whether or not outwardly conforming members of society are more tempted to exceed the speed limit than to expose themselves. The extent of demoralization may also vary with position in the social structure occupied by the conformist. Thus, Ranulf suggested that the middle class was especially vulnerable:

> [T]he disinterested tendency to inflict punishment is a distinctive characteristic of the lower middle class, that is, of a social class living under conditions which force its members to an extraordinarily high degree of self-restraint and subject them to much frustration of natural desires. If a psychological interpretation is to be put on this correlation of facts, it can hardly be to any other effect than that moral indignation is a kind of resentment caused by the repression of instincts.[12]

Once the facts on the rate and the incidence of moral indignation are known, it will become possible to determine whether something must be done to the offender in order to prevent the demoralization of conformists. Suppose that research revealed that a very large proportion of conformists react with moral indignation to *most* violations of the criminal laws. Does this imply that punishment is a functional necessity? Durkheim apparently thought so, but he might have been less dogmatic in his approach to punishment had he specified the functional problem more clearly: making the nonconformist unattractive as a role model. If the norm violation can be defined as unenviable through some other process than by inflicting suffering upon him, punishment is not required by the exigencies of social control.

Punishment can be discussed on three distinct levels: (a) in terms of the motivations of the societal agents administering it, (b) in terms of the definition of the situation on the part of the person being punished, and (c) in terms of its impact on conformists. At this point I am chiefly concerned with the third level, the impact on conformists. Note that punishment of offenders sustains the morale of conformists only under certain conditions. The first has already been discussed, namely that conformists unconsciously wish to violate the rules themselves. The second is that conformists implicitly assume that the nonconformity is a result of *deliberate defiance* of society's norms. For some conformists, this second condition is not met. Under the guidance of psychiatric thinking, some conformists assume that norm violation is the result of illness rather than wickedness.[13] For such conformists, punishment of the offender does not contribute to their morale. Since they assume that the nonconformity is an involuntary symptom of a disordered personality, the offender is automatically unenviable because illness is (by definition) undesirable. Of course, it is an empirical question as to the relative proportions of the conforming members of society who make the "wicked" or the "sick" assumption about the motivation of the offender, but this can be discovered by investigation.

In Western industrial societies, there is increasing tendency to call contemporary methods of dealing with offenders "treatment" rather than "punishment." Perhaps this means that increasing proportions of the population are willing to accept the "sick" theory of nonconformity. Note, however, that the emphasis on "treatment" may be more a matter of symbolism than of substance. Although the definition of the situation as treatment rather than punishment tends to be humanizing—both to the offender and to the persons who must deal with him—there are still kind guards and cruel nurses. Furthermore, it would be an error to suppose that punishment is invariably experienced as painful by the criminal whereas treatment is always experienced as pleasant by the psycho-pathological offender. Some gang delinquents consider a reformatory sentence an opportunity to renew old acquaintances and to learn new delinquent skills; they resist fiercely the degrading suggestion that they need the services of the "nut doctor." Some mental patients are terrified by shock treatment and embarrassed by group therapy.

What then is the significance of the increasing emphasis on "treatment"? Why call an institution for the criminally insane a "hospital" although it bears a closer resemblance to a prison than to a hospital for the physically ill? In my opinion, the increased emphasis on treatment in penological thinking and practice reflects the existence of a large group of conformists who are undecided as between the "wicked" and the "sick" theories of nonconformity. When they observe that the offender is placed in "treatment," their provisional diagnosis of illness is confirmed, and therefore they do not feel that he has "gotten away with it." Note that "treatment" has the capacity to make the offender unenviable to conformists whether or not it is effective in rehabilitating him and whether or not he experiences it as pleasant. Those old-fashioned conformists who are not persuaded by official diagnoses of illness will not be satisfied by "treatment"; they will prefer to see an attempt made to visit physical suffering or mental anguish on the offender. For them, punishment is necessary to prevent demoralization.

Punishment as a Means of Reforming the Offender

Rehabilitation of offenders swells the number of conformists and therefore is regarded both by humanitarians and by scientifically minded penologists as more constructive than punishment. Most of the arguments against imprisonment and other forms of punishment in the correctional literature boil down to the assertion that punishment is incompatible with rehabilitation. The high rate of recidivism for prisons and reformatories is cited as evidence of the irrationality of punishment.[14] What sense is there in subjecting offenders to the frustrations of incarceration? If rehabilitative programs are designed to help the offender cope with frustrations in his life situation, which presumably were responsible for his nonconformity, imprisoning him hardly seems a good way to begin. To generalize the argument, the status degradation inherent in punishment makes it more difficult to induce the offender to play a legitimate role instead of a nonconforming one. Whatever the offender's original motivations for nonconformity, punishment adds to them by neutralizing his fear of losing the respect of the community; he has already lost it.

Plausible though this argument is, empirical research has not yet verified it. The superior rehabilitative efficacy of "enlightened" prisons is a humanitarian assumption, but brutal correctional systems have, so far as is known, comparable recidivism rates to "enlightened" systems. True, the recidivism rate of offenders who are fined or placed on probation is less than the recidivism rate of offenders who are incarcerated, but this comparison is not merely one of varying degrees of punishment. Presumably, more severe punishment is meted out to criminals who are more deeply committed to a deviant way of life. Until it is demonstrated that the recidivism rates of strictly comparable populations of deviants differ depending on the degree of punitiveness with which they are treated, the empirical incompatibility of punishment and rehabilitation will remain an open question.

Even on theoretical grounds, however, the incompatibility of punishment and rehabilitation can be questioned once it is recognized that one may precede the other. Perhaps, as Lloyd McCorkle and Richard Korn think, some types of deviants become willing to change only if the bankruptcy of their way of life is conclusively demonstrated to them.[15] On this assumption, punishment may be a necessary preliminary to a rehabilitative program in much the same way that shock treatment makes certain types of psychotics accessible to psychotherapy.

It seems to me that the compatibility of punishment and rehabilitation could be clarified (although not settled) if it were considered from the point of view of the *meaning* of punishment to the offender. Those offenders who regard punishment as a deserved deprivation resulting from their own misbehavior are qualitatively different from offenders who regard punishment as a misfortune bearing no relationship to morality. Thus, a child who is spanked by his father and the member of a bopping gang who is jailed for carrying concealed weapons are both "punished." But one accepts the deprivation as legitimate, and the other bows before superior force. I would hypothesize that punishment has rehabilitative significance only for the former. If this is so, correctional officials must convince the prisoner that his punishment is just before they can motivate him to change. This is no simple task. It is difficult for several reasons:

1. It is obvious to convicted offenders, if not to correctional officials, that *some* so-called "criminals" are being punished disproportionately for trifling offenses whereas *some* predatory business men and politicians enjoy prosperity and freedom. To deny that injustices occur confirms the cynical in their belief that "legitimate" people are not only as predatory as criminals but hypocritical to boot. When correctional officials act as though there were no intermediate position between asserting that perfect justice characterizes our society and that it is a jungle, they make it more difficult to persuade persons undergoing punishment that the best approximation of justice is available that imperfect human beings can manage.[16]

2. Of course, the more cases of injustice known to offenders, the harder it is to argue that the contemporary approximation of justice is the best that can be managed. It is difficult to persuade Negro inmates that their incarceration has moral significance if their life experience has demonstrated to them that the police and the courts are less scrupulous of *their* rights than of the rights of white persons. It is difficult to persuade an indigent inmate that his incarceration has moral significance if his poverty resulted in inadequate legal representation.[17]

3. Finally, the major form of punishment for serious offenders (imprisonment) tends to generate a contraculture which denies that justice has anything to do with legal penalties.[18] That is to say, it is too costly to confine large numbers of people in isolation from one another, yet congregate confinement results in the mutual reinforcement of self-justifications. Even those who enter prison feeling contrite are influenced by the self-righteous inmate climate; this may be part of the reason recidivism rates rise with each successive commitment.[19]

In view of the foregoing considerations, I hypothesize that

punishment—as it is now practiced in Western societies—is usually an obstacle to rehabilitation. Some exceptions to this generalization should be noted. A few small treatment institutions have not only prevented the development of a self-righteous contraculture but have managed to establish an inmate climate supportive of changed values.[20] In such institutions punishment has rehabilitative significance for the same reason it has educational significance in the normal family: it is legitimate.

To sum up: The social control functions of punishment include crime prevention, sustaining the morale of the conformists, and the rehabilitation of offenders. All of the empirical evidence is not in, but it is quite possible that punishment contributes to some of these and interferes with others. Suppose, for example, that punishment is necessary for crime prevention and to maintain the morale of conformists but is generally an obstacle to the rehabilitation of offenders. Since the proportion of deviants is small in any viable system as compared with the proportion of conformists, the failure to rehabilitate them will not jeopardize the social order. Therefore, under these assumptions, sociological counsel would favor the continued employment of punishment.

Conclusion

A MEMBER OF A SOCIAL SYSTEM who violates its cherished rules threatens the stability of that system. Conformists who identify with the victim are motivated to punish the criminal in order to feel safe. Conformists who unconsciously identify with the criminal fear their own ambivalence. If norm violation is defined by conformists as willful, visiting upon the offender some injury or degradation will make him unenviable. If his behavior is defined by conformists as a symptom of pathology they are delighted not to share, putting him into treatment validates their diagnosis of undesirable illness. Whether he is "punished" or "treated," however, the disruptive consequence of his deviance is contained. Thus, from the viewpoint of social control, the alternative outcomes of the punishment or treatment processes, rehabilitation or recidivism, are less important than the deviant's neutralization as a possible role model. Whether punishment is or is not necessary rests ultimately on empirical questions: (1) the extent to which identification with the victim occurs, (2) the extent to which nonconformity is prevented by the anticipation of punishment, (3) what the consequences are for the morale of conformists of punishing the deviant or of treating his imputed pathology, and (4) the compatibility between punishment and rehabilitation.

NOTES

---

1. Barnes & Teeters, *New Horizons in Criminology* (3d ed. 1959); Caldwell, *Criminology* (1956); Cavan, *Criminology* (1955); Elliot, *Crime in Modern Society* (1952); Korn & McCorkle, *Criminology and Penology* (1959); Reckless, *The Crime Problem* (2d ed. 1955); Sutherland & Cressey, *Principles of Criminology* (5th ed. 1955); Taft, *Criminology* (3d ed. 1956); Tappan, *Crime, Justice and Correction* (1960); von Hentig, *Crime: Causes and Conditions* (1947); Wood & Waite, *Crime and Its Treatment* (1941).

2. Taft, *op. cit. supra* note 1, at 359.

3. Reckless, *op. cit. supra* note 1, at 450.

4. Gouldner, *The Norm of Reciprocity: A Preliminary Statement,* 25 Am. Soc. Rev. 161 (1960).

5. In this connection, it is well to recall that there is less reluctance to steal from corporations than from humans. See A. W. Jones, *Life, Liberty, and Property* (1941).

6. Durkheim, *The Division of Labor in Society* 89 (1947).

7. Parsons, *The Structure of Social Action* 402–03 (1939).

8. Toby, *Social Disorganization and Stake in Conformity: Complementary Factors in the Predatory Behavior of Young Hoodlums,* 48 J. Crim. L., C. & P.S. 12 (1957).

9. *Op. cit. supra* note 6, at 88.

10. Trolle, "Syv Maneder uten politi" ("Seven Months Without Police") (Copenhagen, 1945), quoted in Christie, *Scandinavian Criminology,* 31 *Sociological Inquiry* 101 (1961).

11. Durkheim, *op. cit. supra* note 6, at 108.

12. Ranulf, *Moral Indignation and Middle-Class Psychology* 198 (Copenhagen, 1938).

13. Talcott Parsons has repeatedly suggested the analogy between illness and criminality. See also Aubert & Messinger, *The Criminal and the Sick,* 1 Inquiry 137 (1958), and Wootton, *Social Science and Social Pathology* 203–67 (1959).

14. Vold, *Does the Prison Reform?* 293 Annals 42 (1954).

15. McCorkle & Korn, *Resocialization Within Walls*, 293 Annals 88 (1954).

16. See the interesting discussions of human fallibility in the works of Reinhold Neibuhr—*e.g.*, *The Children of Light and the Children of Darkness* (1950).

17. Trebach, *The Indigent Defendant*, 11 Rutgers L. Rev. 625 (1957).

18. For a discussion of the concept of contraculture, see Yinger, *Contraculture and Subculture*, 25 Am. Soc. Rev. 625 (1960).

19. Sellin, *Recidivism and Maturation*, 4 Nat'l Probation and Parole A.J. 241 (1958).

20. McCorkle, Elias & Bixby, The Highfields Story (1958), and Empey & Rabow, *Experiment in Delinquency Rehabilitation*, 26 Am. Soc. Rev. 679 (1961).

DETERRENCE

CESARE BECCARIA

On Crimes and Punishments

INTRODUCTION

MEN GENERALLY ABANDON the most important regulations either to
the care of ordinary common sense or to the discretion of persons
who have an interest in opposing the wisest laws—laws, that is, of the
kind that naturally promote the universal distribution of advantages
while they resist the force that tends to concentrate them in the
hands of a few, placing the summit of power and happiness on one
side, and on the other, only weakness and misery. It is, therefore,
only after they have passed through a thousand errors in matters most
essential to life and liberty, after they have arrived at the limits of
endurance, exhausted by the wrongs they have suffered, that men
are induced to remedy the disorders that oppress them and to acknowledge the most palpable truths, which, precisely because of
their simplicity, escape the attention of vulgar minds accustomed
not to analyzing things, but to receiving general impressions all of a
piece, rather from tradition than through study.

If we glance at the pages of history, we will find that laws,
which surely are, or ought to be, compacts of free men, have been,
for the most part, a mere tool of the passions of some, or have arisen
from an accidental and temporary need. Never have they been
dictated by a dispassionate student of human nature who might, by
bringing the actions of a multitude of men into focus, consider them
from this single point of view: the *greatest happiness shared by the*

Reprinted from Cesare Beccaria, *On Crimes and Punishments,* translated by
Henry Paolucci, pp. 7–18, 42–44, 55–59, 62–66, 99. Copyright © 1963 by the Bobbs-
Merrill Company, Inc. Reprinted by permission of the publisher.

greatest number.[1] Happy are those few nations that have not waited for the slow succession of coincidence and human vicissitude to force some little turn for the better after the limit of evil has been reached, but have facilitated the intermediate progress by means of good laws. And humanity owes a debt of gratitude to that philosopher who, from the obscurity of his isolated study, had the courage to scatter among the multitude the first seeds, so long unfruitful, of useful truths.[2]

The true relations between sovereigns and their subjects, and between nations, have been discovered. Commerce has been reanimated by the common knowledge of philosophical truths diffused by the art of printing, and there has sprung up among nations a tacit rivalry of industriousness that is most humane and truly worthy of rational beings. Such good things we owe to the productive enlightenment of this age. But very few persons have studied and fought against the cruelty of punishments and the irregularities of criminal procedures, a part of legislation that is as fundamental as it is widely neglected in almost all of Europe. Very few persons have undertaken to demolish the accumulated errors of centuries by rising to general principles, curbing, at least, with the sole force that acknowledged truths possess, the unbounded course of ill-directed power which has continually produced a long and authorized example of the most cold-blooded barbarity. And yet the groans of the weak, sacrificed to cruel ignorance and to opulent indolence; the barbarous torments, multiplied with lavish and useless severity, for crimes either not proved or wholly imaginary; the filth and horrors of a prison, intensified by that cruellest tormentor of the miserable, uncertainty—all these ought to have roused that breed of magistrates who direct the opinions of men.

The immortal Montesquieu[3] has cursorily touched upon this subject. Truth, which is one and indivisible, has obliged me to follow the illustrious steps of that great man, but the thoughtful men for whom I write will easily distinguish my traces from his. I shall deem myself happy if I can obtain, as he did, the secret thanks of the unknown and peace-loving disciples of reason, and if I can inspire that tender thrill with which persons of sensibility respond to one who upholds the interests of humanity.

Adherence to a strictly logical sequence would now lead us to examine and distinguish the various kinds of crimes and modes of punishment; but these are by their nature so variable, because of the diverse circumstances of time and place, that the result would be a catalogue of enormous and boring detail. By indicating only the most general principles and the most dangerous and commonest errors, I will have done enough to disabuse both those who, from a mistaken love of liberty, would be ready to introduce anarchy, and those who would like to see all men subjected to a monastic discipline.

But what are to be the proper punishments for such crimes?

Is the death-penalty really *useful* and *necessary* for the security and good order of society? Are torture and torments *just,* and do they attain the *end* for which laws are instituted? What is the best way to prevent crimes? Are the same punishments equally effective for all times? What influence have they on customary behavior? These problems deserve to be analyzed with that geometric precision which the mist of sophisms, seductive eloquence, and timorous doubt cannot withstand. If I could boast only of having been the first to present to Italy, with a little more clarity, what other nations have boldly written and are beginning to practice, I would account myself fortunate. But if, by defending the rights of man and of unconquerable truth, I should help to save from the spasm and agonies of death some wretched victim of tyranny or of no less fatal ignorance, the thanks and tears of one innocent mortal in his transports of joy would console me for the contempt of all mankind.

II

The Origin of Punishments, and the Right to Punish

No lasting advantage is to be hoped for from political morality if it is not founded upon the ineradicable feelings of mankind. Any law that deviates from these will inevitably encounter a resistance that is certain to prevail over it in the end—in the same way that any force, however small, if continuously applied, is bound to overcome the most violent motion that can be imparted to a body.

Let us consult the human heart, and we shall find there the basic principles of the true right of the sovereign to punish crimes.

No man ever freely sacrificed a portion of his personal liberty merely in behalf of the common good. That chimera exists only in romances. If it were possible, every one of us would prefer that the compacts binding others did not bind us; every man tends to make himself the center of his whole world.[4]

The continuous multiplication of mankind, inconsiderable in itself yet exceeding by far the means that a sterile and uncultivated nature could offer for the satisfaction of increasingly complex needs, united the earliest savages. These first communities of necessity caused the formation of others to resist the first, and the primitive state of warfare thus passed from individuals to nations.[5]

Laws are the conditions under which independent and isolated men united to form a society. Weary of living in a continual state of war, and of enjoying a liberty rendered useless by the uncertainty of preserving it, they sacrificed a part so that they might enjoy the rest of it in peace and safety.[6] The sum of all these portions of liberty sacrificed by each for his own good constitutes the sovereignty of a nation, and their legitimate depositary and administrator is the sovereign. But merely to have established this deposit was not enough; it had to be defended against private usurpations by individuals each of whom always tries not only to withdraw his own share but also to usurp for himself that of others. Some tangible motives had to be introduced, therefore, to prevent the despotic spirit, which is in every man, from plunging the laws of society into its original chaos. These tangible motives are the punishments established against infractors of the laws. I say "tangible motives" because experience has shown that the multitude adopt no fixed principles of conduct and will not be released from the sway of that universal principle of dissolution which is seen to operate both in the physical and the moral universe, except for motives that directly strike the senses. These motives, by dint of repeated representation to the mind, counterbalance the powerful impressions of the private passions that oppose the common good.[7] Not eloquence, not declamations, not even the most sublime truths have sufficed, for any considerable length of time, to curb passions excited by vivid impressions of present objects.

It was, thus, necessity that forced men to give up part of their personal liberty, and it is certain, therefore, that each is willing to place in the public fund only the least possible portion, no more than suffices to induce others to defend it.[8] The aggregate of these least possible portions constitutes the right to punish; all that exceeds this is abuse and not justice; it is fact but by no means right.*

Punishments that exceed what is necessary for protection of the deposit of public security are by their very nature unjust, and punishments are increasingly more just as the safety which the sovereign secures for his subjects is the more sacred and inviolable, and the liberty greater.[9]

III

Consequences

THE FIRST CONSEQUENCE of these principles is that only the laws can decree punishments for crimes; authority for this can reside only with the legislator who represents the entire society united by a social contract. No magistrate (who is a part of society) can, with justice, inflict punishments upon another member of the same society. But a punishment that exceeds the limit fixed by the laws is just punishment plus another punishment; a magistrate cannot, therefore, under any pretext of zeal or concern for the public good, augment the punishment established for a delinquent citizen.

The second consequence is that the sovereign, who represents the society itself, can frame only general laws binding all members, but he cannot judge whether someone has violated the social contract, for that would divide the nation into two parts, one represented by the sovereign, who asserts the violation of the contract, and the other by the accused, who denies it. There must, therefore, be a third party to judge the truth of the fact. Hence the need for a magistrate whose decisions, from which there can be no appeal, should consist of mere affirmations or denials of particular facts.

The third consequence is this: even assuming that severity of

---

* Note that the word "right" is not opposed to the word "might"; the first is rather a modification of the second—that modification, to be precise, which is most advantageous to the greater number. And by "justice" I mean nothing more than the bond required to maintain the unity of particular interests which would otherwise dissolve into the original state of insociability.

Care must be taken not to attach to this word "justice" the idea of some real thing, as of a physical force or of an existent being; it is simply a human way of conceiving things, a way that has an enormous influence on everyone's happiness. Much less have I in mind that other kind of justice which emanates from God, and which relates directly to the punishments and rewards of the life to come.

punishments were not directly contrary to the public good and to the very purpose of preventing crimes, if it were possible to prove merely that such severity is useless, in that case also it would be contrary not only to those beneficent virtues that spring from enlightened reason which would rather rule happy men than a herd of slaves in whom a timid cruelty makes its endless rounds; it would be contrary to justice itself and to the very nature of the social contract.

IV

INTERPRETATIONS OF THE LAWS

A FOURTH CONSEQUENCE: Judges in criminal cases cannot have the authority to interpret laws, and the reason, again, is that they are not legislators. Such judges have not received the laws from our ancestors as a family tradition or legacy that leaves to posterity only the burden of obeying them, but they receive them, rather, from the living society, or from the sovereign representing it, who is the legitimate depositary of what actually results from the common will of all. [The judges] receive them not as obligations of some ancient oath* (null, to begin with, because it pretended to bind wills that were not then existent, and iniquitous, because it reduced men from a social state to that of an animal herd), but as consequences of the tacit or expressed oath of allegiance which the united wills of living subjects have pledged to their sovereign, as bonds necessary for restraining and regulating the internal ferment of private interests. This constitutes the natural and real authority of the laws. Who, then, is to be the legitimate interpreter of the laws? Is it to be the sovereign, that is, the depositary of the actual wills of all, or the judge, whose

---

* Each individual is indeed bound to society, but society is, in turn, bound to each individual by a contract which, of its very nature, places both parties under obligation. This obligation, which descends from the throne to the cottage, which binds equally the loftiest and the meanest of men, signifies only that it is in the interests of all that the pacts advantageous to the greatest number be observed.

The word "obligation" is one of those that occur much more frequently in ethics than in any other science, and which are the abbreviated symbol of a rational argument and not of an idea. Seek an adequate idea of the word "obligation" and you will fail to find it; reason about it and you will both understand yourself and be understood by others.

sole charge is merely to examine whether a particular man has or has not committed an unlawful act?

For every crime that comes before him, a judge is required to complete a perfect syllogism in which the major premise must be the general law; the minor, the action that conforms or does not conform to the law; and the conclusion, acquittal or punishment. If the judge were constrained, or if he desired to frame even a single additional syllogism, the door would thereby be opened to uncertainty.

Nothing can be more dangerous than the popular axiom that it is necessary to consult the spirit of the laws. It is a dam that has given way to a torrent of opinions. This truth, which seems paradoxical to ordinary minds that are struck more by trivial present disorders than by the dangerous but remote effects of false principles rooted in a nation, seems to me to be fully demonstrated. Our understandings and all our ideas have a reciprocal connection; the more complicated they are, the more numerous must the ways be that lead to them and depart from them. Each man has his own point of view, and, at each different time, a different one. Thus the "spirit" of the law would be the product of a judge's good or bad logic, of his good or bad digestion; it would depend on the violence of his passions, on the weakness of the accused, on the judge's connections with him, and on all those minute factors that alter the appearances of an object in the fluctuating mind of man. Thus we see the lot of a citizen subjected to frequent changes in passing through different courts, and we see the lives of poor wretches become the victims of the false ratiocinations or of the momentary seething ill-humors of a judge who mistakes for a legitimate interpretation that vague product of the jumbled series of notions which his mind stirs up. Thus we see the same crimes differently punished at different times by the same court, for having consulted not the constant fixed voice of the law but the erring instability of interpretation.

The disorder that arises from rigorous observance of the letter of a penal law is hardly comparable to the disorders that arise from interpretations. The temporary inconvenience of the former prompts one to make the rather easy and needed correction in the words of the law which are the source of uncertainty, but it curbs that fatal license of discussion which gives rise to arbitrary and venal controversies. When a fixed code of laws, which must be observed to the letter, leaves no further care to the judge than to examine the acts of citizens and to decide whether or not they conform to the law as written; when the standard of the just or the unjust, which is to be the norm of conduct for the ignorant as well as for the philosophic citizen, is not a matter of controversy but of fact; then only are citizens not subject to the petty tyrannies of the many which are the more cruel as the distance between the oppressed and the oppressor is less, and which are far more fatal than those of a single man, for the despotism of many can only be corrected by the despotism of one; the cruelty of a single despot is proportioned, not to his might, but to the obstacles he encounters. In this way citizens acquire that sense of security for their own persons which is just, because it is the object of human association, and useful, because it enables them to calculate accurately the inconveniences of a misdeed. It is true, also, that they acquire a spirit of independence, but not one that upsets the laws and resists the chief magistrates; rather one that resists those who have dared to apply the sacred name of virtue to that weakness of theirs which makes them yield to their self-interested and capricious opinions.

These principles will displease those who have assumed for themselves a right to transmit to their inferiors the blows of tyranny that they have received from their superiors. I would, indeed, be most fearful if the spirit of tyranny were in the least compatible with the spirit of literacy.

V

OBSCURITY OF THE LAWS

IF THE INTERPRETATION of laws is an evil, another evil, evidently, is the obscurity that makes interpretation necessary. And this evil would be very great indeed where the laws are written in a language that is foreign to a people, forcing it to rely on a handful of men because it is unable to judge for itself how its liberty or its members may fare—in a language that transforms a sacred and public book into something very like the private possession of a family. When the number of those who can understand the sacred code of laws and hold it in their hands increases, the frequency of crimes will be found to decrease, for undoubtedly ignorance and uncertainty of punishments add much to the eloquence of the passions. What are we to make of men, therefore, when we reflect that this very evil is the inveterate practice of a large part of cultured and enlightened Europe?

One consequence of this last rejection is that, without writing, a society can never acquire a fixed form of government with power that derives from the whole and not from the parts, in which the laws, which cannot be altered except by the general will, are not corrupted in their passage through the mass of private interests. Experience and reason have shown us that the probability and certainty of human traditions diminish the further removed they are from their source. For, obviously, if there exists no enduring memorial of the social compact, how are the laws to withstand the inevitable pressure of time and of passions?

We can thus see how useful the art of printing is, which makes the public, and not some few individuals, the guardians of the sacred laws. And we can see how it has dissipated the benighted spirit of cabal and intrigue, which must soon vanish in the presence of those enlightened studies and sciences, apparently despised, but really feared, by its adherents. This explains why we now see in Europe a diminishing of the atrocity of the crimes that afflicted our ancestors, who became tyrants and slaves by turns. Any one acquainted with the history of the past two centuries, and of our own time, may observe how from the lap of luxury and softness have sprung the most pleasing virtues, humanity, benevolence, and toleration of human errors. He will see what the real effects were of the so-called simplicity and good faith of old: humanity groaning under implacable superstition; avarice and private ambition staining with blood the golden treasure-chests and thrones of kings; secret betrayals and public massacres; every nobleman a tyrant over the people; ministers of the Gospel truth polluting with blood the hands that daily touched the God of mercy—these, surely, are not the work of this enlightened age that some people call corrupt. [pp. 7–18]

XV

MILDNESS OF PUNISHMENTS

FROM SIMPLE CONSIDERATION of the truths thus far presented it is evident that the purpose of punishment is neither to torment and afflict a sensitive being, nor to undo a crime already committed. Can there, in a body politic which, far from acting on passion, is the tranquil moderator of private passions—can there be a place for this useless cruelty, for this instrument of wrath and fanaticism, or of weak tyrants? Can the shrieks of a wretch recall from time, which never reverses its course, deeds already accomplished? The purpose can only be to prevent the criminal from inflicting new injuries on its citizens and to deter others from similar acts.[10] Always keeping due proportions, such punishments and such method of inflicting them ought to be chosen, therefore, which will make the strongest and most lasting impression on the minds of men, and inflict the least torment on the body of the criminal.

Who, in reading history, can keep from cringing with horror before the spectacle of barbarous and useless torments, cold-bloodedly devised and carried through by men who called themselves wise? What man of any sensibility can keep from shuddering when he sees thousands of poor wretches driven by a misery either intended or tolerated by the laws (which have always favored the few and outraged the many) to a desperate return to the original state of nature—when he sees them accused of impossible crimes, fabricated by timid ignorance, or found guilty of nothing other than being true to their own principles, and sees them lacerated with meditated formality and slow torture by men gifted with the same senses, and consequently with the same passions? Happy spectacle for a fanatical multitude!

For a punishment to attain its end, the evil which it inflicts has only to exceed the advantage derivable from the crime; in this excess of evil one should include the certainty of punishment and the loss of the good which the crime might have produced.[11] All beyond this is superfluous and for that reason tyrannical. Men are regulated in their conduct by the repeated impression of evils they know, and not according to those of which they are ignorant. Given, for example, two nations, in one of which, in the scale of punishments proportioned to the scale of crimes, the maximum punishment is perpetual slavery, and in the other the wheel; I say that the first shall have as much fear of its maximum punishment as the second; whatever reason might be adduced for introducing to the first the maximum punishment of the other could similarly be adduced to justify intensification of punishments in the latter, passing imperceptibly from the wheel to slower and more ingenious torments, and at length to the ultimate refinements of a science only too well known to tyrants.

In proportion as torments become more cruel, the spirits of men, which are like fluids that always rise to the level of surrounding objects, become callous, and the ever lively force of the passions brings it to pass that after a hundred years of cruel torments the wheel inspires no greater fear than imprisonment once did. The severity of punishment of itself emboldens men to commit the very wrongs it is supposed to prevent; they are driven to commit additional crimes to avoid the punishment for a single one. The countries and times most notorious for severity of penalties have always been those in which the bloodiest and most inhumane of deeds were committed, for the same spirit of ferocity that guided the hand of the legislators also ruled that of the parricide and assassin. On the throne it dictated iron laws for vicious-spirited slaves to obey, while in private, hiddenly, it instigated the slaughter of tyrants only to make room for new ones.

Two other baneful consequences derive from the cruelty of punishments, interfering with the avowed purpose of preventing crimes. The first is that it is not easy to establish a proper proportion between crime and punishment because, however much an industrious cruelty may have multiplied the variety of its forms, they cannot exceed in force the limits of endurance determined by human organization and sensibility. When once those limits are reached, it is impossible to devise, for still more injurious and atrocious crimes, any additional punishment that could conceivably serve to prevent them. The other consequence is that impunity itself results from the atrocity of penalties. Men are bound within limits, no less in evil than in good; a spectacle too atrocious for humanity can only be a passing rage, never a permanent system such as the laws must be, for if [the laws] are really cruel, they must either be changed or fatal impunity will follow from the laws themselves.

I conclude with this reflection that the scale of punishments should be relative to the state of the nation itself. Very strong and sensible impressions are demanded for the callous spirits of a people that has just emerged from the savage state. A lightning bolt is necessary to stop a ferocious lion that turns upon the shot of a rifle. But to the extent that spirits are softened in the social state, sensibility increases and, as it increases, the force of punishment must diminish if the relation between object and sensory impression is to be kept constant.[12] [pp. 42–44]

XIX

PROMPTNESS OF PUNISHMENT

THE MORE PROMPTLY and the more closely punishment follows upon the commission of a crime, the more just and useful will it be. I say more just, because the criminal is thereby spared the useless and cruel torments of uncertainty, which increase with the vigor of imagination and with the sense of personal weakness; more just, because privation of liberty, being itself a punishment, should not precede the sentence except when necessity requires. Imprisonment of a citizen, then, is simply custody of his person until he be judged guilty; and this custody, being essentially penal, should be of the least possible duration and of the least possible severity. The time limit should be determined both by the anticipated length of the trial and by seniority among those who are entitled to be tried first. The strictness of confinement should be no more than is necessary to prevent him from taking flight or from concealing the proofs of his crimes. The trial itself should be completed in the briefest possible time. What crueler contrast than the indolence of a judge and the anguish of a man under accusation—the comforts and pleasures of an insensitive magistrate on one side, and on the other the tears, the squalor of a prisoner? In general, the weight of punishment and the consequence of a crime should be that which is most efficacious for others, and which inflicts the least possible hardship upon the person who suffers it; one cannot call legitimate any society which does not maintain, as an infallible principle, that men have wished to subject themselves only to the least possible evils.

I have said that the promptness of punishments is more useful because when the length of time that passes between the punishment and the misdeed is less, so much the stronger and more lasting in the human mind is the association of these two ideas, *crime and punishment;* they then come insensibly to be considered, one as the cause, the other as the necessary inevitable effect. It has been demonstrated that the association of ideas is the cement that forms the entire fabric of the human intellect; without this cement pleasure and pain would be isolated sentiments and of no effect. The more men depart from general ideas and universal principles, that is, the more vulgar they are, the more apt are they to act merely on immediate and familiar associations, ignoring the more remote and complex ones that serve only men strongly impassioned for the object of their desires; the light of attention illuminates only a single object, leaving the others dark. They are of service also to more elevated minds, for they have acquired the habit of rapidly surveying many objects at once, and are able with facility to contrast many partial sentiments one with another, so that the result, which is action, is less dangerous and uncertain.

Of utmost importance is it, therefore, that the crime and the punishment be intimately linked together, if it be desirable that, in crude, vulgar minds, the seductive picture of a particularly advantageous crime should immediately call up the associated idea of punishment. Long delay always produces the effect of further separating these two ideas; thus, though punishment of a crime may make an impression, it will be less as a punishment than as a spectacle, and will be left only after the horror of the particular crime, which should serve to reinforce the feeling of punishment, has been much weakened in the hearts of the spectators.

Another principle serves admirably to draw even closer the important connection between a misdeed and its punishment, namely, that the latter be as much in conformity as possible with the nature of the crime. This analogy facilitates admirably the contrast that ought to exist between the inducement to crime and the counterforce of punishment, so that the latter may deter and lead the mind toward a goal the very opposite of that toward which the seductive idea of breaking the laws seeks to direct it.

Those guilty of lesser crimes are usually punished either in the obscurity of a prison or by transportation, to serve as an example, with a distant and therefore almost useless servitude, to nations which they have not offended. Since men are not induced on the spur of the moment to commit the gravest crimes, public punishment of a great misdeed will be regarded by the majority as something very remote and of improbable occurrence; but public punishment of lesser crimes, which are closer to men's hearts, will make an impression which, while deterring them from these, deters them even further from the graver crimes. A proportioning of punishments to one another and to crimes should comprehend not only their force but also the manner of inflicting them.

XX

THE CERTAINTY OF PUNISHMENT. MERCY

ONE OF THE GREATEST CURBS ON CRIMES is not the cruelty of punishments, but their infallibility, and, consequently, the vigilance of magistrates, and that severity of an inexorable judge which, to be a useful virtue, must be accompanied by a mild legislation. The certainty of a punishment, even if it be moderate, will always make a stronger impression than the fear of another which is more terrible but combined with the hope of impunity; even the least evils, when they are certain, always terrify men's minds, and hope, that heavenly gift which is often our sole recompense for everything, tends to keep the thought of greater evils remote from us, especially when its strength is increased by the idea of impunity which avarice and weakness only too often afford.

Sometimes a man is freed from punishment for a lesser crime when the offended party chooses to forgive—an act in accord with beneficence and humanity, but contrary to the public good—as if a private citizen, by an act of remission, could eliminate the need for an example, in the same way that he can waive compensation for the injury. The right to inflict punishment is a right not of an individual, but of all citizens, or of their sovereign. An individual can renounce his own portion of right, but cannot annul that of others.

As punishments become more mild, clemency and pardon become less necessary. Happy the nation in which they might some day be considered pernicious! Clemency, therefore, that virtue which has sometimes been deemed a sufficient substitute in a sovereign for all the duties of the throne, should be excluded from perfect legislation, where the punishments are mild and the method of judgment regular and expeditious. This truth will seem harsh to anyone living in the midst of the disorders of a criminal system, where pardons and mercy are necessary to compensate for the absurdity of the laws and the severity of the sentences. This, which is indeed the noblest prerogative of the throne, the most desirable attribute of sovereignty, is also, however, the tacit disapprobation of the beneficent dispensers of public happiness for a code which, with all its imperfections, has in its favor the prejudice of centuries, the voluminous and imposing dowry of innumerable commentators, the weighty apparatus of endless formalities, and the adherence of the most insinuating and least formidable of the semi-learned. But one ought to consider that clemency is a virtue of the legislators and not of the executors of the laws, that it ought to shine in the code itself rather than in the particular judgments. To make men see that crimes can be pardoned or that punishment is not their necessary consequence foments a flattering hope of impunity and creates a belief that, because they might be remitted, sentences which are not remitted are rather acts of oppressive violence than emanations of justice. What is to be said, then, when the ruler grants pardons, that is, public security to a particular individual, and, with a personal act of unenlightened beneficence, constitutes a public decree of impunity? Let the laws, therefore, be inexorable, and inexorable their executors in particular cases, but let the legislator be tender, indulgent, and humane. Let him, a wise architect, raise his building upon the foundation of self-love and let the general interest be the result of the interests of each; he shall not then be constrained, by partial laws and tumultuous remedies, to separate at every moment the public good from that of individuals, and to build the image of public well-being upon fear and distrust. Wise and compassionate philosopher, let him permit men, his brothers, to enjoy in peace that small portion of happiness which the grand system established by the First Cause, by that *which is,* allows them to enjoy in this corner of the universe. [pp. 55–59]

XXIII

PROPORTION BETWEEN CRIMES AND PUNISHMENTS

IT IS TO THE COMMON INTEREST not only that crimes not be committed, but also that they be less frequent in proportion to the harm they cause society. Therefore, the obstacles that deter men from committing crimes should be stronger in proportion as they are contrary to the public good, and as the inducements to commit them are stronger. There must, therefore, be a proper proportion between crimes and punishments.[13]

If pleasure and pain are the motives of sensible beings, if, among the motives for even the sublimest acts of men, rewards and punishments were designated by the invisible Legislator, from their inexact distribution arises the contradiction, as little observed as it is common, that the punishments punish crimes which they themselves have occasioned. If an equal punishment be ordained for two crimes that do not equally injure society, men will not be any more deterred from committing the greater crime, if they find a greater advantage associated with it.

Whoever sees the same death penalty, for instance, decreed for the killing of a pheasant and for the assassination of a man or for forgery of an important writing, will make no distinction between such crimes, thereby destroying the moral sentiments, which are the work of many centuries and of much blood, slowly and with great difficulty registered in the human spirit, and impossible to produce, many believe, without the aid of the most sublime of motives and of an enormous apparatus of grave formalities.

It is impossible to prevent all disorders in the universal conflict of human passions. They increase according to a ratio compounded of population and the crossings of particular interests, which cannot be directed with geometric precision to the public utility. For mathematical exactitude we must substitute, in the arithmetic of politics, the calculation of probabilities. A glance at the histories will show that disorders increase with the confines of empires. National sentiment declining in the same proportion, the tendency to commit crimes increases with the increased interest everyone takes in such disorders; thus there is a constantly increasing need to make punishments heavier.

That force, similar to gravity, which impels us to seek our own well-being is restrained in its operation only to the extent that obstacles are set up against it. The effects of this force are the confused series of human actions. If these clash together and disturb one another, punishments, which I would call "political obstacles," prevent the bad effect without destroying the impelling cause, which is that sensibility inseparable from man. And the legislator acts then like an able architect whose function it is to check the destructive tendencies of gravity and to align correctly those that contribute to the strength of the building.

Given the necessity of human association, given the pacts that result from the very opposition of private interests, a scale of disorders is distinguishable, the first grade consisting of those that are immediately destructive of society, and the last, of those that do the least possible injustice to its individual members. Between these extremes are included all the actions contrary to the public good that are called crimes, and they all descend by insensible gradations from the highest to the lowest. If geometry were applicable to the infinite and obscure combinations of human actions, there ought to be a corresponding scale of punishments, descending from the greatest to the least; if there were an exact and universal scale of punishments and of crimes, we would have a fairly reliable and common measure of the degrees of tyranny and liberty, of the fund of humanity or of malice, of the various nations. But it is enough for the wise legislator to mark the principal points of division without disturbing the order, not assigning to crimes of the first grade the punishments of the last.

XXIV

THE MEASURE OF CRIMES

WE HAVE SEEN what the true measure of crimes is—namely, the *harm done to society*. This is one of those palpable truths which, though requiring neither quadrants nor telescopes for their discovery, and lying well within the capacity of any ordinary intellect, are, nevertheless, because of a marvelous combination of circumstances, known with clarity and precision only by some few thinking men in every nation and in every age. But notions of an Asiatic sort, and passions clothed with authority and power, usually with indiscernible but sometimes with violent impressions made on the timid credulity of men, have effaced the simple notions that perhaps formed the first philosophy of primitive societies— notions back to which the present enlightenment seems to be leading us, but with that greater degree of certitude obtainable through precise analysis, through a thousand unhappy experiences and from the very obstacles in its way.

They were in error who believed that the true measure of crimes is to be found in the intention of the person who commits them. Intention depends on the impression objects actually make and on the precedent disposition of the mind; these vary in all men and in each man, according to the swift succession of ideas, of passions, and of circumstances. It would be necessary, therefore, to form not only a particular code for each citizen, but a new law for every crime. Sometimes, with the best intentions, men do the greatest injury to society; at other times, intending the worst for it, they do the greatest good.

Others measure crimes rather by the dignity of the injured person than by the importance [of the offense] with respect to the public good. If this were the true measure of crimes, an irreverence toward the Being of beings ought to be more severely punished than the assassination of a monarch, the superiority of nature constituting infinite compensation for the difference in the injury.

Finally, some have thought that the gravity of sinfulness ought to enter into the measure of crimes. The fallacy of this opinion will at once appear to the eye of an impartial examiner of the true relations between men and men, and between men and God. The first are relations of equality. Necessity alone brought into being, out of the clash of passions and the opposition of interests, the idea of *common utility*, which is the foundation of human justice. The second are relations of dependence on a perfect Being and Creator, who has reserved to himself alone the right to be legislator and judge at the same time, because he alone can be such without inconvenience. If he has established eternal punishments for anyone who disobeys his omnipotence, what insect is it that shall dare to take the place of divine justice, that shall want to vindicate the Being who is sufficient unto himself, who cannot receive from things any impression of pleasure or pain, and who, alone among all beings, acts without suffering any reaction? The weight of sin depends on the inscrutable malice of the heart, which can be known by finite beings only if it is revealed. How then can a norm for punishing crimes be drawn from this? Men might in such a case punish where God forgives, and forgive where God punishes. If men can be in opposition with the Omnipotent in offending him, they may also be so in punishing. [pp. 62–66]

XLII

Conclusion

FROM WHAT HAS THUS FAR been demonstrated, one may deduce a general theorem of considerable utility, though hardly conformable with custom, the usual legislator of nations; it is this: *In order for punishment not to be, in every instance, an act of violence of one or of many against a private citizen, it must be essentially public, prompt, necessary, the least possible in the given circumstances, proportionate to the crimes, dictated by the laws.*[14] [p. 99]

TRANSLATOR'S NOTES

1. "La massima felicità divisa nel maggior numero." Many approximations of this celebrated formula are no doubt to be found in the extensive literature of eudaimonistic and hedonistic ethics which originated with the ancient Greeks, but there is no question that Jeremy Bentham, who made the formula famous, first encountered it here.

2. Perhaps Jean Jacques Rousseau.

3. Charles Louis de Secondat, Baron de la Brède et de Montesquieu (1689–1755). Beccaria was greatly excited and influenced by Montesquieu's *Persian Letters* (1721) and *The Spirit of the Laws* (1748). Book XI of the latter work has been called "the Magna Carta of criminals." See Franz Neumann's Introduction to *The Spirit of the Laws* (New York, 1949), p. 1.

4. This negative view of the political constitution of society as a mere restriction on individual liberty, to be endured as a necessary evil, is, of course, apparently consistent with Rousseau's statement of the "fundamental problem" of the *Social Contract* (I, 6), which is "to find a form of association which will defend and protect the person and property of each associate, and wherein each member, united to all the others, still obeys himself alone, and retains his original freedom."

5. See Montesquieu, *Spirit of the Laws*, I, ii–iii: "Hobbes inquires, 'For what reason go men armed, and have locks and keys to fasten their doors, if they be not naturally in a state of war?' But is it not obvious that he attributes to mankind before the establishment of society what can happen but in consequence of this establishment, which furnishes them with motives for hostile attacks and self-defense? ... As soon as man enters into a state of society he loses the sense of his weakness; equality ceases, and then commences the state of war."

6. Cf. Plato, *Republic* III: "When men have both done and suffered injustice they think they had better agree among themselves. ... Hence there arise laws and mutual covenants." See also Lucretius, *De Rerum Natura* V. 1135ff.: "Affairs sank down to turmoil's lowest dregs, when each one was seeking for himself supremacy and highest place. Then some advised appointing magistrates, and drew up codes, that men might wish to have the use of laws; because mankind, worn out with living lives of violence, lay languishing from feuds; wherefore the more spontaneously they gave submission to strict codes of law."

7. For a critique of this utilitarian concept of the "right" of punishment, see G. W. F. Hegel's *Philosophy of Right*, tr. T. M. Knox (Oxford, 1942), pp. 69–73 and 246–47. According to Hegel, the use of punishment as a deterrent, or preventive "threat," cannot be justified in the political association of free and equal human beings. "To base a justification of punishment on threat," Hegel writes, "is to liken it to the act of a man who lifts his stick to a dog. It is to treat a man like a dog instead of with the freedom and respect due to him as a man. But a threat, which after all may rouse a man to demonstrate his freedom in spite of it, discards justice altogether" (p. 246).

8. Cf. Rousseau, *Social Contract*, II, 4: "It is granted that all which an individual alienates by the social compact is only that part of his power, his property, and his liberty, the use of which is important to the community; but we must also grant that the sovereign is the only judge of what is important to the community."

9. Cf. Aristotle, *Politics* VII. 13: "Just punishments and chastisements do indeed spring from a good principle, but they are good only because we cannot do without them—it would be better that neither individuals nor states should need anything of the sort."

10. Cf. Seneca, *De Clementia* I, 16: "No man punishes because a sin has been committed, but that sin may not be committed. For what has passed cannot be recalled, but what is to come may be prevented."

11. Considering the law of the "state of nature," Locke writes (*Second Treatise*, II, 12): "Each transgression may be punished to that degree and with so much severity as will suffice to make it an ill bargain to the offender, give him cause to repent, and terrify others from doing the like" (Library of Liberal Arts edn., No. 31, New York, 1952, p. 9).

12. Cf. Montesquieu, *Spirit*, VI, 12: "Experience shows that in countries remarkable for the lenity of their laws the spirit of the inhabitants is as much affected by slight penalties as in other countries by severer punishments."

13. Cf. Montesquieu, *Spirit*, VI, 16: "It is an essential point that there should be a certain proportion in punishments, because it is essential that a great crime should be avoided rather than a smaller, and that which is more pernicious to society rather than that which is less."

14. See Article VIII of the "Declaration of the Rights of Man and of the Citizen," passed by the revolutionary National Assembly of France, on August 26, 1789: "The law ought to impose no other penalties but such as are absolutely and evidently necessary; and no one ought to be punished, but in virtue of a law promulgated before the offense, and legally applied."

JOHS ANDENAES

General Prevention—Illusion or Reality?

THE TREND IN PENAL REFORM in the past two generations has
pointed in the direction of wider scope for individual prevention
(specific prevention). As a result, the prosecuting authorities and
the courts have through the years had an ever wider choice of sanctions put at their disposal, adapted to the personality of the offender.
We now have special methods of treatment for juvenile delinquents,
abnormal offenders, habitual criminals, vagrants, and alcoholics.
These methods have been developed partly within and partly outside the framework of the penal system; hence they are partly punitive and partly non-punitive in nature. The catchword for the
whole development is the well-known saying of Frantz von Liszt: It
is not the crime but the criminal that is to be punished.

It would be an exaggeration to say that this development has
proceeded without opposition. But the opposition has been far
weaker than might be expected, inasmuch as most of those who consider the general-preventive function of penal law to be the core of
the punitive system have felt they could make these concessions
without any great danger.

But now and then conflict becomes apparent. It is especially
among doctors and prison administrators that we often note great
skepticism toward the belief in general prevention. Sometimes we
see general prevention characterized as little better than a figment
of the imagination, a fiction used by jurists as a defense for their

Reprinted with permission of the author and by special permission of *The
Journal of Criminal Law, Criminology and Police Science*, Copyright © by the
Northwestern University School of Law, Vol. 43, No. 1 (July–August 1952), 176–
198.

traditional rules and concepts. "I shudder," says the Danish physician, Tage Kemp, director of Copenhagen University's Institute for Hereditary Biology, "when I think what this essentially fictitious concept has cost us, in terms of thousands upon thousands of wasted, bitter man-years of imprisonment—and how many lives it has ruined which could just as well have been saved. We lose much of our belief in the need for general prevention if, instead of looking upon the criminal cursorily, thinking in terms of dry, unrealistic legal formalism, we think in more individualistic terms, as indicated by the latest research in criminology and social biology."

Most jurists take a more positive attitude toward general prevention. Some go so far as to regard the general-preventive function as the only possible argument to support both punishment and the awarding of damages. Lundstedt is a good representative of this view; he in turn attacks the idea of individual prevention. "The idea that punishment aims at adjusting the criminal to society is surely one of the most fantastic to be found even in scholastic jurisprudence," he once wrote with an outspokenness characteristic of his style. "Experience teaches us that punishment has exactly the opposite effect on the criminal. Punishment has a natural tendency to demoralize the convicted person, and it frequently shunts him over to a class of social outcasts."

Even if there are not many who would go so far as Lundstedt, we can see jurists motivating their decisions with considerations of general prevention practically every day. This applies especially to lawmaking. In the premises to the Norwegian Penal Code of 1842 it is clearly stated: "The Theory of Deterrence, which in fact forms the basis for our present legislation . . . [appears] to be the main factor to be borne in mind in determining the nature and magnitude of punishments"—but as a secondary purpose there should also be consideration for the effect of punishment on the individual criminal, "in so far as attainment of the primary object permits this." The Penal Code of 1902 and the special laws passed in connection with it represent in many respects a victory for individual prevention. The father of the new law, Bernhard Getz, said in a lecture on the reform before the Norwegian Association of Criminologists that its aim was to "set up a whole system of institutions by which the state can seek to combat crime at its source or upon its manifestation in a manner adapted to each age group and category of crime." Notwithstanding a broader range of vision today than a century ago, I do not think I go far afield in maintaining that it is a primarily preventive consideration—having an eye to what is necessary to keep the people reasonably law-abiding—which today's legislators have in mind, too, when they define crimes and stipulate punishments. They defer somewhat to individual prevention, to be sure, by permitting the courts to set an appropriate punishment in each individual case.

General prevention often appears in judgments as well—especially in situations new to the courts, when they feel a need to offer a deeper explanation than simple reference to precedent.

The controversial question of the general preventive effect of punishment, therefore, is not merely of theoretical interest: it has a very practical side. And it is especially at the present time that it is important to shed light on the problem. Economic and political developments are responsible for legislation's interfering in the individual's affairs in quite a different way than previously—especially in economic matters. And the cure-all for enforcing these rules is threat of punishment. Thus we find a new category of offenses, whose social consequences can be even more dangerous than the more traditional crimes, but which are not regarded so in the public's moral judgment. Wherever legislation breaks new ground in this way, it becomes vital to learn the answers to questions like these: To what extent are we able to direct people's conduct by threat of punishment? What are the prerequisites for an effective legal prohibition? Can we, for example, maintain a prohibition which is not sanctioned by the public's moral code? How important is magnitude of penalty as compared with the risk of disclosure? What is the effect upon general respect for law of the state's sustaining prohibitions that are openly being disregarded?

It would be interesting to try to explain the reasons for the various attitudes toward general prevention in the various professional groups having contact with crime problems. It would require a rather extensive investigation into the specific views and the grounds given for them. But certain points are already evident. Prison officials and doctors naturally regard it as their chief function to help the individual who has come into conflict with the law to make a new start. By the emotional factor alone, this means a tendency to put the main emphasis on individual prevention, at the expense of the less tangible general prevention. The personal tragedies produced by punishment that is unnecessary or undesirable in terms of individual prevention can readily be perceived, while the indirect effects of punishment escape observation. Another point worth noting is that prison officials and mental examiners are constantly coming across cases where threat of punishment has been ineffective. It is understandable that this constantly recurring observation can induce skepticism as to the efficacy of threat of punishment. Where the mental examiner is concerned, there is also the point that the picture of crime he gets is dominated by the more or less abnormal personalities which it is his lot to deal with. The lawyer, on the other hand, often has little psychological insight and little acquaintance with the sort of persons who most frequently come into conflict with the law. So he can easily lose sight of the irrational factors in human motivation and construct psychologically superficial explanations, based on a view that crime grows out of conscious, rational consideration as to what is most profitable. Such reasoning leads naturally to Feuerbach's formula of psychological coercion: the risk for the lawbreaker must be made so great, the punishment so severe, that he knows he has more to lose than he has to gain from his crime.

So it is easy to find explanations for our problem by referring to the jobs and areas of experience of the different occupational groups. But I believe the differences are a bit more apparent than real. Perhaps they arise because the disputants attach different meanings to the terms "general prevention" and "individual prevention." Or perhaps they think of different types of offenders. The purpose of this paper is to contribute to a tidying up of the discussion.

II

BEFORE I START my exposition I should perhaps pause for a moment to offer a precise definition of the concepts in question and their interrelationship.

By general prevention we mean the ability of criminal law and its enforcement to make citizens law-abiding. If general prevention were 100 percent effective there would be no crime at all. General prevention may depend on the mere frightening or deterrent effect of punishment—the risk of discovery and punishment outweighing the temptation to commit crime. This was what Feuerbach had in mind when he designed his famous theory of punishment as psychological coercion directed against the citizen. Later theory puts much stress on the ability of penal law to arouse or strengthen inhibitions of another sort. In Swedish discussion the *moralizing*—in other words the *educational*—function has been greatly stressed. The idea is that punishment as a concrete expression of society's disapproval of an act helps to form and to strengthen the public's moral code and thereby creates conscious and unconscious inhibitions against committing crime. Unconscious inhibitions against committing forbidden acts can also be aroused without appealing to the individual's concepts of morality. Purely as a matter of habit, with fear, respect for authority or social imitation as connecting links, it is possible to induce favorable attitudes toward this or that action and unfavorable attitudes toward another action. We find the clearest example of this in the military, where extended inculcation of discipline and stern reaction against breach thereof can induce a purely automatic, habitual response—not only where obeying specific orders is concerned, but also with regard to general orders and regulations. We have another example in the relationship between an occupying power and an occupied population. The regulations set down by the occupier are not regarded by the people as morally binding; but by a combination of terror and habit formation a great measure of obedience can be elicited—at any rate in response to commands which do not conflict too greatly with national feelings.

We can say that punishment has three sorts of general-preventive effects: it may have a *deterrent* effect, it may strengthen *moral inhibitions* (a *moralizing* effect), and it may stimulate habitual *law-abiding conduct*. I have reason to emphasize this, since many of those who are most skeptical of general prevention think only of the deterrent effect. Even if it can be shown that conscious fear of punishment is not present in certain cases, this is by no means the same as showing that the secondary effects of punishment are without importance. To the lawmaker, the achievement of inhibition and habit is of greater value than mere deterrence. For these apply in cases where a person need not fear detection and punishment, and they can apply without the person even having knowledge of the legal prohibition.

By individual prevention we mean the effect of punishment on the punished. At best this results in genuine moral improvement or in the acquisition of pro-social habits. Here the contrast to general prevention is quite clear. The same holds where the punished is rendered harmless—for good, by means of capital punishment or banishment, or temporarily by means of definitive prison sentences. In other cases the effect on the convict is simple deterrence, without any change in character being induced. When a motorist is fined $5.oo for illegal parking he is neither improved nor rendered harmless, but he will presumably be more careful the next time he parks. Thenceforth the motorist's thinking in such situations will be influenced both general-preventively and individual-preventively. The deterrent effect which the law by itself has on every citizen will be strengthened in his case by the fact that he knows from personal experience that the law means what it says.

The disagreement over the importance of general prevention is of course largely due to the fact that its effectiveness cannot be measured. We do not know the true extent of crime. In certain areas of crime there is reason to believe that the figures available for offenses which are prosecuted and punished corresponds roughly to the true incidence of crime. In other areas recorded crimes represent only a small fraction of the true incidence. We know still less about how many people *would* have committed crimes if there had been no threat of punishment. There is a certain lesson to be drawn from the events following upon changes in the law or in other circumstances important to general prevention—such as police efficiency. We can also get somewhere by the use of common sense and psychology. But even so, it can hardly be denied that any conclusion as to the real nature of general prevention involves a great deal of guesswork. Claims based on the "demands of general prevention," therefore, can often be used to cloak strictly retributive demands for punishment or mere conservative resistance to change. On the other hand, it is just as possible that the importance of general prevention is seriously overlooked by those who are mainly interested in a more efficacious treatment of the individual offender.

On the other hand we might also ask, what do we really know about the individual-preventive effect of punishment? We have figures on recidivism to tell how large a proportion of ex-convicts commit new crimes. Yet, even aside from the significant error that comes from the fact that figures on recidivism only cover cases where the ex-convict is *caught* committing a new crime, the figures can tell us nothing of how great the recidivism would have been if there had been no punishment, or a different punishment. We might compare recidivism according to the different methods of treatment —e.g. recidivism after the use of probation or recidivism after use of special non-penal measures, as opposed to recidivism after ordinary punishment. But the results can hardly be sure, because the different methods of treatment will always be applied against different sorts of law-breakers. If the most promising of these are selected for probation and their recidivism figures are better than others', this is no proof that probation is superior in terms of individual prevention. (If the result were the opposite, however, there would be grounds for more concrete conclusions.) On the whole we can say that recidivism statistics are no more useful in measuring the individual-preventive effect of punishment than the ordinary crime statistics are useful in measuring its general-preventive effect. Both in an evaluation of individual prevention and of general prevention we can resort only to judgment based on psychology, practical experience and common sense.

III

IN OUR ATTEMPT to get a better understanding of the problem, it is of primary importance that we should not take all crime together but take each important group of crimes separately. One reason why the discussion on general prevention is often so fruitless, and why there is such sharp disagreement is, in my experience, that the protagonists generalize too much. They talk about general prevention in the general case, yet tend to draw from experience they have gained in particular areas. This is, in fact, a common error in jurisprudence: on the basis of a limited material a theory is built to cover a much wider area than is logically justified. Psychological attitudes vary markedly in the different categories of law-breaking, and they can also vary markedly in the various groups and strata of the society. As obvious as it is that it is impossible to do a criminological study throwing together thieves and murderers, rapists and usurers, swindlers and thugs, it should be just as obvious that a study of the general-preventive effect of punishment must also be differentiated.

In a short paper like this it is of course not possible to give any more than samples from selected areas.

1) I shall begin with a group of crimes which play a modest role in the literature but which have a good deal of practical importance and are good for illustration, all these *police regulations* which are such commonplaces in modern times: traffic ordinances, building codes, laws governing the sale of alcoholic beverages, regulations governing commerce, etc. Here there is no doubt that punishment for infraction has primarily a general-preventive function. Here nearly all of us are potential criminals. A public-spirited citizen has, of course, certain inhibitions against breaking laws and regulations. But experience shows that moral and social inhibitions against breaking the law are not enough in themselves to insure obedience, where there is conflict with one's private interests. Thus the extent to which there can be effective enforcement by means of punishment determines to what extent the rules are actually going to be observed. As an example of rules which are just about 100 percent effective, because one must count on detection and punishment of all infractions, we can take blackout regulations during war. Deterrence alone suffices here, even without support of the moral authority which the law usually has. Consider a blacked-out city in an occupied country. The occupier's order has no moral authority at all—on the contrary, he is the enemy and must be resisted. But even so, hundreds of thousands of families take great care each night to prevent the least crack of light from showing. As if guided by an unseen hand, these countless householders go into action as soon as darkness falls. No one defies the order, because everyone knows that there is not enough to be gained to make the risk worthwhile. And eventually it becomes a habit, which is followed automatically, practically without thought. It would be hard to find a more impressive example of the "terror effect" of the threat of punishment under favorable circumstances.

It is not hard to find examples of the opposite: regulations which are not observed because there is no punishment of offenders against them. The Danish state prosecutor, Jorgen Trolle, has described the problem presented by Danish tourists to Sweden in an article in *Ugeskrift for Retsvæsen*, 1947 (Weekly Law Review).[1] There were no restrictions on travel to Sweden, although one could only buy a one-way ticket, not round trip. It was forbidden to take

Danish or Swedish money out of Denmark, and this was strictly enforced; travelers were even searched occasionally. It was forbidden to borrow money in Sweden, and any assets already there were to be called home. The logical conclusion, says Trolle, was that traffic would be minimal, comprising only those few who could persuade the National Bank to sell them some Swedish currency or who had close and prosperous relatives in Sweden. But on the contrary, we witnessed great hordes, some days up to several thousand, crossing over to Sweden and returning laden down with goods. The travelers were so numerous that the customs officials and police had to throw up their hands. They checked to see if the travelers had tobacco or other highly dutiable items, but they did not bother to ask how they had got the Swedish money.

Trolle observes that "although everyone knows that the great majority of the numerous travelers who cross the Sound with a passport issued by the Ministry of Justice and on a ship belonging to the Ministry of Transport are lawbreakers, infringing Ministry of Trade regulations, nevertheless the customs officials, who are subject to the Ministry of Finance, and the police, who are subject to the Ministry of Justice, do nothing."

His conclusion is as follows: "It is unjust that the less law-abiding portion of the population should have advantages which the more conscientious ones are deprived of. And it taxes respect for law that everyone and his brother can see and can draw the lesson that one can with impunity allow oneself a wide margin in observing the law."

This is a good example of how undesirable it is to pass laws which cannot be enforced. It is a common failing in legislation. It is so natural to resort to threat of punishment when the authorities decide they want to channel the citizen's actions in one direction or another. The legislators probably realize that many will break the rules but reason that many will observe them, so that something, at least, will be gained. Looked at from the point of view of the individual administrative branch, this can be valid enough, but if the reasoning is followed first in one area and then in another, it can hardly fail to demoralize respect both for the law and for public authority. It makes sense, therefore, that certain thinkers have warned against this "inflation in the administration of criminal law."

I have cited two examples above to show the two extremes. In most cases the efficiency of law enforcement lies between them. How strict the enforcement must be to effect a reasonable degree of general prevention, a reasonable degree of obedience in a given area of administration, depends on many factors—including, how much a person stands to gain by breaking the law and from which strata of the society the lawbreakers are recruited. For example, it makes a difference that it is not the same sort of people who break parking regulations and who break the regulations against drunkenness in public places.

2) The example of Danish tourists to Sweden has taken us, strictly speaking outside the area of true police regulations and into a new area, which we can call *economic crimes.* I do not mean primarily the traditional crimes against property like theft, embezzlement, fraud and receiving stolen goods—I shall come back to these later. I refer here to crimes against governmental regulation of the economy: price violations, rationing violations, unlawful foreign exchange transactions, offenses against workers protection, disregard of quality standards, and so on. Psychologically we can also put customs and tax evasion in this group, although logically these crimes belong in the fraud category.

In time of war and crisis economic crime of this sort can have immense importance to the nation. Outside Scandinavia we have drastic examples of the entire distribution of foodstuffs being disrupted because the goods find their way onto the black market. From postwar Germany, for instance, we have heard how the starving urban population roamed the countryside carrying their family treasures, with the hope of bartering a little food for themselves— food which the farmers withheld from the controlled channels of distribution. Even under fairly normal conditions, however, the political trend in Western Europe seems to be in the direction of more public control of the economy. If the trend continues, the problem of making these controls effective will become a paramount question in penal law—indeed, a question of far greater dimensions than the sort usually discussed in criminological circles. For whatever our opinion may be on the question of free versus controlled economy, there is no denying that ineffective regulation is the worst arrangement of them all.

Psychologically the economic crimes tend to be rather clear-cut. A large number of the people who are affected by economic regulations or by the levying of taxes and fees feel no strong moral inhibition against infraction. They often find excuses for their behavior in political theorizing: they oppose the current government's regulative policies; they find taxes unreasonably high; and they find support for such views in their newspapers, which daily represent the state as a great vampire and governmental agencies as business enemy number one. Yet the matter of obedience or disobedience can often have important economic consequences. It is to be expected that many will calculate in cold blood the risk of being caught, and act accordingly. It is rather significant that a Norwegian religious newspaper of January 1949 carried an article with roughly the following headline: "Time for Taxpayers to Prepare their Annual Evasion." In this area, at any rate, Feuerbach's law of general prevention has a certain validity: it is necessary that consideration as to the risk involved in breaking the law should outweigh consideration of the advantages to breaking the law. The amount of threat needed varies greatly, of course, from person to person. One is a timid, cautious type; another likes to take chances. One has a social position he is afraid to lose; another has no such fear. Generally speaking, the biggest crimes in this area are committed by people with a certain economic and social position, people who can be deterred by even a rather modest risk of detection and punishment. When they break the law nevertheless, it is because they reckon it as overwhelmingly probable that all will go well.

In this connection we might consider what happened upon the calling in of paper money and the forced registration of bank accounts and securities in Norway in 1945.[2] Enormous values came to light which had previously escaped assessment. In some districts only a small percent of the actual bank holdings had previously been declared. On the basis of the registration we can almost lay down the rule that everyone was a tax evader who could be so without risk. The result is striking confirmation of what we could have inferred by ordinary psychological reasoning: the importance of policing to the enforcement of penal provisions. If there were such policing as to produce a risk of 25 percent in making false tax declarations, tax evasion on a grand scale would be practically eliminated.

From this reasoning I draw the following significant conclusion: in discussions on the introduction of new economic regulations, the question of the feasibility of effective enforcement should occupy a central place. And if it is found that such policing is not feasible, that the law will in effect reward dishonesty, the lawmakers should think twice and three times before legislating it—no matter how fine it looks on paper.

3) When we come to the traditional crimes against property, the picture is a bit more complicated. Strong moral and social inhibitions against the criminal act appear alongside regard for the penal code. Now the question is: are not these moral and social inhibitions enough in themselves to keep most people from committing thefts, frauds, and so on? And then: will these moral and social inhibitions retain their strength if the risk of punishment is removed? Is not the methodical use of punishment or other forms of reaction as an answer to such infractions of the law one of the most important factors in arousing the public's taboo attitude toward them?

The question here is not whether you or I would remain law-abiding even if there were no "switch behind the back." The question is whether there is not a fairly large group on the moral borderline who might go wrong, and whether they might not in turn draw others with them. What we are concerned with is, of course, a long-term process, where the full effect of a weakening in the judicial reaction to crime will not be felt before the passage of a generation or more.

In discussing these questions we must not overlook the fact that for numerically important groups, especially in the cities, the social reaction against crime means little, because the moral standard in these groups is too low to be of account. Likewise we must not overlook the fact that the social reaction is connected in many ways to the judicial. This means not simply that general behavior with regard to a category of acts is affected by the law's attitude toward them: but also that *it would be much easier to keep one's acts secret and thus avoid all social reprobation, if one did not have to consider the risk of their being brought to public notice through criminal prosecution.*

The exceptional conditions that prevailed during the German occupation have given us new and valuable experience, even if it must be evaluated cautiously.

In Denmark the Germans arrested the entire Danish police force in September 1944. During the rest of the occupation the policing was done by an improvised and unarmed watch corps, which was all but ineffectual except when the criminal was caught red-handed. Jorgen Trolle headed the Copenhagen state prosecutor's office at the time, and in an extremely interesting book, *Syv Maaneder uden Politi* (Seven Months without Police), he has described what happened. The crime rate rose immediately, but there was wide discrepancy here between the various types of crime. While in the whole of 1939 only ten cases of robbery were reported in Copenhagen, the figure by 1943 had risen to ten a month, as a result of wartime conditions. After the action against the police the figure quickly rose to over 100 a month and continued to rise. Theft insurance benefits quickly rose ten-fold and more. The fact that punishment was greatly increased for criminals who were caught and brought before the court could not prevent this. Crimes like embezzlement and fraud, where the perpetrator is generally known do not seem to have increased notably.

As Trolle points out, every big city has its quota of underworld types who will exploit the opportunity given them by a crippling of the law enforcement system. In the next round new circles will be drawn into crime, weak persons who are tempted when they see crimes go unpunished. The experiment in Denmark was imperfect and of short duration. What would happen if the state's punishing function were discontinued completely and for a rather long period can only be guessed. My own opinion is that such a complicated mechanism as a modern industrial society can hardly be kept going without police and penal courts. The gangster syndicates in America between the first and second World Wars show how powerful organized crime can become, when conditions are right for it. Just imagine what would have happened if the state had not stepped in resolutely with police, penal courts and other measures, so that the gangs would have had free play: the individual law-abiding citizen would have been helpless, not only against the existing gangs, but against any newcomer who wanted to equip himself with a revolver and try his luck. If we carry the reasoning further, we can imagine how the big gangs would have found it profitable to divide the country among themselves, hauling in money by assessing the population and in return providing it with a certain security by cracking down on upstart competitors. There were actually strong tendencies in this direction. The existing society would have succumbed, and a new one would have risen to take its place—this would have corresponded remarkably to the Marxist definition of the state as a power combination whose purpose is to safeguard the ruling class's exploitation of the oppressed!

The Danish experiment is instructive, but such a radical crippling of law enforcement will hardly be experienced under normal conditions. To illustrate the way demoralization spreads as a result of slack law enforcement under more normal conditions, I can refer to something that happened here in Norway a number of years ago and caused a small sensation. There had been thieving from a military arsenal over a fairly long period of time. It ended finally in violence, as a watchman was shot and killed by two boys caught in the act of breaking in. Now the police got busy; there were house searches and many arrests. Great quantities of stolen goods were recovered. According to newspaper accounts, whole truckloads of stolen military goods were rounded up—weapons, ammunition, radio sets, telephone equipment, fur coats, tarpaulins, searchlights, saddles, uniforms and helmets. And here I quote a newspaper report based on information given by the police and concluding with an analysis into the cause of the thefts:

> There is no escaping the fact that the thefts were entirely due to poor guarding. The boys all say they heard from comrades how easy it was to steal from the arsenal, and so they went out and tried it. It is characteristic that most of the boys know the names of the two "watchdogs," and that none were afraid of them. The lax guarding at the main arsenal became known to all the boys; when some tried to break in, and it went well every time, the thieving gained momentum.

Such a development is no rarity. The process is as follows: Some begin to steal because it is easy and safe. Others hear about it and try their luck, too. The bigger the group implicated, the less each individual in it is able to feel he is doing anything wrong. In the above case it was a question of state property, to boot, which people seem to have comparatively little respect for. But it would hardly have made any great difference if the stores had belonged to a private firm instead.

4) When we look at *moral offenses*, we find there are entirely different factors to be dealt with. The urge for economic gain is a universal motive for crime, even if its intensity varies from case to case. Practically no one can claim to be entirely immune to the temptations of Mammon. Many sex offenses, on the other hand,

grow out of abnormal or unharmonious sexual adjustments. Homosexuality, exhibitionism, sexual assaults on children, incest, and the like, have no appeal for the normal personality. The scope of general prevention is thus here limited to those few people who because of their sex impulses are especially vulnerable. At the same time, these acts are strongly disapproved socially, so that mere anticipation of discovery affords a powerful deterrent. And because the acts are determined by sex impulses, often being performed as outlets for strong mental tensions, the psychological mechanism is quite different from that at work in, for instance the economic crimes which I have discussed above.

For this and for other reasons, sex offenses belong in the area of crime where there is reason to be somewhat skeptical about the general-preventive validity of threat of punishment. It might be noted, incidentally, that the amount of rape and other sex offenses did not appear to increase particularly during the policeless period in Copenhagen. It is hard to calculate, however, what the effect of slackness in enforcement would be in the long run. In all probability the effect would be quite different for the different offenses. In some countries, such as France, incest is usually unpunishable. Whether this has had any influence on the prevalence of incest cannot, of course, be determined with any exactness. But there is at least nothing to indicate that such intercourse has become a commonplace. That rape, on the other hand, is a crime not alien to the normal human personality, can be verified in times of war and occupation. In an occupation army where discipline in this matter is lax, the incidence of rape is commonly high. If discipline is strict, on the other hand, as with the German army of occupation in Norway during the war, the crime hardly ever occurs.

5) The reader probably expects me to take up *murder* next. To mystery story writers—and often to criminologists as well— murder is the crime par excellence. Criminology is mainly the study of murder. But in the every-day administration of justice in Scandinavia murder plays an extremely modest role. In the decade 1931- 1940, 43 persons were convicted of first degree murder in Norway, or four to five per year, about one-tenth of a percent of all criminal convictions. And motivation varies so markedly that it is impossible to evaluate the effect of criminal law in this area without further

differentiation than there is space for here. The holdup man who kills simply for gain, the sex murderer whose crime assuages the darkest drives of his sick mind, the uxoricide who seeks desperate relief for a mental torment that is more than he can bear—there is a world of difference between these types; all they have in common is the judicial name for the act. I could hardly do better here than quote Stephens' famous words of 1863:

> Some men, probably, abstain from murder because they fear that if they committed murder they would be hanged. Hundreds of thousands abstain from it because they regard it with horror. One great reason why they regard it with horror is that muderers are hanged with the hearty approbation of all reasonable men.

6) A similar difficulty greets us as we attempt to evaluate the general-preventive usefulness of threatening punishment for rebellion, treason and other political crimes. There can be little doubt that the provisions against treason, for example, have a certain moral weight in emphasizing the extremely reprehensible nature of treason and thereby inducing an attitude of repugnance toward oneself committing the crime; but here as elsewhere the effect is not really ascertainable. It is also noteworthy that the risk element can even attract the opportunist who coldbloodedly calculates which course of action will be most profitable. On the other hand, it is often said that threat of punishment has no effect on the "genuine" political criminal, who is impelled by belief in the justice of his cause. That can be true enough for some, but hardly for the great mass of people to whom such political movements direct their appeal. To take an example from nineteenth-century Norwegian history: the prosecution of Marcus Thrane—the socialistic agitator whose remains have only recently been returned to Norway from America to be interred with full official honors—completely crippled the movement he had founded. The labor movement's later progress had nothing to do with this pioneer movement. From the dictatorships of our own times we know that it is possible for a brutal, relentless police system to eliminate all organized resistance to the regime. By accompanying the political trials with a vigorous propaganda, it may also be possible to induce a conviction in the people that such resistance is morally wrong. I am of course not proposing that these

examples be followed: I mention them simply to show that punishment can be a deterrent and a moral force in this area as well.

It must be admitted, of course, that these uses of penal provisions are highly dependent upon the political balance of power, and on many other circumstances. During an enemy occupation threat of punishment against traitors will have little weight for those who feel certain that the occupier will win the war. And in certain cases—e.g. after a civil war—it can happen that prosecution of the rebels will not increase respect for the state's authority, but indeed perpetuate a split, in a way that can have serious repercussions. In such cases it can become difficult for the lawmakers to decide which is wiser: to overlook the crime by resorting to a partial or general amnesty, or to hold the guilty ones responsible to the fullest extent of the law.

IV

Up to now I have intentionally avoided the question, in what way the general-preventive effect depends on the *nature and magnitude* of the reaction. In some respects this is the most immediate side of the problem. The magnitude of punishment is a factor which the lawmakers and the courts can regulate as they see fit, while it is harder for them to vary the other factors that are important—notably the intensity of policing and the set of mind of the public. The simplest way to make people more law-abiding, therefore, is to increase the punishment. When a certain type of crime threatens to get out of hand—blackout infringements or black market trading in wartime, for instance—the authorities often resort to stiffening the penal provisions. And when the courts are faced with the question of general prevention, they usually regard the choice as one between severe and light sentences in the individual case.

The best known example in modern Norwegian experience of such reasoning is the increased punishment for sex offenses called for in the penal code revision of 1927. The motive for the change was primarily general-preventive. The reasoning was that sex offenses were becoming more numerous, and this was thought to be due to laxness on the part of the courts. But the effect of the change as reflected in crime statistics was astonishing. Instead of the decline in sex offenses that was expected, there was a notable rise. Comparing the five-year period before the change with the five-year period after the change, the average rose from 136 sex crimes per year to 229, or a rise of 68 percent. In the following years the figure has remained at about this level.

The example hardly tells us much about the general-preventive effect of threat of punishment, but it does show how careful we must be in drawing conclusions from the ordinary crime statistics. The figures for other crimes remained fairly constant in these years, and regardless of what we may think of the efficacy of harsh sentences in preventing crime, we certainly cannot conclude that they increase it. The explanation for the rise in incidence must be that this group of crimes now received more attention than before. The discussion and agitation that went with the revision and the stricter view that the new provisions gave expression to, doubtless caused many sex offenses that would not have been reported before to be reported now—and perhaps the police now investigated such cases more energetically, as well. That this must be the explanation is supported by a glance at a breakdown of the statistics on sex offenses: the rise is found overwhelmingly in the types of cases that one would assume would often go unreported or unsolved—e.g. illicit relations with girls fourteen to sixteen years old.

If we think first of the purely deterrent value of threat of punishment—and with certain penal provisions this is the main point, as we have seen—it is clear that deterrence depends not simply on the risk of being punished, but also on the nature and magnitude of punishment. How important this factor is depends on the characteristic motivation for the crime, and on many other circumstances. Magnitude of punishment should mean more for crimes usually committed after careful consideration pro and con (e.g. tax evasion or smuggling of foreign currencies) than for crimes which grow out of emotions or drives which overpower the individual (e.g. the so-called crimes of passion). Another point is the moral condemnation attached to the deed. If this is strong, the magnitude of punishment is of minor importance. The social position of the potential criminal, incidentally, is also a factor. Embezzlement, for instance, is a crime which is often committed by persons in responsible positions and having some social prestige. To the respectable cashier, fear of detection is more fear of shame and scandal, and economic and social ruin, than it is fear of the punishment itself. Such a view is certainly alien to the bootlegger, however, for whom threat of punishment is just one of the risks of the trade.

That maximum deterrence does not follow from the severest punishment even Orsted, the great Danish legal thinker of a century ago, was able to point out, in his treatise "On the First Rules of Criminal Law." He shows how a penal system which the citizens and the administrators themselves regard as cruel will lead them to hold a protecting hand over the criminal rather than to cooperate in bringing him to justice. "With general enmity toward the penal code, it will lose its force, and impunity will be the real consequence of the law's always threatening the most severe punishment." Modern experience—e.g. the tendency of the jury to acquit when it fears that a verdict of guilty will mean too severe punishment for the defendant—confirm the correctness of Orsted's reasoning.

Turning next to the moral, the educative value of punishment, we find that magnitude of punishment is of importance here too. Punishment is an expression of society's disapproval of the act, and the degree of disapproval is expressed by the magnitude of punishment. A serious crime must be answered with a severe punishment, a minor misdemeanor with a lenient reaction. But here it is rather a question of the *relative* severity of the punishment than of its absolute magnitude. The humanizing of penal law in the past generations has led to a marked lowering of the general level of punishment. What was punishment for a minor crime a century ago is today punishment for a major crime. So long as this development does not take place faster than the public has a chance to adjust its ideas on appropriate punishment, it need have little effect on the ability of punishment to express society's disapproval. It is the same as with marks in school: the same mark can be expressed on a scale from 1 to 2 as on a scale from 1 to 6 or on one from 1 to 100. But a transition from one scale to another can cause some confusion.

A question of practical importance in this connection is: can the law influence the public's attitude toward a group of punishable acts by changing their position on the marking scale? In other words, by increasing the punishment for a group of crimes can we not only increase its deterrent effect but also increase the moral inhibitions against them? It is impossible to say for sure. Personally

I think it probable that such an influence can occur in certain areas and to a limited degree, but that it is at best a long-term proposition. A deterrent effect can be achieved quickly; a moral effect takes longer.

These views on the relationship between general prevention and the magnitude of punishment are built upon abstract reasoning. No doubt there are some skeptical readers who are impatient to ask: can you give any practical examples in which the magnitude of punishment has had influence on its general-preventive effect?

It must be admitted at once that only very little support for the proposition is to be educed from experience—in the first place because the general-preventive effect is always hard to ascertain, and second because there has never been a systematic gathering of material which could illuminate the question. I believe I can, however, give a few examples by way of illustration.

Normally it cannot be shown that it makes any difference to crime whether death or life imprisonment is the maximum penalty which can be imposed.[3] But that there are situations in which the death sentence can have a distinctly different effect than other punishments became apparent during the occupation. The great majority of the people came to feel that it was nationally and morally right to sabotage the occupation authorities. Thus no social opprobrium went with being arrested for illegal activity—quite the contrary. And toward the end of the occupation, when the duration was being reckoned in weeks and months, even the threat of life imprisonment became just a question of short internment. The only thing that could really worry a member of the underground was the thought of torture or death. I remember so well the day in October, 1942, when the *Reichskommissar* issued his ordinance promising death for having any traffic at all with illegal newspapers. There were many that day who got to work tidying up their effects, and the production and distribution of illegal newspapers suffered a serious setback. It was not long, however, before people realized that the ordinance was not to be taken seriously, and activity was resumed. Experience during the war also showed how the risk affects people differently according to their individual attitudes and sensitivity to danger. A large share of the population was unwilling to take any risk—they were against the Germans, to be sure, but their main consideration was their own pockets. Another large share was willing to take part in illegal work where the risk was small, and especially where they would not be risking their lives. A third group, numerically smaller and the heart of the resistance movement, was not to be deterred at all by risk.

All this is of a certain practical value in planning the treatment to be accorded revolutionary movements whose members can be assumed to have about the same attitude toward the lawful authorities as the majority of the Norwegian people had toward the Germans during the occupation. In their recent proposal for a revision of the treason and rebellion paragraphs of the Penal Code, the Norwegian Penal Code Commission has described what might happen if an armed rebellion should be started while the international situation is tense: "If the rebellion is not at once suppressed, it can easily lead to intervention by a foreign power. Then the situation might arise where there is reason to think that a death sentence against a leader of the rebellion is the only way to bring others to their senses and thereby win mastery of the situation for the lawful authorities."

Another practical example of the preventive value of heavy punishment is enactment of a rule in Norway calling for prison sentences without access to probation in cases of drunken driving. The subject is so familiar that it hardly requires elaboration. Most Norwegians are able to see on looking about their own circle of friends that it is becoming more common to leave the car at home when going to a party at which alcohol is likely to be consumed. There is unquestionably a certain preventive effect at work here. How great it is, and how it is distributed over the different social groups among motorists, and whether it is due simply to the deterrent effect or whether the law has succeeded in bringing about a change in attitude toward driving while intoxicated: all this is something we have no exact knowledge of; it could well be made the subject of a sociological study.

I have given a couple of examples of the effect of especially heavy sentences.[4] The other side of the question is whether special leniency to certain groups of offenders might not undermine respect for the law.

Attorney General Aulie, in his lecture on youthful offenders before the Association of Norwegian Criminologists in 1947, touched upon gangsterism, which is so typical in juvenile delinquency. He said:

We know from experience that when members of the gang are released after questioning pending the winding up of investigation, the young people almost invariably flock back together, usually with the idea of planning new escapades. They regard the intervention of the police as a temporary inconvenience, of negligible importance. They count on prosecution being waived for those with clean records, or at worst their being given suspended sentences. And they have reason to believe that a dozen or so new thefts on top of those already counted against them will not make much difference if they are discovered.

If this observation is correct, it shows with all desirable clarity that the humanizing of penal practice must be kept within certain limits if it is not to lead to an undermining of respect for law and authority. But it would take us far afield to go into this problem here.

V

WITH THE LAST EXAMPLE I come to the relation between general and individual prevention. Usually there is no great conflict between the two. This is clearly the case when measures designed for individual prevention go farther than punishment designed along general-preventive lines—such as in the case of forced labor for vagrants and alcoholics or indeterminate sentences for recidivists. Such long sentences are of course sufficient for deterrence. Neither are they objectionable from the point of view of the moralizing function of punishment—at any rate when it is clear to citizens that there is no question here of retribution for the crime but rather of a measure which aims to educate the prisoner or render him harmless. There is greater objection from a general-preventive point of view when individual considerations motivate an especially lenient treatment. But neither here should there be any real danger, so long as the milder special treatment does not become such a commonplace that the potential criminal can count on it and behave accordingly. Both the deterrent and the moralizing sides of general prevention are based primarily on the *average* reaction to certain offenses. Waiving of prosecution and the use of suspended sentence are so widely practiced that the conflict here has become acute.

More common than an out-and-out conflict between individual

and general prevention is the circumstance that a punishment that is necessary for general prevention is often superfluous for individual prevention. In certain crimes there will practically never be an individual-preventive need for punishment—or at any rate, not a severe punishment: such things as perjury (so few persons are called in as witnesses more than once in a lifetime), or bigamy. In other cases the circumstances governing the behavior of the individual offender may lead to the conclusion that punishment is not needed for his benefit—"that execution of the sentence is not necessary to prevent the offender from committing new crimes," to quote the Penal Code's §52 on conditions for probation.

Thus the judge is often put in a difficult position. A single judgment has, to be sure, seldom any concrete effect on general prevention. The question is: would general prevention be significantly impaired if it became the practice to apply probation or minimum sentence in similar cases? Something else to think about is whether people are likely to learn of the decisions and let their conduct be guided by them.

This problem came up in a treason case after the war.[5] A young man was charged with having served in the German army—in itself a serious crime, meriting several years at hard labor. In this case, however, the circumstances were unusual. The defendant, who was still under 20, was arrested by the Germans during the war and put into a concentration camp as a hostage for his mother, who had fled to Sweden. He felt depressed while in the camp and hit on the idea of getting out by volunteering for German war service and then escaping. He had, in fact, heard of people getting out in this way. He volunteered and was accepted, but for a while he was unable to escape. He was sent to Germany and then to serve six months at the front. But when he came home on leave at the end of 1944 he seized the opportunity to flee to Sweden.

In the lower court the defendant was sentenced to one year and put on probation. The majority in the Supreme Court, however, reversed the probation. The writer of the majority opinion held that for the sake of precedent it was indefensible to let a person who had been guilty of such a desperate act as to join the enemy's army get by with a suspended sentence. The reasoning is psychologically a bit unrealistic. One justice dissented, holding that the use of probation in a single case which is clearly different from the majority of cases cannot be said to weaken the future preventive value of the reckoning with Norway's traitors. "This would presuppose knowledge in the future not only of the general lines of the present reckoning, but of its details—a knowledge which is theoretically possible in isolated cases, but which in my opinion can be disregarded in practice."

VI

More than seventy years ago Lombroso wrote his famous book, *L'Uomo delinquente*, based on a study of prisoners in Italian penal institutions. Not many of his conclusions have stood the test of time. Most have been rejected as fanciful hypotheses and untenable generalizations. But he was a pioneer in his use of the empirical method in investigating the causes of crime. Psychiatrists, anthropologists, sociologists and others have continued his work. An enormous body of empirical data has been amassed to aid in appraising lawbreaker's physical and mental traits, family conditions, economic position, and so on. As a result every generalizing theory has had to be abandoned. The time for broad slogans in criminology has passed.

No comparable empirical study of the psychology of *obedience to law* has been undertaken. In a word, we are still in the pre-Lombrosian era in this field. And the discussion often gives way to cock-sure general statements like "I believe (or I do not believe) in general prevention." Much has been written about general prevention; much talented effort has been spent in exploring its operation and importance. But the empirical data are still lacking. If any attempt has been made to include it at all, it has usually—as in this paper—occurred by the use of chance observations, plus ordinary psychological theories. I believe we can make some progress in this way. But we shall not have firm ground to stand on before a systematic investigation is made into the effect of penal law and its enforcement on the citizen's behavior, and into the interrelation between the legal system and the other factors which govern behavior.[6] This task is in a sense much more difficult than the one Lombroso undertook. He had his material nicely collected and concentrated for him in the state prisons. One who wishes to study general prevention, on the other hand, must examine the whole population. Therefore it is a field for sociologists and psychologists.

And it is difficult for one uninitiated into sociological methods of research to judge how the work should be tackled, or how far it is at all possible to go. I, at any rate, do not feel qualified to enlarge on the matter for the time being. But in this paper I have tried to point out how important these problems are.

NOTES

---

1. Just after the war Sweden was a land of plenty compared to Denmark, and some Danes used to make the two-hour boat trip across the Sound to buy scarce commodities. In the Swedish vernacular they became known as "locusts." (Transl.)

2. This was a measure, also resorted to in other European countries, to flush out ill-gotten gain from the war. The idea was that all liquid assets would have to be declared, and the tax authorities and investigators for economic treason would be able to trap profiteers—since the alternative to declaring the assets was to let them become worthless. (Transl.)

3. In Dano-Norwegian legal history there is one remarkable example of the death penalty being abandoned because in a certain type of crime it defeated its purpose. It was done in the Ordinance of December 18, 1767, which replaced the death penalty with penal servitude for life in cases where "melancholy and other dismal persons [committed murder] for the exclusive purpose of losing their lives." The background for the provision was, in the words of Orsted, "the thinking that was then current among the unenlightened that by murdering another person and thereby being sentenced to death, one might still attain salvation, whereas if one were to take one's own life, one would be plunged into external damnation." (Eunomia, Part III, p. 147.)

4. In discussion of this paper a participant (Police Chief Rode) cited as another example of the significance for prevention of magnitude of punishment, his experience from smuggling during prohibition. In his district, at least rumrunning was dealt a severe blow after the courts began to adjudge prison sentences instead of fines. The effect was not alone deterrent: the change was important also to the public's attitude toward crime. Prison, as opposed to fines, was regarded as shameful, and while smuggling had previously been looked upon as a thrilling sport, which even "decent citizens" could engage in, it now became something to stay away from.

5. The Norwegian Case Review (Norsk Retstidende), 1946, p. 854.

6. A limited investigation of this type is Schmidt, Grantze, and Ross, Work and Vacations Among Agricultural Laborers: A Study in the Sociology of Law (1946; in Swedish).

GORDON HAWKINS

Punishment and Deterrence: The Educative, Moralizing, and Habituative Effects

IT IS A WELCOME SIGN that in more recent discussions of deterrence its conceptual aspect has been brought to the forefront. This may constitute one of the most significant advances since deterrence theory was first formulated and elaborated in the writing of Beccaria, Bentham, Blackstone, Romilly, Pailey, and Feuerbach. Indeed, it is probably the most significant advance; for prior to this development, discussion of deterrence has been almost exclusively in terms of the simple conceptual model of the classical theorists.

That model was conceived in terms of man as "a lightning calculator of pleasures and pains," to use Veblen's phrase, directly responsive to systematic intimidation by threat of punishment designed to outweigh any pleasure to be derived from crime. It is a model which plainly fails to fit all the facts. Yet, most critics would agree that the existence of the institution of punishment exerts some control over some types of crime. This conceptual scheme appears to be compatible with some aspects of experience and yet incompatible with others.

To conceive the preventive effects of punishment as simply a matter of deterrence or intimidation is to miss more subtle points

Reprinted from *The Wisconsin Law Review*, Vol. 1969, No. 2, 550 565, with permission of the publishers.

The author wishes to acknowledge that in the course of writing this article he has had the benefit of lengthy discussion with Professor Johannes Andenaes, Dean of the Faculty of Law and Director of the Institute of Criminology and Criminal Law at the University of Oslo, who has been largely responsible for the current renewal of serious interest in the subject of deterrence.

which are fundamental; the whole thing is considerably more complex than the classical theory suggests. Classical theory is misleading in that it neglects what is called variously "the educative-moralizing function of the law," "the moral or socio-pedagogical influence of punishment," or the "educative and habituative effects of our penal sanctions."[1]

It has been noted (1) that the extent to which punishment has moral or educative effects, and (2) that the location of the social conditions instrumental in creating them are empirical problems answerable through empirical research.[2] Empirical investigation requires that we have some idea of the character of the phenomena to be investigated.[3] Yet, both those who assert and those who deny that deterrence is an important aspect of punishment and that the threat and infliction of punishment provide a powerful means of social control, do not provide more than alternative slogans or catch words. And assertions to the effect that punishment has educative, moralizing, and habituative effects have to be formulated in ways that make it clear what such statements mean in terms of practical implications. Only then can there be the possibility of their being tested in experience and by observation. So it is necessary to attempt to identify the empirical referents involved and clarify the issues under consideration.

As a preliminary point, the way in which these educative, moralizing, and habituative functions of punishment relate to the traditionally recognized deterrent function must be considered. Sometimes it is made clear that these functions are regarded as something distinct from mere deterrence.[4] But this is not always the case.

One suggested redefinition of deterrence occurs in the following passage from Professor Tappan's *Crime, Justice and Correction:*

> One difficulty with the classical theory was its implication that prevention occurred merely through repression by fear. Deterrence may be and, indeed, it commonly is defined in this limited sense. . . . General prevention is also served, however, by the educative-moralizing function of the law in strengthening the public's moral code. . . . We would define deterrence as the term is generally used here today as "the preventive effect which actual or threatened punishment of offenders has upon potential offenders."[5]

Unfortunately, this solution of the "difficulty with the classical theory" presents some difficulties itself. It may be true that the classical theorists overestimated the efficiency of "repression by fear" as a means of social control and oversimplified the process of crime prevention or control. It is a different matter, however, to imply that they were mistaken in defining deterrence in the "limited sense" of discouraging action through fear of unpleasant consequences. This not only conforms with ordinary usage but also refers to a familiar pattern of action and reaction. The proposed redefinition does neither for it is unclear what is included within the redrawn boundaries or what is involved in the new concept.[6]

Yet it is clear that something quite different from, and independent of, deterrence as ordinarily understood is involved. For the situation of an individual deterred from offending by conscious fear of punishment is basically dissimilar to that of one refraining because of the operation of some unconscious controls. In one instance, he may still wish to commit the offense "but he no longer dares to do it."[7] In the other, presumably there will be no conscious fear of punishment present and possibly even no awareness of the law or the relevant penal sanctions.

Similar contradictions would seem to apply to some of the other behavior patterns mentioned. Habit, for example, specifically implies a doing unconsciously or without premeditation. When settled patterns of conduct are established, deterrence is no longer relevant, for we need not discourage persons through fear from actions they do not wish to take in the first place.

This is not to say that the suggestion that punishment has general preventive effects other than deterrence is mistaken. But, it seems unwise to formulate a theory of punishment so that those not consciously conforming to a legal prohibition because of the penalty threat are said to be deterred by it. To subsume such varied behavior patterns within one process not only obscures basic distinctions but also begs fundamental etiological questions; indeed, questions which "meaningful empirical research . . . directed toward discovering the effectiveness of punishment"[8] cannot ignore.

Professor Andenaes specifically distinguishes these other effects from "the mere frightening or deterrent effect of punishment."[9] Moreover, he also provides some descriptive detail. "We can say that punishment has three sorts of general preventive effects: it may have a *deterrent* effect, it may strengthen *moral inhibitions* (a *moralizing* effect), and it may stimulate habitual *law-abiding con-*

duct."[10] In another place, he distinguishes "the *moral* or *socio-pedagogical* influence of punishment,"[11] the establishment of a "condition of habitual lawlessness,"[12] and *"mere deterrence,"*[13] as the three principal general preventive effects of punishment. For convenience of exposition, I shall deal first with what is called the educative-moralizing function of punishment and then with the question of its habituative effect providing in both instances a critique and a reappraisal.

I. THE EDUCATIVE-MORALIZING FUNCTION OF PUNISHMENT

PROFESSOR ANDENAES has written that

[i]n Swedish discussion, the *moralizing*—in other words the *educational*—function has been greatly stressed. The idea is that punishment as a concrete expression of society's disapproval of an act helps to form and strengthen the public's moral code and thereby creates conscious and unconscious inhibitions against committing crime.[14]

It may be said that from law and the legal machinery there emanates a flow of propaganda which favors such respect. Punishment is a means of expressing social disapproval. In this way the criminal law and its enforcement supplement and enhance the moral influence acquired through education and other non-legal processes.[15]

Of course, the idea that the enforcement of punishment expresses society's moral condemnation and, at the same time, helps to form and strengthen the public's moral code is not novel. It is not clear either. But the *Report of the Royal Commission on Capital Punishment 1949-53* not only embodies this idea but also provides a concrete example of how it is supposed to operate in practice.

We think it reasonable to suppose that the deterrent force of capital punishment operates not only by affecting the conscious thoughts of individuals tempted to commit murder but also by building up in the community, over a long period of time, a deep feeling of peculiar abhorrence for the crime of murder. "The fact that men are hung for murder is one great reason why murder is considered so dreadful a crime." This widely diffused effect on the moral consciousness of society is impossible to assess but it must be at least as important as any direct part which the death penalty may play as a deterrent in the calculations of potential murderers.[16]

But, what the Royal Commission put forward as a "reasonable" supposition is not entirely convincing. While it may be true that it is "impossible to assess" the "widely diffused effect on the moral consciousness of society," it is reasonable to question whether, if it exists, it can be of the kind suggested. Indeed, over two hundred years ago, Beccaria used the same example to draw the opposite conclusion.

> The death penalty cannot be useful, because of the example of barbarity it gives men. If the passions or the necessities of war have taught the shedding of human blood, the laws, moderators of the conduct of men, should not extend the beastly example, which becomes more pernicious since the inflicting of legal death is attended with much study and formality. It seems to me absurd that the laws, which are an expression of the public will, which detest and punish homicide, should themselves commit it. . . .[17]

It might seem, at first glance, that, because of its unique character, the death penalty belongs in a different category from all other penalties and that, therefore, discussion of the moral effect of that penalty is not really relevant to consideration of the educative-moralizing function of other penalties. But the doctrine we are considering might be viewed as little—if at all—more plausible when seen in relation to any other penalty.

For, as Professor Kenny pointed out in explaining the "special attractiveness" of the criminal law both for students and ordinary readers, "the vivid and violent nature of the events which criminal courts notice and repress" is matched by the character "of those by which they effect the repression." He continues:

> Forcible interferences with property and liberty, with person and life, are the causes which bring criminal law into operation; and its operations are themselves directed to the infliction of *similar acts of seizure, suffering, and slaughter.*[18]

There seems to be no obvious reason to think that any other item from this collection of threats is more likely to engender respect for values than the threat of the death penalty. Indeed, it could be argued that the only sort of respect which systems of compulsion commonly inspire is precisely that which is implied in the concept of mere deterrence and no more.

Yet, this line of argument, which seems to suggest that punishment has no effect, apart from deterrence, which could be described as educative or moralizing, is not only not probative, but also doubtfully relevant to the point at issue. This is because what is called the educative-moralizing function of punishment is largely independent of the nature of the penalties employed. It is true that some penalties may be regarded as poetically appropriate (castration for dangerous sex offenders) or inappropriate (imprisonment in a wholly male institution for male homosexuals) for particular types of offenders and offenses. However, there is nothing in the intrinsic nature of any punishment which makes it either fitting or unfitting. Extrinsic factors deriving from the context in which punishment is used are determinative.

The argument we have been considering fails to meet the point that the educative-moralizing function of punishment derives simply from the fact that "[p]unishment is a means of expressing social disapproval."[19] In other words, punishment is a ritualistic device designed to influence persons by intimating symbolically social disapproval and society's moral condemnation. In this connection, some methods may be regarded as preferable on aesthetic or humanitarian grounds but this is independent of the ritual function. The essential point is that, whatever their nature, "penal provisions may symbolize values which various groups within the populace cherish."[20]

When both this ritualistic aspect of punishment and the way in which the machinery of the traditional criminal legal process achieves "the dramatization of evil"[21] is recognized, it is evident that it is not inappropriate to talk of punishment as in some sense educational. That punishment is effective in conveying social reprobation is clearly reflected in the stigmatization and the loss of social status commonly involved in criminal punishment. That ex-prisoners have severe problems re-establishing themselves in society may be regarded as empirical evidence of the stigma's effectiveness.[22]

From this point of view, a criminal trial followed by conviction and sentence can be seen as a public degradation ceremony in which the public identity of the convicted individual is lowered on the social scale. It has been maintained that "only in societies that are completely demoralized, will an observer be unable to find such ceremonies, since only in total anomie are the conditions of degradation ceremonies lacking."[23] Such ceremonies are described as "a secular form of communion" which help to "reinforce group solidarity" and "bind persons to the collectivity."[24] Although all societies do not have "degradation ceremonies [which] are carried on in accordance with publicly prescribed and publicly validated measures" *we* have "our professional degraders in the law courts." For, in our society, it is said, "the arena of degradation . . . has been rationalized, at least as to the institutional measures for carrying it out. The court and its officers have something like a fair monopoly over such ceremonies, and there they have become an occupational routine."[25]

It is, moreover, a mistake to say as was said above that the only sort of respect inspired by the criminal law is that which is implied in the concept of mere deterrence and no more.[26] The criminal law is more than a neutral system of compulsion; respect for legal authority is different from mere response to threats. To ignore this confuses authority with coercive power. Although coercive power may sometimes be a necessary condition for the exercise of authority and for securing obedience, respect for authority depends on recognition of its legitimacy.

It is not necessary to consider here the various principles of legitimacy upon which authority is said to depend, nor to discuss their sociological and ideological bases. It is sufficient to note that in any society, if it is to continue in existence, there must be general acceptance of authoritative regulation as a means of achieving social control. This affirmative attitude toward obedience to rules is probably a more powerful factor than the fear of punishment in securing conformity. Moreover, the respect, or deference, which the law attracts makes it possible for the law to exercise a socializing influence by securing the acceptance by members of society of rules and regulations in areas where custom, tradition, morality, or religion provide no guidance.

That punishment can be and is used as an educational technique is, of course, recognized even by those dubious about its value as an instrument of moral education. Thus, it is significant that Hart says "there is very little evidence to support the idea that morality is *best* taught by fear of legal punishment."[27] Similarly, R. S. Peters says of the argument that punishment might "help to mark out what is right and wrong and . . . help to stamp in desirable habits which will later make a solid foundation for a rational moral code," that "whether punishment *often* has this effect on individuals is an empirical question."[28] Nevertheless, he goes on to say that "isolated punishments of the 'sharp shock' variety . . . may function in a beneficial way by focusing awareness on social realities";[29] and he also suggests that punishment which brings home to offenders "imaginatively the consequences of actions as they effect other people" may have some "effectiveness . . . in moral education."[30]

These statements do not constitute evidence that punishment does operate in the manner suggested, but they represent acknowledgment that it makes sense to suggest that it might and in some circumstances does. The extent to which it does is, of course, an empirical question.

However, it may be unwise to use the term "moralizing" in reference to this aspect of the law's functioning. There are a number of reasons why this term may be inappropriate.

In the first place, the criminal law is designed to secure conformity in response to sanctions. But the notion of morality, both in ordinary usage and in philosophical and psychological literature, refers to action in accordance with internalized standards or rules as opposed to mere response to sanctions. "Rules are said to be internalized if they are conformed to in the absence of situational incentives or sanctions, *i.e.*, if conformity is intrinsically motivated."[31] Thus, the concept of morality implies internalized values which may call for behavior which conflicts with self-interest whereas the threat of punishment depends for its effectiveness on an appeal to self-interest. And as Professor Andenaes points out, "while the law certainly serves to strengthen the moral inhibitions against crime in general, it is not very successful in pressing upon the public its own evaluation of various types of conduct."[32] Certainly an affirmative attitude toward obedience to rules does not imply even agreement with, much less the internalization of, the content of particular rules. Nevertheless, if this were the only argument against the use of the term "moralizing" it would not in itself constitute a very powerful objection.

Secondly, morality implies more than a behavioral response to psychological conditioning so that it is something of a contradiction to speak of a "threat-induced conscience."[33] Whether we think of conscience as merely the "exercise of the ordinary judgment on moral questions"[34] or as some kind of internal oracle, we ordinarily distinguish between actions in accordance with moral scruples and response to threats. The antimony is reflected in the fact that conscientious offenders, such as conscientious objectors to military service, are commonly unresponsive to threats. Indeed, by referring to such persons as conscientious we mean that their conduct is governed by considerations of principle rather than material interest. It is significant that, both in respect of conscientious offenders and others, the process of status degradation and stigmatization, which may well be of value as a means of reinforcing group solidarity and social cohesion, relies on an emotive response rather than an exercise of moral judgment.

Moreover, although punishment may in some degree facilitate the process of moral learning, its moralizing role is essentially accessory. This hypothesis can never be entirely proved empirically; for morality transcends the law in the sense that moral considerations belong to a more fundamental level of discourse than juristic ones. Indeed, it has been said that "critical rejection or acceptance of custom or law is what is distinctive of morality. . . . Moral philosophy . . . presupposes a critical attitude to rules and the refusal to equate what is right with what is laid down by custom, law or any other authoritative source."[35]

An illustration may serve to demonstrate this point and indicate the paradoxical consequences of failure to draw the relevant distinction. In Bruno Bettelheim's eye witness account of the behavior of political prisoners in two German concentration camps, the author comments:

> In their behavior became apparent the dilemma of the politically uneducated German middle classes when confronted with the phenomenon of National socialism. They had no consistent philosophy which would protect their integrity as human beings. . . . They had obeyed the law handed down by the ruling classes, without ever questioning its wisdom. . . . They could not question the wisdom of law and of the police, so they accepted the behavior of the Gestapo as just. What was wrong was that *they* were made objects of a persecution which in itself *must* be right, since it was carried out by the authorities.[36]

Some relatives of those in the camps

> just would not believe that the prisoners in the camps had not committed outrageous crimes since the way they were punished permitted only this conclusion.[37]

These examples illustrate not only the way in which respect for legal authority may help to secure social control but also why it is important not to confuse acceptance of, and submission to, authority with morality. To identify morality with social or behavioral conformity ignores that morality "implies that fully internationalized moral norms should determine behavior, not only when they conflict with impulse or ego-interest but also when they conflict with external authority."[38]

The essential point is that because the constraints set by the criminal law are designed to achieve social control rather than moral improvement, "socializing" rather than "moralizing" better describes their nature and purpose, and better indicates the criteria by which their success or failure can be measured. De Tocqueville's skepticism about the possibility of reforming the morals of an individual by using the penal system reflects the distinction I am making. Although "radical reformation" was an almost illusory objective "another kind of reformation, less thorough than the former, but yet useful for society" was possible. For one might hope, in regard to the offender "leaving the prison" that

> if he is not more virtuous, he has become at least more judicious; his morality is not honor, but interest. . . . [H]is mind has contracted habits of order, and he possesses rules for his conduct in life; . . . if he has not become in truth better, he is at least more obedient to the laws, and that is all which society has the right to demand.[39]

This distinction is reflected also in Nigel Walker's statement that we "learn prudentially, not ethically, to abstain from traffic offenses."[40]

The significance of the distinction from the viewpoint of research lies in the fact that, as was indicated at the start,[41] identification of the phenomenon to be investigated is a necessary preliminary to empirical investigation. Of course, it may be that in practice this distinction will have no specific research implications. And certainly the fundamental point that criminal punishment has educative or socializing effects which are clearly distinguishable from its deterrent effects is in no way invalidated, nor is its importance diminished, by any of the qualifications suggested above.

II. The Habituative Function of Punishment

The criminal and penal law in providing standards of conduct and penalties, stimulates the habit of law-abiding conduct. . . .[42]

[W]ith fear or moral influence as an intermediate link, it is possible . . . perhaps to establish a condition of habitual lawfulness.[43]

Punishment . . . sometimes has an habituative effect in conditioning human behaviour; but when and how?[44]

The concept of habitual criminality is familiar, and there would be general agreement that it can be defined in terms of "a settled practice in crime."[45] But the concept of habitual lawfulness is relatively new and unfamiliar. Nor does any consensus exist as to its definition. Moreover, the analogy with habitual criminality with its implication of repetition or regularly repeated actions seems to be inappropriate, for the criminal law does not usually prescribe positive actions, the regular performance of which could be regarded as evidence of habitual lawfulness.[46]

However, the emphasis on repetition has not always been regarded as an essential feature of habit. John Dewey, for example, wrote:

Repetition is in no sense the essence of habit. . . . The essence of habit is an acquired predisposition to ways or modes of response. . . . Habit means special sensitiveness or accessibility to certain classes of stimuli, standing predilections and aversions, rather than bare recurrence of specific acts.[47]

This, however, is more like what would, at the present time, be called "attitude."[48]

Professor Andenaes provides two examples of how these habits or attitudes are acquired.

We find the clearest example of this in the military where extended inculcation of discipline and stern reaction against breach thereof can induce a purely automatic habitual response—not only where obeying specific orders is concerned, but also with regard to general orders and regulations.[49]

We have another example in the relationship between an occupying power and occupied population. The regulations set down by the occupier are not regarded by the people as morally binding; but by a combination of terror and habit formation a great measure of obedience can be elicited—at any rate in response to commands which do not conflict too greatly with national feelings.[50]

Yet it is questionable how far either of these examples is relevant to ordinary social life.

The first illustration relates to a highly specialized organized group which has a variety of distinctive features. "The Army," as Hans Mattick has pointed out, "provides a total environment . . . a disciplined, structured, and predictable social environment."[51] It is a social environment in which every individual's life is carefully regulated and ordered, and his status and functions are precisely defined. There is, of course, no doubt that under a regime based on military conceptions of authority and discipline, where obedience is enforced by close control and supervision, a remarkable degree of conformity can be achieved. But what happens in a military context is hardly analogous to the control of behavior in civilian life.

Although the second model refers to society at large, it also deals with a singular situation. It is a situation where there are no customary or legal limitations on the exercise of authority, and the technique of social control employed is not the traditional institution of punishment but terror. Terrorism can produce a great measure of obedience and a large degree of conformity. However,

[s]uch a regime is characterised by the fact that fear of sanctions is the immediate and dominating motive for lawful conduct. It is well known how strict and unrelenting a terroristic regime must be if it is to be at all effective. Fear is insufficient as a barrier unless it is sustained by very drastic and unflinching menaces.[52]

Possibly some sort of habit formation takes place in such situations also, but again the analogy with the operation of the penal system in normal circumstances is exceedingly tenuous.

All this is not to say that no habituative effect exists. It might very well be that although a habituative function does operate it is not a major influence on behavior. Alternatively, it might be that it is so pervasive a feature of our existence that it is impossible to isolate it for objective examination or to provide satisfactorily discrete examples.

Yet, Professor Andenaes does cite an example which seems to illustrate the habituative process very effectively. With regard to the Norwegian legislation dealing with drunken driving he suggests "that the legislation has been instrumental in forming or sustaining the widespread conviction that it is wrong, or irresponsible, to place oneself behind the wheel when intoxicated."[53] He also says:

> When a man goes to a party where alcoholic drinks are likely to be served, and if he is not fortunate enough to have a wife who drives but does not drink, he will leave his car at home or he will limit his consumption to a minimum.[54]

It is precisely this kind of patterned behavior or tendency to behave automatically in a certain way which we ordinarily refer to as a habit. And there can be no doubt that such settled practices or customary manners of acting are a powerful factor in preventing infringements of the law.[55] In so far as observation of the rules of the road or highway codes becomes, as it does for many drivers, a matter of habit, it is clear that the habituative effect of the law is a major factor in legal social control; for such habits are not acquired in infancy. It is an important aspect of this process that repeated observation of a rule which may initially be conscious and deliberate can induce an habitual disposition and ultimately automatic compliance.

However, it seems likely that over a very large area of conduct the habituative effect of the law may take the form of negative reinforcement in the inhibition of types of undesirable behavior which are already largely controlled by habit. Thus it is probably true that the principal importance of habit in relation to social control derives from the fixity of habit organization and the consequent relative dependability of human conduct. As Gardner Murphy puts it:

> The genuine importance of habit as a social stabilizer appears then not to reside so much in the sheer painfulness of forming new habits as in the attitude of condemning what one has condemned since childhood.[56]

Since he also points out that "the family must be considered to be in western Europe and the United States the most important of habit forming institutions,"[57] it might seem that the direct influence of the criminal law in regard to habit formation is likely to be limited to the sort of behavior which is precluded from children. Yet it would be unwise to ignore the possibility that there may be a good deal of habit formation in relation to compliance with *"police regulations* . . . [such as] traffic ordinances, building codes, laws governing the sale of alcoholic beverages, regulations governing commerce, etc."[58] It seems likely that in many cases of this kind, observance of the law eventually becomes a habit which is followed automatically without reflection. And although these crimes "play a modest role in the literature [they] have a good deal of practical importance. . . . "[59]

Nor can one rule out the possible indirect influence of the criminal law in relation to what habits are formed in childhood.

> It is arguable that the criminal law may cause his parents to teach him (the child) rules which they would not otherwise have bothered about. . . . If so, the legislation of one generation might become the morality of the next.[60]

Whether the law by means of the creation or abolition of offenses can and does have this or some other kind of long term effect upon attitudes is an empirical question; this does not necessarily mean that it is capable of being tested empirically.

It would be unwise, however, to assume that because some evidence suggests that the short term effects of change in the law are negligible[61] that the long term effects are also likely to be insignificant. Such an inference rests on the unlikely hypothesis that no accruement of effect takes place over time. It also ignores the potential effect of the fact that "[a] substantial minority of people believe that it is morally wrong to disobey a prohibition which is embodied in the law, irrespective of the morality of the prohibited action itself."[62] The existence of people who believe that the "law automatically govern(s) the morality of conduct"[63] cannot be ignored in considering the general preventive effects of the law; nor can their influences be ruled out in relation to its possible long term effects.

III. CONCLUSION

The foregoing discussion of the moralizing, educative, and habituative effects of the law has been principally concerned with the conceptual question: What does it mean to say that the law has such effects? It has been suggested that, although there are a number of objections to using the term "moralizing," the reference to educative and habituative effects draws attention to important aspects of punishment which have long been obscured by adherence to an inadequate theoretical model and, consequently, largely ignored. This sort of schematic reorientation must be done before meaningful empirical investigation can be begun.

NOTES

1. "Educative-moralizing function of the law," P. Tappan, Crime, Justice and Correction 247 (1960); "the moral or socio-pedagogical influence of punishment," Andenaes, *The General Preventive Effects of Punishment*, 114 U. Pa. L. Rev. 949, 950 (1966); "educative and habituative effects of our penal sanctions," Morris, *Impediments to Penal Reform*, 33 U. Chi. L. Rev. 631 (1966).

This approach is most clearly and fully expounded in the writings of Professor Johannes Andenaes with whose name it is most widely associated. This commentary is largely responsive to the text of his two well known articles, *General Prevention—Illusion or Reality?** 43 J. Crim. L., C. & P.S. 176 (1952), and *The General Preventive Effects of Punishment, supra,* and with the treatment of these topics in his book, The General Part of the Criminal Law of Norway 66–79 (1956).

2. Andenaes, *The General Preventive Effects of Punishment*, 114 U. Pa. L. Rev. 949, 951–78 (1966).

3. "To understand a proposition means to know what is the case if it is true." L. Wittgenstein, Tractatus-Logico-Philosophicus 41 (1961).

4. See text accompanying notes 11–13 *infra.*

5. P. Tappan, *supra* note 1, at 247.

6. It is true that Professor Tappan says that the "moralizing task of the penal law" is one which "involves the introjection of conscious and unconscious controls against violations." He also says that "the criminal and penal law, in providing standards of conduct and penalties, stimulates the habit of law-abiding conduct; it aids in the conditioning of accepted norms." But the processes of introjection, habit formation and conditioning are not further described; nor is the way which penal law functions so as to stimulate or aid them. *Id.*

7. 1 J. Bentham, *Principles of Penal Law* in Works 396 (1843).

8. P. Tappan, *supra* note 1, at 252.

9. Andenaes, *General Prevention—Illusion or Reality?,** 43 J. Crim. L., C. & P.S. 176, 179 (1952). [p. 141 this volume].

* Also reprinted in this volume.

10. *Id.* at 180. [p. 142 this volume]

11. Andenaes, *supra* note 2, at 950.

12. *Id.* at 951.

13. *Id.* at 950.

14. Andenaes, *supra note* 9, at 179. [p. 142 this volume]

15. Andenaes, *supra* note 2, at 950.

16. REPORT OF ROYAL COMMISSION ON CAPITAL PUNISHMENT 1949–1953, at 20 (1953). Professor Andenaes also discusses this point. "The moral effects of capital punishment also must be considered. It may be said that capital punishment for murder exerts a moral influence by indicating that life is the most highly protected value." Andenaes, *supra* note 2, at 967.

17. C. BECCARIA, ON CRIMES AND PUNISHMENTS 50 (Bobbs-Merrill ed. 1963). [excerpts in this volume]

18. C. S. KENNY, OUTLINES OF CRIMINAL LAW 2 (13th ed. 1929) (emphasis added). "Criminal law is itself a system of compulsion on the widest scale. It is a collection of threats of injury to life, liberty, and property if people do commit crime." J. F. STEPHEN, HISTORY OF THE CRIMINAL LAW OF ENGLAND 107 (1883).

19. Andenaes, *supra* note 2, at 950. "Punishment is the way in which society expresses its denomiation of wrong-doing." ROYAL COMMISSION ON CAPITAL PUNISHMENT, MINUTES OF EVIDENCE 207 (1953).

20. J. ANDENAES, THE GENERAL PART OF THE CRIMINAL LAW OF NORWAY 78 (1956). It is, of course, perfectly legitimate to ask why the punishment of offenders should be regarded as an appropriate way of expressing moral condemnation. *See* H. L. A. HART, LAW, LIBERTY AND MORALITY 66 (1963). But the fact is that such ritualistic procedures have long been used in the sphere of education to foster commitment to values. *See* Berstein, Peters, & Elvin, *The Role of Ritual in Education*, PROCEEDINGS OF THE ROYAL SOCIETY (1965).

21. F. TANNENBAUM, CRIME AND THE COMMUNITY 19 (1938).

22. *See* J. P. MARTIN, OFFENDERS AS EMPLOYEES 39 (1962); McSally, *Finding Jobs for Released Offenders*, 24 FED. PROBATION 12 (June 1960); Schwartz & Skolnick, *Two Studies of Legal Stigma*, 10 SOCIAL PROBLEMS 133 (1962). *See also* E. GOFFMAN, STIGMA (1963); Freidson, *Disability as Social Deviance* in SOCIOLOGY AND REHABILITATION 71–79 (M. Sussman ed. 1966).

Because it relates to conduct, such evidence is more convincing than evidence derived from attitude studies, the results of which are derived from verbal responses: Walker & Argyle, *Does the Law Affect Moral Judgment?*, 4 BRIT. J. CRIM. 570 (1964). This article reports an attitude survey, the results of which suggest that knowledge that a form of conduct or type of action is criminal appears to have little bearing on peoples' moral attitude toward the behaviour in question.

No matter how much people may disclaim censorious feelings, their conduct is apt to belie their professions.

23. Garfinkel, *Conditions of Successful Degradation Ceremonies*, 61 AM. J. SOC. 420 (1956).

24. *Id.* at 421.

25. *Id.* at 424.

26. *See* text following note 18 *supra.*

27. H. L. A. HART, *supra* note 20, at 58 (emphasis added).

28. R. S. PETERS, ETHICS AND EDUCATION 274 (1966) (emphasis added).

29. *Id.* at 275.

30. *Id.* at 279.

31. Kohlberg, *Moral Development and Identification*, in CHILD PSYCHOLOGY 277 (H. Stevenson ed. 1963).

32. Andenaes, *supra* note 2, at 966.

33. Schwartz & Orleans, *On Legal Sanctions*, 34 U. CHI. L. REV. 274, 292 (1967). This article reports the results of a field experiment on motivational factors affecting compliance with federal income tax laws conducted at Northwestern University. It is stated that interviews "aimed at inducing sanction threat" produced an increase in "normative sentiments" on the part of upper and middle class Americans. *Id.* at 286 n.45. Working or upper lower class individuals showed a decline in such sentiments following threat, however, and in neither case are the authors able "to report changes in payment in relation to . . . attitudinal responses." *Id.* at 294. Consequently the study is somewhat inconclusive even in regard to taxpaying, which as the authors point out differs significantly "from other forms of legal compliance." *Id.* at 284 n.37. Schwartz and Orleans also point out that "[A]n appeal to conscience could, of course, heighten the determination to *resist* taxes," for there are those "for whom reflection on the intended use of taxes might *decrease* the tendency to comply." *Id.* at 288 n.47 (emphasis added). They cite in this connection, E. WILSON, THE COLD WAR AND THE INCOME TAX: A PROTEST (1963).

34. 2 THE OXFORD ENGLISH DICTIONARY 845 (1893).

35. S. BENN & R. S. PETERS, SOCIAL PRINCIPLES AND THE DEMOCRATIC STATE 26–28 (1959).

36. Bettelheim, *Individual and Mass Behaviour in Extreme Situations*, 38 J. AB. & SOC. PSYCH. 417, 426 (1943). The two camps were Dachau and Buchenwald.

37. *Id.* at 441.

38. Kohlberg, *supra* note 31, at 324. We must recognize that the kinds of behavior forbidden by the criminal law are not necessarily regarded as morally wrong; especially in a pluralistic democratic society, they may sometimes be seen as morally neutral, morally acceptable, or even morally desirable.

39. G. DE BEAUMONT & A. DE TOCQUEVILLE, ON THE PENITENTIARY SYSTEM IN THE UNITED STATES, AND ITS APPLICATION IN FRANCE 89–90 (Lantz ed. 1964).

40. N. WALKER, CRIME AND PUNISHMENT IN BRITAIN 79 (1965).

41. *See* text accompanying and following notes 2–3 *supra.*

42. P. TAPPAN, *supra* note 1, at 247.

43. Andenaes, *supra* note 2, at 951.

44. Morris, *supra* note 1, at 631.

45. N. MORRIS, THE HABITUAL CRIMINAL 6 (1951).

46. There are, of course, exceptions to the general rule. Most criminal codes do establish some duties and punish omissions, but there are comparatively few such instances—too few for a meaningful concept of habitual lawfulness to be derived from them.

47. J. DEWEY, HUMAN NATURE AND CONDUCT 42 (Mod. Lib. ed. 1957).

48. "An attitude can be defined as an enduring organization of motivational, emotional, perceptual and cognitive processes with respect to some aspect of the individual's world." D. KRECH & R. CRUTCHFIELD, THEORY AND PROBLEMS OF SOCIAL PSYCHOLOGY 152 (1948). This definition seems close to what Professor Andenaes has formulated. In relation to habitual law-abiding conduct, Professor Andenaes states: "*Purely as a matter of habit*, with fear, respect and authority or social imitation as connecting links, it is possible to induce *favorable attitudes* toward this or that action and *unfavorable attitudes* toward that action." Andenaes, *supra* note 9, at 179 (emphasis added). [p. 142 this volume]

49. Andenaes, *supra* note 9, at 179. [p. 142 this volume]

50. *Id.* at 179–80. [p. 142 this volume]

51. Mattick, *Parolees in the Army During World War II*, 24 FED. PROBATION 49, 54 (Sept. 1960).

52. K. OLIVECRONA, LAW AS FACT 149 (1938).

53. Andenaes, *supra* note 2, at 969. "The awareness of hazards of imprisonment for intoxicated driving is in our country [Norway] a living reality to every driver, and for most people the risk seems too great." *Id.*

54. *Id.*

55. This particular example refers to a motoring offence. But this is not to say that it can be regarded as of negligible importance. Motoring offences are among the "most deadly and destructive of all contemporary offences." B. WOOTEN, CRIME AND THE CRIMINAL LAW: REFLECTIONS OF A MAGISTRATE AND SOCIAL SCIENTIST 25 (1963).

"Delinquent motorists overwhelmingly outnumber all other offences: two out of every three people found guilty in court are traffic offenders. . . . [I]t is clear that anti-social use of vehicles is a much more important source of death, bereavement, physical suffering and disablement than any intentional forms of violence." N. WALKER, *supra* note 40, at 32–33.

56. Murphy, *Habit*, in 4 ENCYCLOPAEDIA OF THE SOCIAL SCIENCES 239 (E. Seligman ed. 1937).

57. *Id.* at 238.

58. Andenaes, *supra* note 9, at 182. [p. 145 this volume]

59. *Id.*

60. Walker, *Morality and the Criminal Law*, 11 HOWARD J. 214 (1964).

61. Walker & Argyle, *supra* note 22.

62. *Id.* at 574.

63. *Id.*

KARL F. SCHUESSLER

The Deterrent Influence of the Death Penalty

THIS ARTICLE ANALYZES certain statistical material as it bears on the question of how much the death penalty deters people from committing murder. This material, consisting principally of United States homicide and execution data for the period 1925–49, has been organized around six topics expressed for the most part as questions: (1) the adequacy of United States statistics for purposes of measuring the deterrent influence of the death penalty; (2) the deterrence viewpoint as an explanation of murder and punishment trends in this country during the last twenty-five years; (3) whether fewer murders occur in places where murder is punishable by death than in places where it is not; (4) whether differences in the use of the death penalty correspond to differences in the relative occurrence of murder; (5) the consistency between the deterrence viewpoint and differentials in the murder rate by sex, race, and other population classifications; and (6) a general appraisal of the deterrent value of the death penalty.

This analysis in a sense represents a continuation of similar work done intermittently in this country during the last thirty-five years.[1] These previous studies have uniformly concluded that the death

Reprinted from *The Annals of the American Academy of Political and Social Science*, Vol. 284 (November 1952), 54–62, with permission of the author and of the publishers.

This paper was aided immensely by Professor Thorsten Sellin who made available to the author his extensive *Memorandum on Capital Punishment* prepared in 1950 for the British Royal Commission on Capital Punishment. The author is also indebted to Professor Clifford Kirkpatrick who read this paper critically but who is, of course, in no way responsible for its contents, and also to Mrs. Vada Gary who assisted with the statistical work.

penalty is inconsequential as a deterrent and that the relative frequency of murder in a given population is a function of the cultural conditions under which the group lives, Deficiencies in United States data that handicapped earlier investigations of this kind have been remedied somewhat during the last twenty years, but many difficulties still face the analyst who wishes to generalize about murder and the death penalty. Before going to the data and their interpretation, the belief in the death penalty as a deterrent is briefly set forth.

The Deterrence Viewpoint

In brief, people are believed to refrain from crime because they fear punishment. Since people fear death more than anything else, the death penalty is the most effective deterrent, so runs the argument. It is further alleged that the effectiveness of the death penalty as a deterrent depends both on its certain application and on knowledge of this fact in the population; hence, the argument continues, regular use of the death penalty increases its deterrent value. It was largely on grounds of this sort that the death penalty was recently (1950) restored in New Zealand after a ten-year period of abolition, demonstrating that the deterrence line of reasoning still has considerable practical force.

Involved in the deterrence argument is the assumption that men deliberately choose among rival courses of action in the light of foreseeable consequences, the criterion of choice being personal gratification. This psychological hedonism, needless to say, is not in accord with modern psychology and sociology, which see human behavior as largely unplanned and habitual, rather than calculated and voluntary. The belief in the deterrent value of the death penalty is thus seen not as a scientific proposition, but rather as a social conviction widely used to justify and reinforce existing ways of treatment that perhaps rest mainly on feelings of vengeance. Consequently, this study does not constitute a test of a carefully drawn sociological hypothesis that intends to explain differences in the prevalence of murder among human societies, but rather assembles factual evidence to test the validity of a popular belief. We now return to the topics posed in the introduction to this article.

Karl F. Schuessler

United States Homicide and Execution Data

THE HOMICIDE STATISTICS collected by the United States Census Bureau[2] are ordinarily used as an index of murder, figures on murder being generally inaccessible as well as fragmentary. The use of homicide statistics for purposes of estimating the deterrent influence of the death penalty has been criticized on the grounds that (*a*) they include justifiable and excusable homicides and (*b*) they do not distinguish among differing degrees of murder. The reasoning behind this criticism is that the proportion of nonfelonious homicide and the relative amount of different kinds of murder may vary in time and space in such a way as to make unreliable regional comparisons and time trends.

Over against these reasonable objections is the fact that the homicide rate closely corresponds, both geographically and temporally, to the murder figures given in *Uniform Crime Reports*,[3] which exclude nonfelonious homicide, though they include non-negligent manslaughter. Also, the homicide rate is closely correlated, on both a geographic and a temporal basis, with murder conviction rates given in *Judicial Criminal Statistics*, and with murder commitment rates based on information in *Prisoners in State and Federal Prisons and Reformatories*.[4]

This consistency among four independent indexes of murder is probably due to the fact that the relative occurrence of different kinds of murder is similar among states and fairly constant during the last twenty-five years. If this interpretation is correct, then the homicide rate is a reliable index of murder in general and first degree murder in particular, during approximately the last twenty-five years.

National statistics on executions have been readily available in this country only since 1930, when they were reported in *Mortality Statistics* and also in *Prisoners in State and Federal Prisons and Reformatories*. From the standpoint of measuring the temporal relation between execution and murder, these figures are of limited value because they cover such a short period of time. The fact that executions-by-offense were not published for the period 1931–36 adds to this difficulty, although for certain states it may be safely assumed that all executions during that period were for murder.

Some material on murder convictions and death sentences is available in *Federal Judicial Statistics*. But for purposes of relating conviction and punishment trends to concurrent trends in murder, this source is limited as follows: (*a*) this series covers only a thirteen-year period, 1933–45; (*b*) the largest number of states reporting in any single year was thirty; (*c*) only eighteen states (including the District of Columbia) reported each year during the entire period; and (*d*) except for the first few years, the number of persons convicted of murder is not given, but rather the number of murder indictments resulting in conviction.

In spite of the forenamed shortcomings in murder statistics for the period 1925–49, they are probably more adequate than data hitherto employed as a check on the alleged deterrent influence of the death penalty. In consequence, conclusions based on this study are less vulnerable to the objection that murder data are so unreliable as to make worthless generalizations about the death penalty as a deterrent.

United States Homicide and Capital Punishment Trends

THE UNITED STATES homicide rate moved steadily upward from 1900 until the middle of the thirties, dropped sharply during the next ten-year period, and then at the close of World War II started an upward swing. Although homicide statistics are not available for 1950 and 1951, national police statistics indicate that the upward trend was checked in 1951; in any case, the rate is still far below the high levels of the late 1920's and early thirties.

State trends in the period 1925–49 generally correspond to the national trend, although there are several exceptions, important from the standpoint of an explanation of murder. (1) Vermont exhibited an almost constant rate during this period. (2) By 1949, Virginia, North Carolina, and South Carolina had returned to or exceeded the high level of the depression years. (3) Michigan, Nevada, and Florida started their downward trend before 1930. (4) At least one state—Connecticut—continued to climb until 1940. The homicide rate continued to exhibit large regional differences, the highest rates persisting in the South, the lowest in New England.

Also, the homicide rate continued to display large differentials by sex, race, ecological area, and season, the effect of each classification being conditioned to a certain extent by its relation to the others. These differentials suggest at once that murder is a complex sociological event rather than a simple response controlled altogether by the deterrent influence of the death penalty.

Two somewhat contradictory capital punishment trends in the United States characterize the period 1925–49. On the one hand, a trend to extend capital punishment, starting just after World War I, continued with the restoration of the death penalty in Kansas (1935) and South Dakota (1939). The move to re-establish capital punishment in Michigan in 1951 exemplifies the persistence of this trend. On the other hand, a tendency to make the death penalty permissive rather than mandatory on conviction of first degree murder continued. By 1951 the death penalty was mandatory in only one state, in contrast with 1924 when it was mandatory in eight states.

The speculation has been advanced that nowadays a smaller proportion of persons sentenced to death for murder are executed than formerly, the tendency to administer clemency being in line with a general trend to moderate punishment. This was not borne out by an analysis of available judicial and penal statistics, although this evidence is very scanty. Of those sentenced to death for murder in the courts of 25 states during the period 1933–39, 80 per cent were executed; during the period 1940–45, 81 per cent were executed—practically no change. The idea of a downward trend in the use of the death penalty is also opposed, though indirectly, by the fact that the decline in executions from 1930–39 to 1940–49 was roughly proportional to the drop in homicides. The number of executions for murder dropped from 1,507 in the period 1930–39 to 1,063 in the following decade, a 29 per cent drop, while homicides dropped from 107,514 to 78,443, a 27 per cent drop.

By way of summary, capital punishment policy and practice in this country was fairly stable in the period 1925–49; consequently, the movement of the homicide rate and differentials in the homicide rate by various population classifications cannot be attributed to changes in the use of the death penalty. This suggests once again that differences in the homicide rate correspond to differences in social structure and culture setting, and that murder and the death penalty are unrelated except in the circular sense that more murder involves more death penalties.

COMPARISON OF DEATH PENALTY AND ABOLITION STATES

A COMPARISON OF states that provide the death penalty for murder with those that do not shows the homicide rate to be two to three times as large in the former states as in the latter (Table 1). Such a

TABLE 1

HOMICIDE RATES PER 100,000 POPULATION IN DEATH PENALTY
STATES AND ABOLITION STATES[a] FOR FIVE SELECTED YEARS

U56

Year	Abolition States	Death Penalty States
1928	4.2	8.8
1933	3.7	10.5
1938	2.2	7.6
1943	2.1	5.5
1949	2.2	6.0

[a] These two groupings include all states in the national registration area in any given year. All states were in the registration area after 1932.

comparison is usually declared invalid because the two groupings are not uniform with respect to population composition, social structure, and culture pattern. This criticism, though methodologically sound, affirms indirectly that the relative occurrence of murder is the result of a combination of social circumstances of which punishment is only one, possibly an immaterial one.

To meet the foregoing objection, the usual practice is to compare the homicide rate in states that have abolished the death penalty with their neighbors where the death penalty is legal. This comparison is illustrated in Table 2, and it will be seen that Rhode Island, an abolition state since 1852, is very similar to Connecticut, where the death penalty has been retained. Maine also, though not shown in the table, has been abolition since 1887, and is quite similar to the New England states which have the death penalty. The homicide rate in Michigan, where the death penalty was abolished in 1847 (except for treason), closely resembles Indiana and Illinois homicide rates, while Wisconsin, an abolition state for practically a hundred years, has a rate significantly below Michigan, indicating that the homicide rate is indifferent to the presence or absence of capital punishment. Homicide rates in Minnesota, where the death penalty was abandoned in 1911, and in Iowa are very nearly alike with respect to both level and trend during the last twenty-five years. Similarly, homicide rates in Arizona and New Mexico, both death penalty states, have been practically identical both in level and movement during the period 1930–50, although Arizona executed 27 and New Mexico but 4 in this period.

Kansas and South Dakota are of special interest because they make possible a before-and-after comparison, though extremely limited in scope. Kansas abolished the death penalty in 1907 and reestablished it in 1935. The annual average homicide rate in Kansas for the period 1931–35, ~~as shown in Table 2,~~ was considerably

TABLE 2

ANNUAL AVERAGE HOMICIDE RATES IN FIFTEEN STATES
SELECTED ACCORDING TO CONTIGUITY

State	1931–35	1939–40	1941–46
Rhode Island[a]	1.8	1.5	1.0
Connecticut	2.4	2.0	1.9
Michigan[a]	5.0	3.6	3.4
Indiana	6.2	4.3	3.2
Wisconsin[a]	2.4	1.7	1.5
Illinois	9.6	5.7	4.4
Minnesota[a]	3.1	1.7	1.6
Iowa	2.6	1.7	1.3
Kansas[b]	6.2	3.6	3.0
Colorado	7.5	5.5	3.7
Missouri	11.1	6.6	5.3
Nebraska	3.7	1.7	1.8
Oklahoma	11.0	7.2	5.6
Arizona	12.6	10.3	6.5
New Mexico	12.5	8.4	5.3

[a] Abolition state.
[b] Abolition between 1931 and 1935

higher than the average rate for the following five-year period, giving plausibility to the deterrence argument. However, an identical trend characterized the states bordering on Kansas (Table 2), and these states had the death penalty throughout this period. The experience of Kansas, then, when viewed in context, merely emphasizes that homicide trends are the resultant of social conditions rather than the resultant of changes in death penalty policy.

This notion is borne out by a comparison of homicide trends in South Dakota, an abolition state between 1915 and 1939, and North Dakota, where the death penalty has not been in force since 1915. The annual average homicide rate in South Dakota dropped from 1.8 for the period 1930–39 to 1.5 for the following ten-year period, while in North Dakota the rate dropped from 1.8 to 1.1. If changes in the homicide rate were due solely to differences in capital punishment policy, then North Dakota's greater proportional drop in homicides must have been due to the fact that the death penalty was not restored.

European Data

Since the middle of the last century there has been a sustained though uneven movement among European countries to abolish capital punishment by legal annulment or by allowing it to fall into disuse. Certain European statistics therefore bear on the question of whether the removal of the death penalty has a perceptible effect on the incidence of murder. Several examples[5] are cited primarily to illustrate the fact that the independence between the murder rate and the death penalty is not a peculiarity of American culture.

Sweden formally abolished the death penalty in 1921; but the last execution occurred in 1910, this being the only one since 1900. During the preceding period, 1869–1900, there were 12 executions, roughly averaging 4 per decade. There is nothing in the Swedish homicide series (Table 3) to suggest that its movement has in any way been conditioned by the abandonment of the death penalty during the twentieth century.

The death penalty in the Netherlands was not used after 1860 and was formally abolished in 1870. Although there was an upward trend (Table 4) in the murder and attempted murder conviction rate in the twenty-year period immediately following abolition, during this period the rate never attained the level of 1860–70 when the death penalty was still legally in force. The rate reached its lowest level in the 1920's when the death penalty was, of course, not in effect. Moreover, the decade immediately following abolition, 1870–79, was the lowest but one in the approximately eight-decade period covered by this series.

TABLE 3
ANNUAL AVERAGE HOMICIDE RATE PER 100,000 POPULATION OF
SWEDEN FROM 1754 TO 1942

Period	Homicide Rate
1754–1763	.83
1775–1792	.66
1793–1806	.61
1809–1830	1.09[a]
1831–1845	1.47
1846–1860	1.24
1861–1877	1.12
1878–1898	.90
1899–1904	.96
1905–1913	.86
1914–1916	.72
1920–1932	.52
1933–1938	.46
1939–1942	.47

[a] Exclusive of 1814 and 1818.

TABLE 4
ANNUAL AVERAGE MURDER AND ATTEMPTED MURDER CONVICTION RATES
PER MILLION INHABITANTS IN THE NETHERLANDS, 1850–1927

Period	Homicide Rate
1850–1859	.96
1860–1869	1.46
1871–1880	.83
1881–1890	1.17
1891–1900	1.41
1901–1910	1.25
1911–1920	1.32
1921–1927	.60

CERTAINTY AS A DETERRENT INFLUENCE

THE POINT HAS OFTEN BEEN MADE that it is not so much the legal existence of the death penalty that deters potential murderers, but rather the certainty of its being used. In fact, a common criticism of the death penalty is that juries do not convict readily if the punishment is death, thereby reducing the certainty of punishment, and, in consequence, its deterrent value. The problem as to whether differences in the use of the death penalty are in some way related to variations in the homicide rate may be approached by correlating execution and homicide data distributed geographically or temporally.

That the risk of execution is not uniform among the states that have a death penalty for murder is demonstrated by the lack of consistency between homicide and execution rates. The correlation coefficient of a homicide rate based on the period 1937–49 and an execution rate for the same period was .48 for 41 death penalty states.[6] The question therefore arises as to whether the relative occurrence of murder decreases regularly as the risk of execution increases, since, under deterrence theory, the value of the death penalty as a deterrent is thought to depend on its certain application.

To test this idea, though somewhat crudely, the risk of execution, operationally defined as the number of executions-for-murder per 1,000 homicides for the period 1937–49, was statistically compared with the homicide rate in 41 death penalty states. The correlation between these two indices was —.26, indicating a slight tendency for the homicide rate to diminish as the probability of execution increases. Next, as a check on consistency in this trend, the ratio of the average execution rate to the average homicide rate was computed for four groupings of states according to size of the homicide rate, as shown in column 3 of Table 5. This analysis shows that

TABLE 5
AVERAGE HOMICIDE AND EXECUTION RATES IN 41 STATES
GROUPED ACCORDING TO SIZE OF HOMICIDE RATE

Quartile by Homicide Rate	Average Homicide Rate (HR)	Average Execution Rate (ER)	$\dfrac{ER}{HR}$
Highest	15.4	.32	.21
Upper middle	7.8	.14	.18
Lower middle	4.2	.08	.19
Lowest	2.0	.05	.25

the homicide rate does not consistently fall as the risk of execution increases.

To illustrate: the average homicide rate for the ten states having the highest homicide rates is almost twice as large as the average homicide rate for the states in the next quartile, but the risk of execution is slightly greater in the former group of states than in the latter group. This evidence, included primarily because of its suggestiveness, must be classed as negative from the standpoint of deterrence theory, since (*a*) the homicide rate does not drop consistently as the certainty of the death penalty increases, and (*b*) the geographic correlation between the risk of execution and the homicide rate is not impressive, failing to reach the 5 per cent significance level and statistically accounting for only 7 per cent (r^2) of the variability in the homicide rate.

To investigate further how differences in the use of the death penalty affect the homicide rate, the relationship between homicide and execution data as time series was measured within certain death penalty states. States which displayed little variability in executions for murder from year to year were not included in this analysis; also, states not having execution-for-murder figures complete for the period 1930–49 were omitted. This left a total of eleven states. On the assumption, implicit in deterrence theory, that a large number of executions relative to the frequency of murder should be followed by a reduction in the murder rate, a one-year time lag was established, with the execution risk, defined as the number of executions-for-murder to 1,000 homicides per year, as the forerunner.

The most general finding is that the homicide rate and the execution risk as time series move independent of one another. None of the correlation coefficients reached .35, and the number of negative correlation coefficients, 4, was less than the number of positive coefficients, 7, but not significantly so. This evidence, like that just preceding, fails to substantiate the belief that the deterrent influence of the death penalty is enhanced by its frequent use, as changes in the homicide rate do not correspond in a systematic way to variations in the probability of its being used.

DIFFERENTIAL HOMICIDE RATES AND THE DEATH PENALTY

A FINAL PROBLEM is whether the deterrence viewpoint is consistent with certain population classifications. First, the death penalty is hardly ever used with women in the United States, but women, in contrast with men, seldom commit murder. Very likely the conditions of life surrounding women in most human societies operate to develop and sustain lawful attitudes and habits. Lawfulness in the female population, specifically the fact that women generally refrain from committing murder, is probably due to these positive sociocultural influences rather than to fear of the death penalty.

Second, the number of Negro murderers is relatively larger than the number of white murderers; yet it is doubtful whether the death penalty is used less often with Negro murderers than with white murderers. Suggestive in this connection is the fact that white executions for murder, 166, were 1.1 per cent of all white homicides, 15,494, in the period 1946–49, while Negro executions for murder, 265, constituted 1.5 per cent of all Negro homicides, 18,327, during the same period. The environmental factors influencing Negroes are analogous but opposite to those influencing women. The circumstances of life surrounding large numbers of Negroes in the United States generate violence, assault, and murder,[7] and this kind of behavior, to a certain extent socially expected and socially sanctioned among Negroes, is indifferent to the use of the death penalty.

Finally, the homicide rate exhibits differentials by age, social class, ethnic background, community size, and season, but in no instance can these differences be ascribed to corresponding differences in the application of the death-penalty.

DISCUSSION AND CONCLUSION

THE RESULTS OF the foregoing analysis are consistent with the results of previous investigations of this kind. The findings of this study, then, sustain the conclusion that the death penalty has little if anything to do with the relative occurrence of murder. Studies of this sort have been criticized on the ground that they do not *prove* that the death penalty is completely without deterrent value. Although logically sound in a very strict sense, this objection is unrealistic, since there is no way at present of contrasting personal and social situations so as to assure that all differences in murder behavior are due solely to differences in the use of the death penalty. As usual, inferences have to be based on evidence collected under conditions that most nearly approximate the methodological ideal.

Moreover, the inference drawn from statistical data that the death penalty is inconsequential as a deterrent is borne out by case studies and expert opinion, material not surveyed in this paper but now briefly noted.

The alleged deterrent influence of the death penalty is contradicted by the following recurrent case study data, expressed as four rough generalizations: (1) In the events preceding murder, the murderer is usually preoccupied to the point that reflection over future consequences is virtually impossible. (2) The fear of death is relative to the situation; consequently, the death penalty may appear on reflection to be a necessary though unfortunate sequel to murder. (3) Certain cultural circumstances (underworld, marital, and others) often make murder imperative, thereby nullifying the supposed deterrent effect of the death penalty. (4) The relation between murderer and victim is usually primary, hence, one that is likely to be suffused with emotionality. This emotionality, probably heightened during a crisis, doubtless interferes with the objective assessment of future consequences. The indifference of the murderer to the death penalty is well illustrated by the following conversation between Lawes and a prisoner.

> Before Morris Wasser's execution, when I told him that the governor had refused him a last-minute respite, he said bitterly: "All right, Warden. It doesn't make much difference what I say now about this here system of burning a guy, but I want to set you straight on something."
>
> "What's that?" I asked.
>
> "Well, this electrocution business is the bunk. It don't do no good, I tell you, and I know, because I never thought of the chair when I plugged that old guy. And I'd probably do it again if he had me on the wrong end of a rod."
>
> "You mean," I said, "that you don't feel you've done wrong in taking another man's life?"
>
> "No, Warden, it ain't that," he said impatiently. "I mean that you just don't think of the hot seat when you plug a guy. Somethin' inside you just makes you kill, 'cause you know if you don't shut him up it's curtains for you."
>
> "I see. Then you never even thought of what would happen to you at the time."
>
> "Hell, no! And lots of other guys in here, Harry and Brick and

Luke, all says the same thing. I tell you the hot seat will never stop a guy from pullin' a trigger." That was Wasser's theory, and I've heard it echoed many times since.[8]

To summarize: statistical findings and case studies converge to disprove the claim that the death penalty has any special deterrent value. The belief in the death penalty as a deterrent is repudiated by statistical studies, since they consistently demonstrate that differences in homicide rates are in no way correlated with differences in the use of the death penalty. Case studies consistently reveal that the murderer seldom considers the possible consequences of his action, and, if he does, he evidently is not deterred by the death penalty. The fact that men continue to argue in favor of the death penalty on deterrence grounds may only demonstrate man's ability to confuse tradition with proof, and his related ability to justify his established way of behaving.

NOTES

1. See, for example, Raymond T. Bye, *Capital Punishment in the United States,* Philadelphia: Committee on Philanthropic Labor of Philadelphia Yearly Meeting of Friends, 1919; Edwin H. Sutherland, "Murder and the Death Penalty," *Journal of the American Institute of Criminal Law and Criminology,* Vol. 15, 1925, pp. 522–29; Clifford Kirkpatrick, *Capital Punishment,* Philadelphia: Committee on Philanthropic Labor of Philadelphia Yearly Meeting of Friends, 1925; George B. Vold, "Can the Death Penalty Prevent Crime?" *Prison Journal,* October 1932, pp. 3–8.

2. *Mortality Statistics,* Bureau of the Census, United States Department of Commerce, Washington, D.C. Also, *Special Reports,* National Office of Vital Statistics, Public Health Service, Federal Security Agency, Washington, D.C.

3. *Uniform Crime Reports,* Federal Bureau of Investigation, United States Department of Justice, Washington, D.C.

4. Both publications issued by the Bureau of the Census. The results of this correlational analysis are omitted because of lack of space, except to say that the correlation coefficients were uniformly high ($r \geq .8$).

5. Taken from Thorsten Sellin's *Memorandum on Capital Punishment,* London, 1951.

6. Includes states that had a death penalty for murder during the period

1937–49, except South Dakota where the death penalty was restored in 1939 and Idaho where no executions occurred during this period. The product-moment correlation method was used throughout this analysis, not because it necessarily gave the best fit in all cases, but rather because its limitations and signification are well known.

7. Gunnar Myrdal, *The American Dilemma* (New York, 1944), pp. 558–60.

8. Lewis E. Lawes, *Meet the Murderer!* (New York, 1940), pp. 178–79.

WILLIAM J. CHAMBLISS

The Deterrent Influence of Punishment

The general disrepute of the "classical" school of criminology and of the theory that capital punishment deters murder has led many investigators to assume that punishment, as administered through formal sanctioning agencies, does not prevent norm violation. An intensive study of parking violators indicates that, at least in this limited area, an increase in the severity and certainty of punishment does act as a deterrent to further violation. These findings suggest the necessity for a reappraisal of current thinking. Studies demonstrating the ineffectuality of punishment as a deterrent to certain types of offenses should not be interpreted to mean that punishment is ineffective in deterring all types of offenses.

WHEN SOCIAL SCIENCE was still speculating on the number of teeth in the horse's mouth before it had gone into the stable to count them, Jeremy Bentham was advocating a total revision of the criminal law based on a conception of man as "hedonist."[1] Among Bentham's many fascinating and intriguing notions was the theory that man would be deterred from crime if punishment for offenses were applied swiftly, certainly, and severely. While this proposition has been inextricably associated with Bentham and others of the "classical" school of criminology, it currently serves as a straw man for contemporary criticisms of the notion that punishment is an effective deterrent to *anything*, including crime.

The assumption that man is a complexity of hidden drives, motives, desires, and needs which push him to behave (in some

Reprinted from *Crime and Delinquency*, Vol. 12, No. 1 (January 1966), 70–75, with permission of the author and of the publishers.

cases) criminally is obviously incompatible with a "rational" conception of man which views him as selecting certain courses of action in line with his assessment of the "pleasure" or "pain" likely to result from these actions. Furthermore, the theory of punishment as a deterrent has been rejected because the question of deterrence has frequently turned into a debate over the *morality* of *capital* punishment. Social scientists have generally opposed capital punishment on moral grounds and have, as an extension of this, put themselves in the position of arguing against punishment of any kind. Finally, the social scientists' opposition to the notion that punishment might act as a deterrent has been supported by a great deal of research which demonstrates that *capital* punishment does not act as an effective deterrent to *murder*.[2] This finding emerges consistently, regardless of the particular techniques used to assess the impact of capital punishment on the incidence of murder. In states where capital punishment has been abolished the murder rates have not changed. In addition, when we compare a state where capital punishment is a possibility with another "culturally similar" contiguous state where it is not, we arrive at the same conclusion: there is no difference between the percentages of murder in the two areas. Even an execution that is particularly well publicized has no subsequent effect on the propensity of others to murder.[3]

As important as these studies are in indicating that the death penalty is ineffective as a deterrent to murder, their very broad interpretation has rendered a disservice to the more general issue of punishment as a deterrent to all kinds of criminal behavior. Such an expansive conclusion is obviously not justified since murder is, in many ways, a unique kind of offense often involving very strong emotions.

In view of the foregoing it seems essential that studies be conducted on the deterrent influence of punishment on crimes other than murder.

An opportunity for conducting such an investigation presented itself in 1956 when changes were made in the policies and practices pertaining to the violation of parking regulations on a midwestern university campus. A dramatic increase in the certainty and severity of punishment for the violation of parking regulations occurred at this time and a study was made to assess the impact of these changes on the behavior of the group affected.

BACKGROUND OF THE STUDY

BECAUSE OF THE RAPID INCREASE of students and faculty in the early fifties, the university was faced with the problem of insufficient parking space. The university made several attempts to provide a system of control to assure parking space for all faculty and students, but eventually it became apparent that adequate space could not be provided for all the cars on campus. As a result, an attempt was made to restrict student parking to a few parking lots on the periphery of the campus; parking on curbs, in alleyways, and (as had sometimes occurred) on the grass was prohibited for everyone.

In 1951 the faculty council instituted a system of fines for violation of these rules. Faculty members were required to pay one dollar for each parking ticket received; students were required to pay one dollar for the first offense, three dollars for the second, and five dollars for the third. If a student received more than three citations in one academic year his "right to drive" in the county was revoked. Failure to pay fines or continuing to drive after receiving four or more tickets resulted in disciplinary action by the dean.

These procedures remained in effect until January 1956. Although the seriousness of the parking problem was somewhat reduced, the measures taken were far from sufficient. The university administration was plagued with complaints from faculty, students, and the campus police. It was argued that since no provision was made in the regulations for forcing faculty to pay fines, many of the faculty continued to park wherever they wished, frequently blocking traffic or taking up two parking spaces.

In 1956, responding to considerable bitterness and dissatisfaction with the system, the faculty council established a set of rules which attempted, once more, to alleviate the problem. These new rules provided that faculty members would be fined the same as students—one dollar for the first ticket, three dollars for the second, and five dollars for the third. Further, if a faculty member failed to pay his fine his right to park on campus would be automatically revoked, and if he parked on campus his car would be towed away at his own expense.

In addition to these rule changes, the staff employed by the safety division was greatly expanded, a new director (formerly a state police captain) was appointed, and the necessity of enforcing the regulations was pointed out to all the campus police (who had concluded that it was useless to give tickets to the faculty because they would "merely tear them up").

These changes increased the likelihood of a violator's receiving a parking citation (because of the increased number of personnel assigned to patrol parking areas and the increased efficiency of the safety division) and increased the severity of penalties (by increasing the amount of the fine to be paid for the second, third, and subsequent violations and by providing for a tow-away for failure to pay fines).

It would then follow that if punishment is an effective deterrent, the number of violations of the regulations should have decreased after January 1956, when the new policies were instituted.

THE SAMPLE

TO SEE WHETHER the number of violations did, in fact, decrease, we studied the faculty's pattern of violation before and after the changes in policy. Although there was consensus among the administrators of the university that the new procedures had "solved the problem," their conclusion was impressionistic and did not rest on an empirical analysis.

A sample of forty-three faculty members was taken at random from all faculty members who had been on campus for at least 2½ years before January 1956 and for an equivalent period after that date. They were interviewed and were asked simply to "discuss the parking situation at the university." The parking problem and the resultant turmoil were, apparently, of so much concern to the faculty that most of them talked at length about the events of the preceding five to six years with very little further prompting from the interviewer. The most important information sought, of course, was whether or not the interviewee had violated the regulations in either or both of the two periods and, if so, how often.

RESEARCH FINDINGS

TABLE I SHOWS THE BREAKDOWN, by reported frequency, of violations for the two periods. Respondents were considered frequent violators if they reported breaking the regulations five times or more. Thus, to be classified as a "frequent" violator *before* the change in regulations, the respondent had to report violating the regulations at least five times from 1953 to 1955. Similarly, to be a frequent violator *after* the change, he would have to have violated the regulations at least five times from 1955 to 1957. "Occasional" violators were those who broke the rules three or four times during the periods specified; "seldom" violators were those who violated once or twice; and "nonviolators" were those who reported no violations.

It is significant that fifteen of the forty-three respondents reported that they never violated the regulations during either period. Thus, the rules were obeyed by 35 per cent of the population not only when severe restrictions were instituted, but also when relatively light penalties were applied.

Of the remaining twenty-eight respondents, thirteen reported frequent violation of the regulations prior to the change. Of these, six became nonviolators after the change, four became seldom violators, one became an occasional violator, and two remained frequent violators.

These data indicate clearly that the change in regulations (and the corresponding increase in the certainty and severity of punishment) greatly reduced the number of transgressions and the number of transgressors and served as an effective deterrent. The differences are statistically significant, as shown in Table I.

Even the two persons who remained frequent violators after the change in regulations did so in a qualified manner. One of them reported violating the regulations every day by parking in an alley beside his office. Although he said he knew that this was against the rules, he had never received a citation for parking in this alley. In this case, then, the certainty of punishment had not increased as it had for the others. The other frequent violator said that although he still violated as often as he had before, he was now limiting his transgressions to "emergency" stops of only a few minutes rather

TABLE 1

RESPONDENTS BY REPORTED FREQUENCY OF VIOLATION
BEFORE AND AFTER CHANGE IN REGULATIONS
(June 1, 1953, to December 31, 1955, and January 1, 1956, to June 1, 1958)

BEFORE CHANGE	AFTER CHANGE				
Frequency of Violations	*None*	*Seldom*	*Occasional*	*Frequent*	*Total*
None (15)	15	0	0	0	15
Seldom (12)	0	12	0	0	12
Occasional (3)	1	0	2	0	3
Frequent (13)	6	4	1	2	13
Total (43)	22	16	3	2	43

χ^2 (change in number of persons violating *zero times* in two periods) = 5.1, P<.05

χ^2 (change in number of persons violating *one or two times* in two periods) = 2.25, not significant

χ^2 (change in number of persons violating *three or four times* in two periods) = n too small to be meaningful

χ^2 (change in number of persons violating *five or more times* in two periods) = 9.1, P<.05

χ^2 (change in total number violating in two periods) = 5.1, P<.05

NOTE: For an explanation of the χ^2 formula used to compute these significance tests see Helen M. Walker and Joseph Lev, *Statistical Inference* (New York: Henry Holt, 1953), pp. 102–03.

than leaving his car parked illegally for sustained periods of time. Thus he attempted to reduce the likelihood of apprehension, albeit violating the rules with some regularity.

In summary, except for those who violated the regulations once or twice (seldom violators), the differences in the number of violations prior to the change in regulations and the number of violations after the change are significant at the .05 level and in the direction of a reduced number of violations.

Similar results obtain from an analysis of the frequency of receiving tickets in the two periods (Table 2). Seventeen persons indicated receiving no tickets in either period. As can be seen, there was a rather startling reduction in the number of persons receiving tickets after the change despite the fact that the likelihood of receiving a ticket for violating the regulations was greater after the change than it had been before. It is also significant that no one in the sample received "five or more" tickets after the change in the regulations, whereas nine persons were in the "five or more" tickets category before the change. These findings, then, tell essentially the

TABLE 2
RESPONDENTS BY REPORTED FREQUENCY OF RECEIVING TICKETS
BEFORE AND AFTER CHANGES IN REGULATIONS
(June 1, 1953, to December 31, 1955, and January 1, 1956, to June 1, 1958)

BEFORE CHANGE Frequency of Receiving Tickets	AFTER CHANGE None	Seldom	Occasional	Frequent	Total
None (19)	17	2	0	0	19
Seldom (12)	5	7	0	0	12
Occasional (3)	1	1	1	0	3
Frequent (9)	5	4	0	0	9
Total (43)	28	14	1	0	43

same story as the above analysis of the reported frequency of violations before and after the change in the regulations: the changes had the effect of substantially reducing the number of violations.

Another indication of the deterrent influence of the change in the regulations is the degree to which respondents reported greater caution in avoiding violations. Of the forty-three persons interviewed, twenty-five (58 per cent) reported being more cautious about violating the regulations after the changes. Among those not reporting more caution, five were nonviolators and six were seldom violators before the change. Like the other findings, this indicates that the most outstanding changes took place among the most frequent violators.

DISCUSSION

THE FINDINGS GIVE evidence that an increase in the certainty and the severity of punishment deters violation of parking regulations, except for one group. All twelve persons who reported that they were seldom violators before the change in the regulations reported that they were *still* seldom violators after the change in the regulations. In short, the change in the certainty and severity of punishment did in fact deter the more frequent violators, but it had no effect upon those who violated the rules only once or twice in a 2½-year period. The change had no effect because the seldom violators paid their fines during *both* periods where other categories of offenders did not. During the period before the change, sixteen persons violated the regulations occasionally or frequently (Table 1); twelve of them had received tickets (Table 2): but only *three* of them, according to their own admissions, had paid a fine. Clearly, then, the new regulations represented a rather drastic change for the frequent and occasional violators but did not represent much of a change for the seldom violators.

During the study period there were, of course, changes in the parking facilities. Space previously used for parking was put to other uses, and new parking space was made available. Although the total number of parking spaces for faculty did not change appreciably during the time studied, it is possible that the facilities after 1956 were, in general, better suited to faculty demands and that this, rather than the increased punishment imposed, accounts for the reduction in the number of violations. We assessed this possibility by asking all of the forty-three respondents whether they found it less difficult to find parking space during the second period covered by the study. Only six reported less difficulty after the change; nineteen reported that it was more difficult to find a parking space *after* January 1956 than it had been before. Thus, thirty-seven (86 per cent) of the respondents in our sample reported that they had at least as much difficulty in finding a parking space after the change as they had had before. The reduction in the number of violations, then, cannot be attributed to more accessible or "better" facilities.

CONCLUSION

WE CANNOT, OF COURSE, infer from the findings of this study of parking regulations that "punishment does deter" any more than we should infer from the studies of murder that "punishment does not deter." Because we are dealing with specialized groups of offenders in both instances, generalizations to other groups are extremely hazardous. Rather than attempt to answer the question of deterrence in such an all-encompassing manner, we should pursue investigations, of the kind reported here, on other types of offenders and examine *those circumstances under which particular types of punishment do in fact act as a deterrent and those circumstances under which particular types of punishment have little or no effect*. It is naïve to suppose that punishment exists in a vacuum and is unrelated to the specific kinds of acts and the meaning which the punishment has for the actor. By keeping such differences in mind we can go beyond the polemics which have, unfortunately, characterized scientific as well as lay thinking on the subject of punishment as a deterrent.

NOTES

1. For an excellent summary of Bentham's position, see Gilbert Geis, "Pioneers in Criminology: Jeremy Bentham," *Journal of Criminal Law and Criminology*, July–August 1955, pp. 159–71.

2. See, for example, Karl Schuessler, "The Deterrent Influence of the Death Penalty," *Annals of the American Academy of Political and Social Science*, November 1952, pp. 54–62.*

3. Leonard D. Savitz, "A Study in Capital Punishment," *Journal of Criminal Law and Criminology*, November–December 1958, pp. 338–41.

* Also reprinted in this volume.

Dorothy Miller, Ann Rosenthal, Don Miller,
Sheryl Ruzek

Social Psychiatry Research Associates

Public Knowledge of Criminal Penalties:
A Research Report

IN EVERY ORGANIZED SOCIETY in the world, the problem of illegal or harmful acts perpetrated by one man upon others has presented a control problem. Every type of punishment, from banishment to death, from incarceration to maiming, has been tried. The current rising incidence of crime seems related to factors other than the deterrent power of punishment, no matter how severe or cruel it may be. However, retaliation and revenge against a wrongdoer have a morality older than recorded history. Indeed the course of civilization might be traced in terms of its treatment of, and attitude toward, its deviant members. Further, a man is believed to be accountable for his acts, and a penalty is the sanction that supports accountability.

In this humane age, Californians recognize the futility of retribution and seek to rehabilitate rather than to retaliate. We call our prison system a correction and or rehabilitative unit; we assign indeterminate sentences so that a criminal might be freed when he is rehabilitated rather than when he has served a specific time behind bars.

Yet all of this has developed from an older philosophy of penalty, of punishment, and of incarceration. Thus, we convict, insti-

Reprinted from *Deterrent Effects of Criminal Sanctions,* Progress Report of the California Assembly Committee on Criminal Procedure, Sacramento, California (May 1968), 10-18 (excluding Table 1), with permission of the authors.

tutionalize, and attempt to reconstruct a person at the same time. Such conflictual ends produce disappointing results.

Most experts maintain that increasing penalties has no effect upon decreasing crime, but that efficiency of law enforcement, of the certainty of being "caught," is the strongest deterrent to crime. Auditors, for example, try to develop systems which make embezzlement difficult to carry out and to set up controls which lead to certainty of detection. Banks do not rely solely upon legal sanctions to protect them against embezzlers, but develop efficient control and detection systems.

As we have moved from rural to urban society, many of the informal social control and detection systems have broken down. Strangers are not good order-keepers. As urbanization increases, crime increases. As crime increases, many people suggest increasing penalties. Very few would suggest decreasing urbanization.

In the face of the rising incidence of crime, numerous measures have been enacted by legislative bodies in an attempt to impede the runaway rise of unlawfulness. While it can be argued that the *existence* of penalties may in fact deter *some* crime, it is not clear that the increasing of already existing penalties has an equally increasing deterrent effect. A traditional response to an increase in crime has been to increase penalties to deter increased criminal activity. That such an increase in penalties does, in fact, deter crime, however, remains to be demonstrated.

In order to examine the deterring effect of increased penalties, a potential criminal must be viewed as considering the penalty for the crime prior to committing the unlawful deed—to weigh the consequences, as it were. Theoretically, then a crime would occur only if the possible gain from the commission of the crime exceeded the penalty for that crime. Illustrative of the reason for increasing penalties for a crime against persons or property is the following consideration a potential lawbreaker would give the situation: "The penalty for forgery is one year, which really is not a very long time. Therefore, I will chance the penalty and forge a $1,000 check. If, however, the penalty for forgery were five years, which really is a very long time, I would not chance that penalty for the gain of $1,000." This kind of thinking would constitute the rationale for a recommendation to increase the penalty for forgery.

However, if a deterrent is to be effective, it follows then that a potential criminal must *know* which penalties go with which crimes—knowledge essential in the process of weighing consequences. The foregoing conclusion, if acceptable, prompts the queries: *How knowledgeable are criminals, potential criminals, and law-abiding citizens on the subject of crime and punishment?* Would those persons with the greatest knowledge about a crime—which is to say those persons who know specific penalty—be the least likely to commit a crime? If the deterrent theory is valid, persons with the most knowledge of the penalty would engage in the least amount of the crime, as the knowledge of the penalty would prevent the criminal act. It follows, therefore, that knowledge about a penalty would decrease that crime.

How effective are penalties, and in what areas is it reasonable to expect penalties to be related to controlling crime? It is generally recognized that increased penalties are ineffective in controlling crimes committed against the self, such as homosexual behavior, drug addiction, and prostitution. Similarly, penalties are regarded as ineffective deterrents of the crimes of passion, such as murder and assault.[1]

The issue at hand is whether or not increased penalties decrease the incidence of crimes which arise from an individual's decision to act toward realizing a specific goal, such as robbery, embezzlement, or forgery. The person engaging in the criminal act had intended to so engage himself despite his knowledge that a law is being broken for which *a* penalty exists.

The issue of the deterrent value of penalties has been investigated by a number of criminologists. Andenaes,[2] in an historical review, concludes that penalties and repressive measures may deter, but only in the context of the interplay between moral reprobation and legal implementation. He emphasizes that the greatest determent is the fear of apprehension and conviction in a complex, total social consequence, only a part of which may be the penalty per se!

The problem of "bad checks" was studied extensively by Beutel[3] who found that those states in which this was a felony offense were actually plagued with a higher rate of the passing of bogus checks than were states in which the crime was merely a misdemeanor. By way of explanation he suggests that the excessively severe penalties imposed by felony states may reduce the risk of conviction, thereby leading to results contrary to their purposes.

The relative ineffectiveness of penalties is further documented by Schwartz and Orleans[4] in a field experiment with taxpayers. They found that conscience appeals were significantly more effective than sanction threats in influencing tax compliance—although both had some effect. The threat of punishment, however, appeared to produce a resistance to compliance, unless compliance was also secured through appeals to conscience and a sense of civic responsibility.

A psychological approach taken by Claster[5] in his study of delinquent and nondelinquent boys adds another dimension to the assertion that penalties do not deter. He found that delinquents view themselves as more likely to commit criminal acts than do nondelinquents, and that delinquents also have a distorted view of themselves vis-à-vis the legal structure which leads them to believe that they are immune to arrest. If this is in fact the case, increasing penalties would have no deterring effect, as the potential criminal would not consider himself as likely to be arrested and subsequently subject to the increased punishment.

In spite of research findings which suggest the contrary, the belief persists that penalties are effective deterrents to crime. In an extensive study of the public's attitudes toward crime and the police, Ennis[6] found that the ordinary citizen's sense of justice includes a vengeful element—a desire for punishment over and above monetary compensation for loss. While this vengeance embedded within the citizenry is no indication that punitive measures reduce crime, it does perhaps offer a clue as to why the practice persists and is not discarded in spite of scientific evidence which documents its ineffectiveness.

While there have been many studies in this area, a crucial assumption has been ignored: *If penalties are to deter, we must assume that members of society know what the penalties are.* If we are to assume that the consequences of an act will deter persons from committing that act, they obviously know what those consequences are. That they do, in fact, know the penalties, however, has not been empirically examined.

Dorothy Miller et al.

Scope of this Study

In an attempt to investigate public knowledge regarding criminal penalties in California, with the use of social survey methods, we asked a number of citizens to answer the following questions:

1. How knowledgeable are the people in California about penalties for various crimes?

2. What is the public's perception of the "crime problem" and what do they think should be done to lessen the crime rate?

3. What is the relationship between knowledge of penalties and criminal behavior?

4. If knowledge about penalties does not deter crime, what might?

All of these questions may be viewed differently by different social and ethnic groups in our communities. We, therefore, also were concerned about the effect of race, age, educational, and occupational categories upon responses to such questions.

Methodology

In order to examine these questions, a questionnaire was designed and administered to various groups and subgroups in California.

The questionnaire was designed to tap the respondents' knowledge of penalties for specific crimes, knowledge of the cost of incarcerating criminals, and knowledge of the recent changes in criminal penalties. Questions were also posed regarding attitudes about how serious respondents felt the crime problem to be, and what they felt would help ease the crime rate. Hypothetical situations were presented to elicit ideas about what would deter the respondents from potential criminal activity. Data on the respondent's age, education, occupation, and race were obtained. Additional comments made on the questionnaire by the respondents were coded. These comments which reflected their attitudes toward criminals fell into the following categories: (1) punitive, (2) somewhat punitive, (3) rehabilitative or ameliorative, (4) admission of ignorance, or (5) miscellaneous or mundane comment.

Prior to the final study, a pilot study was conducted to test the questionnaire. A group of male registered voters, chosen at random, along with a group of prisoners, California Youth Authority wards, and classes of boys from high and low delinquency area high schools participated in this pilot study. As a result of the pilot, the revised questionnaire was developed for this survey.

This representative sample includes 3,348 male registered voters selected at random from Alameda, Contra Costa, San Francisco, Los Angeles, Kern, and San Bernardino Counties. (Since most crime occurs in large urban areas, we selected four urban counties and two rural, suburban counties for this study.) An equal number of Democrats and Republicans were selected from lists of registered male voters. Questionnaires were then administered, largely by mail, to these subjects. A letter from the Chairman of the Criminal Procedure Committee accompanied the questionnaire which requested the cooperation of each subject.

The questionnaire was also administered to two adult subsamples: 115 male inmates of the Deuel Vocational Institute and 54 students at the University of the Pacific.

As most crimes in California are committed by males between the ages of fifteen and twenty-nine, 96 boys from a low-delinquency high school in San Francisco, 165 inmates of the CYA Preston School of Industry, and 98 students at a high-delinquency San Francisco high school were selected for a subgroup.

A total of 3,348 questionnaires were administered to these variously selected groups. The total number of usable questionnaires returned was 1,567 or nearly one-half of the total number administered. This rate of return for a survey is relatively high, since only one mail-out was used. Had a careful followup or additional time been available, the return rate could have been increased. However, we feel this group is representative of the most vocal and articulate of Californians, and represents the opinion-leaders. Information in this report is based on these 1,567 completed forms.

How Representative was this Sample?

THE SPECIAL SUBGROUPS SELECTED for study were representative young men who live in high and low delinquency areas. The mailed survey sample, when evaluated for possible bias, was found to be largely representative of the urban adult California population as reflected by comparison with the distribution of the sample with U.S. census figures and projections. The age, ethnic, and occupational distribution compared closely, while the sample group were better educated than the general California population.

The education of the sampled group as measured by years of completed formal schooling revealed that the sample contained an overrepresentation of the college-educated group. Presumably these college-educated citizens who are overrepresented in this sample are representative of those persons most likely to participate in surveys, most likely to be community leaders, most likely to be influential, and most likely to symbolize the opinions and attitudes of the younger, more active, and better educated citizenry in California. Since population trends indicate that this group will be ever-growing in the future, perhaps the responses from this sample point to attitude trends of the future.

MAJOR FINDINGS

THE MAJOR FINDINGS from the survey relate to the four central questions investigated.

Each of these central questions raises other questions, some of which were analyzed, others of which remain for further study.

1. *How knowledgeable are the people in California about penalties for various crimes?* Eleven questions were asked about penalties for various crimes.

Among the general public there was considerable variation in the extent of knowledge about sentences for selected felonies. First of all, a range of 21 percent to 49 percent of the respondents had complete ignorance or were unable to even guess the maximum sentences for these crimes. Furthermore, even among those who made an estimate, the percent of correct responses ranged from 8 percent to 39 percent. If one combined the number of correct responses into a single index score of accuracy, *no one person correctly answered all eleven questions about penalties,* while, at the other extreme, *69 percent of the respondents answered 3 or less items correctly.* This finding is evidence that there is profound lack

TABLE I
AVERAGE NUMBER OF CORRECT ANSWERS REGARDING PENALTIES FOR CRIMES
AND PERCENT OF POSSIBLE ANSWERS FOR ALL GROUPS
TESTED. (N = 1567)

	Mean number correct responses	Percent of total items correct	N
General Population	M = 2.6	24	1,024
College men	M = 3.2	29	54
Low-delinquent high school boys	M = 3.0	27	96
High-delinquent high school boys	M = 3.0	27	113
Youth authority	M = 3.4	31	165
Adult corrections	M = 6.3	57	115
			1,567

of information concerning criminal penalties. This finding is less true for the delinquent or institutionalized groups since first-hand experience would presumably expose such groups to information about penalties. But, while criminal groups knew more about penalties than did the general population, such knowledge had seemingly not deterred them from criminal acts.

The general population had the least amount of knowledge about criminal penalties, while those who had engaged in crime had the greatest knowledge of penalties. It appears that knowledge of penalties comes *after* the crime—that is, penalties cannot act as deterrents since these are unknown until after a person has committed a crime or become a prisoner. Since approximately one-third of all persons who are imprisoned once continue to engage in crime after their release, it would appear that even when they have knowledge about penalties, it does not act as a strong deterrent to their continuation of criminal activity.

Knowledge of criminal penalties varied among the population tested according to certain crimes, as shown in Table II.

As can be seen, the general population had the most knowledge about penalties for assault with a deadly weapon and borrowing a car; among college men, the penalty for borrowing a car was best known; among low delinquency high school boys, the car borrowing penalty was also the best known one; among the high delinquency high school boys, the penalty for cashing a check from a closed account was best known; among boys now in a Youth

TABLE II
PERCENT OF CORRECT RESPONSES REGARDING PENALTIES FOR
SPECIFIC CRIMES BY CALIFORNIA CITIZENS, HIGH SCHOOL,
COLLEGE, AND INSTITUTIONAL POPULATION

| | | LOW-DELINQUENCY | | High delin- quency, | INSTITUTIONAL | |
Knowledge of penalties	General popu- lation (percent correct)	College (percent correct)	High School (percent correct)	High School (percent correct)	Youth Author- ity (percent correct)	Adult Correc- tions (percent correct)
(4) Assault and deadly weapon ...	35	26	24	33	30	59
(5) Second degree burglary ..	15	22	26	26	16	63
(6) First degree robbery ..	8	11	11	10	21	85
(7) Forcible rape	24	30	14	22	36	52
(8) Taking a car and leaving it .	35	44	35	31	40	65
(9) Check from closed account ..	17	20	27	42	33	50

Authority institution, the best known penalty was for borrowing a car; while convicts were most knowledgeable about penalties for first degree robbery. Between these groups, the differences in amount of correct knowledge about criminal penalties was marked, as can be seen by comparing the general population's knowledge against the Deuel Vocational Institution inmates' percent of correct answers. Criminals have the greatest knowledge about penalties, yet seemingly have been deterred the least from crime.

Did respondents under- or overestimate penalties? Among the general population, the tendency *was to underestimate* the penalties, as can be seen in Table III which examines the knowledge of penalties for six crimes.

As can be seen, over one-half of the population underestimated the penalties for second degree burglary, first degree robbery, and writing a check on a closed account. Could this finding indicate that

TABLE III
GENERAL POPULATION RESPONSES INDICATING UNDER-, CORRECT,
OVER-, OR NO ESTIMATE OF SEVERITY OF SENTENCES
FOR SIX CRIMES. (N = 1,024)

	Under-estimate (percent)	Correct answer (percent)	Over-estimate (percent)	No estimate (percent)	Total (percent)
Assault with deadly weapon	..	35	40	25	100
Second degree burglary	52	15	5	28	100
First degree robbery	65	8	1	26	100
Rape	35	24	20	21	100
Joy riding	28	35	15	22	100
Check on closed account	59	17	..	24	100

the actual maximum penalties now levied for those crimes are viewed by the public as being excessive?

The finding that over one-fourth of all the respondents could not *even* guess what the penalty for these crimes were, indicates the great lack of knowledge about criminal penalties in the community.

Several crimes were reviewed by the Legislature in the 1967 session and penalties increased. In general, this action reflected an attempt on the part of the Legislature to respond to growing public concern over the rise of "crime in the streets." All of the crimes for which the penalties were raised involved great bodily injury to the victim—the crimes which have created the greatest fear in the minds of the public. These crimes were rape, robbery, and burglary where great bodily injury was involved. The minimum for all these crimes was increased to fifteen years imprisonment.

The penalties for these crimes as well as two additional crimes were included in the questionnaire. Driving under the influence of alcohol, and possession of marijuana were added to the three crimes with increased penalties. Both of these offenses are currently of public concern, as both have received much attention from public media. The last Legislature had not increased penalties for these crimes.

These five items received greater percentages of "don't know" responses than other questions about criminal penalties. Nearly 50 percent of the population answered that they did not know if the

Legislature had acted or not on the crimes involving great bodily injury. For the other two crimes, about a third of the population could not answer the questions.

When answers were given, people were more likely to respond that the *Legislature* had not acted at all. Very few were able to give correct answers. While the Legislature had supposedly responded to public appeal and increased the penalties for crimes of violence to victims, this was not known by the public. Table IV shows the percent of correct responses made to these five questions.

TABLE IV

PERCENT OF CORRECT ANSWERS ON RECENTLY INCREASED
PENALTIES FOR CRIMES BY GENERAL PUBLIC, HIGH
AND LOW DELINQUENCY GROUPS, AND
INSTITUTIONAL POPULATIONS

Knowledge of increased penalties	General population (percent)	College (percent)	Low delin-quency high school (percent)	High delin-quency high school (percent)	Institutional	
					Youth Authority (percent)	Adult Correc-tions (percent)
Rape	16	17	30	27	24	43
Drunk driving ...	39	46	48	34	26	37
Robbery with bodily injury	20	20	23	33	30	76
Burglary with bodily injury	16	15	25	29	21	57
Possession of marijuana .	36	65	38	16	25	47

The public was as likely to say they did not know as to guess one of the answers to questions involving crimes of a personal nature—driving under the influence of alcohol or possession of marijuana. Where an incorrect answer was given, it was most likely to be that these *penalties* had been *decreased*. (The Legislature did not decrease any penalties.)

Thus, people were in general unaware that the Legislature had taken any action at all when in fact the Legislature had increased the minimum penalties for crimes involving bodily injury to the victim. The public was inclined to answer "don't know" as often as to give a correct response on questions concerning drunk driving and possession of marijuana. (The only major exception occurred among college students who were correct in 65 percent of cases on the question about marijuana.)

When the public did answer these items, they tended to underestimate the amount of the penalty, as is shown in Table V.

TABLE V
GENERAL PUBLIC'S ESTIMATE OF SEVERITY OF PENALTY
FOR FIVE CRIMES. (N = 1,024)

	Under-estimate (percent)	Correct answer (percent)	Over-estimate (percent)	Can't guess (percent)	Total (percent)
Rape with bodily injury	22	16	13	49	100
Driving under influence of alcohol	21	39	4	36	100
Robbery and bodily injury	28	20	6	46	100
Burglary and bodily injury	30	16	5	49	100
Possession of marijuana	16	36	10	38	100

When there seems to be a public outcry against crimes, this finding may indicate that a legislative body should pause and reflect that most people in the general public will *not* know of their action of increasing legal penalties. Further, the public thinks that *penalties for most crimes are actually less than they really are!*

We asked the respondents their concern about the crime rate. Over one-half of the respondents indicated that the present crime rate is so great that it constitutes a public problem. Another one-fourth indicated that the crime rate is higher than it should be. Hence, among the population responding to the survey, nearly three-fourths indicated concern about California's rising crime rate.

2. *What is the public's perception of the "crime problem" and what do they think should be done about it?*

What do people feel will help to lessen the rising crime rate in California? A question was asked about various alternatives.

As can be seen in Table VI, responses to the question varied.

TABLE VI

RESPONSES TO "WHAT DO YOU THINK WOULD HELP
MOST TO LESSEN THE CURRENT CRIME RATE?"

	N	Percent
Better opportunities for poor people	246	24
More law enforcement officers	109	11
Social and psychiatric help for offenders	81	8
Stiffer sentences and longer imprisonment	250	24
Increased scientific study of the causes of crime, etc.	291	28
No response	47	5
Total	1,024	100

One-fourth of the respondents felt that stiffer sentences and longer imprisonments would be the greatest help in lessening the current crime rate. Who are these people, and how knowledgeable are they about the dimensions of the problem?

Respondents from the general population averaged a correct score of 2.8 responses out of a possible 11 responses regarding the penalties for various crimes. However, people who felt that stiffer sentences and longer periods of imprisonment should be applied correctly answered questions about criminal penalties in only 18 percent of the cases, i.e., to answer correctly an average of 2 questions out of the total of 11. Thus those respondents who felt stiffer penalties were needed were even *less* knowledgeable about present penalties than was true for the general population. For this group, the lack of knowledge about existing penalties was not a consideration in suggesting increased penalties as a solution to the crime problem.

In general, the older, retired, and less well-educated groups were more primitive in their general attitude about crime as compared with the younger, better-educated, or employed respondents. Conversely, the better-educated group suggested more scientific study about the causes of crime or better opportunities for jobs and education. In general, there were two groups of respondents. One group wanted short-term answers for the present crime situations, i.e., more law enforcement officers and stiffer sentences. The other group felt attention should be paid, with a long-range view, to the indirect causes of crime, such as poverty, poor education, lack of opportunities, etc. For example, the better educated the respondent, the more likely he was to see the need for more scientific study regarding the causes of crime. Persons from the lower socioeconomic groups, such as laborers or semiskilled workers, were more likely to suggest better opportunities for the poor as a remedy for the rising crime rate in California.

Forty percent of the respondents added comments on their forms. Of those who commented, 18 percent felt that judges were too lenient, that police should have more power, and in general, indicated a sense of irritation of the present administration of justice. An additional one-third were mildly punitive in their attitude toward the courts and police power. Only a few respondents commented about penalties, per se. Most comments calling for stricter law enforcement pointed at the courts and their administration of the present laws. Twenty percent of those who wrote comments expressed concern about individual rights, or the guarantees of protection from excessive legal harassment. It was also of interest to note that one-fourth of those who commented noted their ignorance of the penalties and expressed some amazement at how little they knew about such laws. Many also commented favorably upon the work of the Criminal Procedure Committee.

Since some respondents suggested longer imprisonment, how much did the public know about the cost of prison? The average cost per year for caring for a prisoner in California is $2,560. The respondents were asked to estimate this cost, and the results are shown in Table VII.

Only one-fourth of the people knew the actual cost of keeping

TABLE VII

ESTIMATE OF COST OF PRISON AMONG GENERAL POPULATION AND OTHER SUBGROUPS.

	Don't know (percent)	Under-estimate $1,500 (percent)	Correct $2,560 (percent)	Over-estimate $3,100 (percent)	Total (percent)
General population..	36	9	23	32	100
College men	26	4	24	46	100
Low delinquency high school	42	18	26	15	100
High delinquency high school	47	18	22	13	100
Youth Authority ...	32	24	24	20	100
Adult Corrections ..	23	30	30	17	100

a prisoner for each year, while another one-third couldn't even guess. It is of interest to note that the respondents who are presently in an institution, tended to underestimate the actual cost of their care while one-third of the general public overestimated the cost of caring for a prisoner.

3. *What is the relationship between knowledge of penalties and criminal behavior?*

As was shown in Table I, persons who have already engaged in crime have the most knowledge about penalties. This seems paradoxical, i.e. that if knowledge of penalties is an essential ingredient for deterrence, then how is it that criminals have the most knowledge and are seemingly the least deterred?

Two-thirds of the institutionalized persons also indicated that the crime rate is too high and constitutes a public problem, similar to the responses of the general population. But they differed as to what they thought should be done to remedy this high crime rate.

What do criminals think would lower the crime rate? As can be seen in Table VI both institutionalized groups felt that better opportunities for poor people (32 percent), social and psychiatric help for offenders (23 percent) and increased study of causes of crime (26 percent) would help in lessening the crime rate.

In Chart I, the influence of criminal activity upon knowledge about penalties is shown.

As can be seen, as the group's identity as a deviant one increases, so does the amount of correct knowledge about criminal penalties. To put it another way, those who knew the least about criminal penalties were the least likely to engage in crime.

Of course, *this does not mean that knowledge of criminal penalties causes crime.* It may simply mean that a penal institution is a fine training ground for learning law and criminology. But it also seems to indicate that penalties become of interest to a person only *after* he engages in criminal behavior. Knowledge of penalties does not seem to deter, but it may be important for "copping a plea" or making the best "deal" in court.

It can be conjectured that the cause of criminal behavior lies elsewhere, and the understanding of the motivation for criminal actions does not involve a balance sheet of penalty vs. gain. Rather, people engage in crime and learn of the penalties, not as deterrents, but only as factors of a criminal career faced *after the* fact.

CHART I
COMPARISON BETWEEN GROUPS ON PERCENTAGE OF
CORRECT RESPONSES TO PENALTY QUESTIONS

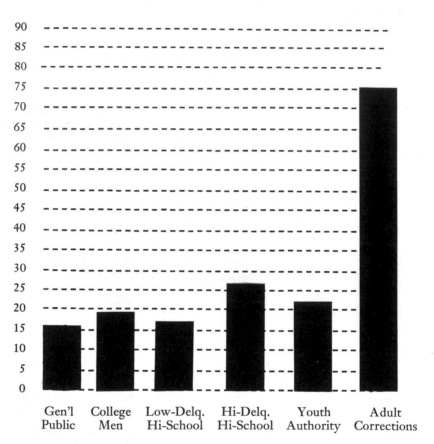

| | Gen'l Public | College Men | Low-Delq. Hi-School | Hi-Delq. Hi-School | Youth Authority | Adult Corrections |

4. *If knowledge about penalties does not deter a person's criminal actions, what might?*

The questionnaire included two items which attempted to learn about personal deterrence factors. The first question was: "If you were convicted of a serious crime, such as forging your employer's signature to a $1,000 check or stealing a color TV, what would bother you the most?"

The question elicited responses regarding "external controls," i.e. sanctions involving the law, prison, stigma of a bad record, etc., and "internal controls," i.e., family sanction, loss of reputation, or self-feelings of guilt.

Table VIII shows that the general public, college men, and high school adolescents would be bothered most, if convicted, by feelings of guilt, or by concern about what their families would think of them.

TABLE VIII
RESPONSES TO "WHAT WOULD BOTHER YOU MOST ABOUT
COMMITTING A CRIME?" FOR ALL GROUPS

	General public (percent)	*College men (percent)*	*Low delin- quency (percent)*	*High delin- quency (percent)*	*Youth Authority (percent)*	*Adult Corrections (percent)*
External controls	32	23	40	42	59	61
Internal controls	68	78	60	58	41	39

(percentages rounded)

However, those now confined in a correctional institution, i.e., those who *have* been convicted of a crime, are bothered more by the external sanctions, i.e., the loss of a job, or imprisonment, than they are by feelings of guilt or concern about what others might think.

Does such a finding indicate that internal sanctions prevent criminal activity, or is such a finding a reflection of the change in attitude which accompanies criminal action?

In order to explore such a question further, each respondent was asked: "If you had suffered such a run of bad luck that you needed money *badly,* and found that you were in a position to accept a bribe or a fix without much fear of getting caught, what, if anything, would stop you?"

As can be seen in Table IX, the more delinquent or criminal the group, the less important are internal sanctions as deterrent to crime. That is, those who look only to external sanctions as a deterrent to thievery are much more likely to, in fact, engage in stealing than are those who feel internal sanctions would deter them.

Thus, from these two findings one might argue that the best deterrent for crime would be to develop social systems that would strengthen internal sanctions rather than to depend solely upon stiffer penalties or more law enforcement officers. In short, it is

TABLE IX
WHAT WOULD DETER CRIMINAL BEHAVIOR?
COMPARISON OF ALL GROUPS

	General public (percent)	College men (percent)	Low delin- quency (percent)	High delin- quency (percent)	Youth Authority (percent)	Adult Corrections (percent)
External controls	23	31	45	44	57	60
Internal controls	77	69	55	56	43	40
Total	100	100	100	100	100	100

man's view of himself as a lawful and responsible person that will deter crime, not just the legal sanctions applied by strangers in authority positions.

SELECTED DEMOGRAPHIC FACTORS

IN ORDER TO STUDY the possible influence of education, occupation, age, and race upon public knowledge about penalties, the data were analyzed for each of those variables.

Education: Those respondents in the general population with more than a high school education had the same amount of knowledge about criminal penalties as did those with less than a high school education. Chi-square shows no significant difference between high school and college-educated respondents with relation to the number of correct answers made.

Occupation: Respondents from the general public were divided into three occupational groups: white collar, blue collar, and other. When compared on the number of correct responses to the criminal penalty questions, there was no statistical significant differences among the groups, using a chi-square. That is, about 70 percent of all groups answered fewer than three questions correctly. (It is of interest to note that questionnaires were returned by 21 attorneys; 4 of whom answered 9 of the 11 penalty questions correctly, 8 answered 8 correctly, etc. Thus, even attorneys and other legal professionals were unable to correctly answer the criminal penalties questions.)

Age: The respondents were scored as being above or below the average on the number of correct answers ($M = 3$) and classified by age as shown in Table X.

TABLE X
AGE OF RESPONDENTS FROM GENERAL PUBLIC COMPARED ON
ABOVE AND BELOW MEAN SCORES ON CORRECT ANSWERS
TO CRIMINAL PENALTIES PERCENTAGE ($M = 3$ CORRECT
RESPONSES OUT OF 11 POSSIBLE RESPONSES)

Age	Below mean score (percent)	Above mean score (percent)	Total (percent)
20-29	66	34	100
30-39	66	34	100
40-49	78	22	100
50-59	73	27	100
60+	71	29	100

Younger respondents tended to have slightly better knowledge of penalties than did other respondents although this was not statistically significant.

Race: The general population sample was classified according to the number of correct answers made above and below the average correct responses to the questions regarding criminal penalties. As shown in Table XI, there were no significant differences in the knowledge of criminal penalties among the three major race divisions.

TABLE XI

Race	Below mean correct response (percent)	Above mean correct response (percent)	Total (percent)
White	71	29	100
Black	70	30	100
Oriental, other	74	26	100

Thus, the social and demographic variables of the respondent's education, occupation, age, and race did not differentiate on the amount of knowledge these groups had about criminal penalties. All groups in the general population were generally unaware of the penalties now in existence for the various crimes.

SUMMARY

A TOTAL OF 3,348 questionnaires were administered to registered voters and others from four urban counties and two suburban-rural counties in California as well as to deviant subgroups. A questionnaire regarding knowledge of criminal penalties and persons' concerns and attitudes toward crime was administered to males from the general public and to other selected groups. A total of 1,567 forms was collected. The sample of the general public used in this research totaled 1,024 completed questionnaires. The general public sample was compared with the U.S. census figures for the six counties studied, and the sample was found to be representative by age and race, and to be overrepresented in education by the college educated. Thus, the sample represents a better-educated group within the population than would be expected. Thus, among the general population, respondents were likely to be the most articulate, most concerned, and most motivated among those sampled. Time did not permit extensive followup, so that these returns represent the most cooperative of the subjects chosen. These respondents are likely to be the opinion-leaders of their community, and as such, their responses should be of great concern to the California State Legislature. Since these respondents represented the better educated and most highly motivated group, how did this group view the crime problem, what did they know of criminal penalties, and what did they think would help lessen the crime rate?

1. *How knowledgeable were Californians about penalties for crimes?* They were extremely ignorant about penalties for crimes. Out of 11 possible items, the means score was only 2.6 answers correct. In fact, most persons underestimated the severity of the penalties now in existence, although one-fourth of these respondents felt that in order to lessen the crime rate, penalties should be increased. When questioned about the recent legislative action in increasing penalties for certain crimes, about one-half of the respondents couldn't even guess whether the penalties had been changed or in which direction. In short, the general public simply *does not know* what the penalties are for various crimes. How then could increased penalties deter crime?[7]

2. *What is the public's perception of the "crime problem" and*

what to they think should be done about it? About three-fourths of all respondents felt the crime rate was too high and many felt crime constituted a public problem. In general, the public seemed to form two opinion groups about what should be done to lessen the California crime rate. The better educated, younger, employed group looked to indirect or long-range solutions aimed at removing the causes for crime, such as better opportunities for poor, social and psychiatric help for the offenders, or increased scientific study of the problem. The older, less well-educated, and unemployed group felt that a more direct, immediate reaction seemed indicated, i.e., stiffer sentences and longer imprisonment, or more law enforcement officers. Some of this group complained, in written comments, about the leniency of judges and the lack of effective law enforcement. This group did not seem to wish increased penalties, per se, but focused upon the problems they saw in the administration of justice. Also, this group was somewhat less well informed about present penalties, even when they were advocating "stiffer sentences."

3. *What is the relationship between knowledge of penalties and criminal behavior?* While this question could not be answered directly, there was some evidence that the more delinquent the group of respondents, the more knowledgeable they were about penalties. That is, the more criminal their behavior, the less likely they were to have been deterred by knowledge of penalties. Penalties appear to be important to delinquent or criminal groups, not as deterrents but as bargaining items after their arrest.

4. *If knowledge about penalties does not deter criminal actions, what might?* Two questions were asked about personal attitudes toward criminal behavior. It was found that the less delinquent groups were controlled and concerned by "internal sanctions," i.e., by guilt, opinions of others, family attitudes, etc., while the more delinquent the group, the less concerned they were with internal, personal sanctions against crime. Rather, they were concerned about not getting caught and about going to prison. But evidently "external sanctions" are not as effective as deterrents against crime as "internal" personal attitudes and self-sanctions. The best program for prevention of crime would have to strengthen these "internal sanctions" if real deterrence of criminal behavior was to develop.

The responses about criminal penalties were not influenced by the respondent's age, education, occupation, or race. They were influenced by identification with a delinquent or criminal subgroup. Those persons now in correctional institutions, who while most knowledgeable about criminal penalties, were least deterred by their greater knowledge about criminal penalties.

NOTES

---

1. Despite increasing the penalty for murder to the death penalty etc., the murder rate in the United States has remained constant for the last thirty years. (F.B.I. Statistics.)

2. Andenaes, Johannes, "The General Preventive Effects of Punishment," *University of Pennsylvania Law Review*, Vol. 114, 7, May 1966, pp. 949–983.

3. Beutel, Frederick K., "Results of a Study of the Bad Check Problem," *Experimental Jurisprudence*.

4. Schwartz, Richard D. and Orleans, Sonya, "Our Legal Sanctions," *University of Chicago Law Review*, Vol. 34:274, pp. 274–300.

5. Claster, Daniel, "Comparison Risk Perception, Between Delinquents and Non-Delinquents," *Journal of Criminal Law, Criminology and Police Science*, Vol. 58, No. 1, 1967, pp. 80–86.

6. Ennis, Phillip H., "Crime, Victims and the Police," *Trans-Action*, June 1967, pp. 36–44.

7. A return rate of .47 is fairly high for a "one-shot" mailout for such a survey. See the sections on mailed questionnaires in Stephens, S. F. and T. J. McCauley, *Sampling Opinion* and Kish, Leslie, *Survey Sampling*, pp. 539–540.

REHABILITATION

ENRICO FERRI

The Positive School of Criminology

LECTURE III [REMEDIES]

IN THE PRECEDING TWO LECTURES, I have given you a short review of
the new current in scientific thought, which studies the painful and
dangerous phenomena of criminality. We must now draw the logical conclusions, in theory and practice, from the teachings of experimental science, for the removal of the gangrenous plague of crime.
Under the influence of the positive methods of research, the old
formula "Science for science's sake" has given place to the new
formula "Science for life's sake." For it would be useless for the
human mind to retreat into the vault of philosophical concentration,
if this intellectual mastery did not produce as a counter-effect a
beneficent wave of real improvement in the destinies of the human
race.

What, then, has the civilized world to offer in the way of
remedies against criminality? The classic school of criminology,
being unable to locate in the course of its scientific and historical
mission the natural causes of crimes, . . . was not in a position to deal
in a comprehensive and far-seeing manner with this problem of the
remedy against criminality. Some of the classic criminologists, such
as Bentham, Romagnosi, or Ellero, with a more positive bent of
mind than others, may have given a little of their scientific activity

From *The Positive School of Criminology*, edited by Stanley E. Grupp, ©
1968 by the University of Pittsburgh Press. Excerpts 95-104, 106-112, reprinted by
permission of the University of Pittsburgh Press.

This is the third of three lectures given by Enrico Ferri at the University of
Naples, Italy, April 22, 23, and 24, 1901.

to the analysis of this problem, namely the prevention of crime. But Ellero himself had to admit that "the classic school of criminology has written volumes concerning the death penalty and torture, but has produced but a few pages on the prevention of criminality." The historical mission of that school consisted in a reduction of punishment. For being born on the eve of the French revolution in the name of individualism and natural rights, it was a protest against the barbarian penalties of the Middle Ages. And thus the practical and glorious result of the classic school was a propaganda for the abolition of the most brutal penalties of the Middle Ages, such as the death penalty, torture, mutilation. We in our turn now follow up the practical and scientific mission of the classic school of criminology with a still more noble and fruitful mission by adding to the problem of the *diminution of penalties* the problem of the *diminution of crimes*. It is worth more to humanity to reduce the number of crimes than to reduce the dread sufferings of criminal punishments, although even this is a noble work, after the evil plant of crime has been permitted to grow in the realm of life. Take, for instance, the philanthropic awakening due to the Congress of Geneva in the matter of the Red Cross Society, for the care, treatment, and cure of the wounded in war. However noble and praiseworthy this mission may be, it would be far nobler and better to prevent war than to heal the mutilated and wounded. If the same zeal and persistence, which have been expended in the work of the Red Cross Society, had been devoted to the realization of international brotherhood, the weary road of human progress would show far better results.

It is a noble mission to oppose the ferocious penalties of the Middle Ages. But it is still nobler to forestall crime. The classic school of criminology directed its attention merely to penalties, to repressive measures after crime had been committed, with all its terrible moral and material consequences. For in the classic school, the remedies against criminality have not the social aim of improving human life, but merely the illusory mission of retributive justice, meeting a moral delinquency by a corresponding punishment in the shape of legal sentences. This is the spirit which is still pervading criminal legislation, although there is a sort of eclectic compromise between the old and the new. The classic school of criminology has substituted for the old absolutist conceptions of justice the eclectic theory that absolute justice has the right to punish, but a right modified by the interests of civilized life in present society. This is the point discussed in Italy in the celebrated controversy between Pasquale Stanislao Mancini and Terencio Mamiani,[1] in 1847. This is in substance the theory followed by the classic criminologists who revised the penal code, which public opinion considers incapable of protecting society against the dangers of crime. And we have but to look about us in the realities of contemporaneous life in order to see that the criminal code is far from being a remedy against crime, that it remedies nothing, because either premeditation or passion in the person of the criminal deprive the criminal law of all prohibitory power. The deceptive faith in the efficacy of criminal law still lives in the public mind, because every normal man feels that the thought of imprisonment would stand in his way, if he contemplated tomorrow committing a theft, a rape, or a murder. He feels the bridle of the social sense. And the criminal code lends more strength to it and holds him back from criminal actions. But even if the criminal code did not exist, he would not commit a crime, so long as his physical and social environment would not urge him in that direction. The criminal code serves only to isolate temporarily from social intercourse those who are not considered worthy of it. And this punishment prevents the criminal for a while from repeating his criminal deed. But it is evident that the punishment is not imposed until after the deed has been done. It is a remedy directed against effects, but it does not touch the causes, the roots, of the evil.

We may say that in social life penalties have the same relation to crime that medicine has to disease. After a disease has developed in an organism, we have recourse to a physician. But he cannot do anything else but to reach the effects in some single individual. On the other hand, if the individual and the collectivity had obeyed the rules of preventive hygiene, the disease would have been avoided 90 times in 100, and would have appeared only in extreme and exceptional cases, where a wound or an organic condition break through the laws of health. Lack of providence on the part of man, which is due to insufficient expression of the forces of the intellect and pervades so large a part of human life, is certainly to blame for the fact that mankind chooses to use belated remedies rather than to observe the laws of health, which demand a greater methodical control of one's actions and more foresight, because the remedy must be applied before the disease becomes apparent. I say occasionally that human society acts in the matter of criminality with the same lack of forethought that most people do in the matter of tooth-ache. How many individuals do not suffer from tooth-ache, especially in the great cities? And yet any one convinced of the miraculous power of hygiene could easily clean his teeth every day and prevent the microbes of tooth rot from thriving, thereby saving his teeth from harm and pain. But it is tedious to do this every day. It implies a control of one's self. It cannot be done without the scientific conviction that induces men to acquire this habit. Most people say: "Oh well, if that tooth rots, I'll bear the pain." But when the night comes in which they cannot sleep for tooth-ache, they will swear at themselves for not having taken precautions and will run to the dentist, who in most cases cannot help them any more.

The legislator should apply the rules of social hygiene in order to reach the roots of criminality. But this would require that he should bring his mind and will to bear daily on a legislative reform of individual and social life, in the field of economics and morals as well as in that of administration, politics, and intelligence. Instead of that, the legislators permit the microbes of criminality to develop their pathogenic powers in society. When crimes become manifest, the legislator knows no other remedy but imprisonment in order to punish an evil which he should have prevented. Unfortunately this scientific conviction is not yet rooted and potent in the minds of the legislators of most of the civilized countries, because they represent on an average the backward scientific convictions of one or two previous generations. The legislator who sits in parliament today was the university student of thirty years ago. With a few very rare exceptions he is supplied only with knowledge of outgrown scientific research. It is a historical law that the work of the legislator is always behind the science of his time. But nevertheless the scientist has the urgent duty to spread the conviction that hygiene is worth as much on the field of civilization as it is in medicine for the public health.

This is the fundamental conviction at which the positive school arrives: That which has happened in medicine will happen in criminology. The great value of practical hygiene, especially of social hygiene, which is greater than that of individual hygiene, has been recognized after the marvelous scientific discoveries concerning the origin and primitive causes of the most dangerous diseases. So long as Pasteur and his disciples had not given to the world their discovery of the pathogenic microbes of all infectious diseases, such as typhoid fever, cholera, diphtheria, tuberculosis, etc., more or less absurd remedies were demanded of the science of medicine. I remember, for instance, that I was compelled in my youth, during an epidemic of cholera, to stay in a closed room, in which fumigation was carried on with substances irritating the bronchial tubes and lungs without killing the cholera microbes, as was proved later on. It was not until the real causes of those infectious diseases were discovered, that efficient remedies could be employed against them. An aqueduct given to a center of population like Naples is a better protection against cholera than drugs, even after the disease has taken root in the midst of the people of Naples. This is the modern lesson which we wish to teach in the field of criminology, a field which will always retain its repressive functions as an exceptional and ultimate refuge, because we do not believe that we shall succeed in eliminating all forms of criminality. Hence, if a crime manifests itself, repression may be employed as one of the remedies of criminology, but it should be the very last, not the exclusively dominating one, as it is today.

It is this blind worship of punishment which is to blame for the spectacle which we witness in every modern country, the spectacle that the legislators neglect the rules of social hygiene and wake up with a start when some form of crime becomes acute, and that they know of no better remedy than an intensification of punishment meted out by the penal code. If one year of imprisonment is not enough, we'll make it ten years, and if an aggravation of the ordinary penalty is not enough, we'll pass a law of exception. It is always the blind trust in punishment which remains the only remedy of the public conscience and which always works to the detriment of morality and material welfare, because it does not save the society of honest people and strikes without curing those who have fallen a prey to guilt and crime.

The positive school of criminology, then, aside from the greater value attributed to daily and systematic measures of social hygiene for the prevention of criminality, comes to radically different conclusions also in the matter of repressive justice. The classic school has for a cardinal remedy against crime a preference for one kind

of punishment, namely imprisonment, and gives fixed and prescribed doses of this remedy. It is the logical conclusion of retributive justice that it travels by way of an illusory purification from
moral guilt to the legal responsibility of the criminal and thence on
to a corresponding dose of punishment, which has been previously
prescribed and fixed.

We, on the other hand, hold that even the surviving form of
repression, which will be inevitable in spite of the application of the
rules of social prevention, should be widely different, on account of
the different conception which we have of crime and of penal
justice.

In the majority of cases, composed of minor crimes committed
by people belonging to the most numerous and least dangerous class
of occasional or passionate criminals, the only form of civil repression will be *the compensation of the victim for his loss.* According
to us, this should be the only form of penalty imposed in the majority of minor crimes committed by people who are not dangerous.
In the present practice of justice the compensation of the victim for
his loss has become a laughing stock, because this victim is systematically forgotten. The whole attention of the classic school has been
concentrated on the juridical entity of the crime. The victim of the
crime has been forgotten, although this victim deserves philanthropic sympathy more than the criminal who has done the harm.
It is true, every judge adds to the sentence the formula that the
criminal is responsible for the injury and the costs to another authority. But the process of law puts off this compensation to an indefinite time, and if the victim succeeds a few years after the passing of
the sentence in getting any action on the matter, the criminal has
in the meantime had a thousand legal subterfuges to get away with
his spoils. And thus the law itself becomes the breeding ground of
personal revenge, for Filangieri says aptly that an innocent man
grasps the dagger of the murderer, when the sword of justice does
not defend him.

Let us say at this point that the rigid application of compensation for damages should never be displaced by imprisonment, because this would be equivalent to sanctioning a real class distinction.
For the rich can laugh at damages, while the proletarian would have
to make good a sentence of 1000 lire by 100 days in prison, and in
the meantime the innocent family that tearfully waits for him out-

side would be plunged into desperate straits. Compensation for damages should never take place in any other way than by means of the labor of the prisoner to an extent satisfactory to the family of the injured. It has been attempted to place this in an eclectic way on our law books, but this proposition remains a dead letter and is not applied in Italy, because a stroke of legislator's pen is not enough to change the fate of an entire nation.

These practical and efficient measures would be taken in the case of lesser criminals. For the graver crimes committed by atavistic or congenital criminals, or by persons inclining toward crime from acquired habit or mental alienation, the positive school of criminology reserves segregation for an indefinite time, for it is absurd to fix the time beforehand in the case of a dangerous degenerate who has committed a grave crime.

The question of indeterminate sentences has been recently discussed also by Pessina, who combats it, of course, because the essence of the classic school of criminology is retribution for a fault by means of corresponding punishment. We might reply that no human judge can use any other but the grossest scale by which to determine whether you are responsible to the extent of the whole, one half, or one third. And since there is no absolute or objective criterion by which the ratio of crime to punishment can be determined, penal justice becomes a game of chance. But we content ourselves by pointing out that segregation for an indefinite time has so much truth in it, that even the most orthodox of the classic school admit it, for instance in the case of criminals under age. Now, if an indeterminate sentence is a violation of the principles of the classic school, I cannot understand why it can be admitted in the case of minors, but not in the case of adults. This is evidently an expedient imposed by the exigencies of practical life, and only the positive school of criminology can meet them by a logical systematization. For the rest, indefinite segregation, such as we propose for the most dangerous atavistic criminals, is a measure which is already in use for ordinary lunatics as well as for criminal lunatics. But it may be said that this is an administrative measure, not a court sentence. Well, if any one is so fond of formulas as to make this objection, he may get all the fun out of them that he likes. But it is a fact that an insane person who has committed a crime is sent to a building with iron bars on its gates such as a prison has. You may call it an administrative building or a penal institute, the name is unessential, for the substance alone counts. We maintain that congenital or pathological criminals cannot be locked up for a definite term in any institution, but should remain there until they are adapted for the normal life of society.

This radical reform of principles carries with it a radical transformation of details. Given an indeterminate segregation, there should be organs of guardianship for persons so secluded, for instance permanent committees for the periodical revision of sentences. In the future, the criminal judge will always secure ample evidence to prove whether a defendant is really guilty, for this is the fundamental point. If it is certain that he has committed the crime, he should either be excluded from social intercourse or sentenced to make good the damage, provided the criminal is not dangerous and the crime not grave. It is absurd to sentence a man to five or six days imprisonment for some insignificant misdemeanor. You lower him in the eyes of the public, subject him to surveillance by the police, and send him to prison from whence he will go out more corrupted than he was on entering it. It is absurd to impose segregation in prison for small errors. Compensation for injuries is enough. For the segregation of the graver criminals, the management must be as scientific as it is now in insane asylums. It is absurd to place an old pensioned soldier or a hardened bureaucrat at the head of a penal institution. It is enough to visit one of those compulsory human beehives and to see how a military discipline carries a brutal hypocrisy into it. The management of such institutions must be scientific, and the care of their inmates must be scientific, since a grave crime is always a manifestation of the pathological condition of the individual. In America there are already institutions, such as the Elmira Reformatory, where the application of the methods of the positive school of criminology has been solemnly promised. The director of the institution is a psychologist, a physician.[2] When a criminal under age is brought in, he is studied from the point of view of physiology and psychology. The treatment serves to regenerate the plants who, being young, may still be straightened up. Scientific therapeutics can do little for relapsed criminals. The present repression of crime robs the prisoner of his personality and reduces him to a number, either in mass imprisonment which corrupts him completely, or in solitary confinement, which will turn him into a stupid or raving beast. . . .

You must, therefore, give a scientific management to these institutions, and you will then render humane even the treatment of those grave and dangerous criminals, whose condition cannot be met by a simple compensation of the injury they have done to others.

This is the function of repression as we look upon it, an inevitable result of the positive data regarding the natural origin of crime.

We believe, in other words, that repression will play but an unimportant role in the future. We believe that every branch of legislation will come to prefer the remedies of social hygiene to those symptomatic remedies and apply them from day to day. And thus we come to the theory of the prevention of crime. Some say: "It is better to repress than to prevent." Others say: "It is better to prevent than to repress." In order to solve this conflict we must remember that there are two widely different kinds of repression. There is the immediate, direct empirical repression, which does not investigate the cause of criminality, but waits until the crime is about to be committed. That is police prevention. There is on the other hand a social prevention which has an indirect and more remote function, which does not wait until crime is about to be committed, but locates the causes of crime in poverty, abandoned children, trampdom, etc., and seeks to prevent these conditions by remote and indirect means. In Italy, prevention is anonymous [synonymous] with arrest. That is to say, by repression is understood only police repression. Under these circumstances, it is well to take it for granted that some of the expected crimes will be carried out, for crimes are not committed at fixed periods after first informing the police. The damage done by criminality, and especially by political and social criminality, against which police repression is particularly directed, will be smaller than that done by the abuse inseparably connected with police power. In the case of atavistic criminality, prevention does not mean handcuffing of the man who is about to commit a crime, but devising such economic and educational measures in the family and administration as will eliminate the causes of crime or attenuate them, precisely because punishment is less effective than prevention.

In other words, in order to prevent crime, we must have recourse to measures which I have called "substitutes for punishment," and which prevent the development of crime, because they go to the source in order to do away with effects.

Bentham narrates that the postal service in England, in the eighteenth century, was in the hands of stage drivers, but this service was not connected with the carrying of passengers, as became the custom later. And then it was impossible to get the drivers to arrive on time, because they stopped too often at the inns. Fines were imposed, imprisonment was resorted to, yet the drivers arrived late. The penalties did not accomplish any results so long as the causes remained. Then the idea was conceived to carry passengers on the postal stages, and that stopped the drivers from being late, because whenever they made a halt, the passengers, who had an interest in arriving on time, called the drivers and did not give them much time to linger. This is an illustration of a substitute for punishment.

Another illustration. In the Middle Ages, up to the eve of our modern civilization, piracy was in vogue. Is there anything that was not tried to suppress piracy? The pirates were persecuted like wild beasts. Whenever they were caught they were condemned to the most terrible forms of death. Yet piracy continued. Then came the application of steam navigation, and piracy disappeared as by magic. And robbery and brigandage? They withstood the death penalty and extraordinary raids by soldiers. And we witness today the spectacle of a not very serious contest between the police who want to catch a brigand, Musolino;[3] and a brigand who does not wish to be caught.

Wherever the woods are not traversed by railroads or tramways, brigandage carries on its criminal trade. But wherever railroads and tramways exist, brigandage is a form of crime which disappears. You may insist on death penalties and imprisonment, but assault and robbery will continue, because it is connected with geographical conditions. Use on the other hand the instrument of civilization, without sentencing any one, and brigandage and robbery will disappear before its light. And if human beings in large industrial centers are herded together in tenements and slum hotels, how can a humane judge aggravate the penalties against sexual crimes? How can the sense of shame develop among people, when young and old of both sexes are crowded together in the same bed, in the same corrupted and corrupting environment, which robs the human soul of every noble spark?

I might stray pretty far, if I were to continue these illustrations of social hygiene which will be the true solution of the problem and the supreme systematic, daily humane, and bloodless remedy against the disease of criminality. However, we have not the simple faith that in the near or far future of humanity crimes can ever be wholly eradicated. Even Socialism, which looks forward to a fundamental transformation of future society on the basis of brotherhood and social justice, cannot elevate itself to the absolute and naive faith that criminality, insanity, and suicide can ever fully disappear from the earth. But it is our firm conviction that the endemic form of criminality, insanity, and suicide will disappear, and that nothing will remain of them but rare sporadic forms caused by lesion or telluric and other influences.

Since we have made the great discovery that malaria, which weighs upon so many parts in Italy, is dependent for its transmission on a certain mosquito, we have acquired the control of malarial therapeutics and are enabled to protect individuals and families effectively against malaria. But aside from this function of protecting people, there must be a social prevention, and since those malarial insects can live only in swampy districts, it is necessary to bring to those unreclaimed lands the blessing of the hoe and plow, in order to remove the cause and do away with the effects. The same problem confronts us in criminology. In the society of the future we shall undertake this work of social hygiene, and thereby we shall remove the epidemic forms of criminality. And nine-tenths of the crimes will then disappear, so that nothing will remain of them but exceptional cases. There will remain, for instance, such cases as that of the bricklayer which I mentioned, because there may always be accidents, no matter what may be the form of social organization, and nervous disorders may thus appear in certain individuals. But you can see that these would be exceptional cases of criminality, which will be easily cured under the direction of science, that will be the supreme and beneficent manager of institutes for the segregation of those who will be unfit for social intercourse. The problem of criminality will thus be solved as far as possible, because the gradual transformation of society will eliminate the swamps in which the miasma of crime may form and breed.

If we wish to apply these standards to an example which today attracts the attention of all Italy to this noble city, if we desire to carry our theories into the practice of contemporaneous life, if science is to respond to the call of life; let us throw a glance at that form of endemic criminality known as the Camorra in this city, which has taken root here just as stabbing affrays have in certain centers of Turin, and the Mafia in certain centers of Sicily. In the first place, we must not be wilfully blind to facts and refuse to see that the citizens will protect themselves, if social justice does not do so. And from that to crime there is but a short step. But which is the swampy soil in which this social disease can spread and persist like leprosy in the collective organism? It is the economic poverty of the masses, which leads to intellectual and moral poverty.

You have lately had in Naples a very fortunate struggle, which seems to have overcome one of the representatives of the high Camorra. But can we believe that the courageous work of a few public writers has touched the roots of the Camorra in this city? It would be self-deception to think so. For we see that plants blossom out again, even after the most destructive hurricane has passed over them.

The healing of society is not so easy, that a collective plague may be cured by the courageous acts of one or more individuals. The process is much slower and more complicated. Nevertheless these episodes are milestones of victory in the onward march of civilization, which will paralyze the historical manifestations of social criminality. Here, then, we have a city in which some hundred thousand people rise every morning and do not know how to get a living, who have no fixed occupation, because there is not enough industrial development to reach that methodical application of labor which lifted humanity out of the prehistoric forests. Truly, the human race progresses by two uplifting energies: War and labor.

In primitive and savage society, when the human personality did not know the check of social discipline, a military discipline held the members of the tribe together. But war, while useful in primitive society, loses its usefulness more and more, because it carries within itself the cancer that paralyzes it.

While war compels collective groups to submit to the co-ordinating discipline of human activity, it also decreases the respect for human life. The soldier who kills his fellow man of a neighboring nation by a stroke of his sword will easily lose the respect for the life of members of his own social group. Then the second educational energy interferes, the energy of labor, which makes itself felt at the decisive moment of prehistoric development, when the human race passes from a pastoral, hunting, and nomadic life into an agricultural and settled life. This is the historic stage in which the collective ownership of land and instruments of production is [are] displaced by communal property, family property, and finally individual property. During these stages, humanity passes from individual and isolated labor to collective, associated, co-ordinated labor. The remains of the neolithic epoch show us the progress of the first workshops, in which our ancestors gathered and fashioned their primitive tools and arms. They give us an idea of associated and common labor, which then becomes the great uplifting energy, because, unlike war, it does not carry within itself a disdain or violation of the rights of others.

Labor is the sole perennial energy of mankind which leads to social perfection. But if you have 100,000 persons in a city like Naples who do not enjoy the certainty and discipline of employment at methodical and common labor, you need not wonder that the uncertainty of daily life, an illfed stomach, and an anemic brain, result in the atrophy of all moral sentiment, and that the evil plant of the Camorra spreads out over everything. The processes in the law courts may attract the fleeting attention of public opinion, of legislation, of government, to the disease from which this portion of the social organism is suffering, but mere repression will not accomplish anything lasting.

The teaching of science tells us plainly that in such a case of endemic criminality social remedies must be applied to social evils. Unless the remedy of social reforms accompanies the development and protection of labor; unless justice is assured to every member of the collectivity, the courage of this or that citizen is spent in vain, and the evil plant will continue to thrive in the jungle.

Taught by the masterly and inflexible logic of facts, we come to the adoption of the scientific method in criminal research and conclude that a simple and uniform remedy like punishment is not adequate to cure such a natural and social phenomenon as crime, which has it own natural and social causes. The measures for the preservation of society against criminality must be manifold, complex and varied, and must be the outcome of persevering and systematic work on the part of legislators and citizens on the solid foundation of a systematic collective economy.

Let me take leave of you with this practical conclusion, and give my heart freedom to send to my brain a wave of fervent blood, which shall express my enduring gratitude for the reception which you have given me. Old in years, but young in spirit and energetic aspiration to every high ideal, I tender you my sincere thanks. As a man and a citizen, I thank you, because these three lectures have been for me a fountain of youth, of faith, of enthusiasm. Thanks to them I return to the other fields of my daily occupation with a greater faith in the future of my country and of humanity. To you, young Italy, I address these words of thanks, glad and honored, if my words have aroused in your soul one breath which will make you stronger and more confident in the future of civilization and social justice.

NOTES

1. Terencio Mamiani, 1799–1885, Italian writer, philosopher, political theorist, and professor; noted for the series of letters exchanged with Mancini in 1841. Mamiani argued, in opposition to Mancini, that the objectives of law and morality were identical and that punishment must reward evil with evil.

2. The reference is apparently to Zebulon Reed Brockway. However, Brockway was not a physician. Similarly, only very liberal use of the term psychologist would warrant this label today.

3. Benedetto Musolino, 1809–1885, Italian political roustabout, founder of the "Sons of Young Italy," active on the Left, and a leader of the Calabrian Revolt.

KARL MENNINGER

Love against Hate

WE COME TO a final chapter and, in keeping with the classic formula, the reader no doubt expects a happy ending. The minor chords which have filled so many of the pages of the long score must dissolve into cheery and conclusive tonic majors, so that the reader may close the book with a sigh of relief and a feeling that, in spite of blunder and turmoil, all's right with the world, or getting to be so.

But all is *not* right with the world in respect to crime and criminals—not yet. And if the reader closes this book with a sense of relief, I have failed. He must close it rather with a disturbed feeling of shared guilt and responsibility, perhaps even a sense of mission. I will have succeeded if he has begun to feel that it may be *up to him* whether or not crime is to be better controlled and public safety insured. Only through such a sense of disturbed concern on the part of intelligent readers and leaders are these results likely to be achieved.

Fifty years ago, Winston Churchill declared that the mood and temper of the public in regard to crime and criminals is one of the unfailing tests of the civilization of any country. Judged by this standard, how civilized are we?

The chairman of the President's National Crime Commission, Nicholas Katzenbach, declared recently that organized crime flourishes in America because enough of the public wants its services, and most citizens are apathetic about its impact. It will continue

From *The Crime of Punishment*, by Karl Menninger, M.D. (Copyright © 1966, 1968 by Karl Menninger, M.D. All rights reserved. Chapter 10, "Love against Hate," excerpts 249-251, 253-254, 257-266. Reprinted by permission of The Viking Press, Inc.

uncurbed as long as Americans accept it as inevitable and, in some instances, desirable. Do we *believe* crime is an inescapable part of our civilization, the eradication of which would requre the surrender of our "freedom," our personal liberty, to a painful degree? Were we to limit the range of individuality, would we sacrifice the courage of innovation, the spark of initiative which delights in taking risks and courting dangers?

The famous simile of the shivering porcupines applies today more accurately than ever. We human porcupines multiply in numbers but remain confined within a limited life area, surrounded by the intense cold of outer space. But the more we seek to huddle together for warmth and comfort and communication, the more we wound and are wounded. What shall we do?

Human beings have one advantage over porcupines: we can see what the problem is. Are there steps that we can take which will reduce the aggressive stabs and self-destructive lurches of our less well-managing fellow men? Are there ways to prevent and control the grosser violations, other than the clumsy traditional maneuvers which we have inherited? These depend basically upon intimidation and slow-motion torture. We call it punishment, and justify it with our "feeling." We know it doesn't work.

Yes, there *are* better ways. There are steps that could be taken; some *are* taken. But we move too slowly.

The reader knows by now some things which I think would hasten the improvement. I have suggested various changes which seem to me to recommend themselves during the discussion of the obvious faults in the system. Much better use, it seems to me, could be made of the members of my profession and other behavioral scientists than having them deliver courtroom pronunciamentos. The consistent use of a diagnostic clinic would enable trained workers to lay what they can learn about an offender before the judge who would know best how to implement the recommendation.

This would no doubt lead to a transformation of prisons, if not to their total disappearance in their present form and function. Temporary and permanent detention will perhaps always be necessary for a few, especially the professionals, but this could be more effectively and economically performed with new types of "facility" (that strange, awkward word for institution). I also favor enabling and expecting offenders to make restitution to the state and to the injured parties, if feasible, although I recognize the complications of framing this requirement legally.[1]

I assume it to be a matter of common and general agreement that our object in all this is to protect the community from a repetition of the offense by the most economical method consonant with our other purposes. Our "other purposes" include the desire to prevent these offenses from occurring, to reclaim offenders for social usefulness, if possible, and to detain them in protective custody, if reclamation is *not* possible, But how? . . .

TREATMENT

THE WORD *treatment* has many meanings. Applied to human beings, it may mean kindness or it may mean cruelty. "Alcoholics should be treated like sick people, not like criminals," someone exclaimed in my hearing recently; two different meanings of treatment were obviously implied.

The medical use of the word *treatment* implies a program of presumably beneficial action prescribed for and administered to one who seeks it. The purpose of treatment is to relieve pain, correct disability, or combat an illness. Treatment may be painful or disagreeable but, if so, these qualities are incidental, not purposive. Once upon a time, we must admit, we doctors with the best of intentions did treat some patients with torture. That, thank God, was long ago.[2]

But the treatment of human failure or dereliction by the infliction of pain is still used and believed in by many non-medical people. "Spare the rod and spoil the child" is still considered wise warning by many.

Whipping is still used by many secondary schoolmasters in England, I am informed, to stimulate study, attention, and the love of learning. Whipping was long a traditional treatment for the "crime" of disobedience on the part of children, pupils, servants, apprentices, employees. And slaves were treated for centuries by flogging for such offenses as weariness, confusion, stupidity, exhaustion, fear, grief, and even overcheerfulness. It was assumed and stoutly defended that these "treatments" cured conditions for which they were administered.

Meanwhile, scientific medicine was acquiring many new healing methods and devices. Doctors can now transplant organs and limbs; they can remove brain tumors and cure incipient cancers; they can halt pneumonia, meningitis, and other infections; they can correct deformities and repair breaks and tears and scars. But these wonderful achievements are accomplished on *willing* subjects, people who voluntarily ask for help by even heroic measures. And the reader will be wondering, no doubt, whether doctors can do anything with or for people who *do not want* to be treated at all, in any way! Can doctors cure willful aberrant behavior? Are we to believe that crime is a *disease* that can be reached by scientific measures? Isn't it merely "natural meanness" that makes all of us do wrong things at times even when we "know better"? And are not self-control, moral stamina, and will power the things needed? Surely there is no medical treatment for the lack of those!

Let me answer this carefully, for much misunderstanding accumulates here. I would say that according to the prevelant understanding of the words, crime is *not* a disease. Neither is it an illness, although I think it *should* be! It *should* be treated, and it could be; but it mostly isn't. . . .

When the community begins to look upon the expression of aggressive violence as the symptom of an illness or as indicative of illness, it will be because it believes doctors can do something to correct such a condition. At present, some better-informed individuals do believe and expect this. However angry at or sorry for the offender, they want him "treated" in an effective way so that he will cease to be a danger to them. And they know that the traditional punishment, "treatment-punishment," will not effect this.

What *will?* What effective treatment is there for such violence? It will surely have to begin with motivating or stimulating or arousing in a cornered individual the wish and hope and intention to change his methods of dealing with the realities of life. Can this be done by education, medication, counseling, training? I would answer *yes*. It can be done successfully in a majority of cases, if undertaken in time.

The present penal system and the existing legal philosophy do not stimulate or even expect a change to take place in the criminal. Yet change is what medical science always aims for. The prisoner, like the doctor's other patients, should emerge from his treatment experience a different person, differently equipped, differently functioning, and headed in a different direction from when he began the treatment.

It is natural for the public to doubt that this can be accomplished with criminals. But remember that the public *used* to doubt that change could be effected in the mentally ill. Like criminals, the mentally ill were only a few decades ago regarded as definitely unchangeable—"incurable." No one a hundred years ago[3] believed mental illness to be curable. Today *all* people know (or should know) that *mental illness is curable* in the great majority of instances and that the prospects and rapidity of cure are directly related to the availability and intensity of proper treatment.

In the city in which I live there had been for many years a gloomy, overcrowded, understaffed place of horror called "the insane asylum." In its dark wards and bar-windowed halls, as late as 1948, one psychiatrist and one nurse were on duty for nearly two thousand sick people. There was no treatment for them worthy of the name. There was no hope. There were few recoveries.[4]

Today this old asylum is a beautiful medical complex of forty one- and two-story buildings, with clinics and laboratories and workshops and lecture halls surrounded by parks and trees and recreational areas. Some patients are under intensive treatment; others are convalescent; many are engaged in various activities in the buildings or about the grounds. Some leave their quiet rooms each morning to go to work in the city for the entire day, returning for the evening and their night's rest at the hospital. The average length of time required for restoring a mentally ill patient to health in this hospital has been reduced from years, to months, to weeks. Four-fifths of the patients living there today will be back in their homes by the end of the year. There are many empty beds, and the daily census is continually dropping.

What Is This Effective Treatment?

If these "incurable" patients are now being returned to their homes and their work in such numbers and with such celerity, why not something similar for offenders? Just what are the treatments used to effect these rapid changes? Are they available for use with offenders?

The forms and techniques of psychiatric treatment used today number in the hundreds. Psychoanalysis; electroshock therapy; psychotherapy; occupational and industrial therapy; family group therapy; milieu therapy; the use of music, art, and horticultural activities; and various drug therapies—these are some of the techniques and modalities of treatment used to stimulate or assist the restoration of a vital balance of impulse control and life satisfaction. No one patient requires or receives all forms, but each patient is studied with respect to his particular needs, his basic assets, his interests, and his special difficulties. In addition to the treatment modalities mentioned, there are many facilitations and events which contribute to total treatment effect: a new job opportunity (perhaps located by a social worker) or a vacation trip, a course of reducing exercises, a cosmetic surgical operation or a herniotomy, some night school courses, a wedding in the family (even one for the patient!), an inspiring sermon. Some of these require merely prescription or suggestion; others require guidance, tutelage, or assistance by trained therapists or by willing volunteers. A therapeutic team may embrace a dozen workers—as in a hospital setting—or it may narrow down to the doctor and the spouse. Clergymen, teachers, relatives, friends, and even fellow patients often participate informally but helpfully in the process of readaptation.

All of the participants in this effort to bring about a favorable change in the patient, i.e., in his vital balance and life program, are imbued with what we may call a *therapeutic attitude*. This is one in direct antithesis to attitudes of avoidance, ridicule, scorn, or punitiveness. Hostile feelings toward the subject, however justified by his unpleasant and even destructive behavior, are not in the curriculum of therapy or in the therapist. This does not mean that therapists approve of the offensive and obnoxious behavior of the patient; they distinctly disapprove of it. But they recognize it as symptomatic of continued imbalance and disorganization, which is what they are seeking to change. They distinguish between disapproval, penalty, price, and punishment.

Doctors charge fees; they impose certain "penalties" or prices, but they have long since put aside primitive attitudes of retaliation toward offensive patients. A patient may cough in the doctor's face or may vomit on the office rug; a patient may curse or scream or even struggle in the extremity of his pain. But these acts are not "punished." Doctors and nurses have no time or thought for inflicting unnecessary pain even upon patients who may be difficult, disagreeable, provocative, and even dangerous. It is their duty to care for them, to try to make them well, and to prevent them from doing themselves or others harm. This requires love, not hate. . . .

Right You Are If You Think You Are

THERE IS ANOTHER ELEMENT in the therapeutic attitude not explicitly mentioned by me in that paragraph. It is the quality of hopefulness. If no one believes that the patient can get well, if no one—not even the doctor—has any hope, there probably won't be any recovery. Hope is just as important as love in the therapeutic attitude.

"But you were talking about the mentally ill," readers may interject, "those poor, confused, bereft, frightened individuals who yearn for help from you doctors and nurses. Do you mean to imply that willfully perverse individuals, our criminals, can be similarly reached and rehabilitated? Do you really believe that effective treatment of the sort you visualize can be applied to people *who do not want any help*, who are so willfully vicious, so well aware of the wrongs they are doing, so lacking in penitence or even common decency that punishment seems to be the only thing left?"

Do I believe there is effective treatment for offenders, and that they *can* be changed? *Most certainly and definitely I do.* Not all cases, to be sure; there are also some physical afflictions which we cannot cure at the moment. Some provision has to be made for incurables—pending new knowledge—and these will include some offenders. But I believe the majority of them would prove to be curable. The willfulness and the viciousness of offenders are part of the thing for which they have to be treated. These must not thwart the therapeutic attitude.

It is simply not true that most of them are "fully aware" of what they are doing, nor is it true that they want no help from anyone, although some of them say so. Prisoners are individuals: some want treatment, some do not. Some don't know what treatment is. Many are utterly despairing and hopeless. Where treatment is made available in institutions, many prisoners seek it even with the full knowledge that doing so will not lessen their sentences. In some prisons, seeking treatment by prisoners is frowned upon by the officials.

Various forms of treatment are even now being tried in some progressive courts and prisons over the country—educational, social, industrial, religious, recreational, and psychological treatments. Socially acceptable behavior, new work-play opportunities, new identity and companion patterns all help toward community reacceptance. Some parole officers and some wardens have been extremely ingenious in developing these modalities of rehabilitation and reconstruction—more than I could list here even if I knew them all. But some are trying. The secret of success in all programs, however, is the replacement of the punitive attitude with a therapeutic attitude.

A therapeutic attitude is essential regardless of the particular form of treatment or help. Howard Gill of the American University's Institute of Correctional Administration believes that thirty per cent of offenders are overwhelmed with situational difficulties, and for such individuals crisis intervention often works wonders. Case work, economic relief, or other social assistance often will induce a favorable behavior pattern change in these offenders. In another thirty per cent, he estimates, personal psychological problems exist in the offender which require technical treatment efforts. For these the help of psychiatrists, physicians, and psychologists are needed. Still another thirty per cent of prisoners are essentially immature individuals whose antisocial tendencies have never found the proper paths of distribution and transformation in socially acceptable ways. These men are usually amenable to redirection, education, and guidance. They can achieve development of self-control and social conformity by the various programs which we call milieu treatment. In other words, one can think of the categories of treatment as falling largely into the three modalities of sociological, psychological (medical), and educational.

The reflective reader, recalling the history of our mental hospital reformation, may now feel prompted to ask, "Could not sufficient diagnosis and treatment be provided for offenders who need it in our presently existing psychiatric hospitals? We read that the population in these hospitals is diminishing rapidly; could not this empty space be used to treat offenders who might be transferred there?"

Unfortunately, the answer is not clearly in the affirmative at present. In the first place, the victims of our penal system are usually so embittered and, indeed, so outright aggressive that a degree of security is necessary for them, especially in the beginning, which the average psychiatric hospital is not physically prepared to insure. Even more significantly, our psychiatric hospitals are not psychologically prepared at the present time to be assigned the task of detaining and treating patients who have been labeled prisoners. We have had a long, painful experience with this in my own State of Kansas.

Please remember that psychiatric hospitals have themselves only recently emerged from a state of public obloquy which was nearly as bad as that now affecting prisons. Those hospitals which have raised their standards are proud of their achievement, proud of their respectability and good name, proud of being known as places where people come to be made well by the best of scientific medical effort. Ailing, faltering, erring, or even dimly conscious patients brought to them are soon surrounded by new-found friends who take in the newcomer and minister to him as companions, aides, fellow sufferers, amateur repairmen.

But if, into such an environment, there is introduced an individual who is not only angry and unsocial and generally hostile but who has a public record of having been caught and convicted for something heinous, the atmosphere immediately changes. No matter how obvious his suffering, sympathy and therapeutic idealism will not always be sufficient to neutralize the suspicion and negative feelings aroused in patients and staff members alike.[5]

Treatment for the Many

In thinking of ways to provide truly corrective therapy for large numbers of offenders at minimal expense, penologists might take a leaf from the book of modern psychiatry. It was long assumed that only under detention, i.e., *in the hospital,* was it possible to effectively control and treat and change severely disturbed individuals. Early in the twentieth century an experiment of "out-patient" psychiatric treatment was made in Boston by Ernest Southard of Harvard. Today, half a century later, the *majority* of all psychiatric patients are in outpatient status! Furthermore, there is a steadily rising preponderance of outpatients over inpatients. "Day hospitals," where patients spend some daylight hours in scheduled activities with other patients but go home in the evening for sleep, privacy, and family adaptation, have also proved useful. Similarly, "night hospitals" came into use for patients who could adapt themselves well enough to a work situation or a school setting but who did better by spending their nights under the protective care of the friendly hospital.

Thus there has developed the outpatient principle, which holds that it is optimal for the patient to continue living and working in his ordinary, everyday-life ways as much as possible, seeing his psychiatrist, psychologist, social worker, therapist, teacher, or clergyman in successive sessions at intervals *in their offices*. Obviously this is a great saving of time and money for everyone. And, curiously, it has proved to be just as effective, statistically measured, in nurturing favorable change in patients as were our carefully planned and elaborated inpatient hospital programs. Not the least advantage was the diminished stigmatization of the non-confined patient.

All this the correctional system might emulate—and in some progressive jurisdictions it does. Some individuals have to be protected against themselves, some have to be protected from other prisoners, some even from the community. Some mental patients must be detained for a time even against their wishes, and the same is true of offenders. Offenders with propensities for impulsive and predatory aggression should not be permitted to live among us unrestrained by some kind of social control. *But the great majority of offenders, even "criminals," should never become prisoners if we want to "cure" them.*

What we want to accomplish is the reintegration of the temporarily suspended individual back into the main stream of social life, preferably a life at a higher level than before, just as soon as possible. Many, many precariously constituted individuals are trying to make it on the outside right now, with little help from us. We all have to keep reminding ourselves that *most offenders are never even apprehended.* Most of those who are caught and convicted, we must remember, are released either free or on probation. But they rarely have the benefit of treatment.

Parole and probation officers are thus indispensable, and the profession should be vastly elevated in numbers, in prestige, and in salary. Its responsibility is great and should be greater. By their counsel, encouragement, warning, and befriending, many one-time offenders, with whom they keep in touch, are supported in new life efforts by these skilled and experienced guides and friends.[6] . . .

NOTES.

1. See for example the study of Ellen Bersheid of the University of Minnesota and Elaine Walster of the University of Rochester, "When Does a Harm-Doer Compensate a Victim?" (*Journal of Personality and Social Psychology*, 6:435, 1967).

2. The intentional infliction of pain for the treatment of any physical illness or disability is rare today except in the most ignorant circles. A persistent exception is the treatment of bed-wetting in children by whipping and various humiliations. I discovered recently that convulsions in children are treated with beatings in some families in certain communities.

3. The curability of mental illness was statistically demonstrated *over* a hundred years ago at the Worcester State Hospital in Massachusetts, and in a number of other hospitals in New England and New York. But this magnificent demonstration was forgotten in the confusion of Irish immigration and the Civil War and Reconstruction in our country (and comparable upheavals in other lands). For one hundred years there was no progress in the treatment of the mentally ill. Despair, waste, neglect, and public scandal obscured the whole scene of psychiatry, and few doctors concerned themselves with the gloomy and unsavory mental-illness problem. It was left to politicians. (See Norman Dain, *Concepts of Insanity in the United States: 1789–1865*. New Brunswick, N.J.: Rutgers University Press, 1964; and Gerald N. Grob, *The States and the Mentally Ill*. Chapel Hill: University of North Carolina Press, 1966.)

4. Some years previously the staffing was much better! The year 1948 was a low point which really triggered the "revolution." Unhappily, however, many such asylums still exist in the United States for lack of legislative action. In twenty-one of them there is not a single psychiatrist on duty today! (See "What Are the Facts About Mental Illness?" compiled in 1966 by the National Committee on Mental Illness, Inc., Washington, D.C.)

5. Dr. Linda Hilles has described this phenomenon vividly in a case which was really most pitiful. A fifty-four-year-old grocer, after several futile attempts to get psychiatric treatment in a small university town, suddenly turned a shotgun on his wife and then ran from the house to his store, where he cut off both his own hands by laying his arms before an electric

meat-cutting saw. He was found guilty of murder but was sent to one of our best state hospitals for treatment of both his handlessness and his disturbed mental state. I was a party to this recommendation.

As can well be imagined, he was deeply melancholic and, of course, almost utterly helpless, and required much personal attention. In spite of his obvious demoralization, his presence in the hospital seemed to be resented by all members of the nursing staff, by the other patients, and even by one doctor. This continued even after his helplessness was reduced by equipping him with artificial hands. The failure to deal effectively with him did not stem from indifference or lack of interest and effort; an inordinate amount of time and energy was invested by the staff members in meetings, discussions, and reviews of the problem. These produced no gratifying results.

Dr. Hilles analyzed these unscientific attitudes and feelings as well as she could and concluded that in dealing with a patient who is also a murderer, the prime asset of the psychotherapist trained to work with the mentally ill, his empathy, may prove a liability and he may become disturbed by an awareness of the murderous impulses within himself. (Hilles, Linda: "Problems in the Hospital Treatment of a Disturbed Criminal." *Bull. Menninger Clin.*, 30: 141–149, 1966.)

6. "Denver courts have gained nation-wide attention through their pioneer work rehabilitating probationers and have made probation services and pre-sentence investigation possible to misdemeanants. This program . . . was started in July of 1966 through the interest and efforts of Denver County's Chief Judge William Burnett even before such a recommendation was made by the President's Crime Commission. . . . Two features of the program are of paramount importance. These are the use of volunteers as probation supervisors, and the rapid evaluation of, and reporting on, the misdemeanant." (Afton, W. E.: "Denver Courts Blaze Trail with New Probation Services." *Bethesda Bulletin*, 43:4–6, Summer 1967.)

HENRY WEIHOFEN

Punishment and Treatment: Rehabilitation

§ 13. HUMANITARIANISM AND PSYCHOLOGY

THE HISTORIC "Declaration of Principles" adopted in 1870 by the leaders of what is now the American Correctional Association said that "the supreme aim of prison discipline is the reformation of criminals, not infliction of vindictive suffering."[1] Today most of the academic writers emphasize rehabilitation of the offender and protection of society by measures specifically aimed at rendering him unlikely to relapse to crime. To a large extent the movement in this direction was originally humanitarian, a shocked revulsion against degrading physical conditions in prisons. Decent treatment, together with moral exhortation, was hopefully expected to induce prisoners to reform. The results proved disappointing, for reasons examined elsewhere in this work.[2] But in the middle third of the twentieth century, psychiatry and scientific criminology became established fields of inquiry and have contributed enormously to our understanding of human behavior and of criminal behavior in particular. "These developments," writes Francis A. Allen, "have been accompanied by nothing less than a revolution in public conceptions of the nature of crime and the criminal, and in public attitudes toward the proper treatment of the convicted offender." One common theme or element in current public thinking and action, he says, is the rise of the rehabilitative ideal, which contains these essential points: Human behavior is the product of antecedent causes. These causes

Reprinted from *The Law of Criminal Correction*, Sol Rubin, Henry Weihofen, George Edwards, and Simon Rosenzweig, West Publishing Company (1963), 665–672, with permission of the publishers.

255

can be identified, and it is the function of the scientist to discover and describe them. Knowledge of the antecedents of human behabior is essential for scientific control of that behavior. "Finally, and of primary significance for the purposes at hand, it is assumed that measures employed to treat the convicted offender should serve a therapeutic function, that such measures should be designed to effect changes in the behavior of the convicted person in the interests of his own happiness, health, and satisfactions and in the interest of social defense."[3]

The rehabilitative ideal, then, not only is projected as the most efficient way to protect society against the likelihood of later relapses into crime, but also is motivated by humanitarianism, a belief in the worth and dignity of every human being and a willingness to expend effort to reclaim him for his own sake and not merely to keep him from again harming us.[4]

Today it is said that efforts at reform should be aimed primarily at the prisoner's social and psychological readjustment. As the writer of an important English work on penal reform puts it, "This conception of readjustment makes no presumptuous claims to produce a religious conversion or a moral rebirth . . . nor does it pretend to make a man a law-abiding citizen by a wise handling of his economic and social problems alone. The efforts are to be focused on the man himself. . . . Penal and reformative treatment has taken over this outlook from social work. Constructive methods today owe much to the experience of social casework, and to a psychological insight into man's personal conflicts."[5]

The main objective is to change the person's attitudes and to help him cope with his circumstances, gain insight into his own motivations, reorient his feelings, and achieve a measure of self-control. Attitudes are largely a product of social contacts. "The contacts that are of greatest importance in determining attitudes are those that are frequent and intimate, as in the family, the playgroup, and the neighborhood. The procedure for modifying attitudes consists essentially in changing the person's group relations."[6]

The new aims are being urged in institutions as well as in probation and parole services. The introduction of classification systems, psychiatric services, and techniques such as group therapy is evidence of a growing recognition by penal authorities that mental and emotional disturbance is at the root of much criminal behavior.

To some extent the legislatures have explicitly accepted this approach in juvenile court and youthful offender laws,[7] the use of presentence investigations, probation and parole statutes, and the occasional establishment of psychiatric and other diagnostic clinics as adjuncts of the courts and institutions. The new Wisconsin Criminal Code avoids the word "punish." The New York Correction Law was amended to refer to "person" rather than "prisoner."[8] The Advisory Council of Judges of the National Council on Crime and Delinquency has suggested that the term "penal code," which implies that the disposition of criminals is solely by way of punishment, is archaic.

§ 14. Limitations on Rehabilitative Policy

Any attempt to make rehabilitation a primary objective for *all* offenders creates certain difficulties. Not every person whose conduct is deemed criminal is in need of rehabilitation. As George Dession pointed out, "The repressive sanctions of criminal law are and will continue to be applied not only to those who should by anyone's standards be considered dangerously unfit for society, but also to those whom organized majorities may choose at any time to treat as so unfit."[9] Organized majorities (or sometimes organized minorities) may decide that conduct which, in other places or in other times, is legal shall henceforth be criminal; homosexuality is an example. No sensible, scientific treatment program can be devised to change the character of such persons, whose behavior is criminal only because the law chooses to differentiate them from other citizens.

§ 15. Individualization and the Principle of Equality

A rehabilitative approach is necessarily an individual approach. But by individualizing treatment, we necessarily ordain unequal treatment for offenses in themselves alike. On the surface at least, this seems a violation of the democratic principle of equality; and it may be especially resented by the offender. Although "equality between crime and punishment is a fiction,"[10] equal punishment for equal crimes is still a popular concept of justice as well as a tenet of constitutional law.[11]

Some years ago a seventeen-year-old boy escaped from an Illinois training school and proceeded to commit a series of burglaries. After two months he was caught and brought before the criminal court in Chicago. His family background had afforded him little opportunity for healthy development. The presiding judge took an interest in his case and, after careful investigation, decided to release him under conditions that would give him an opportunity to make good. A court official helped him find a job and living quarters that would remove him from the undesirable home influence. From the standpoint of individualized treatment, this seemed a proper and even commendable disposition of the case. But it created an immediate problem in the training school. Many of the boys bitterly resented what was being done for him. He had broken discipline by escaping and then committed further crimes, and now he was being treated so much better than they. They felt this was most unfair and discriminatory. A disposition that was, let us grant, the best possible for the rehabilitation of the person concerned impaired the rehabilitative program of perhaps fifty others. We cannot overlook the effect that the treatment accorded one person may have on others.

§ 16. Punishment in the Guise of Rehabilitation

If we believed strongly enough in the rehabilitation objectives (and had great faith in rehabilitative techniques) we might wish to lock up all potentially dangerous people, no matter how trivial the crime they actually committed (or perhaps even if they have not as yet committed any crime?), and "treat" them until we were sure they would not offend in the future. This would protect society from a lot of people and in the meantime presumably rehabilitate them. But it would make the "treatment" approach, which is often attacked as too "soft," much harsher than a frankly punitive policy, especially so far as petty offenders are concerned. The history of our sexual psychopath laws is an example of legislation which, influenced by fear of "sex criminals," subjected persons to the possibility of long terms of incarceration less because of what they *did* than because of what they *might* do if left at liberty.[12]

Jerome Hall has warned that this trend may subvert the fundamental principle, *nulla poena sine lege:* only conduct defined as criminal at the time it occurred may be punished, and the punishment must be one which has previously been fixed by law. We cannot assume that the actions of administrative boards of psychiatric and sociological experts will always be wise and good. "Unfortunately," says Hall, "history records other eventualities—and in places where 'scientific criminology' reached its highest peak."[13]

The point was cogently presented some years ago when the model Youth Correction Authority Act was promulgated. The avowed aim was "to substitute for retributive punishment methods of training and treatment directed toward correction and rehabilitation." But the Act provided for incarceration in generous allotments. Professor Hall opposed it. "One would need to revert to long forgotten barbarism," he wrote, "to find a law equaling the potential brutality of Section 13, (2) (i), which provides for the commitment of youths convicted of crimes *punishable by fine or imprisonment for less than 30 days* if the youth has previously been convicted of any 'violation of law,' which provision, combined with Section 29, would permit the incarceration of such youths for the balance of their lives if the 'treatment experts' decided they had not reformed. It was 'the sheerest pretense' to assert that this was not punishment. In cases of extremely long incarcerations for relatively minor offenses, it would be cruel and unusual punishment if these terms have any contemporary significance whatever."[14] Evidently "treatment" and "punishment" are not necessarily discrete concepts.

We must never lose sight of the elementary truth that measures depriving persons of their liberty against their will are essentially punitive in nature no matter how well-intentioned the authorities administering those measures. Indeed, such persons may all too easily delude themselves that their good motives and professional approach and devotion to science are a sufficient safeguard against abuse of power. But personal liberties cannot be left to depend on the beneficence of those in power. Criminal justice is fundamentally an exercise of political power, and the problems of its administration are fundamentally problems of political science and political philosophy, and not only of psychiatry, sociology, or social psychology.[15] Where to draw the line between the interests of the state and the interests of the individual is a fundamental issue in modern government, far transcending criminal law. It echoes through all the debates about totalitarianism and democracy, the welfare state, social security, regulation of business, socialized medicine, freedom of speech and of the press, and other political questions of the day.

Developing procedures that are scientifically sound and yet conformable to our traditional concepts of "ordered liberty" is a task that taxes our ingenuity, but it should not be beyond us. Certainly we should not return to the older assumption that even-handed justice requires nothing more than making the punishment fit the crime. We should be able to comply with the principles of legality and equality and yet distinguish various categories, not only such obvious ones as juveniles, the mentally disordered, and persons acting under extenuating or aggravating circumstances, but also subtler physical, psychological, and emotional conditions and various components in the socio-economic and cultural background. If we continue to expand our understanding of antisocial personalities and to develop methods of dealing with them, we should be able to take such factors into account, not in a discriminatory way but by the application of classification principles. As we increase our knowledge we should be able to multiply the relatively few categories we now recognize, without making the classifications any more arbitrary than they now are.

§ 17. The Model Sentencing Act

The Model Sentencing Act, promulgated by the Advisory Council of Judges of the National Council on Crime and Delinquency,[16] is a direct attempt to achieve a classification of offenders according to a concept of dangerousness that is based on what appear to be sound sociological and psychological principles. It undertakes to define three categories of "dangerous offenders," who may be subject to terms up to thirty years (but not a life term, except for murder):

1. A person who (a) is convicted of a felony in which he inflicted or attempted to inflict serious bodily harm and (b) is found to be suffering from a severe personality disorder indicating a propensity

toward criminal activity. 2. A person who (a) is convicted of a felony which seriously endangered the life or safety of another, (b) had previously been convicted of a felony, and (c) is found to be suffering from a severe personality disorder indicating a propensity toward criminal activity. 3. A person who is convicted of extortion, compulsory prostitution, selling or knowingly and unlawfully transporting narcotics, or other felony committed as part of a continuing criminal activity in concert with one or more other persons. Offenders other than those classified as dangerous may be placed on probation or may be committed for terms not exceeding five years.[17] All prisoners are eligible for parole.

This formulation has the philosophical merit of translating into statutory form the oft-repeated goal of criminologists—that we should sentence the individual, not the crime; it is the only statutory formulation that avoids sentencing by offense. The "severe personality disorder" dangerous offender categories 1 and 2 must be established by a diagnostic clinic, upon whose diagnosis (along with other information) the sentencing judge makes the necessary findings.

Such a statutory framework encourages the expanded use of probation, suspended sentence, and other dispositions that allow the "nondangerous" offender to remain in the community, which, together with a maximum commitment of five years for such persons, helps to establish an image of the great majority of offenders as nondangerous (in the terms of the Act).

§ 18. REHABILITATION THE PRIMARY OBJECTIVE

For the vast majority of the general run of delinquents and criminals, the *corrective theory*, based upon a conception of multiple causation and curative-rehabilitative treatment, should clearly predominate in legislation and in judicial administrative practices. No other single theory is as closely related to the actual conditions and mechanisms of crime causation; no other gives as much promise of returning the offender to society not with the negative vacuum of punishment-induced fear but with the affirmative and constructive equipment—physical, mental and moral—for law-abidingness. Thus, in the long run, no other theory and practice gives greater promise of protecting society.[18]

As we come to understand the motivations, rational and irrational, that lie behind the way criminals behave, and the motivations, sometimes no more rational, that lie behind the way we behave towards criminals, we shall be increasingly able to supplant an emotionally colored, illogical, and inconsistent aggregation of criminal sanctions with a systematic correctional policy soundly based on social dangerousness, deterrability, and treatability. Half a century ago, Sir Winston Churchill, then Home Secretary, said:

The mood and temper of the public in regard to the treatment of crime and criminals is one of the most unfailing tests of the civilization of any country. A calm and dispassionate recognition of the rights of the accused against the State, and even of convicted criminals against the State, a constant heart-searching by all charged with the duty of punishment, a desire and eagerness to rehabilitate in the world of industry all those who have paid their dues in the hard coinage of punishment, tireless efforts towards the discovery of curative and regenerating processes, and an unfaltering faith that there is a treasure, if you can only find it, in the heart of every man—these are the symbols which in the treatment of crime and criminals mark and measure the stored-up strength of a nation, and are the sign and proof of the living virtue in it.[19]

NOTES

1. Transactions of the National Congress on Penitentiary and Reformatory Discipline, Cincinnati, Ohio, 1870 (Wines ed. 1871), p. 541.

2. *Supra* [THE LAW OF CRIMINAL CORRECTION] ch. 8.

3. Allen, *Criminal Justice, Legal Values and the Rehabilitative Ideal*, 50 J. CRIM. L., C. & P.S. 226 (1959). [p. 317 this volume]

4. "The principle of forgiveness and the doctrine of redemption are too deep in our philosophy to admit that there is no return for those who have once erred." Black, J. dissenting in Harisiades v. Shaughnessy, 342 U.S. 580, 72 S.Ct. 512, 96 L.Ed. 586 (1951), rehearing denied 343 U.S. 936, 72 S. Ct. 767, 96 L.Ed. 1344 and Coleman v. McGrath, 343 U.S. 936, 72 S.Ct. 768, 96 L.Ed. 1344 (1952).

5. GRÜNHUT, PENAL REFORM 449 (1948).

6. SUTHERLAND & CRESSEY, PRINCIPLES OF CRIMINOLOGY 434 (5th ed. 1955).

7. *Supra* [THE LAW OF CRIMINAL CORRECTION] ch. 12.

8. New York Correction Law § 282, Amended Laws of 1954 ch. 803.

9. Dession, *Psychiatry and the Conditioning of Criminal Justice*, 47 YALE L.J. 319, 335–36 (1938). On the problem of what conduct *should* be made criminal, see KENNEY, OUTLINES OF CRIMINAL LAW 28 (15th ed. 1936); Gause-witz, *Considerations Basic to a New Penal Code*, 11 WIS. L. REV. 346, 368–71 (1936).

10. Grünhut, *op. cit. supra* note 5, at 4.

11. *Supra* [THE LAW OF CRIMINAL CORRECTION] ch. 4, § 4.

12. See *supra* [THE LAW OF CRIMINAL CORRECTION] ch. 11, § 14.

13. HALL, GENERAL PRINCIPLES OF CRIMINAL LAW ch. 2, especially at 53, 59 (1947).

14. Hall, *The Youth Correction Authority Act: Progress or Menace?* 28 A.B.A.J. 317 (1942). See the reply of the director, Lewis, *The Youth Correction Authority Act: A Model*, ibid., 322.

15. Allen, *op. cit. supra* note 3, at 230. [p. 324 this volume]

16. Adopted by the Advisory Council of Judges at its meeting, May, 1962; published April 15, 1963.

17. The Model Act also has an optional section that does authorize sentencing by offense: terms of up to ten years for certain "atrocious" crimes, such as second degree murder, arson, forcible rape, and others. A comment on this section states: "Inclusion of this optional section in the Act is supported by a number of members of the Advisory Council of Judges in the belief that persons who commit the crimes listed, even if they are not suffering from a severe personality disorder, may require more control than the average offender, whose commitment is limited to a five-year term. Other ACJ members consider that the other provisions of the act amply deal with all requirements of public protection, deterrence, and treatment and that one of the new principles of the Act—sentencing on the basis of the offender rather than the offense—is contradicted by the provision regarding named offenses."

18. HALL & GLUECK, CRIMINAL LAW AND ENFORCEMENT 19 (2d ed. 1958). See also Glueck, *Principles of a Rational Penal Code*,* 41 HARV. L. REV. 453 (1928), reprinted in GLUECK, CRIME AND CORRECTION 72 (1952).

19. Quoted in FOX, ENGLISH PRISONS AND BORSTAL SYSTEMS (1952).

* Also reprinted in this volume.

Torsten Eriksson

Society and the Treatment of Offenders

THE TREATMENT OF THE OFFENDER must be based on the characteristics of the culture in which it is given and adapted to the prevailing
economic, social and political conditions. Despite many differences,
some of them deeply rooted, the various nations still have numerous
characteristics in common. This was confirmed in Geneva in 1955,
when the First United Nations Congress on the Prevention of Crime
and the Treatment of Offenders was able to agree on the well-
known Standard Minimum Rules for the Treatment of Prisoners.
Then as now, all the participating countries were united by the
common desire to humanize the treatment of the criminal, to respect
his human dignity regardless of the nature of his crime. This was the
principle by which we were guided in developing the Standard
Minimum Rules.

All nations are under-developed with respect to the treatment
of offenders. Even countries which, due to fortunate circumstances,
are justified in calling themselves economically and socially developed must admit that their correctional methods lag far behind developments in other areas. Sweden, my mother country, is generally
regarded in international penological circles as one of the pioneers in
the treatment of offenders. This may be so, but we must nevertheless confess that we have not attained the level which could justifiably be required of a country which has enjoyed the favorable
social and economic development of Sweden. All countries, without

Reprinted from *Studies in Penology*, edited by Manuel Lopez-Rey and Charles
Germain, Martinus Nijhoff, The Hague, Netherlands (1964), 85-91, with permission
of the author and of the publishers.

exception, are engaged in a struggle to evolve more effective means of treating offenders.

The task of the correctional system is twofold: to protect society from the dangerous criminal and to rehabilitate the same dangerous criminal so that he can return to society as a law-abiding citizen. The correctional system shall provide good care and satisfactory security. This, however, is easier said than done. Traditionally, the correctional system is cursed by the fact that the offender is regarded as a pariah, that he has been rejected by society for hundreds of years, exiled to a foreign land or to the wilderness, branded and restricted to certain occupations, confined in prisons, and banished from the society of his fellow-men. The great reform movements in criminal policy began scarcely one century ago. The social re-establishment of the offender after he has served his sentence is a problem which still has not been solved even in the most advanced nations. Although the mark on his brow is no longer visible, the ex-prisoner remains a spiritually branded individual, shunned by the law-abiding. The achievement of effective methods of restoring the sentenced man to a decent place in society is inevitably the foremost objective of the progressive correctional system.

What has been done in various parts of the world to advance this process of integration? The most significant innovations are undoubtedly the suspended sentence and the suspension of prosecution. In the former case the offender is prosecuted for his crime but is not institutionalized. In the latter he is not even brought before a court. The greater the anonymity surrounding the crime and the criminal, the greater the chance that the offender can be rehabilitated and restored to a normal way of life. In countries which have adopted the suspended sentence—whether as probation or in some other form—there is a clear tendency to use it to excess. Relying on precedent, the courts are inclined to go to the limit permitted by the laws. The courts are, of course, motivated by humanitarian considerations. They know only too well that the offender has a better chance with a suspended sentence than with an unconditional sentence. As a result of this knowledge, maximum use is made of the suspended sentence.

Let us now consider probation: the chief characteristic of this form of suspended sentence is that it is associated with certain conditions and with supervision of the offender. If the offender does not fulfill the conditions, his sentence may be made unconditional. There are two main methods of supervision. According to one system, stemming chiefly from Anglo-Saxon law, the offender is supervised by an official, i.e. a probation officer. In other systems of jurisprudence, e.g. the Swedish, supervision is carried out by laymen as a commission of trust. In my small country with a population of only 7.5 million, there are today approximately 5,000 persons in prisons and no less than 15,000 under supervision in the form of probation. All of the latter are supervised by volunteers. These volunteers may turn for advice to special officials known as protective officers, who also exercise control over all supervisors and instruct them in their duties.

Here I should like to mention my first thesis concerning the integration of the treatment of offenders with the social order. If this objective is to be achieved, it is essential that our citizens in general participate in the treatment of criminals. By this I mean that the correctional system must not continue to be a restricted area to which only officials have access. There is no better way of correcting the misconceptions and dispelling the mystique surrounding crime and the criminal and the prerequisites for his treatment than to bring as many as possible of the thinking members of our population into closer contact with the offender and his offense.

By learning to recognize the human being underneath the offender, the ordinary citizen's understanding is deepened and his attitude toward criminals in general becomes less harsh. A series of happy circumstances have made it possible in our small country to achieve a relatively high standard of correctional methods. Uninterrupted peace for almost 200 years and an economic development resulting from favorable natural resources have been of importance in this connection. Most important, however, is that the Swedish people themselves have become deeply involved in the problems of the treatment of the offender. This has not only come about because we have engaged so many thousands of individuals as supervisors of offenders under suspended sentence. Of great significance also is that the entire Swedish court system is based on the collaboration of citizens. Instead of a jury, the Swedish judge has a committee of laymen who, with him, judge not only major crimes but all those offenses which may lead to deprivation of liberty.

In those countries which apply the system of suspended sentence, we have thus come to the point that the general public has at least learned that all offenders need not and should not be imprisoned for their offenses. But what can be done to integrate into society that part of the treatment of criminals which takes place in institutions?

As a result of the reform of the treatment of criminals by the State of Pennsylvania, when the single-cell prison was introduced, it was understood that the cooperation of the layman was important to the re-integration of the offender in civilian society. Prison visitors were introduced. England is probably a pioneer in this respect and has a very large body of prison visitors who have, indeed, formed an association. Each prison visitor in England shall agree to pay regular calls on one or two inmates in their cells in specific prisons. The inmates are to consider their visitors their true and understanding friends, whose duty it also is to help find employment for their protegees when they are discharged. It is the consensus in England that these prison visitors play a tremendously important part in informing the public about the facts of the correctional system and about the true nature of criminals. I myself have participated in numerous meetings in England, at which criticism has been leveled at the English correctional system and at which one prison visitor after another has stood up to defend prison officials and to explain why conditions are as they are. This is particularly important in a country like England, where officials have not the right to make public statements, either verbally or in writing, concerning conditions in correctional institutions without special permission.

In the United States the prison visitor concept is applied most widely in institutions for juveniles. These visitors are usually called "Big Brothers" or "Big Sisters." Many years ago I visited a youth institution outside New York. When I entered the director's office, I saw a crimson-faced man sitting there, who had obviously been discussing a matter of great concern to him personally. When the man left the director told me what had happened. He had come to complain that he had not been made a Big Brother for any of the young inmates of the institution. He wondered what was wrong with him and explained that his reputation had suffered in the small neighbourhood in which he lived and in which so many of his friends had been appointed Big Brothers. He was also upset because his failure made him wonder whether he had some defect of character which others noticed but of which he was unaware. A great deal is expected of these Big Brothers and Big Sisters, but recruitment is nevertheless not particularly difficult. In any case, it is quite obvious that they, like prison visitors, play an important part in shaping public opinion.

Another means of giving the public insight into the institutional treatment of offenders is to establish special visits committees. These exist in many places, and in my country each institution has a special committee consisting of a small number of persons whose duty it is to make an informed judgment of life in the institution and to have conversations with all the inmates.

Prison officials themselves frequently object strongly to the public becoming familiar with institutional conditions. They are primarily opposed to newspaper publicity concerning the internal workings of prisons. The calm of the institution is disturbed, they say, and they also are inclined to stress the inmate's right to anonymity, a right which is protected by law in many countries. Personally I am convinced that the correctional system has everything to gain and nothing to lose from complete frankness about the conditions in its institutions. The more isolated the prison is from civilian society, the greater is the mysticism created around it and the more serious are the effects on the institutional personnel and especially on the inmates. In my opinion there should be no more secretiveness about the conditions in a penal institution than in a hospital. This is my thesis number two.

More direct lines of communication between the institution and the free world can be achieved in various ways without endangering security. The first that comes to mind in this respect is the open institution. As we know, the First United Nations Congress in 1955 clearly recommended open institutions. Some countries have gone far along this line, while others have not yet taken the first step. The concept is based on differentiation, on the assumption that in the mass of offenders we can recognize those who, in all probability, do not represent a real danger to society and whose behavior in prison cannot be expected to present major problems. The open institution is unquestionably more humane and also is generally more effective therapeutically, as well as consistently less expensive to operate, than the closed one.

More than one-third of all prisoners are in open institutions in my country. In this connection, it should be borne in mind that, as I have already intimated, the suspended sentence is widely used in Sweden. This means that an initial differentiation takes place which puts the simplest cases under open care and leaves only the more problematic elements for the institutions. Nevertheless, we have found it possible to sentence as many as one-third of the latter category to open institutions. Nor are we alone in this, since our neighbor, Finland, has as many offenders as we do under open treatment. By open treatment we refer to the definition of the First United Nations Congress, namely, that the open institution is equipped with no escape-preventive devices and is based entirely on the honor system. An unwalled institution may still be a closed one if, for example, it is patrolled by armed guards. The officials of open institutions are not there to prevent escapes, but to maintain order and to make sure that life in the institution functions according to regulations. It is scarcely assumed that they will pursue an escaping inmate. We often find in many countries that the open institutions are relatively primitive and that they do not offer the inmates the same comforts as certain closed institutions. This is a mistake, in my view. The open institution should in all respects be more attractive to the inmate than the closed one.

The open institution is a powerful battering-ram on the public image of a criminal as a dangerous individual. When we initiated open institutions in Sweden, we often heard vociferous protests from nervous inhabitants of the areas where we located them. Only the experience of having an open institution in the vicinity for several years with little if any of the trouble they had anticipated could rid people of their initial fears. Our great success with open institutions in Sweden and in many other countries refers not only to the treatment itself, but to the fact that we have evolved more humane methods of treating the more reliable elements in our clientele. It also reflects a significant change in the attitude of the public to the criminal, a more profound understanding of the philosophy of the treatment of offenders, without which no progress can be made.

The great majority of individuals sentenced to imprisonment want to return to society as law-abiding citizens. Only a few are definitely asocial and have no intention of changing their lawless ways after their discharge. Our Swedish system of furloughs for inmates is based on this observation. It represents still another phase of our efforts to make the abnormal life in prison less abnormal. One of our prisoners who behaves well and who is not believed to be dangerous to his fellow-men may, after a certain period of his sentence has been served, receive so-called regular furloughs in order to visit his family for three days. This privilege is granted every third month to inmates of open institutions. Extra furloughs may also be given under special circumstances, including serious illness in the family.

It is extremely difficult if not impossible to find work for prisoners in countries with a high rate of unemployment. In fact, it is even a problem in many countries with little unemployment. Businesses and trade unions are often hostile to prison work. You shouldn't steal jobs from "honest" citizens to give them to the "dishonest," they claim. In a country like mine, where there are no unemployed, we have had little trouble in settling this problem in the institutions. We have also been able to construct real factories in our institutions. In fact, in recent years we have built our institutions on the principle that first we build a factory and then we add a prison to it.

We have actually come to the point where Swedish prison work constitutes one of the main industries in the country. If work in the prisons can be organized so as to approximate conditions in the open market, this too will dispel one of the prejudices that help to build the wall between the prisoner and his free fellow-man.

My conclusion is: to rehabilitate the man who has served a sentence for a criminal offense and integrate him into civilian life, it is essential to abolish the isolation of the institution, whether open or closed, from society at large.

SHELDON GLUECK

Principles of a Rational Penal Code

THE RECENT WIDESPREAD INTEREST on the part of individuals, institutions of learning and of less learning, research foundations and
governmental organizations in the problem of criminality is the outcome of an alleged collapse of the administration of criminal justice
in the American city. Thus far, effort has taken the form of popular
articles, crime surveys, commissions, conferences. But in all of the
survey reports thus far published, and in the work of commissions
and conferences, no serious attempt seems to have been made at a
basic analysis of the presuppositions and prejudices crystallized in
the substantive and procedural criminal law. And no suggestions of
principles for fundamental revision of the existing régime seem to
have been made. Not even the standard-setting Cleveland survey,
which remains unique in the thoroughness of its execution and
scholarliness of its interpretation, made any attempt to suggest the
prolegomena to a criminal procedure more scientific than that under
which society now is so ineffectively waging the struggle against
crime.[1]

One need hardly defend the thesis that what is required in this
field is a fundamental reexamination[2] of the foundations of criminal
law and procedure in the light of what is known today of psychiatry, psychology, and social case work—that rapidly growing trinity
of the yet to be developed master-discipline, the "science of human
nature." Such a reexamination, however, must go more deeply than
the drafting of logically-articulated but wrongly-premised penal

From *Harvard Law Review*, Vol. 41 (1928), 453–482, copyright 1928 by the
Harvard Law Review Association. Reprinted with permission of the author and of
the publishers.

codes. It can certainly not be limited to "getting a law passed." It cannot be satisfied by "speeding up justice," when nobody has any clear notion of what justice is, and just why, and at what link in a complicated procedural chain speed is desirable. Finally, it cannot be made by persons whose only qualification, profound as that may be, is learning in "dogmatic law," and whose minds move logically, but provincially, within the ambit of "legal reasoning." The most creative legal treatises and judicial opinions have come from scholars whose disciplined learning in the law has not blinded them to the possibilities of infusion therein of wisdom from other arts and sciences. The twentieth century sociological school of jurisprudence expresses the movement to interrelate the social sciences, of which the law is but one. Law is no longer regarded as a self-sufficient, cabalistic discipline, isolated from the general stream of culture. We are realizing more and more that methods and attitudes from outside the realm of the formal law must be imported into the legal order as powerful catalyzers to creativity. We can no longer be content with the use of exclusively legal materials in the critique of the law.[3]

It is not easy, however, to find the means of this creative cross-fertilization, especially with regard to the penal régime. Deep-rooted fears and prejudices are embalmed in our penal law. For the purpose of focusing thought upon this problem, we set down some tentative principles for a penal code that, in the light of modern ethical, psychological-psychiatric, and sociological views give some promise of being more rational and just than the procedure under which we are ineffectively laboring.

Underlying Social-Ethical Principle of Penal Code

The basic social-ethical principle of any system of penal law should express the *raison d'être* of that system. Too often in the past has the basic principle of penal codes been implied, rather than expressed and defended, with the result that our penal statutes are full of confusions and inconsistencies, containing statutory and case-law accretions of many epochs and philosophies. We submit the following basic principle: *Society should utilize every scientific instrumentality for self-protection against destructive elements in its midst, with as little interference with the free life of its members as is con-*

sistent with such social self-protection. This proposition is basic to any discussion of social problems. If one denies that a society should protect itself, he not only denies to it the fundamental right of self-preservation, but jeopardizes his own security. Only by repelling criminal attacks against itself or its members can organized society offer the peace, security, and traditional expectancy of orderliness which are indispensable to the pursuit of the affairs of life by itself and its members. One who denies this indirectly advocates his own destruction.

In this basic work of self-protection, society should utilize every available scientific instrumentality. This is dictated both by the principle of justice and that of economy. While society has a primary interest in maintaining the general security, it also has an interest in the welfare of the individual life, and a duty to use every reasonable instrumentality for the rehabilitation of its anti-social members. Even a socially harmful criminal has a right, in justice, to be treated with those instrumentalities that give him the greatest promise of self-improvement and rehabilitation.

Justice demands also that, in its work of self-protection, society interfere as little as possible with the free life of its members. If one conceives of society as a necessary instrument for the harmonious integration of the more or less conflicting desires of human beings with the demands of the general welfare, one must acknowledge that social interference should cease at the point where such integration cannot be brought about by interference. A law or procedure, which, in the general opinion, unnecessarily or arbitrarily overemphasizes the social interest in the general security to the undue interference with the social and individual interests in the life and well-being of each person, is unjust, for it unnecessarily enslaves human beings.[4]

Not only justice but economy dictates the employment of scientific devices in the work of social self-protection. It is wasteful for society to be satisfied with a continuance of the present judicial and peno-correctional régimes, because the large figures of recidivism[5] are an indication that the present methods are not preventing criminals from repeating their anti-social behavior.

Rationale of punishment: Retributive-expiative theory. The chief means which society has long relied upon to maintain the general security is punishment either on a retributive-expiative theory, or for the pragmatic purposes discussed below. The old argument was that punishment was necessary as a "just retribution" or requital of wickedness. No thoughtful person today seriously holds this theory of sublimated social vengeance, nor that "expiative theory" which is the reverse of the shield of retribution. Official social institutions should not be predicated upon the destructive emotion of vengeance, which is not only the expression of an infantile way of solving a problem, but unjust and destructive of the purpose of protecting society. The official social institutions of criminal law and penal treatment should not be occupied with the criminal's expiation of his sins; that is properly the domain of religion. Society's legal institutions are concerned with the utilitarian possibilities of a punishment régime, possibilities which are founded upon the social purpose of the machinery of justice, namely, the maintenance of the general security with as little interference with the individual's rights as a human being and citizen as is necessary for the achievement of that social purpose.

It is sometimes argued that it is "natural" and thus "right and proper" that we "hate the criminal" and show our hatred. But (aside from the question whether everything that is "natural" is necessarily right) much of our hate-reaction toward criminals has been conditioned by education. Men used to hate the insane, and punished them accordingly. To hate acts that are socially harmful may be proper; but to base a policy of social protection upon the hatred of those who commit such acts is both uneconomical and unjust. It is uneconomical because, far from the vengeful attitude having produced socially desirable results, it has failed throughout to stem the tide of recidivism.[6] It is unjust because every human being has the right to be considered as such, with his hereditary and acquired weaknesses, as well as his strengths. This is to some extent feasible with modern scientific instrumentalities; but no device yet invented can dive into the heart and mind of an individual and come up with that exact apportionment of blame and blamelessness which even a rationalized vengeance called "solemn justice" demands as a prerequisite to castigation.

The attitude we are discussing may also be conceived of as a "rationalization" of something which is psychologically more profound. To one unfamiliar with the data of psychoanalytic psychology the following analyses of this attitude will doubtless be a surprise; but upon mature and honest reflection such a reader will gradually become convinced that there is more than "a grain of truth" in these suggestions. Says Dr. William A. White, dean of American psychiatrists:

> The criminal thus becomes the handy scapegoat upon which he [the ordinary citizen] can transfer his feeling of his own tendency to sinfulness and thus by punishing the criminal he deludes himself into a feeling of righteous indignation, thus bolstering up his own self-respect and serving in this roundabout way, both to restrain himself from like indulgences and to keep himself upon the path of cultural progress. The legal punishment of the criminal today is, in its psychology, a dramatic tragic action by which society pushes off its criminal impulses upon a substitute. The principle is the same as that by which an emotion such as anger is discharged upon an inoffensive lifeless object.[7]

Discussing Spinoza's views on determinism and psychology, Dr. M. Hamblin Smith gives a similar analysis of the "righteous indignation" rationalization of man's fear and anger responses and its social crystallization into a program of punishment *qua* punishment:

> It is often said that determinism leaves practical questions exactly as they were before. Generally speaking this statement is true. But it is not true in one important particular. All ground for blame, in the ordinary sense of that word, has been removed. This deprives the ordinary man of what he finds a great comfort. . . . We may point out that man always wants to blame others for what he finds in himself. The matter goes much deeper than the influence of the primitive instinct of vengeance. Man is always trying to get rid of something that makes him unhappy. If this something happens to be wrong, according to the ethical standards of the herd, he attempts to escape his personal responsibility for it. In punishing an offender, man is trying to get rid of a wrong which he feels is resident in himself. Hence the offender becomes a convenient scapegoat.[8]

Turning now to the utilitarian justifications of punishment, much confusion in the discussion of this subject can be avoided by referring to the influence of the *threat* of arrest, imprisonment, or execution, as the *deterrent* effect of punishment, and the influence of the memory of past punishment upon the individual punished as the *preventive* effect of punishment. The first is the psychological effect of a continuous appeal to the fear emotion in the form of a threat of enforced suffering in making "the rest of us" behave in conformity with the law; the second, the psychological effect of

e recollection of past punishment in influencing the future conduct of an ex-prisoner to bring it within legal bounds.

Punishment as a deterrent. As to the first influence, knowledge of psychology must convince one that much of conduct can
be and in fact is influenced by the threat of punishment. Fear plays
an important role in deterring most persons from the commission of
legally prohibited acts, although other motives are, of course, also
operative. Since the threat of arrest and punishment is an appeal to
fear, which for most persons is probably the strongest motive, it
doubtlessly has a deterrent value. It is fallacious to argue, as many
do, that because the volume of crime in proportion to the population has not diminished, or is rising (if such be the case), such a
condition proves that the threat of punishment is no deterrent. No
one can say how much *more* crime there would be on the part of
the law-abiding public were the restraint of the threat of punishment removed. During the Boston police strike, for example, not
all of the increased crime was due to "imported criminals," or local
habitual criminals. Some of it was probably brought about by persons on the brink of criminality who needed just that removal of
the threat of apprehension and punishment to push them over into
the criminal ranks. The same phenomenon is observable after every
great public catastrophe when among those who steal from the
bodies of dead and wounded there are a number of people who
formerly were law-abiding but who commit crimes, upon the removal of organized restraint in the post-catastrophic confusion.

But though the threat of punishment has some deterrent value,
it must be pointed out that a scientific system of penal law taking
the point of view of modern psychiatry would not, in any real
sense, deprive society of whatever deterrent effect such threat might
have. The modern psychiatric school of criminology does not ask
that we pass by, unnoticed, the acts of criminal aggression committed by individuals, and thus break down the defensive breastworks
of the threat of punishment. Under the regime proposed herein,
for example, anti-social persons would still be deprived of their liberty. Nay more, it may justly be claimed that the proposed procedure of scientific individualization would have a greater deterrent
effect than does the present mechanized and bargaining procedure.
Under the existing system, prospective criminals know in advance
the chances of probation, and, essentially, the length of imprisonment as related to contemplated crimes; and they know that with

the mechanically applied rules as to "time off for good behavior," parole as an automatic "reward" after the minimum limit of a sentence euphoniously designated "indeterminate" has been reached, and similar unscientific devices, they will be given their freedom *regardless of their improvement or further deterioration.* This is so because the present system bases penal treatment on a single or a few isolated acts of a person rather than upon knowledge of the personality and motivations of the offender and his social background.

With the emphasis shifted, as is proposed, from the isolated criminal act to the personality of the offender—his potentialities for good and evil, his response to treatment and so on—and his social setting, a prospective wrongdoer will not be able to estimate in advance the length of his incarceration, on the basis of the seriousness of the contemplated offense as set down in the statute books or the mechanized treatment of judges and parole boards. For an offense relatively venial in itself, it is conceivable that a socially-dangerous *personality* may remain incarcerated for life; and for one relatively serious it is likewise conceivable that a person who has profited by institutional or extra-mural treatment and gives reasonable scientific promise of permanent rehabilitation, will be given his liberty after a comparatively short period. The vital element of the possibility of lifelong incarceration if the individual is shown by scientific investigation to require it, may reasonably be expected to reinforce the natural deterrent effect of the threat of punishment.[9]

Punishment as a preventive. Considering now the second question, the prevention of further wrongdoing by the recollection of the punishment for the last, here again we cannot go along with most of the modern radicals in criminology. It cannot be seriously denied that the fear of the repetition of a painful experience of the past plays an important role in the guidance of conduct. Such anticipation of a painful reaction to a certain form of behavior (founded upon the psychological phenomenon of memory or whatever its neurological correlate may be) acts as a powerful influencer of conduct. The role of punishment and reward as determinants of behavior is clear in the laboratory when one deals experimentally with animals. Punishment is recognized also as an instrument for influencing the conduct of children and adults. It is daily used in the affairs of life and in penal institutions to influence conduct.

It is submitted, however, that punishment is an instrumentality ıat should not be used blindly, but by trained scientists, and only where "indicated," as the physicians would say. Moreover, punishment is but one of numerous "medicines" or devices that are more and more being put at the disposal of trained experts. It, as well as these other instrumentalities, should be utilized only after careful examination of the individual criminal has demonstrated his peculiar needs. It is the conviction of psychologists and psychiatrists that the emotion of fear is not the only motive of conduct, lawful or unlawful. It is certainly not the highest motive to appeal to, and not necessarily the most effective. It may well be that in the excitement of a criminal act the memory of the former suffering is beclouded; that in particular individuals (whether they are mentally "abnormal" or not) such former punishment has had little, if any, lasting effect; that the appeal to other motives promises to "build in" a more lasting change of character and habit than the appeal to fear alone or primarily; that in certain individuals, emphasis of the appeal to fear is the worst possible method of treatment, resulting, as it so often does with juvenile delinquents, in the building up of strong defensive or compensatory bulwarks of defiance, distrust, grudgefulness, or "low cunning," which in turn lead to further misconduct.

Our discussion indicates, then, that to continue in operation a penal system grounded largely upon the appeal to fear is unjust and uneconomical; but that a rational approach to the problems of crime and its treatment would not ignore the possible utility of punishment either as a deterrent or a preventive. It seeks merely to evaluate it according to its true worth, and to control it in accordance with a well-rounded, preventive-therapeutic program. Moreover, such a view of the role of the appeal to the emotion of fear promises not only to retain whatever present effectiveness there may be in punishment, as a preventive or deterrent, but to increase it.

INDIVIDUALIZATION, WITH THE AID OF APPROPRIATE SCIENCES, AS THE MEANS OF ENFORCEMENT

THE NEED, *and the technical instruments, of individualization.* As long as the legal order confined itself to a reliance upon fear as the principal instrument for the protection of society against criminal aggression, there was not much need for scientific individualization of peno-correctional treatment. The criminal law defined the crimes, the penal statutes set down for each offense the precise dosage of punishment fatuously believed to "fit the crime," and the judge mechanically sentenced convicted persons on the basis of this schedule of punishments. But with the recognition of the futility of that system because of the complex mental and social factors which enter into the commission or failure to commit crimes, individualization of treatment must be recognized as indispensable. Effective individualization must be based upon as complete an understanding of each offender as modern science will permit. Hence psychiatry, psychology, and social case work—not to mention those disciplines more remotely concerned with the problems of human motivation and behavior—must be drawn into the program for administering criminal justice. And this is true not alone in those cases in which a definite mental disorder is present, but in the general run of cases. For only by recognition of the motives behind and the social setting of criminal conduct can the treatment prescribed by the judge be intelligently calculated to protect society, through the rehabilitation of those who respond to treatment and the permanent isolation of those who do not so react.

Only through the systematic assistance of psychiatrists, psychologists, and social investigators can even the existing individualizing instrumentalities—probation, the indeterminate sentence, parole, the juvenile court—be effectively utilized. Thus, "probation" in some jurisdictions means the evil practice of releasing almost every first offender and many a dangerous repeater "to give him another chance." The hoped-for rehabilitation is ostensibly to be brought about by some miracle. For in such jurisdictions no effort whatsoever is made, either in the way of examination into the social-psychiatric conditions of the offender to determine his fitness for probation, or in the way of constructive supervision during the probation period. Thus an instrumentality, the very creation of which was due to recognition of the importance of individualization, is used mechanically, perfunctorily, and in some cases even corruptly. Probation in a few jurisdictions,[10] however, is based on careful, individualized examination and treatment, in which psychiatrists, psychologists, and social workers are the interpretive agencies, while the judge represents the tempering wisdom of the gally-experienced magistrate. The same distinctions could be made between so-called "indeterminate sentences," "parole," and "juvenile courts," and the genuine devices whose titles have thus been wrongly pre-empted. In a word, individualization is necessary on the part of the court and other institutions dealing with the offender; and effective individualization is not based on guesswork, mechanical routine, "hunches," political considerations, or even (as so many judges seem to think) on past criminal record alone. It must rest on a scientific recognition and evaluation of those mental and social factors involved in the criminal situation which make each crime a unique event and each criminal a unique personality.

Objection to utilization of scientific instrumentalities in administration of criminal justice. The objection has been made against the consistent use of psychiatry, psychology, and social case work in the administration of criminal justice, that these instrumentalities are still in a highly experimental and formative state and that experts representing these disciplines frequently disagree when asked to give opinions. The principle is self-evident that in a wise legal order we should proceed cautiously in absorbing methods or attitudes from outside of the law. But it must be said that the disagreement between experts has been "greatly exaggerated." On fundamental symptomatology of the various mental and behavior disorders most psychiatrists are agreed. On basic mental "mechanisms"[11] many of them are coming more and more to agree. True, there are some real differences of opinion on questions of *theory*, on attempts to account for the phenomena observed. But this is a healthy sign of a growing discipline; it is not absent in the law itself. There is also disagreement as to the effectiveness of various methods of therapy, which is likewise a sign of vitality. Again, in the realm of psychology, standardized intelligence tests of various kinds are admittedly far from perfect and are undergoing continuous improvement on the basis of experimentation. Yet their use is becoming more and more widespread if also more critical. Further, a complete, perfectly logical set of principles of social case work has not yet been developed; but a body of wisdom, based on experience, is gradually crystallizing, and scientific method is little by little being infused into social case work.[12] The imperfection in social service technique did not prevent the rapid spread of the movement to substitute "constructive social work" for indiscriminate, mass-treating, wasteful, pauperizing "charity." Though the instruments for "constructive social work" are still far from ideally suitable to the purpose, nobody would seriously propose the return to the old methods of almsgiving. In the field of criminal justice, society has experimented for many years with mass-treatment, unscientific methods. Is it not time to make a serious effort at experimentation with the more promising techniques? Any system of diagnosis and treatment of the individual delinquent, based on a responsible application of such scientific instrumentalities as exist, few and imperfect as these may be, is superior to a practice which treats human acts *in vacuo*, and human beings mechanically, perfunctorily, and in the mass, on the basis of impossible rules set down by the legislature in advance of the events to which they are to be applied by perplexed judges.

Types and stages of existing individualization. Assuming the necessity of individualization, at what stage in the procedure of criminal justice shall it be made and by what legal agency? The work of individualization of one kind or another may, of course, be attempted at various stages and by differing means. The district attorney may crudely "individualize" as to types of cases he is going to stress in prosecution out of a mass of cases. Again, definitions in the substantive criminal law itself, such as the historical distinction between murder and manslaughter,[13] distinctions between voluntary and involuntary manslaughter, or between burglary and larceny, represent crude judicial and legislative categorizations of types of somewhat analogous criminal acts, on the ground that the individual acts differ in degree of seriousness. So also, the breaking up of crimes into rather detailed "degrees," which was so common a phenomenon in American codes and statutes in the nineteenth century and which is still a characteristic, represents a later and less crude process of legislative individualization in the trial and punishment of varieties of a similar type of criminal act rather than of classes of criminal.[14] Such code or statutory provisions are customarily accompanied by stipulations as to fixed length and type of punishment, leaving the trial judge, or (in states where the jury has anything to do with fixing the punishment) the jury, relatively little discretion as to penal treatment. These are very crude individualizations of various classes of offenses by the legislature. Within such crime categories, however, there is no distinction made between individual delinquents; all offenders committing the same crime are punishable equally.

The "indeterminate sentence" movement which began late in

the nineteenth century as a recognition of the need of individualization of punishment has in practice had but little effect upon these fixed provisions regarding punishment or upon the attitude which inspired them. For, in the first place, not all states have indeterminate sentences; secondly, indeterminate sentence provisions apply in most jurisdictions only to specified types of crime or to persons within specified age limits; and thirdly, the aims of the proponents of the indeterminate sentence have frequently been defeated on the one hand by judges imposing sentences which practically make the minimum limit identical with the maximum (as a sentence, say, of from twenty-four years and six months to twenty-five years), and, on the other, by parole boards automatically releasing prisoners after the minimum limit of the sentence has been served. We may fairly say then that although crude attempts have been made at individualization of penal treatment on the basis of type of crime, and by use of the so-called "indeterminate sentence," the mass-treatment method of dealing with offenders, founded on legislative prescription in advance of detailed rules for the guidance of the judiciary is, by and large, still in vogue in the American criminal court.

The provision for pleas in mitigation or aggravation of punishment after conviction but prior to sentence represents another stage and method of individualization of penal treatment. This is, however, also a crude and unreliable instrument, the appeal to judicial discretion consisting, as it frequently does, of one-sided emotional or irrelevant pleas to the judge rather than unbiased reports founded on scientific examination. Then there is the crude, mechanical, unimaginative individualization of the judge who has made up his mind in advance to impose heavy sentences on offenders against certain laws, or on second offenders, or to place only offenders against certain legislation on probation, and that regardless of how often they have already failed under such extramural treatment in the past, and of how promising of redemption offenders against other laws might be.

As to all these methods of "separating the sheep from the goats," one may safely say that they do not constitute efficient instruments of that scientific individualization which we found to be the *sine qua non* to economical as well as just administration of criminal law. Legislative prescription in advance of detailed degrees of offenses is individualization of acts and not of human beings, and is, therefore, bound to be inefficient. Judicial "individualization," without adequate scientific facilities in aid of the court, is bound to deteriorate into a mechanical process of application of certain rules of thumb or of implied or expressed prejudices.

Essence of Professor Ferri's scheme of individualization. It is along the lines of an even more detailed legislative prescription of rules to be applied by trial courts in individualizing punishment of future criminals than exists in America today that Professor Enrico Ferri's penal code commission has drafted its basic provision. American experience, however, both with the detailed definitions of the pre-indeterminate-sentence era, and with the indeterminate sentence as applied by judges, would suggest that this setting down of detailed rules of individualization by the legislature in advance, for the guidance of the bench in the imposition of sentence, is not the best road out of the jungle of the present inefficient judicio-penal practice.

Ferri's commission recommends that a schedule of "conditions of dangerousness" and "conditions of less dangerousness" be adopted for the guidance of judges in individualizing punishment. The basic criterion of his scholarly project for an Italian Penal Code, is "the principle of the dangerousness of the offender."[15] The penal code and the penal and correctional institutions take this principle as their point of departure. This must be admitted to be a great stride in advance, when one compares it with the basis of our criminal law as expounded by Dean Pound:

> Historically, our substantive criminal law is based upon a theory of punishing the vicious will. It postulates a free agent confronted with a choice between doing right and doing wrong and choosing freely to do wrong. It assumes that the social interest in the general security and the social interest in the general morals are to be maintained by imposing upon him a penalty corresponding exactly to the gravity of his offense.[16]

This existing criminal law stresses but one act of the offender, without going into the causes of that act or considering other acts or the personality of the actor. Since it thus treats *a symptom* instead of regarding the entire symptom complex and its causes, it is bound to be almost as ineffective as a medical régime which prescribes for a single symptom, not troubling with its relation to other symptoms nor with the causes of the symptoms.

But in the light of what was said above, it must be obvious that to found a new penal code on the sole principle of the dangerousness of the offender[17] which condition is to be arrived at by judicial application of a legislative schedule of "conditions of dangerousness" and those of "less dangerousness" is open to objections. First, it emphasizes a single feature (although it improves upon existing practice in that that feature is a more or less lasting *condition* rather than an individual act), and, secondly, it employs in the work of individualization an instrument that has already been shown to be inadequate.

As to the first point—which is incidental to the main discussion at this stage—if the offender is "dangerous," is not that but one feature of his personality make-up? To look only at his dangerousness is both unjust and unscientific. In overemphasizing the social interest in the general security to the underemphasis of the social interest in the individual life, it is unjust. The easiest way to dispose of criminals, when one stresses their social dangerousness, is to execute them all. But such a principle, standing alone, does not recognize the social justice of constructive rehabilitative work with delinquents on the basis of individual case-study and need. It is uneconomical, for it does not recognize that the most efficient way of coping with the problem, in the long run, is this same constructive rehabilitative effort with the individual delinquent, on the basis of scientific understanding. For while executed criminals do not destroy, neither do they build; and this latter possibility is certainly not to be ignored merely because the traditional, mechanical, punitive régime has failed to reform many criminals. Besides, if we are ever going to learn anything about criminal motivation, it is short-sighted to destroy our "laboratory material" without study.

It is true that, as to the penal organization, Ferri agrees with the soundest American thought on the problem, when he says: "In place of the traditional system of prison penalties for a fixed period, there must be substituted segregation for a period relatively or absolutely unlimited, while the necessary guarantees for individual rights are secured."[18] Nevertheless, by stressing the dangerousness of the offender, Ferri unduly underemphasizes the rehabilitative possibilities of the offender.

Basic criterion of penal system. We would therefore substitute for Ferri's basic criterion the following: *The legal and institutional provisions for the protection of society must be based not so much upon the gravity of the particular act for which an offender happens to be tried, as upon his personality, that is, upon his dangerousness,*[19] *his personal assets, and his responsiveness to peno-correctional treatment.*

This criterion takes account of the well known fact that a relatively innocuous act may happen to be, and not infrequently is, committed by one who fundamentally is socially dangerous, while a relatively serious offense (even murder)[20] may be committed by one who fundamentally is no longer socially dangerous. But it also takes account of the fact that when we speak of "personality," rather than "crime" or "act," we are dealing with a developing, dynamic phenomenon rather than a static fact, a complex phenomenon of which dangerousness at the time of conviction is but one symptom.

The second point of criticism of Ferri's system is more serious. It is doubtful whether any scheme of individualization based on a schedule of minute rules set down by the legislature to govern judges in future cases can be successful. This can no more be done by the legislature as to a person's character than it can (as at present attempted) as to single acts. The legislature cannot possibly conceive in advance the subtle *nuances* that distinguish different offenders from each other, nor the types or lengths of treatment required by various individuals. What the legislature can do is to set down broad penological standards and leave to trained judges, psychiatrists , and psychologists, forming a quasi-judicial treatment body, the application of those standards in the individual case.

An examination of the details of Ferri's scheme will indicate that this criticism is sound. In accordance with his policy of emphasizing the dangerousness of the offender and at the same time providing for "necessary guarantees" of individual rights, Ferri furnishes an elaborate, narrowly-defined schedule of "conditions of dangerousness" and "conditions of less dangerousness," to be prescribed by the code in advance and to be applied by judges as a basis for computation of the type and length of the individual convict's incarceration. At the same time, he stresses the necessity of "segregation for a period relatively or absolutely unlimited." The "degree of dangerousness" is to "be determined according to the gravity and modalities of the offense, the determining motives and the personality of the offender."[21]

From a perusal of the items quoted in note 21, it must be admitted that Professor Ferri and his colleagues have evidenced an enviable ingenuity in analyzing and defining the conditions of "dangerousness" and "less dangerousness" to be used as a schedule of individualization by judges. It will be noticed, however, that practically all of the "circumstances" listed are those mental and physical accompaniments of the criminal act itself which today are taken into account in definitions distinguishing degrees of crimes in American penal statutes, or as conditions in aggravation or mitigation of sentence, or by some judges in determining fitness for probation, by some prison officials in dealing with prisoners within the institution, by some parole boards in considering their release on parole;[22] and it is a serious question whether more is not lost than gained by removing the application of such criteria from the discretion of the last-named agencies and putting the criteria into the code to be applied by judges. For example, to the extent that it substitutes the application of criteria of dangerousness and less dangerousness *at the time of original sentence* for application of similar criteria at a later-stage, the procedure provided for is inferior to that of the better parole boards. How can a judge possibly know in advance how long it will take to rehabilitate a person or even what type of institutional or extra-mural régime is required, without a provision for observation of the progress of treatment, and for the trial and error method of continuous modification of treatment in the light of results?[23] In Ferri's scheme not only are the criteria solely those of "dangerousness," but the prisoner is permanently labeled in advance of treatment.

Such detailed legislative prescription of criteria to be judicially applied to individual cases constitutes a peculiarly unsatisfactory and confusing solution of the dilemma of which judicial discretion is one horn and detailed legislative prescription the other. Subsequent articles of the Code only increase the confusion. They provide for the judicial application of the "sanctions"[24] in a manner that would transform the judge into a computer of his own sum of discretion in different types of cases.[25]

The details given in the notes abundantly indicate the mechanical nature of the individualization provided for. They are quite on a parity with the traditional practice in the criminal law which Dean Pound has criticized as based on an erroneous assumption. While ostensibly reforming this situation, what does Ferri's scheme propose but the substitution of minute rules, mechanically to be applied by judges, the difference being that now, instead of the legislature measuring the exact gravity of the *offense* in advance, it is provided that it measure the exact dangerousness of every type of *offender* in advance. The practice is so mechanical and complicated in its conception that one has a picture of a judge checking up whether, say, "circumstances of greater dangerousness," numbered 1, 3, 7 and 14, and "circumstances of less dangerousness," numbered 5, 9 and 11 are applicable to a defendant before him, ascertaining which of the numerous "sanctions" or combinations thereof are pertinent, then using a computing machine to figure out just how much incarceration the so-called "unlimited" sentence really calls for. Both in making such provisions to be used at the time of sentence in a judicial computation of the length of incarceration[26] and in setting down a schedule of periods of time before which prisoners may not apply for conditional release, the purpose of individualized treatment is largely defeated.

Machinery of individualization. This discussion brings us to the conviction that instead of the penal code setting down in advance, and in great detail, rules of "dangerousness" and "less dangerousness," numerous "sanctions," and mathematical formulae for figuring out sentences and determining the length of incarceration and time for release from custody on the basis of such rules—all this practice to be resorted to by a trial judge—we must seek some instrumentality which will retain the essence as well as the name of individualization. But this does not mean that to provide for true individualization the treatment of the offender must be left to judges or other officials wholly without guidance and without control as to the length or nature of that treatment. A more promising method out of the dilemma than the Italian must probably be based upon four principles which should underlie individualizing criminal procedure:

(1) The treatment (sentence-imposing) feature of the proceedings must be sharply differentiated from the guilt-finding phase.
(2) The decision as to treatment must be made by a board or tri-

bunal specially qualified in the interpretation and evaluation of psychiatric, psychological, and sociologic data. (3) The treatment must be modifiable in the light of scientific reports of progress. (4) The rights of the individual must be safeguarded against possible arbitrariness or other unlawful action on the part of the treatment tribunal.

As to the first point, although it has long been urged by psychiatrists, it was not until the Ninth International Prison Congress of London, in 1925, that the following resolution was adopted:

> The trial ought to be divided into two parts: In the first the examination and decision as to . . . guilt should take place; in the second one the punishment should be discussed and fixed. From this part the public and the injured party should be excluded.[27]

This resolution expresses the general recognition that while the public may be concerned with the trial proceedings, the inquiries pertaining to treatment should be of a scientific, non-sensational nature not deliberately accommodated, as so many modern trials are, to the greedy appetites of "yellow journalism."

The second principle has abundant reason to support it. While a legally trained judge can act as an impartial referee during a technical trial, ruling upon the exclusion or inclusion of evidence, giving a legally unimpeachable charge to the jury, and performing similar functions, his education and habit of mind have not qualified him for the more difficult task of determining the type of treatment best suited to the individual delinquent on the basis of reports of scientific investigations. It would therefore seem that the work of the ordinary criminal court should cease with the finding of guilt or innocence. Recognition of the illogical and unscientific present procedure led us to propose the establishment of a "Socio-Penal Commission,"[28] or treatment board to be composed, say, of a psychiatrist or psychologist, a sociologist and a lawyer. Such a tribunal would begin to function beyond the point where the substantive and procedural criminal law has prepared the case for the imposition of sentence. The primary duty of such a board would be to determine the psychiatric, social, or peno-correctional treatment appropriate to the individual delinquent, as well as its duration. But such treatment and its duration would, in accordance with the general essence of the treatment board idea, have to be extremely flexible. This treatment tribunal would perform its functions on the basis of psychiatric, psychological and social reports of the investigations of each delinquent.

The third principle of wise individualization—modifiability of the length and type of treatment in the light of progress thereunder —is dictated by the logic of the foregoing. For a treatment tribunal to carry out its functions more intelligently than do the present criminal courts it is not only necessary that it be an independent, specially qualified body, but that it evolve methods for the observation of the individual delinquent's progress under the treatment originally ordered, so that, if necessary, such treatment may be modified, much as the physician modifies treatment, in the light of progress.[29] Probably periodic reports upon, and review of cases as a routine procedure of the treatment board would have to be provided for.

The fourth proposition raises the greatest technical difficulties. Here one must look to the fertile field of administrative law for devices which with appropriate modification can be adapted to criminal procedure. Indeed it must already be evident that the problem in its essence is analogous to those of various types of administrative instrumentalities. At least that phase of criminal law and procedure which begins with the sentencing function has or should have some of the earmarks of what is commonly called "administrative law." First, it is "public law"; that is, it involves the relationship of the individual to the state, or the social interest in the general welfare (security), instead of private litigation. Secondly, it contains an element of "preventive justice," in that, for effectiveness, it requires continuity of effort with an aim to prevention of recidivism. The present procedure discharges criminals from penal institutions automatically, without much regard to whether or not further crime might be prevented by their continued incarceration. As long as the end of criminal procedure was punishment for the sake of punishment or even for the sake of prevention and deterrence as ordinarily conceived, the notion of continuity of treatment did not enter the minds of legal scholars; and indeed few students of criminal law seem even today to be aware of the vital significance of this point. The sentence disposed of the convict until the end of the precise term prescribed in advance by a legislature which fatuously measured the length of punishment to make it just enough to restore the imaginary "balance" of the disturbed "jural order." In the meantime the convict was forgotten until his next appearance in court; and even then his past misconduct was frequently unknown to the trial judge. Nobody concerned himself with the response of the prisoner to the dosage of punishment prescribed him by this judicial medicine man. Unfortunately the use of the past tense in this criticism is not precisely justified; many legislatures still prescribe the length of punishment in advance, and many trial judges still mechanically apply this treatment without ever going near the penal institutions to which they daily sentence criminals. A third evidence of the administrative law essence of the problem is that criminal procedure, beginning with the stage of sentence, if it is to be at all effective, requires technical experts learned in matters outside of the ken of the law—psychiatrists, psychologists, social workers, penologists.

Finally, when once we recognize that punishment *qua* punishment does not bring about the desired result of protection of society, and that constructive individualized treatment of offenders against the law is more likely to achieve it, we are met with the basic problem in administrative law—the need and the methods of safeguarding individual rights against the possible arbitrary action of a technically skilled, yet "all too human," administrative board.

In the light of these evidences of the administrative essence of penal procedure, it is surprising that Continental criminologists, such as Ferri, have resorted to the clumsy device described above—legislative prescription of detailed rules of individualization—as a way out of the dilemma of free judicial discretion versus protection of individual liberty. The field of administrative law would have suggested the much more simple and effective device of a treatment board. Discussion of the scope of such a tribunal's jurisdiction, its manner of functioning, its relation to existing services (parole, probation, peno-correctional régimes), and, above all, the legal means for safeguarding individual rights against possible arbitrariness on the part of the treatment body is beyond the scope of this paper.[30] The idea raises many vexing problems of policy and law, and much thorough-going study will be required to sketch in the vital details.

To make the work of such a treatment body effective, a temporary detention institution or "clearing house" manned by able psychiatrists, psychologists and social investigators would have to form an integral part of the board's equipment.[31] Careful records of examinations and field investigations of each offender would have to be maintained. Above all, however, the actual work of peno-correctional treatment—probation, institutional régimes, parole—would have to be greatly improved, and new devices experimented with. The possibilities of various types of the newer psychotherapy in the treatment of offenders, for example, have thus far been prac-tically ignored by those who deal with the problems of penology. Nor have different schemes of inmate self-government been suffi-ciently experimented with.

The substantive law. The system briefly sketched above would not necessarily involve changes in the substantive law; but no doubt modifications would gradually be suggested on the basis of carefully accumulated, scientific experience with treatment. Modifications in substantive law have not infrequently followed in the wake of pro-cedural changes. Perhaps, eventually, the basic mode of analysis of crimes into act and intent, which Dean Pound has pointed out to be faulty,[32] will be radically modified. One can conceive, for exam-ple, that the effective operation of the type of board described will have its influence on the "tests" of the irresponsibility of the insane; it might even render them superfluous. It would probably also have its effect on the reduction of the number and variety of "degrees" in the definition of homicide, robbery, rape, larceny, and so on. It might, further, influence the substantive law of attempts. The minute splitting up of offenses into degrees and the distinguishing of attempts from completed criminal acts, with the meticulous setting down of supposedly appropriate dosages of punishment, belongs to an era when punishment based upon degrees of "vicious will" as re-flected in types of crime was thought to be the only or best means of coping with anti-social behavior.

Indeterminate sentence. The system under consideration should logically have as a basic provision a wholly and truly indeterminate sentence.[33] The present "indeterminate sentence" is indeterminate only within maximum-minimum limits or embraces variations of this principle. The so-called indeterminate sentence of Ferri is, as was indicated, even less satisfactory. But even if concessions will have to be made to public opinion in such matters as murder and rape (that is, even if, as to certain serious offenses, *minimum* limits of an indeterminate sentence will have to be retained), the system ought to work more effectively than the present order. Similarly, if concessions will have to be made to public opinion in regard to such crimes as larceny (that is, even if, as to certain less serious offenses, *maximum* limits of an indeterminate sentence will have to be retained) the machinery ought to operate more satisfactorily than the present régime. It should constitute a promising as well as interesting social experiment.

Summary

The underlying principles of a rational penal code are:

1. Society should utilize every scientific instrumentality for self-protection against destructive elements in its midst, with as little interference with the free life of its members as is consistent with such an aim.

2. To put this principle into practice, scientific individualization of peno-correctional diagnosis and treatment is necessary.

3. Professor Ferri's scheme of judicial individualization on the basis of a detailed legislative schedule of "conditions of dangerousness" and "conditions of less dangerousness" and a penal calculus is unsatisfactory. Individualization should be effected by a scientifically qualified treatment board, to begin to function after the individual offender has been found (or has pleaded) guilty in the existing criminal court. In addition to the original disposition of cases, the treatment tribunal should periodically review the progress of offenders under treatment, modifying the original prescription ("sentence") if found necessary. The board should utilize existing scientific facilities (psychiatry, psychology, social work) in individualizaton.

4. Provision is necessary for protecting individual rights against possible arbitrariness or other unlawful conduct of the treatment board.

5. Certain modifications in substantive law may be expected to result from this basic change in procedure, and these, together with a truly indeterminate sentence provision and improvements in peno-correctional practice, would facilitate the work of the treatment body.

NOTES

---

1. Dean Pound's summary of the Cleveland survey findings, and his philosophical interpretation of the inherent and acquired difficulties of the situation in which the administration of American criminal justice now finds itself, is, however, of the utmost value in an understanding of the principal reasons for the inefficiencies and conflicting aims of the present regime.

2. The Italian penal code commission headed by Professor Enrico Ferri, appointed September 14, 1919, was faced at the outset with the choice of making "a simple revision and technical correction of the statutes now in force," or propounding "a new and autonomous systematization of legislative norms in accord with the advance in scientific doctrines." The president of the commission said that the reason why it chose the latter alternative was "to avoid the inconveniences already experienced in Italy and abroad from attempting reforms that are fragmentary and often contradictory," and insisted that the reforms proposed "ought to respond to one general direction and one organic system." 1 Ferri, Relazione sul Progetto Preliminare di Codice Penale Italiano (1921) 3–4, 180–81. This volume will hereinafter be referred to as the Italian Project. For an able discussion of this code project, see Collin, Enrico Ferri et L'avant-projet de Code Penal Italien de 1921 (1925).

The London Times for November 23, 1927, reports that the draft of the Fascist penal code, prepared largely by Signor Rocco, the Fascist Minister of Justice, affirms as a basic principle the criterion which Ferri's code abandoned as unsatisfactory because unscientific. As a preliminary to enunciation of the penal philosophy of the positive school of criminology (Lombroso, Garofalo, Ferri), Professor Ferri many years ago pulled the foundation from the classical theory which bases criminal responsibility on freedom of will, substituting "social accountability" therefor. The new code, however, which appears to have every chance of adoption, is supported by Signor Rocco's statement that "there must be no modification of the principle of responsibility, which has rested for centuries on the basis of the individual capacity of understanding and will, and of consciousness and volition in human action." London Times, *supra*. For the text of the Rocco code, see Progetto Preliminare di un Nuovo Codice Penale (1927). See also Ferri, *Il Progetto Rocco di Codice Penale* (1927) 7 Scuola Positiva (N.S.) no. 11–12.

3. See Ogburn and Goldenweiser, The Social Sciences and their Interrelations (1927), for abundant evidences of the recognition of the need for an assault upon the more or less artificial barriers between the sciences. A few colleges of political science and one or two law schools are beginning to

recognize the possible value of systematic collaboration among the social scientists.

4. It is much easier to formulate this general principle than to apply it in any specific instance. It cannot be denied, however, that a society which interferes substantially more with the liberty of its members than is dictated by a scientific conception of the general welfare is to that degree unjust.

5. Almost every prison census and work on criminology refers to the problem of recidivism. See Bernard Glueck, *A Study of 608 Admissions to Sing Sing Prison* (1918) a Mental Hygiene 177. On the basis of his Sing Sing studies, Glueck found that 66.8 percent of 608 consecutive admissions to Sing Sing Prison were recidivists, i.e., persons who had been previously sentenced to penal institutions. First Annual Report of the Psychiatric Clinic in Collaboration with Sing Sing Prison (1917) 11, 16. In a relatively recent examination by the National Committee for Mental Hygiene, of 1288 unselected prisoners of 34 county jails and penitentiaries in New York State (exclusive of New York City) it was found that 66 percent were repeated offenders. This figure for petty offenders (drunkards, vagrants, prostitutes, and those who have committed petty larceny) is strangely about the same as that for the more serious offenders of Sing Sing Prison. "This is but in keeping with similar studies in penal and correctional institutions throughout the country, and means that we are in a large measure dealing with the same material over and over again—locking up and turning out the same individuals, and failing adequately to protect society from their depredations." A Plan for the Custody and Training of Prisoners Serving Sentences in the County Jails in New York State (1924) 16.

6. It is a well known fact that when punishment becomes so severe as to suggest the revenge motif rather than the idea of social protection, juries are loath to convict.

7. White, Insanity and the Criminal Law (1923) 13–14.

8. Cited by Root, A Psychological and Educational Survey of 1916 Prisoners in the Western Penitentiary of Pennsylvania (1927) 11–12.

9. Another advantage of a change in basic principle of the penal system along the lines proposed herein is suggested by the following words of Professor Ferri "Since [under the present regime] the judges have before them a man and not an objective fact, a contrast often arises in their consciences and in their sentences between the law and the human reality, and their judgments do not carry public approval because deemed too rigorous or too inadequate." Italian Project, 183–84. This public attitude is founded on the old notion that the sentence is the payment to society of an amount of suffering precisely proportionate to the amount of harmfulness of the crime, something in itself impossible of measurement.

The principle of penocorrectional treatment of the offending personality rather than of punishment supposedly commensurate to the precise gravity of an act will gradually become prevalent. Indeed, the widespread use of probation and the juvenile court is already transforming the public attitude toward the entire problem. We may expect the gradual replacement of the bargaining attitude by one in which length of deprivation of liberty will be recognized to depend upon the response of the offender to treatment.

10. As indicative of what probation ought to be and of its tremendous importance in the protection of society through rehabilitation of promising offenders, the reader should consult COOLEY, PROBATION AND DELINQUENCY (1927). Notice particularly the sub-title—The Study and Treatment of the Individual Delinquent. See also VAN WATERS, YOUTH IN CONFLICT (1925).

11. See WHITE, MECHANISMS OF CHARACTER FORMATION (1918), HART, PSYCHOLOGY OF INSANITY (1920), and Barrett, *Mental Disorders in Medicolegal Relations* in 1 PETERSON, HAINES AND WEBSTER, LEGAL MEDICINE AND TOXICOLOGY (1923).

12. See, e.g., RICHMOND, SOCIAL DIAGNOSIS (1917), and WHAT IS SOCIAL CASE WORK? (1922). Consult COOLEY, *op. cit. supra* note 10, for striking illustrations of the possibilities of constructive social case work methods in the service of the court.

13. See authorities collected in SAYRE, CASES ON CRIMINAL LAW (1927) 767 *et seq.*

14. Such, e.g., are the distinctions in varieties of arson found in the N. Y. PENAL LAW §§ 221–23, dividing the crime into three degrees dependent largely on the type of structure burned and whether the burning was by day or night; the familiar practice of breaking up burglary into degrees, depending upon whether or not the entry is accompanied by one or more of the common law requisites of burglary or not; the division of murder and manslaughter into degrees based on such mental and other accompaniments of the homicide as whether or not the act was done with "deliberately premeditated malice aforethought" (MASS. GEN. LAWS (1921) c. 265, § 1), whether or not it was committed in the perpetration or attempted perpetration of specified other crimes, such as rape, arson, robbery, or burglary, whether the means were poison (Pa. Act of April 22, 1794, § 2), or interference with railroad tracks (N. Y. PENAL LAW § 1044).

15. ITALIAN PROJECT, 7, 49 *et seq.*, 153, 183 *et seq.*, 229 *et seq.*, 342.

16. Introduction to SAYRE, *op. cit. supra* note 13 at xxxvi–xxxvii.

17. The other principle Ferri employs "social defense," while broader is still subject to the same criticism, when used as Ferri proposes.

18. ITALIAN PROJECT, 15, 192.

19. It is quite true as Ferri points out, that the emphasis of the dangerousness of the offender becomes of vital significance in treating of the law of attempts. It is conceivable, for example, that one who attempts a crime but does not for some reason bring about its completion may be a much more dangerous person than another whose attempt has ripened into a completed act. Both would ordinarily be guilty of some offense at present, but the former would be punishable far less, i.e., only for an attempt, the latter for the more serious, completed crime. But the question is, shall dangerousness be the sole criterion, and provided for in the substantive law, or by its inclusion

among the "conditions of dangerousness," or shall its recognition, together with the many other factors disclosed by scientific examination of the individual case, be by a "treatment board" with wide administrative discretion?

20. Mrs. Jessie D. Hodder, one of the foremost prison administrators in the country, has on several occasions said that the inmates of her institution (The Massachusetts Reformatory for Women) who make the least trouble and who are the most trustworthy are those who have committed certain types of homicides.

21. ITALIAN PROJECT, 153, 342. The following are the "circumstances which indicate a greater dangerousness in the offender":

"(1) Dissoluteness or dishonesty of prior personal, family or social life; (2) Prior judicial and penal record; (3) Abnormal organic and mental conditions before, during and after the offense, which do not constitute mental infirmity and which reveal criminal tendencies; (4) Precocity in committing a grave offense; (5) Having acted through ignoble or trivial motives; (6) Family and social relationship with the injured or damaged party; (7) Deliberate preparation of the offense; (8) Time, place, instruments, manner of execution of the offense, when these have rendered more difficult the defence by the injured or damaged party or indicate a greater moral insensibility in the offender; (9) The execution of the offense by means of ambush or stratagem or through the commission of other offenses or by abusing the aid of minors, the deficient, the unsound of mind, the alcoholic, or by employing the assistance of other offenders; (10) The execution of the offense during a public or private calamity or a common danger; (11) Having acted by pre-arranged complicity with others; (12) Abuse of trust in public or private matters or malicious violation of special duties; (13) Execution of the offense on things confided to the public good faith or kept in public offices or destined for public utility, defence or reverence; (14) Abuse of personal conditions of inferiority in the injured party or of circumstances unfavorable to him; (15) Having aggravated the consequences of the offense or having through the same act and not by mere accident damaged or injured more than one person, or having through one and the same crime violated various provisions of law, or the same provision of law at various times, by acts carrying out one and the same resolve; (16) Blameworthy conduct after the offense towards the injured or damaged party or his relations, the person present at the time of the offense or those who gathered at the time of the offense; (17) In offenses by imprudence (negligence) having caused the damage in circumstances which made it very probable and easy to foresee." ITALIAN PROJECT, 153–54, 342–43.

The following circumstances are presumed to indicate "less dangerousness in the offender":

"(1) Honesty of prior personal, family and social life; (2) Having acted from excusable motives or motives of public interest; (3) Having acted in a state of excusable passion or of emotion through intense grief or fear or impulse of anger unjustly provoked by others; (4) Having yielded to a special and transitory opportunity or to exceptional and excusable personal or family conditions; (5) Having acted in a state of drunkenness or other form of intoxication not to be foreseen by the offender, through transitory conditions of health or through unknown material circumstances; (6) Having acted through suggestion coming from a turbulent crowd; (7) Having used, spontaneously and immediately after having committed the offense, all exertion to diminish the consequences or to make good the damage, even in part, if it be done with sacrifice of one's own economic condition; (8) Having in repentance confessed the offense not yet discovered or before being interrogated by the judge, or having in repentance presented oneself to the authorities immediately after the offense." ITALIAN PROJECT, 154, 344–45.

22. The schedules of "dangerousness" and "less dangerousness" are further complicated by exceptions and special provisions. Thus Chapter III, Art. 74, provides that "the judge shall apply the sanction set forth for each offense within the limits established by the law and according to the criteria of Art. 20" (see note 21, *supra*), with certain elaborate exceptions.

23. While provision is made for "conditional condemnation" (analogous to suspension of execution of sentence), and "judicial pardon," and while at varying periods application may be made by inmates to the judge for "conditional release" (parole), still, as to these functions as well as the original determination of the length of incarceration, Ferri sets down in advance a sort of penal mathematic by which the judge is more or less mechanically bound. Thus, Art. 83 provides: "The person sentenced to simple detention, to the workhouse, or agricultural colony for minors, or to simple or rigorous temporary segregation for a minimum not less than three years, may, after serving such period as corresponds to one half of the difference between the minimum and the maximum, and at least two thirds where he be an habitual offender, apply for release on condition. The convicted person who has been sentenced for one offense only and is not a recidivist and who has been placed [by the penal institution] in the category *best*, may apply for conditional release after he has served a period corresponding to one third of the difference between the minimum and the maximum. The person sentenced to rigorous segregation for a period absolutely unlimited for an ordinary offense, may apply for release on condition after twenty years; the habitual offender after twenty-four [Note the arbitrary precision.] years; the social-political offender after ten years."—ITALIAN PROJECT, 165, 356. Other articles provide for application for release from various types of institutions to be made not before nine and three years, respectively; and give the judge power "to shorten by not more than one-third" the various terms provided for, after considering the mode of the offense and the personality of the offender.

24. Ferri's code provides an elaborate set of punishments ("sanctions") which must be taken into account by judges in connection with the conditions of dangerousness and "less dangerousness," thus further complicating the process of individualization. For *ordinary offenses by majors* over eighteen: The mulct (a species of fine); local relegation (prohibition from residence in the place of the offense for from three months to three years); confinement (compulsion to reside in the commune named in the sentence, which must be "distant not less than 100 kilometres" from that where the

offense occurred, where the injured party resides, and from the offender's residence); obligatory day labor (in workhouse or agricultural colony, without night detention, for from one month to two years); simple segregation in workhouse or agricultural colony (with compulsory industrial or agricultural day labor and night isolation, for from three months to fifteen years, the type of labor to conform to "the previous life and aptitudes for labor" of the convict); rigorous segregation in "an establishment of seclusion" (with compulsory day labor and night isolation for from three to twenty years, or for an indeterminate period but not less than ten years, if "temporary," and for life if "perpetual"). For *social-political offenses by majors:* General relegation (banishment from Italian territory for from three months to ten years); simple detention ("isolation during the night and, on request of the prisoner, also during the day, in a special establishment," for from one month to ten years, the prisoner being at liberty to choose one of the forms of labor provided and to have other privileges); rigorous detention (which is indeterminate for from two to fifteen years, but may also be for not less than ten years). For *juvenile offenders:* Supervised freedom, professional correctional school or schoolship, workhouse or agricultural colony for minors, house of custody. For *majors in a state of "mental infirmity":* House of custody (night isolation with compulsory industrial or agricultural day labor, when possible, for at least one year, "under the direction of a physician expert in criminal anthropology"); criminal insane asylum (same régime for at least three years); special labor colony (for alcoholics and "others infirm of mind"; régime of "simple" or "rigorous" segregation "for a period equal to that of the simple or rigorous segregation applied for the offense committed"). "*Complementary sanctions*" (where they do not constitute sanctions standing alone): Special publication of the sentence, suspension from exercise of trade or profession, interdiction from public office, expulsion of foreigner, "caution for good behavior" (depositing money or mortgage conditioned upon good behavior within probationary period of from two to five years). Italian Project, 158–61, 348–52.

25. These provisions completely demonstrate the underlying weakness of the Ferri proposal for individualization of punishment:

"If there occurs only one circumstance of greater dangerousness, the judge shall apply the sanction in a measure not less than half between the minimum and the maximum set forth for the offense committed by the accused.

"If there concur more than one circumstance of greater dangerousness, the judge shall apply the maximum of the sanction and shall be empowered to exceed it, but not beyond one third.

"If the circumstances of greater dangerousness be exceptionally grave the judge shall be empowered to apply the sanction of the next grade of severity." Italian Project, 163, 354.

Articles 76 and 77 similarly set down detailed directions for a perplexed judge's penal arithmetic:

"If there occurs only one circumstance of less dangerousness the judge shall apply the sanction in a measure less than half between the minimum and the maximum.

"If there concur more than one circumstance of less dangerousness the judge shall apply the minimum of the sanction and shall be empowered to lower it, but not beyond one third.

"If the circumstances of less dangerousness be exceptionally important, the judge shall be empowered to apply the sanction which is immediately inferior in gravity or else the judicial pardon according to art. 82.

"If there occur together circumstances of greater dangerousness and circumstances of less dangerousness, the judge shall establish which are prevalent, in order to graduate the dangerousness of the accused and to apply . . . the sanction best adapted to his personality." ITALIAN PROJECT, 164, 354.

26. The determination, in advance, of how long the anti-social patient will be confined in the peno-correctional hospital!

27. PRISON ASS'N OF NEW YORK, EIGHTY-FIRST ANNUAL REPORT (1926) 74.

28. "The jury could still pass upon the mental element of the crime—the *mens rea;*—but the work of scientific determination of the *peno-correctional consequences of conviction* by a jury would be lodged in a skilled, administrative board specially qualified for such a task." GLUECK, MENTAL DISORDER AND THE CRIMINAL LAW (1925) 486. So practical a statesman as Governor Smith of New York has recently urged the adoption of a treatment board device as a fundamental reform of existing practice. See N. Y. Times, Dec. 8, 1927 (address before New York Crime Commission); *ibid.*, Jan. 5, 1928 (Annual Message).

29. We do not by this mean to suggest that all criminals are "sick people"; but that the same common sense that dictates observation of the results of treatment of various types in medicine is necessary (perhaps even more so) in the case of peno-correctional treatment of the individual offender. In brief, we are in a realm where the trial and error method will have to be resorted to. What must at all events be avoided is the present practice of slapping a man into prison and then forgetting him until he is again brought into court.

30. Without discussing possible means of "judicialization of the administrative act" of determination of appropriate treatment for every "individual delinquent," it may be said that in general the solution of this problem probably involves, first, the definition of broad legal categories of a social-psychiatric nature within which the treatment board will classify individual delinquents; secondly, the safeguarding of individual rights by permitting the defendant to have counsel and witnesses (of fact and opinion), and to examine psychiatric and social reports filed with the tribunal, while at the same time avoiding a technical, litigious procedure, hide-bound by strict rules of evidence; thirdly, provision for judicial review of the administrative action of the treatment tribunal when it is alleged to have acted "arbitrarily" or otherwise unlawfully. I am indebted to Prof. Felix Frankfurter's course in Administrative Law for valuable clues as to the intricacies of this general problem and hints as to the direction which its solution will probably take.

COLLIN, *op. cit. supra* note 2, at 189, rightly points out that since, under Ferri's system of minute legislative prescriptions, judges will not be called upon to "interpret the will of the legislator" but to investigate the nature of the individual delinquent, the course of judicial decision (*"la jurisprudence"*) "will have to adapt itself constantly to the evolution of scientific doctrines," presenting the dangerous alternative that, either the course of decision will have to follow step by step the development of science, "which would give rise to the most conflicting and perhaps most erroneous decisions," or judges will have to continue to apply the ideas of the framers of the project, "at the risk of maintaining, in the courts of justice, a scientific system abandoned by the majority of scholars." The system proposed herein will avoid at least the latter difficulty; since the *content* of the social-psychiatric categories could change with the advance of science, which advance it is presumed would be reflected in the techniques of the experts attached to the treatment tribunals. The former difficulty could be minimized by providing for a specialized appellate tribunal which would tend to unify the findings of the different treatment boards of a state, and for frequent conferences of the officials and associated scientists of the boards, for exchange of ideas on policy and treatment.

31. The training of this personnel is a *sine qua non* to the success of the entire project. Present training facilities and prejudices are not suitable.

32. "We know that the old analysis of act and intent can stand only as an artificial legal analysis and that the mental element in crime presents a series of difficult problems." POUND, CRIMINAL JUSTICE IN CLEVELAND (1922) 586.

33. One of the most important resolutions adopted by the Ninth International Prison Congress in 1925 was "that the indeterminate sentence is the necessary consequence of the individualization of punishment and one of the most efficacious means of social defence." PRISON ASS'N OF NEW YORK, EIGHTY-FIRST ANNUAL REPORT (1926) 73.

Joseph F. Scott, formerly superintendent of reformatories for New York, in discussing the origin of the first American indeterminate sentence law in New York, says that Mr. Brockway's original draft of the bill in 1877 "embodied an indeterminate sentence without limitation, which was approved by the board of managers and incorporated in their report to the legislature. But, previous to its introduction in the legislature, fearing that the bill in this form might not pass, the draft was altered, limiting the sentence to 'the maximum term provided by law for the crime for which the prisoner was convicted and sentenced.' " This has been the model for all subsequent legislation on the subject. Superintendent Scott was of the conviction, in 1910, that, "Undoubtedly, had the section containing the indeterminate sentence clause as originally drafted been left in the bill, it would have become law, as drafted, and would have given to us the purely indeterminate sentence which we have not been able to obtain up to the present time." Scott, *American Reformatories for Male Adults* in HENDERSON, PENAL AND REFORMATORY INSTITUTIONS (1910) 89, 94.

C. S. Lewis

The Humanitarian Theory of Punishment

In England we have lately had a controversy about Capital Punishment. I do not know whether a murderer is more likely to repent and make a good end on the gallows a few weeks after his trial or in the prison infirmary thirty years later. I do not know whether the fear of death is an indispensable deterrent. I need not, for the purpose of this article, decide whether it is a morally permissible deterrent. Those are questions which I propose to leave untouched. My subject is not Capital Punishment in particular, but that theory of punishment in general which the controversy showed to be almost universal among my fellow-countrymen. It may be called the Humanitarian theory. Those who hold it think that it is mild and merciful. In this I believe that they are seriously mistaken. I believe that the "Humanity" which it claims is a dangerous illusion and disguises the possibility of cruelty and injustice without end. I urge a return to the traditional or Retributive theory not solely, not even primarily, in the interests of society, but in the interests of the criminal.

According to the Humanitarian theory, to punish a man because he deserves it, and as much as he deserves, is mere revenge, and, therefore, barbarous and immoral. It is maintained that the only legitimate motives for punishing are the desire to deter others by example or to mend the criminal. When this theory is combined, as frequently happens, with the belief that all crime is more or less pathological, the idea of mending tails off into that of healing or

Reprinted from *20th Century*, Vol. 3, No. 3 (Autumn 1948-49), 5-12, with permission of the editor.

curing and punishment becomes therapeutic. Thus it appears at first sight that we have passed from the harsh and self-righteous notion of giving the wicked their deserts to the charitable and enlightened one of tending the psychologically sick. What could be more amiable? One little point which is taken for granted in this theory needs, however, to be made explicit. The things done to the criminal, even if they are called cures, will be just as compulsory as they were in the old days when we called them punishments. If a tendency to steal can be cured by psychotherapy, the thief will no doubt be forced to undergo the treatment. Otherwise, society cannot continue.

My contention is that this doctrine, merciful though it appears, really means that each one of us, from the moment he breaks the law, is deprived of the rights of a human being.

The reason is this. The Humanitarian theory removes from Punishment the concept of Desert. But the concept of Desert is the only connecting link between punishment and justice. It is only as deserved or undeserved that a sentence can be just or unjust. I do not here contend that the question "Is it deserved?" is the only one we can reasonably ask about a punishment. We may very properly ask whether it is likely to deter others and to reform the criminal. But neither of these two last questions is a question about justice. There is no sense in talking about a "just deterrent" or a "just cure." We demand of a deterrent not whether it is just but whether it will deter. We demand of a cure not whether it is just but whether it succeeds. Thus when we cease to consider what the criminal deserves and consider only what will cure him or deter others, we have tacitly removed him from the sphere of justice altogether; instead of a person, a subject of rights, we now have a mere object, a patient, a "case."

The distinction will become clearer if we ask who will be qualified to determine sentences when sentences are no longer held to derive their propriety from the criminal's deservings. On the old view the problem of fixing the right sentence was a moral problem. Accordingly, the judge who did it was a person trained in jurisprudence; trained, that is, in a science which deals with rights and duties, and which, in origin at least, was consciously accepting guidance from the Law of Nature, and from Scripture. We must admit that in the actual penal code of most countries at most times these high originals were so much modified by local custom, class interests, and utilitarian concessions, as to be very imperfectly recognizable. But the code was never in principle, and not always in fact, beyond the control of the conscience of the society. And when (say, in eighteenth-century England) actual punishments conflicted too violently with the moral sense of the community, juries refused to convict and reform was finally brought about. This was possible because, so long as we are thinking in terms of Desert, the propriety of the penal code, being a moral question, is a question on which every man has the right to an opinion, not because he follows this or that profession, but because he is simply a man, a rational animal enjoying the Natural Light. But all this is changed when we drop the concept of Desert. The only two questions we may now ask about a punishment are whether it deters and whether it cures. But these are not questions on which anyone is entitled to have an opinion simply because he is a man. He is not entitled to an opinion even if, in addition to being a man, he should happen also to be a jurist, a Christian, and a moral theologian. For they are not questions about principle but about matter of fact; and for such *cuiquam in sua arte credendum.* Only the expert "penologist" (let barbarous things have barbarous names), in the light of previous experiment, can tell us what is likely to deter: only the psychotherapist can tell us what is likely to cure. It will be in vain for the rest of us, speaking simply as men, to say, "but this punishment is hideously unjust, hideously disproportionate to the criminal's deserts." The experts with perfect logic will reply, "but nobody was talking about deserts. No one was talking about *punishment* in your archaic vindictive sense of the word. Here are the statistics proving that this treatment deters. Here are the statistics proving that this other treatment cures. What is your trouble?"

The Humanitarian theory, then, removes sentences from the hands of jurists whom the public conscience is entitled to criticize and places them in the hands of technical experts whose special sciences do not even employ such categories as rights or justice. It might be argued that since this transference results from an abandonment of the old idea of punishment, and, therefore, of all vindictive motives, it will be safe to leave our criminals in such hands. I will not pause to comment on the simple-minded view of fallen human nature which such a belief implies. Let us rather remember that the "cure" of criminals is to be compulsory; and let us then watch how the theory actually works in the mind of the Humanitarian. The immediate starting point of this article was a letter I read in one of our Leftist weeklies. The author was pleading that a certain sin, now treated by our laws as a crime, should henceforward be treated as a disease. And he complained that under the present system, the offender, after a term in gaol, was simply let out to return to his original environment where he would probably relapse. What he complained of was not the shutting up but the letting out. On his remedial view of punishment the offender should, of course, be detained until he was cured. And of course the official straighteners are the only people who can say when that is. The first result of the Humanitarian theory is, therefore, to substitute for a definite sentence (reflecting to some extent the community's moral judgment on the degree of ill-desert involved) an indefinite sentence terminable only by the word of those experts—and they are not experts in moral theology nor even in the Law of Nature—who inflict it. Which of us, if he stood in the dock, would not prefer to be tried by the old system?

It may be said that by the continued use of the word punishment and the use of the verb "inflict" I am misrepresenting Humanitarians. They are not punishing, not inflicting, only healing. But do not let us be deceived by a name. To be taken without consent from my home and friends; to lose my liberty; to undergo all those assaults on my personality which modern psychotherapy knows how to deliver; to be re-made after some pattern of "normality" hatched in a Viennese laboratory to which I never professed allegiance; to know that this process will never end until either my captors have succeeded or I grown wise enough to cheat them with apparent success—who cares whether this is called Punishment or not? That it includes most of the elements for which any punishment is feared—shame, exile, bondage, and years eaten by the locust —is obvious. Only enormous ill-desert could justify it; but ill-desert is the very conception which the Humanitarian theory has thrown overboard.

If we turn from the curative to the deterrent justification of punishment we shall find the new theory even more alarming. When you punish a man *in terrorem*, make of him an "example" to others, you are admittedly using him as a means to an end; someone else's end. This, in itself, would be a very wicked thing to do. On the classical theory of Punishment it was of course justified on the ground that the man deserved it. That was assumed to be established before any question of "making him an example" arose. You then, as the saying is, killed two birds with one stone; in the process of giving him what he deserved you set an example to others. But take away desert and the whole morality of the punishment disappears. Why, in Heaven's name, am I to be sacrificed to the good of society in this way?—unless, of course, I deserve it.

But that is not the worst. If the justification of exemplary punishment is not to be based on desert but solely on its efficacy as a deterrent, it is not absolutely necessary that the man we punish should even have committed the crime. The deterrent effect demands that the public should draw the moral, "If we do such an act we shall suffer like that man." The punishment of a man actually guilty whom the public think innocent will not have the desired effect; the punishment of a man actually innocent will, provided the public think him guilty. But every modern State has powers which make it easy to fake a trial. When a victim is urgently needed for exemplary purposes and a guilty victim cannot be found, all the purposes of deterrence will be equally served by the punishment (call it "cure" if you prefer) of an innocent victim, provided that the public can be cheated into thinking him guilty. It is no use to ask me why I assume that our rulers will be so wicked. The punishment of an innocent, that is, an undeserving, man is wicked only if we grant the traditional view that righteous punishment means deserved punishment. Once we have abandoned that criterion, all punishments have to be justified, if at all, on other grounds that have nothing to do with desert. Where the punishment of the innocent can be justified on those grounds (and it could in some cases be justified as a deterrent) it will be no less moral than any other punishment. Any distaste for it on the part of a Humanitarian will be merely a hang-over from the Retributive theory.

It is, indeed, important to notice that my argument so far supposes no evil intentions on the part of the Humanitarian and considers only what is involved in the logic of his position. My contention is that good men (not bad men) consistently acting upon that position would act as cruelly and unjustly as the greatest tyrants. They might in some respects act even worse. Of all tyrannies a tyranny sincerely exercised for the good of its victims may be the most oppressive. It may be better to live under robber barons than under omnipotent moral busybodies. The robber baron's cruelty may sometimes sleep, his cupidity may at some point be satiated; but those who torment us for our own good will torment us without end for they do so with the approval of their own conscience. They may be more likely to go to Heaven yet at the same time likelier to make a Hell of earth. Their very kindness stings with intolerable insult. To be "cured" against one's will and cured of states which we may not regard as disease is to be put on a level with those who have not yet reached the age of reason or those who never will; to be classed with infants, imbeciles, and domestic animals. But to be punished, however severely, because we have deserved it, because we "ought to have known better," is to be treated as a human person made in God's image.

In reality, however, we must face the possibility of bad rulers armed with a Humanitarian theory of punishment. A great many popular blue prints for a Christian society are merely what the Elizabethans called "eggs in moonshine" because they assume that the whole society is Christian or that the Christians are in control. This is not so in most contemporary States. Even if it were, our rulers would still be fallen men, and, therefore, neither very wise nor very good. As it is, they will usually be unbelievers. And since wisdom and virtue are not the only or the commonest qualifications for a place in the government, they will not often be even the best unbelievers. The practical problem of Christian politics is not that of drawing up schemes for a Christian society, but that of living as innocently as we can with unbelieving fellow-subjects under unbelieving rulers who will never be perfectly wise and good and who will sometimes be very wicked and very foolish. And when they are wicked the Humanitarian theory of punishment will put in their hands a finer instrument of tyranny than wickedness ever had before. For if crime and disease are to be regarded as the same thing, it follows that any state of mind which our masters choose to call "disease" can be treated as crime; and compulsorily cured. It will be vain to plead that states of mind which displease government need not always involve moral turpitude and do not therefore always deserve forfeiture of liberty. For our masters will not be using the concepts of Desert and Punishment but those of disease and cure.

We know that one school of psychology already regards religion as a neurosis. When this particular neurosis becomes inconvenient to government, what is to hinder government from proceeding to "cure" it? Such "cure" will, of course, be compulsory; but under the Humanitarian theory it will not be called by the shocking name of Persecution. No one will blame us for being Christian, no one will hate us, no one will revile us. The new Nero will approach us with the silky manners of a doctor, and though all will be in fact as compulsory as the *tunica molesta* or Smithfield or Tyburn, all will go on within the unemotional therapeutic sphere where words like "right" and "wrong" or "freedom" and "slavery" are never heard. And thus when the command is given, every prominent Christian in the land may vanish overnight into Institutions for the Treatment of the Ideologically Unsound, and it will rest with the expert gaolers to say when (if ever) they are to re-emerge. But it will not be persecution. Even if the treatment is painful, even if it is life-long, even if it is fatal, that will be only a regrettable accident; the intention was purely therapeutic. Even in ordinary medicine there were painful operations and fatal operations; so in this. But because they are "treatment," not punishment, they can be criticized only by fellow-experts and on technical grounds, never by men as men and on grounds of justice.

This is why I think it essential to oppose the Humanitarian theory of punishment, root and branch, whenever we encounter it. It carries on its front a semblance of mercy which is wholly false. That is how it can deceive men of good will. The error began, perhaps, with Shelley's statement that the distinction between mercy and justice was invented in the courts of tyrants. It sounds noble, and was indeed the error of a noble mind. But the distinction is essential. The older view was that mercy "tempered" justice, or (on the highest level of all) that mercy and justice had met and kissed. The essential act of mercy was to pardon; and pardon in its very essence involves the recognition of guilt and ill-desert in the recipient. If crime is only a disease which needs cure, not sin which deserves punishment, it cannot be pardoned. How can you pardon a man for having a gumboil or a club foot? But the Humanitarian theory wants simply to abolish Justice and substitute Mercy for it. This means that you start being "kind" to people before you have considered their rights, and then force upon them supposed kindnesses which they in fact had a right to refuse, and finally kindnesses which no one but you will recognize as kindnesses and which the recipient will feel as abominable cruelties. You have overshot the mark. Mercy, detached from Justice, grows unmerciful. That is the important paradox. As there are plants which will flourish only in mountain soil, so it appears that Mercy will flower only when it grows in the crannies of the rock of Justice: transplanted to the marshlands of mere Humanitarianism, it becomes a man-eating weed, all the more dangerous because it is still called by the same name as the mountain variety. But we ought long ago to have learned our lesson. We should be too old now to be deceived by those humane pretensions which have served to usher in every cruelty of the revolutionary period in which we live. These are the "precious balms" which will "break our heads."

There is a fine sentence in Bunyan: "It came burning hot into my mind, whatever he said, and however he flattered, when he got me home to his house, he would sell me for a slave." There is a fine couplet, too, in John Ball:

> Be ware ere ye be woe
> Know your friend from your foe.

One last word. You may ask why I send this to an Australian periodical. The reason is simple and perhaps worth recording: I can get no hearing for it in England.

Norval Morris and Donald Buckle

The Humanitarian Theory of Punishment
A Reply to C. S. Lewis

The University of Melbourne has recently established a Department of Criminology. Our Chairman is a Judge of the Supreme Court, and our Board includes specialists in Medicine, Psychology, Sociology, Psychiatry, and Criminology. Already it is clear that we all adhere, to a greater or less degree, to what C. S. Lewis in his entirely delightful article called a "Humanitarian Theory of Punishment."

His thesis is so profoundly opposed to our work as participants in this new Department that it is incumbent upon us to state our position; though we face this task with trepidation, seeing ourselves as Davids with literary slings incapable of delivering a series of blows as incisive as even one phrase from the armoury of Goliath Lewis.

Lewis' vital contention is that the Humanitarian Theory gives to the supposed expert an unwarranted and unjustified power over other men's lives. It is, of course, undeniable that to put a man in a white coat, or to give him a degree a psychology or sociology, does not diminish his sadistic potentialities or the disrupting effects of power on him. Such specialists must be regarded with that healthy scepticism of which Lewis is a fine champion; but scepticism should not lead us to deny their usefulness entirely, and insist—as does Lewis—on purely condign punishment, linked, as he phrases it, to the criminal's "desert." As we shall show, the use of the expert

Reprinted from *20th Century*, Vol. 6, No. 2 (Summer 1951-52), 20-26, with permission of the editor.

does not involve any abandonment of control over him. He can be kept on tap and yet not on top.

Let us attempt a reply to Lewis' article by advancing two propositions contrary to his thesis. First, the possibility of linking with the Humanitarian Theory of Punishment a just consideration of the interest of society and of the criminal. Secondly, the impossibility of his suggested return to the Retributive Theory of Punishment. If these propositions be demonstrated, there is little left of Lewis' argument; though its great worth as a warning against the uncontrolled allocation of powers remains.

Lewis rests his case on a suggested dichotomy in which a contrast is drawn between the "deserved" or "just" punishment on the one hand, and therapy or treatment on the other—the latter being the significant purpose of those upholding the Humanitarian Theory of Punishment. To us, this seems an unreal distinction. Whatever the punishment inflicted as a "just" punishment, whatever theory of punishment one may espouse, it cannot be denied that reformation procured in association with it is a desirable thing. To an extent, therefore, some concept of therapy is involved in every desirable theory of punishment. What Lewis opposes is that therapy should be procured through punishment (not in association with it but by means of it), arguing that if treatment be elevated to a purpose as distinct from a mere subsidiary part of a punishment we shall have been delivered over to omnipotent moral busybodies who will work cruelty without end.

Herein then lies the kernel of the discussion—Lewis regards reformation and deterrence as subsidiary and never as a justification of punishment and suggests that the Humanitarian Theory of Punishment has erected them into its vital aims. This, we believe, is a perversion of the Humanitarian theory. To us, the vital purpose of the criminal law is the *protection of the community*, always limiting and conditioning its punishments in the light of two other factors, namely, a determination by its actions never to deny the fundamental humanity of even the most depraved criminal, and secondly, a critical appraisal of the limits of our understandings of the springs of human conduct and our ability to predict its course. There is a third limitation imposed by the community's expectations of penal sanctions which we shall later consider.

Lewis' article omits any reference to the protection of the community as a valid aim of penal sanctions. He stresses the human personality of each individual criminal, and with this we agree. One human personality he overlooks, however, is the individual humanity of the potential *victim* of the criminal. It is this humanity we defend; the humanity of those whose only likely connection with the criminal law is the law's failure to protect them from clearly dangerous people.

There is, surely, a parallel in the medical sphere. None of us shrinks from imposing considerable limitations on the freedom of action of those suffering from an infectious disease, and it is perfectly clear that over a wide area we have a Humanitarian Theory of Social Medicine. By suggesting this, we do not mean to take up the completely determinist position, and do not argue that criminal actions are as inaccessible to the actor's control as are the germs that may infect him. Crime is not a personal disease; it cannot be equated to personal disease; it is, however, a social disease. Looked at from the point of view of society, crime is a disease of an integral part of that society. And it is a virus from which society must seek protection. Thus, Lewis' suggestion that the humanitarians think "all crime is more or less pathological" is untrue if he means by it that crime is regarded as individually pathological. No responsible authority would accept that crime is an individually pathological phenomenon; but it is quite clearly a socially pathological phenomenon. From the point of view of a society, therefore, the prime function of punishment must clearly be the protection of that society.

The complete absence of any regard for the potential victim of the criminal which runs through Lewis' article is to us somewhat shocking. His insistence on the individual personality of the criminal to the extent that the punishment must in some way be regarded by the community as deserved, as capable of being measured by an efficient punishment system, carries with it a total disregard for the essential personality of the potential victims of the criminal. *Per contra*, it seems to us that an argument for this aim of the criminal law—the protection of the community—is conclusive provided it does not carry with it any serious disadvantages. And the disadvantage Lewis sees, and which is undoubtedly a threat, is the possibility of the abuse of power necessarily given to those aiming to fulfil this purpose. *Can* the expert be kept on tap and not on top?

This risk of administrative abuse of power runs throughout the whole social pattern as we increasingly come to rely on the expert— in economics, in town planning, in many aspects of social organization, indeed in every sphere of our corporate life, including that of the detection and punishment of crime. One of the basic problems of our age is to erect effective controls by which we can make use of the services of experts and yet guard ourselves from their potential authoritarian danger. In the field of penal sanctions, because of our traditional awareness of this danger, this protection can fairly easily be guaranteed.

The Criminal Courts have traditionally represented the common man and the common man's view of morality. The Judges have earned the confidence of the people as unbiased and incorruptible men. The Courts have to hand excellent techniques for controlling the exuberance of the expert in criminology or penology. Let the ultimate control always reside in the Courts, let the expert always be accountable to them, let the criminal always have access to the Court, let the controls of natural justice which the law has built up be applicable, and, it is suggested, the tyranny which Lewis foreshadows will not eventuate. This type of protection of the individual citizen is surely not beyond the wit of a Nation that has built up the concept of a Parliament and the idea of a Jury.

A test case is given by one of the basic demands of those adhering to the Humanitarian theory: for certain types of criminals the Humanitarians wish to substitute for definite sentences some degree of indeterminacy as to the period those criminals will spend in prison. As Lewis points out, herein lies a real risk of tyranny. The answer is again to be found in the existing courts. These should require the expert to give evidence publicly and, subject to cross-examination, to substantiate the reasons for his decision concerning the release of the criminal. The prisoner should have the power to initiate this type of enquiry at regular intervals, and the onus of proof should never shift from the expert.

An example of wise techniques of judicial control of the indeterminate sentence is to be found in the recent Tasmanian Sexual Offences Act 1951, which allows the courts to impose several forms of indeterminate sentence accompanied by re-educative measures on certain sexual offenders. One of these sentences is called a Treatment Order, and section 13(2) of the Act protects the convicted criminal against the tyranny of the expert by providing that:

> A person against whom a treatment order has been made may petition the court to discharge the order upon the ground—
> (a) that the treatment is unreasonable;
> (b) that the treatment is ineffective;
> (c) that the treatment is not being given or is unduly protracted; or
> (d) that the . . . petitioner is cured of the indisposition which the order was made to cure.

The use of "indisposition" is infelicitous, and there may well be other grounds on which the criminal should be allowed to petition the court; but the need to avoid the abuse of power and the establishment of means of achieving this is clearly recognized in this Act as it is throughout Anglo-American jurisprudence. This recognition constitutes a complete rebuttal of Lewis' worst fears.

We therefore submit that we have demonstrated the practical possibility of a Humanitarian theory carrying with it a due regard for the interests both of society and of the individual criminal. Now let us suggest the impossibility of a return, as Lewis recommends, to the Retributive Theory of Punishment.

For certain types of criminals, given our present moral conscience, a return to a pure Retributive Theory is unthinkable. At both ends of the scale of punishment practically every civilized society has abandoned the Retributive Theory. With child criminals we have abandoned it quite explicitly, holding that the welfare of the child must frequently be regarded as a major consideration motivating courts charged with sentencing juvenile delinquents. The cost to the community of rewarding the larceny of a few sweets by a child with a punishment exactly equated to that social harm, has proved too expensive to be tolerated. It has been calculated that an incurable schizophrenic costs the community some £20,000 throughout his life, and it is clear that the adult criminal costs the community a great deal more. Therefore, both for the child's sake and for the community's, it is frequently necessary to reward the delinquent child with a punishment not "justly related," in the sense in which Lewis uses the phrase, to the offence he has committed. The emphasis must be on therapy. We suggest that there would be no responsible opinion reversing this development.

And at the other end of the scale of punishment the community has likewise abandoned any hint of a Retributive Theory. With habitual criminals every civilized society has abandoned any attempt to equate the punishment to the latest crime that that criminal committed. There are various techniques adopted all over the world. By some the habitual criminal is first punished for the crime he has committed and then held in prison for a protracted period on account of his being an habitual criminal. Others add together the man's dangerousness to the community and his latest offence, and impose a sentence on him as an habitual criminal which is clearly unrelated to that offence only. Here again nobody could tolerate the thought of abandoning this Humanitarian approach to punishment and reverting to a purely Retributive one.

It is, we agree, possible to gather some support for a return to the Retributive Theory of Punishment for the graver and more professional type of criminal who has not yet developed into the habitual criminal. It is possible to do this simply because we do not know very much about the causes of crime. It is not possible, however, to find support for such a retrograde step in regard to those people who are at present put on probation. These are asked to atone for their crimes by being good citizens. And the Courts, advised by those who have studied problems of punishment and by those probation officers who are working in society, have decided that the people they put on probation are good risks, that is to say, they are not likely to offend again. A Retributive Theory could not tolerate such an approach to the punishment of these more minor offenders. Agreed, there is room for mercy in a Retributive Theory, but it could not be universally applied mercy for certain types of crimes or criminals—if so, it would no longer be Retributive.

Thus for child delinquents, for habitual criminals, and for those on probation—to take only a few—the punishments accepted by all civilized societies as suitable are not "deserved" punishments in any expiatory talionic sense. This concept of "desert" is really the lynchpin of Lewis' article. As he sees it, the idea of the "deserved" or "just" punishment is an acceptance that for each offence, calculated in the light both of the crime committed and the history of crimes perpetuated by that individual, there is a price of punishment known fairly widely throughout the community—that there is, in other words, a price-list of deserved punishments. This may well be a true picture of what is in many men's minds; but it is only true for those people who consider a static situation in crime, who consider only two parties to any crime—the criminal and his victim. Now the contrast with this is the Humanitarian Theory which sees crime as a dynamic situation, not involving two parties, but involving many parties: not only a criminal and his victim, but a whole list of future potential victims who, unless they are protected with the best means at our disposal, are likely to suffer hardship. In arranging this protection, however, the Humanitarian must always remember that it should be related to the extent of current knowledge, and to the fact that the community must be expected to bear some risk for its dangerous and pathological elements.

We do not go to the extreme of denying importance to the community's conception of a "deserved" punishment. The punishments imposed on criminals serve purposes other than those we have canvassed—they constitute society's official pronouncement of the gravity with which any criminal action is viewed, and therefore assist in reinforcing that community's sense of right. This sense of right, this group super-ego, must never be exacerbated either by the too great leniency or the extreme severity of any punishment imposed. In other words, the community's sense of a just punishment will create the polarities of leniency and severity between which the criminal law may work out its other purposes.

Where we do deny the validity of this concept of the just or deserved punishment is where it is advanced as a basic philosophic justification of punishment, and not merely as a limiting factor. Kant and Hegel built theories of punishment around this concept which had no more connection with the day-to-day realities of our criminal law than with the pieces on the chess board. It is a similar erection of an emotional sense of right, not applied to the factual exigencies of the task faced by those imposing penal sanctions, that leads to such impossibilities as Lewis' suggested return to the Retributive Theory of Punishment.

By constantly making the experts justify to judges and to juries their actions in relation to criminals, punishment may be kept linked to the social conscience of the community. This, we submit, is a more truly comprehended "just" or "deserved" punishment than is the entirely emotional, atavistic approach which Lewis advocates.

It must not be assumed that Lewis' version of the Retributive Theory is itself completely satisfactory. Indeed, arguing from no less an authority than St. Thomas Aquinas, we may describe "retribution" as a deprivation or limitation of the individual's powers to continue to exercise his choice between good and evil acts in the area where his delinquency has occurred. (See Dr. Hawkins' article "Punishment and Moral Responsibility" at page 92 of *The King's Good Servant*—Papers read to the Thomas More Society of London, 1948.) In most cases, therefore, the punishment which will take the form of removal from society is itself the retribution, and should logically continue until the prisoner reaches a sufficient state of grace that he no longer intends to transgress. To us, there is no lack of conformity between theories derived from the Scholastic and Humanitarian philosophies.

Lewis may have been led to his conclusion by what appears to us an over-simplified view of the aetiology of crime. He appears to regard any crime solely as the result of a wrong choice between doing good or doing evil. We do not propose to wander into the morass of the free will-determinism argument, for we agree with Lewis that this is a cause of crime. We do not, however, regard it as the only cause of crime which is to us an extremely complicated moral, physical, psychological, and sociological phenomenon in which the totality of the criminal's inheritance and environment, together with his area of free will, will have causal connection with the crime he commits. To relate punishment to but one aetiological factor is to minimize the difficulty of fixing a rational sentence.

Our argument thus leads to a rejection of the Retributive Theory, not only on philosophical but also on purely practical political grounds, and to an acceptance of a morally just Humanitarian approach to punishment. It may be that a vital cause of our different view of punishment from that accepted by Lewis lies in our lower estimation of the efficacy of law as a means of social control. Law stands below Custom and well below Religion as a means of guiding men to the Good Life. It is a relatively blunt instrument of moral control, and should not be thought of as a means of achieving expiation of sin or completely just retribution for evil-doing.

Francis A. Allen

Criminal Justice, Legal Values and the Rehabilitative Ideal

ALTHOUGH ONE IS SOMETIMES inclined to despair of any constructive changes in the administration of criminal justice, a glance at the history of the past half-century reveals a succession of the most significant developments. Thus, the last fifty years have seen the widespread acceptance of three legal inventions of great importance: the juvenile court, systems of probation and of parole. During the same period, under the inspiration of continental research and writing, scientific criminology became an established field of instruction and inquiry in American universities and in other research agencies. At the same time, psychiatry made its remarkable contributions to the theory of human behavior and, more specifically, of that form of human behavior described as criminal. These developments have been accompanied by nothing less than a revolution in public conceptions of the nature of crime and the criminal, and in public attitudes toward the proper treatment of the convicted offender.[1]

This history with its complex developments of thought, institutional behavior, and public attitudes must be approached gingerly; for in dealing with it we are in peril of committing the sin of oversimplification. Nevertheless, despite the presence of contradictions and paradox, it seems possible to detect one common element in much of this thought and activity which goes far to characterize the

Reprinted with permission of the author and by special permission of *The Journal of Criminal Law, Criminology and Police Science*, Vol. 50, No.3 (September-October 1959), 226-232, © 1959 by the Northwestern University School of Law.

history we are considering. This common element or theme I shall describe, for want of a better phrase, as the rise of the rehabilitative ideal.

The rehabilitative ideal is itself a complex of ideas which, perhaps, defies completely precise statement. The essential points, however, can be articulated. It is assumed, first, that human behavior is the product of antecedent causes. These causes can be identified as part of the physical universe, and it is the obligation of the scientist to discover and to describe them with all possible exactitude. Knowledge of the antecedents of human behavior makes possible an approach to the scientific control of human behavior. Finally, and of primary significance for the purposes at hand, it is assumed that measures employed to treat the convicted offender should serve a therapeutic function, that such measures should be designed to effect changes in the behavior of the convicted person in the interests of his own happiness, health, and satisfactions and in the interest of social defense.

Although these ideas are capable of rather simple statement, they have provided the arena for some of the modern world's most acrimonious controversy. And the disagreements among those who adhere in general to these propositions have been hardly less intense than those prompted by the dissenters. This is true, in part, because these ideas possess a delusive simplicity. No idea is more pervaded with ambiguity than the notion of reform or rehabilitation. Assuming, for example, that we have the techniques to accomplish our ends of rehabilitation, are we striving to produce in the convicted offender something called "adjustment" to his social environment or is our objective something different from or more than this? By what scale of values do we determine the ends of therapy?[2]

These are intriguing questions, well worth extended consideration. But it is not my purpose to pursue them in this paper. Rather, I am concerned with describing some of the dilemmas and conflicts of values that have resulted from efforts to impose the rehabilitative ideal on the system of criminal justice. I know of no area in which a more effective demonstration can be made of the necessity for greater mutual understanding between the law and the behavioral disciplines.

There is, of course, nothing new in the notion of reform or rehabilitation of the offender as one objective of the penal process.

This idea is given important emphasis, for example, in the thought of the medieval churchmen. The church's position, as described by Sir Francis Palgrave, was that punishment was not to be "thundered in vengeance for the satisfaction of the state, but imposed for the good of the offender: in order to afford the means of amendment and to lead the transgressor to repentance, and to mercy."[3] Even Jeremy Bentham, whose views modern criminology has often scorned and more often ignored, is found saying: "It is a great merit in a punishment to contribute to the *reformation of the offender*, not only through fear of being punished again, but by a change in his character and habits."[4] But this is far from saying that the modern expression of the rehabilitative ideal is not to be sharply distinguished from earlier expressions. The most important differences, I believe, are two. First, the modern statement of the rehabilitative ideal is accompanied by, and largely stems from, the development of scientific disciplines concerned with human behavior, a development not remotely approximated in earlier periods when notions of reform of the offender were advanced. Second, and of equal importance for the purposes at hand, in no other period has the rehabilitative ideal so completely dominated theoretical and scholarly inquiry, to such an extent that in some quarters it is almost assumed that matters of treatment and reform of the offender are the only questions worthy of serious attention in the whole field of criminal justice and corrections.

THE NARROWING OF SCIENTIFIC INTERESTS

THIS NARROWING OF INTERESTS prompted by the rise of the rehabilitative ideal during the past half-century should put us on our guard. No social institutions as complex as those involved in the administration of criminal justice serve a single function or purpose. Social institutions are multi-valued and multi-purposed. Values and purposes are likely on occasion to prove inconsistent and to produce internal conflict and tension. A theoretical orientation that evinces concern for only one or a limited number of purposes served by the institution must inevitably prove partial and unsatisfactory. In certain situations it may prove positively dangerous. This stress on the unfortunate consequences of the rise of the rehabilitative ideal need not involve failure to recognize the substantial benefits that have also accompanied its emergence. Its emphasis on the fundamental problems of human behavior, its numerous contributions to the decency of the criminal-law processes are of vital importance. But the limitations and dangers of modern trends of thought need clearly to be identified in the interest, among others, of the rehabilitative ideal, itself.

My first proposition is that the rise of the rehabilitative ideal has dictated what questions are to be investigated, with the result that many matters of equal or even greater importance have been ignored or cursorily examined. This tendency can be abundantly illustrated. Thus, the concentration of interest on the nature and needs of the criminal has resulted in a remarkable absence of interest in the nature of crime. This is, indeed, surprising, for on reflection it must be apparent that the question of what is a crime is logically the prior issue: how crime is defined determines in large measure who the criminal is who becomes eligible for treatment and therapy.[5] A related observation was made some years ago by Professor Karl Llewellyn, who has done as much as any man to develop sensible interdisciplinary inquiry involving law and the behavioral disciplines:[6] "When I was younger I used to hear smuggish assertions among my sociological friends, such as: 'I take the sociological, *not* the legal, approach to crime'; and I suspect an enquiring reporter could still hear much the same (perhaps with 'psychiatric' often substituted for 'sociological')—though it is surely somewhat obvious that when you take 'the legal' out, you also take out 'crime.'"[7] This disinterest in the definition of criminal behavior has afflicted the lawyers quite as much as the behavioral scientists. Even the criminal law scholar has tended, until recently, to assume that problems of procedure and treatment are the things that "really matter."[8] Only the issue of criminal responsibility as affected by mental disorder has attracted the consistent attention of the non-lawyer, and the literature reflecting this interest is not remarkable for its cogency or its wisdom. In general, the behavioral sciences have left other issues relevant to crime definition largely in default. There are a few exceptions. Dr. Hermann Mannheim, of the London School of Economics, has manifested intelligent interest in these matters.[9] The late Professor Edwin Sutherland's studies of "white-collar crime"[10] may also be mentioned, although, in my judgment,

Professor Sutherland's efforts in this field are among the least perceptive and satisfactory of his many valuable contributions.[11]

The absence of wide-spread interest in these areas is not to be explained by any lack of challenging questions. Thus, what may be said of the relationships between legislative efforts to subject certain sorts of human behavior to penal regulation and the persistence of police corruption and abuse of power?[12] Studies of public attitudes toward other sorts of criminal legislation might provide valuable clues as to whether given regulatory objectives are more likely to be attained by the provision of criminal penalties or by other kinds of legal sanctions. It ought to be re-emphasized that the question, what sorts of behavior should be declared criminal, is one to which the behavioral sciences might contribute vital insights. This they have largely failed to do, and we are the poorer for it.

Another example of the narrowing of interests that has accompanied the rise of the rehabilitative ideal is the lack of concern with the idea of deterrence—indeed the hostility evinced by many modern criminologists toward it. This, again, is a most surprising development.[13] It must surely be apparent that the criminal law has a general preventive function to perform in the interests of public order and of security of life, limb, and possessions. Indeed, there is reason to assert that the influence of criminal sanctions on the millions who never engage in serious criminality is of greater social importance than their impact on the hundreds of thousands who do. Certainly, the assumption of those who make our laws is that the denouncing of conduct as criminal and providing the means for the enforcement of the legislative prohibitions will generally have a tendency to prevent or minimize such behavior. Just what the precise mechanisms of deterrence are is not well understood. Perhaps it results, on occasion, from the naked threat of punishment. Perhaps, more frequently, it derives from a more subtle process wherein the mores and moral sense of the community are recruited to advance the attainment of the criminal law's objectives.[14] The point is that we know very little about these vital matters, and the resources of the behavioral sciences have rarely been employed to contribute knowledge and insight in their investigation. Not only have the criminologists displayed little interest in these matters, some have suggested that the whole idea of general prevention is invalid or worse. Thus, speaking of the deterrent theory of punishment, the authors of a leading textbook in criminology assert: "This is simply a derived rationalization of revenge. Though social revenge is the actual psychological basis of punishment today, the apologists for the punitive regime are likely to bring forward in their defense the more sophisticated, but equally futile, contention that punishment deters from [*sic*] crime."[15] We are thus confronted by a situation in which the dominance of the rehabilitative ideal not only diverts attention from many serious issues, but leads to a denial that these issues even exist.

Debasement of the Rehabilitative Ideal

Now PERMIT ME to turn to another sort of difficulty that has accompanied the rise of the rehabilitative ideal in the areas of corrections and criminal justice. It is a familiar observation that an idea once propagated and introduced into the active affairs of life undergoes change. The real significance of an idea as it evolves in actual practice may be quite different from that intended by those who conceived it and gave it initial support. An idea tends to lead a life of its own; and modern history is full of the unintended consequences of seminal ideas. The application of the rehabilitative ideal to the institutions of criminal justice presents a striking example of such a development. My second proposition, then, is that the rehabilitative ideal has been debased in practice and that the consequences resulting from this debasement are serious and, at times, dangerous.

This proposition may be supported, first, by the observation that, under the dominance of the rehabilitative ideal, the language of therapy is frequently employed, wittingly or unwittingly, to disguise the true state of affairs that prevails in our custodial institutions and at other points in the correctional process. Certain measures, like the sexual psychopath laws, have been advanced and supported as therapeutic in nature when, in fact, such a characterization seems highly dubious.[16] Too often the vocabulary of therapy has been exploited to serve a public-relations function. Recently, I visited an institution devoted to the diagnosis and treatment of disturbed children. The institution had been established with high hopes and, for once, with the enthusiastic support of the state legislature. Nevertheless, fifty minutes of an hour's lecture, delivered by a supervising psychiatrist before we toured the building, were devoted to custodial problems. This fixation on problems of custody was reflected in the institutional arrangements which included, under a properly euphemistic label, a cell for solitary confinement.[17] Even more disturbing was the tendency of the staff to justify these custodial measures in therapeutic terms. Perhaps on occasion the requirements of institutional security and treatment coincide. But the inducements to self-deception in such situations are strong and all too apparent. In short, the language of therapy has frequently provided a formidable obstacle to a realistic analysis of the conditions that confront us. And realism in considering these problems is the one quality that we require above all others.[18]

There is a second sort of unintended consequence that has resulted from the application of the rehabilitative ideal to the practical administration of criminal justice. Surprisingly enough, the rehabilitative ideal has often led to increased severity of penal measures. This tendency may be seen in the operation of the juvenile court. Although frequently condemned by the popular press as a device of leniency, the juvenile court is authorized to intervene punitively in many situations in which the conduct, were it committed by an adult, would be wholly ignored by the law or would subject the adult to the mildest of sanctions. The tendency of proposals for wholly indeterminate sentences, a clearly identifiable fruit of the rehabilitative ideal,[19] is unmistakably in the direction of lengthened periods of imprisonment. A large variety of statutes authorizing what is called "civil" commitment of persons, but which, except for the reduced protections afforded the parties proceeded against, are essentially criminal in nature, provide for absolutely indeterminate periods of confinement. Experience has demonstrated that, in practice, there is a strong tendency for the rehabilitative ideal to serve purposes that are essentially incapacitative rather than therapeutic in character.[20]

The Rehabilitative Ideal and Individual Liberty

The reference to the tendency of the rehabilitative ideal to encourage increasingly long periods of incarceration brings me to my final proposition. It is that the rise of the rehabilitative ideal has often been accompanied by attitudes and measures that conflict,

sometimes seriously, with the values of individual liberty and volition. As I have already observed, the role of the behavioral sciences
in the administration of criminal justice and in the areas of public
policy lying on the borderland of the criminal law is one of obvious
importance. But I suggest that, if the function of criminal justice is
considered in its proper dimensions, it will be discovered that the
most fundamental problems in these areas are not those of psychiatry, sociology, social case work, or social psychology. On the
contrary, the most fundamental problems are those of political
philosophy and political science. The administration of the criminal
law presents to any community the most extreme issues of the
proper relations of the individual citizen to state power. We are
concerned here with the perennial issue of political authority: Under what circumstances is the state justified in bringing its force to
bear on the individual human being? These issues, of course, are not
confined to the criminal law, but it is in the area of penal regulation
that they are most dramatically manifested. The criminal law, then,
is located somewhere near the center of the political problem, as the
history of the twentieth century abundantly reveals. It is no accident, after all, that the agencies of criminal justice and law enforcement are those first seized by an emerging totalitarian regime.[21] In
short, a study of criminal justice is most fundamentally a study in
the exercise of political power. No such study can properly avoid
the problem of the abuse of power.

The obligation of containing power within the limits suggested
by a community's political values has been considerably complicated by the rise of the rehabilitative ideal. For the problem today is
one of regulating the exercise of power by men of good will, whose
motivations are to help not to injure, and whose ambitions are quite
different from those of the political adventurer so familiar to history. There is a tendency for such persons to claim immunity from
the usual forms of restraint and to insist that professionalism and a
devotion to science provide sufficient protections against unwarranted invasion of individual right. This attitude is subjected to
mordant crticism by Aldous Huxley in his recent book, "Brave
New World Revisited." Mr. Huxley observes: "There seems to be
a touching belief among certain Ph.D's in sociology that Ph.D's in
sociology will never be corrupted by power. Like Sir Galahad's,
their strength is the strength of ten because their heart is pure—and

their heart is pure because they are scientists and have taken six thousand hours of social studies."[22] I suspect that Mr. Huxley would be willing to extend his point to include professional groups other than the sociologists. There is one proposition which, if generally understood, would contribute more to clear thinking on these matters than any other. It is not a new insight. Seventy years ago the Italian criminologist, Garafalo, asserted: "The mere deprivation of liberty, however benign the administration of the place of confinement, is undeniably punishment."[23] This proposition may be rephrased as follows: Measures which subject individuals to the substantial and involuntary deprivation of their liberty are essentially punitive in character, and this reality is not altered by the facts that the motivations that prompt incarceration are to provide therapy or otherwise contribute to the person's well-being or reform. As such, these measures must be closely scrutinized to insure that power is being applied consistently with those values of the community that justify interferences with liberty for only the most clear and compelling reasons.

But the point I am making requires more specific and concrete application to be entirely meaningful. It should be pointed out, first, that the values of individual liberty may be imperiled by claims to knowledge and therapeutic technique that we, in fact, do not possess and by failure candidly to concede what we do not know. At times, practitioners of the behavioral sciences have been guilty of these faults. At other times, such errors have supplied the assumptions on which legislators, lawyers and lay people generally have proceeded. Ignorance, in itself, is not disgraceful so long as it is unavoidable. But when we rush to measures affecting human liberty and human dignity on the assumption that we know what we do not know or can do what we cannot do, then the problem of ignorance takes on a more sinister hue.[24] An illustration of these dangers is provided by the sexual psychopath laws, to which I return; for they epitomize admirably some of the worst tendencies of modern practice. These statutes authorize the indefinite incarceration of persons believed to be potentially dangerous in their sexual behavior. But can such persons be accurately identified without substantial danger of placing persons under restraint who, in fact, provide no serious danger to the community? Having once confined them, is there any body of knowledge that tells us how to treat and cure them? If so, as a practical matter, are facilities and therapy available for these purposes in the state institutions provided for the confinement of such persons?[25] Questions almost as serious can be raised as to a whole range of other measures. The laws providing for commitment of persons displaying the classic symptoms of psychosis and advanced mental disorder have proved a seductive analogy for other proposals. But does our knowledge of human behavior really justify the extension of these measures to provide for the indefinite commitment of persons otherwise afflicted? We who represent the disciplines that in some measure are concerned with the control of human behavior are required to act under weighty responsibilities. It is no paradox to assert that the real utility of scientific technique in the fields under discussion depends on an accurate realization of the limits of scientific knowledge.

There are other ways in which the modern tendencies of thought accompanying the rise of the rehabilitative ideal have imperiled the basic political values. The most important of these is the encouragement of procedural laxness and irregularity. It is my impression that there is greater awareness of these dangers today than at some other times in the past, for which, if true, we perhaps have Mr. Hitler to thank. Our increased knowledge of the functioning of totalitarian regimes makes it more difficult to assert that the insistence on decent and orderly procedure represents simply a lawyer's quibble or devotion to outworn ritual. Nevertheless, in our courts of so-called "socialized justice" one may still observe, on occasion, a tendency to assume that, since the purpose of the proceeding is to "help" rather than to "punish," some lack of concern in establishing the charges against the person before the court may be justified. This position is self-defeating and otherwise indefensible. A child brought before the court has a right to demand, not only the benevolent concern of the tribunal, but justice. And one may rightly wonder as to the value of therapy purchased at the expense of justice. The essential point is that the issues of treatment and therapy be kept clearly distinct from the question of whether the person committed the acts which authorize the intervention of state power in the first instance.[26] This is a principle often violated. Thus, in some courts the judge is supplied a report on the offender by the psychiatric clinic before the judgment of guilt or acquittal is announced. Such reports, while they may be relevant to the defendant's need for therapy or confinement, ordinarily are wholly irrelevant to the issue of his guilt of the particular offense charged. Yet it asks too much of human nature to assume that the judge is never influenced on the issue of guilt or innocence by a strongly adverse psychiatric report.

Let me give one final illustration of the problems that have accompanied the rise of the rehabilitative ideal. Some time ago we encountered a man in his eighties incarcerated in a state institution. He had been confined for some thirty years under a statute calling for the automatic commitment of defendants acquitted on grounds of insanity in criminal trials. It was generally agreed by the institution's personnel that he was not then psychotic and probably had never been psychotic. The fact seemed to be that he had killed his wife while drunk. An elderly sister of the old man was able and willing to provide him with a home, and he was understandably eager to leave the institution. When we asked the director of the institution why the old man was not released, he gave two significant answers. In the first place, he said, the statute requires me to find that this inmate is no longer a danger to the community; this I cannot do, for he may kill again. And of course the director was right. However unlikely commission of homicide by such a man in his eighties might appear, the director could not be certain. But, as far as that goes, he also could not be certain about himself or about you or me. The second answer was equally interesting. The old man, he said, is better off here. To understand the full significance of this reply it is necessary to know something about the place of confinement. Although called a hospital, it was in fact a prison, and not at all a progressive prison. Nothing worthy of the name of therapy was provided and very little by way of recreational facilities.

This case points several morals. It illustrates, first, a failure of the law to deal adequately with the new requirements being placed upon it. The statute, as a condition to the release of the inmate, required the director of the institution virtually to warrant the future good behavior of the inmate, and, in so doing, made unrealistic and impossible demands on expert judgment. This might be remedied by the formulation of release criteria more consonant with actuality. Provisions for conditional release to test the inmate's reaction to the free community would considerably reduce the strain on administrative decision-making. But there is more here. Perhaps the case reflects that arrogance and insensitivity to human values to which men who have no reason to doubt their own motives appear peculiarly susceptible.[27]

Conclusion

In these remarks I have attempted to describe certain of the continuing problems and difficulties associated with, what I have called, the rise of the rehabilitative ideal. In so doing, I have not sought to cast doubt on the substantial benefits associated with that movement. It has exposed some of the most intractable problems of our time to the solvent properties of human intelligence. Moreover, the devotion to the ideal of empirical investigation provides the movement with a self-correcting mechanism of great importance, and justifies hopes for constructive future development.

Nevertheless, no intellectual movement produces only unmixed blessings. It has been suggested in these remarks that the ascendency of the rehabilitative ideal has, as one of its unfortunate consequences, diverted attention from other questions of great criminological importance. This has operated unfavorably to the full development of criminological science. Not only is this true, but the failure of many students and practitioners in the relevant areas to concern themselves with the full context of criminal justice has produced measures dangerous to basic political values and has, on occasion, encouraged the debasement of the rehabilitative ideal to produce results, unsupportable whether measured by the objectives of therapy or of corrections. The worst manifestations of these tendencies are undoubtedly deplored as sincerely by competent therapists as by other persons. But the occurrences are neither so infrequent nor so trivial that they can be safely ignored.

NOTES

---

1. These developments have been surveyed in Allen, *Law and the Future: Criminal Law and Administration*, 51 Nw. L. Rev. 207, 207–208 (1956). See also Harno, *Some Significant Developments in Criminal Law and Procedure in the Last Century*, 42 J. Crim L., C. and P.S. 427 (1951).

2. "We see that it is not easy to determine what we consider to be the sickness and what we consider to be the cure." Fromm, Psychoanalysis and Religion (1950) 73. See also the author's development of these points at 67–77.

3. Quoted in Dalzell, Benefit of Clergy and Related Matters (1955) 13.

4. Bentham, The Theory of Legislation (Ogden, C. K., ed., 1931) 338–339. (Italics in the original.) But Bentham added: "But when [the writers] come to speak about the means of preventing offenses, of rendering men better, of perfecting morals, their imagination grows warm, their hopes excited; one would suppose they were about to produce the great secret, and that the human race was going to receive a new form. It is because we have a more magnificent idea of objects in proportion as they are less familiar, and because the imagination has a loftier flight amid vague projects which have never been subjected to the limits of analysis," Id., at 359.

5. Cf. Hart, *The Aims of the Criminal Law*, 23 Law and Cont. Prob. 401 (1958).

6. See Llewellyn and Hoebel, The Cheyenne Way (1941). See also *Crime, Law and Social Science: A Symposium*, 34 Colum. L. Rev. 277 (1934).

7. *Law and the Social Sciences—Especially Sociology*, 62 Harv. L. Rev. 1286, 1287 (1949).

8. Allen, *op. cit. supra*, note 1, at 207–210.

9. See, especially, his Criminal Justice and Social Reconstruction (1946).

10. White-Collar Crime (1949). See also Clinard, The Black Market (1952).

11. Cf. Caldwell, *A Re-examination of the Concept of White-Collar Crime*, 22 Fed. Prob. 30 (March, 1958).

12. An interesting question of this kind is now being debated in England centering on the proposals for enhanced penalties for prostitution offenses made in the recently-issued Wolfenden Report. See Fairfield, *Notes on Prostitution*, 9 Brit. J. Delin. 164, 173 (1959). See also Allen, *The Borderland of the Criminal Law: Problems of "Socializing" Criminal Justice*, 32 Soc. Ser. Rev. 107, 110, 111 (1958).

13. But see Andenaes, *General Prevention—Illusion or Reality?** 43 J. Crim. L., C. and P.S. 176 (1952).

14. This seems to be the assertion of Garafalo. See his Criminology (Millar trans. 1914) 241–242.

15. Barnes and Teeters, New Horizons in Criminology (2nd ed. 1954) 337. The context in which these statements appear also deserves attention.

16. See note 25, *infra*.

17. As I recall, it was referred to as the "quiet room." In another institution the boy was required to stand before a wall while a seventy pound fire hose was played on his back. This procedure went under the name of "hydrotherapy."

* Also reprinted in this volume.

18. Cf. Wechsler, *Law, Morals and Psychiatry*, 18 Colum. L. School News 2, 4 (March 4, 1959): "The danger rather is that coercive regimes we would not sanction in the name of punishment or of correction will be sanctioned in the name of therapy without providing the resources for a therapeutic operation."

19. Cf. Tappan, *Sentencing under the Model Penal Code*, 23 Law and Cont. Prob. 538, 530 (1958).

20. Cf. Jerome Hall, General Principles of Criminal Law (1947) 551. And see Sellin, The Protective Code: A Swedish Proposal (1957) 9.

21. This development in the case of Germany may be gleaned from Crankshaw, Gestapo (1956).

22. Huxley, Brave New World Revisited (1958) 34–35.

23. *Op. cit. supra*, note 14, at 256.

24. I have developed these points in Allen, *op. cit. supra*, note 12, at 113–115.

25. Many competent observers have asserted that none of these inquiries can properly be answered in the affirmative. See, e.g., Sutherland, *The Sexual Psychopath Laws*, 40 J. Crim. L., C. and P.S. 543 (1950). Hacker and Frym, *The Sexual Psychopath Act in Practice: A Critical Discussion*, 43 Calif. L. Rev. 766 (1955). See also Tappan, The Habitual Sex Offender (Report of the New Jersey Commission) (1950).

26. A considerable literature has developed on these issues. See, e.g., Allen, *The Borderland of the Criminal Law: Problems of "Socializing" Criminal Justice*, 32 Soc. Ser. Rev. 107 (1958), Diana, *The Rights of Juvenile Delinquents: An Appraisal of Juvenile Court Proceedings*, 44 J. Crim. L., C. and P.S. 561 (1957), Paulsen, *Fairness to the Juvenile Offender*, 41 Minn. L. Rev. 547 (1957); Waite, *How Far Can Court Procedures Be Socialized Without Impairing Individual Rights?* 12 J. Crim. L. and C. 430 (1921).

27. One further recent and remarkable example is provided by the case, In re Maddox, 351 Mich. 358, 88 N.W. 2d 470 (1958). Professor Wechsler, *op. cit. supra*, note 18, at 4, describes the facts and holding as follows: "Only the other day, the Supreme Court of Michigan ordered the release of a prisoner in their State prison at Jackson, who had been transferred from the Ionia State Hospital to which he was committed as a psychopath. The ground of transfer, which was defended seriously by a State psychiatrist, was that the prisoner was 'adamant' in refusing to admit sexual deviation that was the basis of his commitment; and thus, in the psychiatrist's view, resistant to therapy! The Court's answer was, of course, that he had not been tried for an offense."

INTEGRATIVE

F. J. O. Coddington

Problems of Punishment

The Laws Themselves

The origins of Criminal Law and Punishment are, of course, obscure, and there are varied theories on the topic. According to some,
the origins are separate. There may be punishment without law, or
law without punishment. Punishment of a person who has not
broken any rule of law is exemplified where the tribe stones to
death, or exiles, a member supposed to possess the evil eye. One who
is considered to be a danger to the community is eliminated. I do not
think that anything less than elimination is applied at this stage of
development. This is one of the early barbarisms which was revived
by the Nazis.

On the other hand, there have been laws in the sense that there
have been clearly defined and hardened customs which everybody
was supposed to follow. But if a man did not, he did not necessarily
suffer at the hands of the State or Court in any defined manner for
his breach of *mores*.

In later developments, these two methods of tribal behaviour
came into contact with a third, namely, the Vendetta, and redemption by purchase. Later still, came a code of laws and a system of
fines and mutilations as well as of capital punishment and outlawry.

There is little to be learnt from the history of criminal law
except to note that certain very primitive reactions still remain, at
least vestigially. There is the vendetta, revenge—which is replaced

From *Proceedings of the Aristotelian Society*, Vol. 46 (1946), 155-178, © 1946
by the Aristotelian Society. Reprinted by courtesy of the Editor of the Aristotelian
Society.

by the action of the State instead of that of the individual. There is the idea of redemption, the buying off of revenge by the payment of money.

This also develops to the idea of attaching a value to each wrong, which leads to a maximum fine, and also to *lex talionis,* an eye for an eye—a tooth for a tooth. The idea of payment for wrongs done was also used by the King for the purpose of extorting revenue. In the end we come to the three historically leading ideas of Criminal Law: that a specific wrong definable by a formula must have been committed before a man is declared a criminal; that he must pay for this in some form or another; and that there must be a tariff for such payment.

A modern criminal law is usually described as a "prohibition," though, of course, there are many laws, for instance, as to the construction and use of motor vehicles, which are more properly described as "positive" commands. Practically all criminal laws have this peculiarity, that criminal procedure is not invoked until the law has been broken. In other words, no matter how powerful the State is, it is incapable of making every citizen obey its prohibitions. Criminal procedure is in the nature of a post mortem. The law has been broken: what, if anything, is to be done about it? Whether by accident or design, a great many English criminal laws are framed as if to answer or avoid this difficult question, because they run: "If any man shall do so and so, he shall be liable to such and such punishment"—the punishment stated being, of course, in the majority of cases, a maximum. Here, the legislature recognises quite clearly that some people will infringe the prohibition, and sets the maximum pains they shall suffer in consequence. Punishment, therefore, is not enforcement of the law, as it is sometimes inaccurately called, whatever else it be.

There are a few cases in which a minimum penalty is specified: usually it is a minimum fine in a case where the infringement of the prohibition results in an illegal profit to the offender: and the minimum is to be calculated on the basis that the man shall not make a financial profit by his offence.

In some other countries there are minimum punishments as to length of imprisonment, and so on, but I do not know of any in English law, except that there are a few offences, such as murder, where the only punishment is death. Even here, the King, through his Minister, may reduce or remit the punishment.

We are apt to take it for granted that all the Criminal Laws of a nation are closely related to their code of ethics. This is not necessarily true where the King is sufficiently powerful, and is obeyed by the armed forces of the State. Some, at any rate, of the laws of Rome under the Emperors ran contrary to the ethical code of the Romans. In a modern democracy the majority of the criminal laws, particularly the basic ones, such as "Thou shalt not steal," have the approval of the people, while the many detailed regulations for the controlling of conduct in our complex civilisation are taken on trust by the mass of the people as representing rules made for their benefit and more or less consonant with their ideas of right and wrong.

On the other hand, as we could see in Nazi Germany, the legislators and the dictatorship may preach a new morality, and impose corresponding laws, so as gradually to train the public into approval of a new code of behaviour, which may be contrary to that held previously, or by the majority of mankind.

The same thing has happened in England to a lesser extent. For instance, during the war, by means of prohibitions and punishments, the Courts have sought to train people into regarding it as wicked to show a light after dark, or to drive a car more than 20 m.p.h. in a town at night, or to spread alarm and despondency, and so on and so forth. There is, therefore, a constant interaction between the general moral judgment and the body of criminal prohibitions, but certainly, in an outspoken democracy like England, it is dangerous for a Court to attempt to enforce prohibitions which flagrantly contradict the moral sense of the community.

The ideal basic purpose of a code of criminal law, and, in my opinion (though here I tread on dangerous ground), the basis of any practical code of ethics is satisfactory order. It is no accident that law and order are continually bracketed together. Just as we organise our intellectual world into a coherent systematised universe as far as we can, so we organise our judgments of behaviour into a system. We say, in effect, if everybody behaved according to our system, the world would go smoothly, there would be the minimum of quarrelling, of disputes, and of avoidable unhappiness. And, similarly, the English ideal purpose of a criminal code of law is, that men's conduct should be orderly, should interact as smoothly as possible, and that there should be no deprivation of the freedom of any individual except for the corresponding benefit of the community.

Thus, satisfactory order, or something like it, is the ostensible purpose of law. In practice, this may be warped by oppressive laws against one person or class for the benefit of other persons or classes, or for the purpose of obtaining additional revenue for the State, and so on. But whatever in practice may be the imperfections of our laws, the fact that they are intended for the preservation of person and property, of liberty, and of the smooth working of everyday life, is what leads to their support and help in enforcement by the general public in England to a greater extent than in other parts of the world.

THEORY AND PRACTICE

The Purposes of Punishment

I now wish to approach the basic questions: Why should we have any Laws? What are Criminal Laws? Why should we punish an infraction of the Law? What is punishment? and what purposes should we try to achieve in punishment? and if there are several, how should they be balanced? and what is the practical result?

I don't think anybody but an ethical theoretician would seriously ask, either what is a criminal law, or why should we have one? In any organised society of conscious beings there must be rules of conduct, and the more complex the society, and the higher the consciousness of the units, the more rules will there be, and the greater is the likelihood that they will be broken by individuals.

Ideally, a Criminal Law is a command, usually a prohibition, against anti-social conduct; that is to say, against conduct which will interfere with the order and smooth and satisfactory running of the society, and any such explanation of the law demonstrates the necessity that there should be such laws, otherwise chaos would come again. It is of the nature of such a law that practically everybody is ordered to obey it.

What, then, is to happen if an individual disobeys the law? And the first answer to this surely must be that something must be done to demonstrate that the law is a law, and not a mere request, or pious opinion of what conduct is appropriate. Law is not a law, at any rate in modern times, without a sanction. This we may call punishment. Punishment is required to vindicate the law. Vindication is the best word I have been able to find to express in one word the first necessary purpose of punishment. Etymologically, it combines the root meanings of strength and speech, i.e., using power and proclaiming. Historically and in fact this may apply to reward as well as to infliction of pain, and suggests the wide variety available for punishment. What, then, is punishment? In practice, and in my submission, in correct theory also, the basis of punishment is that the offender is put within the power of the Court. The Court has the power to choose whether the offender shall suffer a certain ill up to a maximum, or whether he shall be treated in some other way. He may be made to suffer an actual ill, such as imprisonment, or a fine, or he may be compelled to undergo procedure for his reformation, such as being put on 'probation,' or sent to some educational institution, school, Borstal, hostel, or so on, or he may be merely made to promise not to offend again (for a certain limit of time), or he may even be set free by the Court on that understanding. But in every case, and whatever the Court does, the essence of the matter is that the offender loses his freedom of choice of behaviour to a greater or lesser extent, and that the Court acquires a power to deal with the offender (within defined limits), so that the offender loses freedom, and the Court acquires power, in a manner and to a definite extent, which would not happen but for the proof of the commission of the offence. This loss of freedom and corresponding acquirement of power is the essential vindication of the law in a modern State.

Of course the matter does not stop there. The Court does not merely acquire this power—it exercises it. And it exercises it not in a purely capricious way, but with what we call a judicial discretion, that is to say, appropriately for the achievement of a suitable end.

The exercise of this power is the secondary and the visible vindication of the law. I want to emphasise this vindication of the law because it seems to me to have both theoretical value and historical exemplification.

Our lesser Courts of Criminal Law have throughout the centuries framed their conduct on the model of the greater Criminal Law Courts, presided over by the High Court Judges. They have done this partly from a natural desire to copy the approved model, and partly because of the practical necessity to avoid frequent successful appeals to the High Courts, or to those trained in the High Courts, from their decisions. High Court Judges have always previously been advocates practising in Law Courts for most of their adult lives, living in, for, by, and with, the law. Such men have naturally valued the practice, procedure, and power of the law above everything. They have for generations attached a higher value to correctness of procedure, than to the output of true justice in the conduct of trials. On the one hand, uncounted thousands of obviously guilty criminals, even murderers, have up to this day been acquitted and set free to prey upon the public again, because of some defect in the procedure of their trial, demonstrating quite clearly that the judges regard the safety of the public as far less important than the enforcement of technically correct procedure. On the other hand, where the procedure has been correct, in former times many of the sentences imposed were to modern ideas savage and cruel—but in their very ferocity demonstrating and glorifying the power of the law.

The contrast between procedure and severity was strikingly demonstrated in those days when a thief or a murderer who could claim benefit of Clergy was handed over unpunished to the ecclesiastical authorities, who appear to have done little to him, while the man who could not read was hanged even for what, in modern times, we should regard as a trivial offence.

Let me return from this historical excursion to my central theme. Punishment is essential to differentiate a law from a request. The basis of punishment, the fundamental vindication of law, is that the proved offender is placed within the power of the Court. The action of the Court in using that power, with judicial discretion, is punishment, the essence of which is the imposition of the will of the Court upon the behaviour of the offender for a limited period of time in the future.

As I have pointed out, and shall later detail, the use of the power of the Court may actually result in something which is positively pleasant to the offender, just as a doctor may give his patient a tasty medicine, and for this reason many prefer to speak of the "treatment" of the delinquent, but as whatever is done is done in the exercise of power acquired by reason of the finding of guilt and is imposed upon the offender, I prefer to stick to the original word "punishment" to cover any treatment, pleasant or unpleasant, emanating from the Court.

What is to guide the Court in the exercise of its judicial discretion in choosing what it shall do to the offender? A number of obvious and easy answers to this question have been proposed. None of them is by itself satisfactory. To mention one in passing: some idealists contend that the crime of the individual is the fault of society and that, therefore, society should as it were punish itself by so altering the environment of the criminal it has sinned against that he no longer is tempted to offend. Such a theory obviously has no application to such offences as driving with ineffective brakes, failing to fence machinery, or adulterating wine. Even when it might be thought to apply, it observes environment and overlooks heredity, and both factors are fundamental; and, in any event, it is too remote from the daily facts of life as revealed in Court. In so far as this theory has any value, and I think it has some, it points towards reformation as a leading purpose of punishment.

The fundamental purpose historically has been, and I submit, theoretically, should be, the vindication of the law. Therefore whatever is done should have as its fundamental purpose that the law should in future be better respected and better obeyed, and that thereby the order of society should be improved. This fundamental purpose is, however, by itself, not a sufficient guide to the choice of punishment by the Court.

The next stage, which is often put forward as if it were the fundamental purpose, is nowadays alleged to be the "protection of the public." Those who posit this goal appear to exclude the offender himself from the public. But even if he is sent to prison or school, he will come out again before long, and then will become a member of the public, so that the word "protection" hardly applies to him. Apart from this, the word "protection" suggests that the offender is a perpetual menace to his fellow-citizens and therefore ought to be sent to prison, or otherwise rendered innocuous for the longest possible time. It can, of course, be argued that the reformation of the offender is the best protection to the public, and therefore is included in such an object. This is not untrue, but, so stated, it disregards the effect of the method of reformation upon the attitude to the offence of some other people, such as previous offenders in crime.

Certainly, the protection of the public is a good slogan, so far as it goes, but I do not think it accurately points to the ideal social purpose of punishment. This, I would suggest, is the improvement of the order of society, using order in the sense of that word in the phrase "law and order." What the criminal Courts are for, not from the point of view of lawyers and legally trained judges, but from that of the citizens of a complex modern State, is that, in dealing with each offender, the Court should tend to make the working of the whole complex process of the civilized community more satisfactory and smoother than before. This involves, not merely that well-behaved citizens shall be protected from the further ill-conduct of an offender, but that all people, to whose knowledge the trial and treatment of the offender is brought, may thereby be led to an increased respect for the prohibition concerned, that the offender himself may not merely cease to commit that kind of offence, but that he may become a useful, or at least a harmless, citizen, and that those who have suffered wrong through his ill-conduct, either directly, or indirectly through sympathetic imagination, may be satisfied with the procedure of the Court in dealing with the offender, so that, as the phrase has it, they may say that justice has been done. This, therefore, improved harmony of the community is, I submit, the basic secondary purpose of punishment. In the rare event of the primary and secondary purposes clashing, the lawyer would prefer the first, the statesman the second.

The second, like the previous slogan, is too wide and abstract to be by itself a sufficient guide to appropriate punishment, but it is only with this as background that we can go on to consider those purposes which are usually inaccurately described as the primary purposes of punishment. These tertiary purposes, if I may so call them, have been catalogued as retribution, prevention, deterrence, and reformation. Indeed, in calling these "purposes," we may be accused of confusing the "what" with the "how." Perhaps we should call them "methods"—methods of achieving the primary and secondary purposes.

Retribution

Punishment for the sake of punishment, without regard to the consequences. *Fiat pœna ruat cœlum.* This, as a goal of punishment, is today looked at askance. And for weighty reasons. It is associated with a whole group of ideas, such as divine vengeance, expiation of sin, penance, and the like, now outmoded. Most people do not today believe in a God who uses earthly Courts for the wreaking of vengeance, or for payment of the wages of sin. With this repudiation of old theology is associated a repugnance to the idea of State vengeance, with its implication of emotional hostility in the consciousness of the Court. When Bacon said "Revenge is a kind of wild justice," he implied that justice is a kind of tame revenge. But all forms of revenge, tame or wild, are repugnant to the philosophic mind, though obviously sometimes acceptable to the public of today.

From all such points of view, the idea of retribution seems to imply that to the past evil of the crime, now done and irreversible, is to be added a fresh evil of penal suffering, merely as a theoretical balance to return an indifferent universe to an equilibrium it will never attain anyhow. For these and similar reasons, many theoreticians repudiate the idea of retribution as a factor in punishment.

Yet it is never absent in the sentences imposed for major offences, and is the basis of the tariff attitude, which, whatever they may say to the contrary, is obviously present to the minds of our High Court Judges, and of the common people. Nor is this as wrong as it appears to be at first sight. Retribution is indeed but another aspect of that fundamental vindication of the criminal law which, as we have said, is necessary to make such a law more than a mere request.

Punishment for breach of a criminal law is (in advance) a threat which is a promise; it would be a kind of breach of contract not to impose it. Further, retribution for crime satisfies our inherited reactions; without it, we should feel thwarted. However impossible it be to work out any mathematical equality between a crime and a punishment, neither of which can be quantified beyond a very rough, and really qualitative, classification into great, medium, or trivial, everybody feels that there should usually be some approximate equation between crime and punishment. Many offenders expect a tit for tat. Once, when I asked an old petty thief what he had to say in mitigation, he replied, "Nothing, sir. Give me what you think it's worth." When I replied, "I think it's worth three months" he thanked me, sincerely and cheerfully.

Those who repudiate retribution do not appear to realise that this idea is the only one which justifies the acquittal of a defendant, who has committed all the physical acts of crime, on the ground that his mind did not go with them, owing to insanity, mistake, or accident.

Apart from the retributive theory, it would be much better for the order of the State to find guilty one who had done a wrong through insanity, and should therefore be shut up, through mistake which should not be repeated, or through accident which ought to be prevented—indeed, the matter of insanity is so pregnant with danger that the illogical verdict "Guilty, but insane" is provided for the higher Courts, at once acquitting and conferring the power to "punish," namely to incarcerate the unhappy offender.

To put this matter in another way. Those who are so fond of arguing whether a particular wrongdoer is or is not "responsible for his actions"—a thoroughly misleading phrase, which omits the crucial question "responsible to whom?"—should realise that the background of the whole discussion contains the postulates that punishment is always painful, and that these pains are always imposed by way of retribution, and of retribution only—neither of which is accurate.

This criticism of a common confusion does not however alter the fact that there is a retributive aspect to almost all punishment. But though the retributive factor remains alive, its precise application by the imposition of pains equated to the atrocity of the offence of the offence is no longer compulsory in all offences.

Public opinion seldom demands this. In the case of trivial offences, the opinion of the public, or the desire of the victim that the offender shall suffer or shall not, can within wide limits be safely disregarded. In such cases, the basic fact that the offender is within the power of the Court and can be made to suffer severely is sufficient to satisfy the idea of retribution, where other considerations control the quantum and method of punishment. In practice it is to the other considerations that attention is largely directed, while retribution looks after itself. Still there are cases where the offender cannot be effectively prevented or deterred from repeating his offence, nor can he be reformed, yet something must be done—in other words, there must be retribution.

Prevention

Prevention, as an ideal goal of punishment, is usually impossible or impracticable. There is no means of preventing any but the offender from committing similar offences, while the offender himself can usually only be permanently "prevented" by death, transportation, imprisonment for life, or appropriate mutilation. These methods have all been tried, and abandoned, firstly, as cruel and barbarous, and secondly, because they cause other offenders to resist arrest, and offend, if at all, with ferocity. "As well be hanged for a sheep as for a lamb," and "Kill rather than be taken," are the natural reactions, both harmful to the State.

In a few cases, the purpose of prevention is uppermost in the mind of the Court, but the result of a sentence imposed to achieve that purpose is usually temporary, and may well conflict with public opinion based on the idea of retributive justice. In any event, only a small percentage of offenders can be so treated, and the implication is that these can be neither deterred nor reformed. Indeed, the only effective prevention, in these days, apart from capital punishment, is where the offender is certified insane or mentally defective and permanently restrained accordingly.

Deterrence

Deterrence was undoubtedly the major goal of punishment in recent times, and still is in many cases, and in many Courts, particularly with respect to adults. Deterrence is intended to operate by fear. The idea is that the sentence imposed shall be so unpleasant —so terrible, if the word be understood without exaggeration— that the offender will hereafter be afraid to repeat similar offences, and that others will be afraid to imitate his crime. If this were all, the more savage the sentence the better—as our ancestors apparently thought.

But savage sentences do not work (in England), for the reasons given under "Prevention" supra, and for other reasons such as the state to which public opinion has evolved, the effect of religion, sentiment, and so on. Therefore, the deterrent sentence, nowadays, must be moderate, and carefully calculated to achieve its object of deterrence without offending other criteria of punishment (e.g. the retributive idea), or outraging public opinion and the zeitgeist, too flagrantly.

But a moderated, tariff-regulated, deterrent sentence encounters practical difficulties.

In the first place one must distinguish between deterrence of the offender and deterrence of other potential offenders. In order to deter an offender, by a moderate and calculated sentence which shall be just enough to deter him without being savage, one must consider him personally. What will just deter one man will have no effect on another, yet will crush a third. Here we find the greatest weakness in the attitude of those who champion deterrence. Their method is based on the theory that all men are mentally alike, and something like themselves! Nothing could be farther from the truth. Most judges are horrified by the thought of prison for themselves, but many offenders cannot be deterred by any punishment a modern Court can or dare inflict.

Recidivists, the subnormal, the excitably passionate, slum dwellers who live in an atmosphere of crime, and many others of subnormal mentality, cannot be deterred any more than a moth can be deterred from a candle by the singeing of its wings.

On the other hand, many who are sensitive, or whose society is highly "respectable," are so shocked by the mere fact of trial and guilt, that a simple reprimand and threat is enough to deter them effectively.

When, however, the deterrence, not of the offender, but of others, is in question, the problem, though similar, may lead to different answers.

Where the individual, though mentally abnormal himself, has committed an offence which is likely to be imitated by others who are normal, a punishment imposed, which has no deterrent effect upon him, may be adequate to deter those others. Similarly, the reprimand and threat, appropriate to the individual offender, may not merely not deter but may actually encourage others to offend in the same way—this frequently occurs where Courts habitually treat first offenders leniently. The result may be a widespread opinion that it is safe to commit the type of offence in question repeatedly until one is caught. "Every dog has a first bite free" may lead to widespread offending. This is one of the dangers of leniency, e.g. in cases of "Jackdaw" shoplifting.

The principle of deterrence is most easily applied in two cases: (i) where the offender is obviously a normal person who has systematically offended with calculation with the motive of gain, (ii) where some particular form of offence has become fashionable—such as pilfering from railways, or stealing joy-rides in motor-cars, and it is more socially important to deter others than to give precisely appropriate treatment to the individual, as considered in isolation from such circumstances.

In the first case, what deters the actual offender, being normal, will probably deter other potential offenders similarly normal; in the second case, deterrence of others is the dominant purpose. Whether, for the benefit of society, one should prefer the deterrence of the offender, or the deterrence of other potential offenders, must depend on surrounding circumstances, it is impossible to lay down any general rule. The offender is the only one actually within the power of the Court, and in general it may seem better, or more practicable, to concentrate on deterring him—but, as I have just suggested, this procedure is not always apt.

In most cases, a Court which is guided by the purpose of deterrence should walk warily. First, the mind of the offender should be investigated, by means of reports of Police, Probation Officers, Schoolmasters, Employers, and so on, supplemented in many cases by the diagnoses of doctor and of psychiatrist (or even in some rare cases, psychoanalyst), in order to discover just what punishment (if any) is likely to deter the individual. Next, the type of individual who will learn of the fate of the offender, and whom it is desired to deter, will have to be estimated. It is only after this double estimation that punishment can be imposed which will, if it be possible, achieve both forms of deterrence.

This is often difficult, to the point of impossibility. Beyond this, always to employ, as the guiding purpose, deterrence by fear is to act as a doctor with one cure-all medicine, and that a purge, for all illnesses. Fear, even when it works, is not an ennobling motive, and a person who abstains from crime merely because he fears the consequences is greatly inferior spiritually and as a social asset to the one who behaves well because he wants to be a decent fellow, or is influenced by a more generous motive, such as gratitude to the Court.

There is yet another grave danger in the practical application of deterrence, which, though theoretically included in what I have already said, is so important as to merit special emphasis. It is this, that the only methods of deterrence available may, not merely not deter, but actually make the offender worse than before. Particularly does this apply to the young. Thus, in June, 1945, M. M. Simmons in "Making Citizens" writes of "The burning indignation" (of the early reformers) "against a system which could send so many children to prison and thereby confirm them in a life of crime." But it is not only the young who can be worsened by experience of prison. Some adults are. And the same may be said of the lash. There is still controversy as to whether experience demonstrates that this punishment deters or increases crimes of violence—official statistics are against the whipping of juveniles.

Yet, in spite of all that can be urged against deterrence, here, as in the case of retribution, we have an attitude which is often by force of circumstances willy-nilly adopted by the Court.

The gap between Deterrence and Reformation is in some sense bridged by Binding Over (not accompanied with Probation).

When an offender is Bound Over for a period—usual maximum three years—he does not suffer penalties at the moment, but is told that if he offends again (within the time limit) he will be "punished" (in the penalty sense) for what he has already done wrong, as well as for the further offence. This is a threat, similar to, but more personal than, the threat attaching to the original law he has offended, and as such is intended to deter the offender. At the same time, by refraining from immediate infliction of penalties, the Court appeals to any sense of gratitude of which the offender may be capable (some offenders have none), and also to any capacity of loyalty he may have. "We are trusting you, do not let us down," is an appeal often made, sometimes with success, by the Court. The appeal of Binding Over is therefore to a wider area of the character than is mere deterrence by fear, and from that aspect superior; moreover it does not require so much accuracy of diagnosis as do methods of Reformation. As against this, it may fail to deter others —may even encourage them. Again, the gap between Retribution and Reformation is in some sense bridged by an order to pay compensation. Where monetary compensation to the victim can be combined with Binding Over or Probation, as in some petty larcenies and frauds, the offender knows that his payments (usually made weekly) go towards the financial cure of the harm done by his offence. If, as is not very uncommon, he repents his sin, this is an expiation he is willing to perform—and, in my view, there can be no expiation not done willingly. Even if he does not repent, such precise restoration of the financial status quo may satisfy the primitive sense of justice in those concerned, even including the offender.

Reformation

The manifest difficulties in applying as guiding purposes or methods retribution, prevention, or deterrence, combined with a sense of the guilt of society and with the amelioration of manners of our Christian civilisation, have led to increasing emphasis on the idea of Reformation. Crime, like sin, proceeds from the mind, though committed by the body, and it is obvious that if the mind can be altered so that the individual no longer wishes to do that which transgresses the law, the result will be more satisfactory, so far as the individual is concerned, and so far as society as a whole is concerned, than any other possible treatment. This description of Reformation might well be held to include deterrence, as a special type of reformation; it would also be a perfect prevention, and the Christian's ideal form of retribution—but it would merely confuse the issue so to widen it. Reformation usually connotes something in the nature of Education, not based on fear, not regarded as penitential. But it is with reformation as with deterrence, only more so, one must consider the individual. The first question is, can this individual be reformed by the means at our disposal? This, in many cases, will involve a careful enquiry, without which the Court is uninformed and blind.

It is perhaps partly the association of Reformation with Education which has led to such special efforts to redeem the young— the creation of the Juvenile Court, the Approved School, the Borstal Institution, the Probation machinery and so forth. Such efforts are essentially experimental and experiential—"you never know till you try" is the attitude. As we know, a considerable percentage of youngsters are reformed and become satisfactory citizens, and we hope that as these methods are further applied and developed they may become more effective.

Reformation is, however, not confined to the young. Though their elders cannot be sent to school or Borstal, some of them can be sometimes persuaded to reside at suitable hostels and institutions and these and many others can be put upon probation. It is perhaps even more obvious in the case of the adult than of the youngster that before we attempt to reform we must investigate the individual's character, his mental and moral potentialities, as much as possible. Any such enquiry involves, besides his history and environment, medical and psychical diagnoses by experts who should be wise as well as trained and experienced.

Reformation of offenders was very much in the air just before the war and—in spite of the fact that the so-called crime wave has compelled the Courts to increase the number and severity of deterrent sentences—in spite of all this, Reformation is still the main tendency of penological development.

But it should not be forgotten—as it tends to be—that there are three fundamental limitations to Reformation. The first is that one can only hope to reform those (e.g. thieves) whose offences are also sins against the general ethical code of the community. No penologist would attempt to reform one who drank after hours, or indulged in cash betting, or pawned a watch on Xmas Day. The second is that there are many offenders whom it is impossible to reform. These may be classified as follows: (1) Those who are so subnormal as to be incapable of responding to reformative efforts. Here we have, amongst others, the mass of hopeless individuals who pass through Approved School, Borstal, prison, and end up as habitual criminals, if they have not already been certified as mentally defective or insane. (2) Clever, wicked people who make a profession or hobby of crime, such as confidence tricksters. These may learn that lowest of moralities, "Crime does not pay," by experience of heavy penalties, but seldom otherwise. (3) Business men, and the like, previously "indifferent honest," who have been led by a careful calculation of profit and dangers into systematic deception of customer or tax gatherer. The same remarks apply to these as to the last, and both classes are susceptible to deterrence by example, if it be severe enough. (4) Men of previous good character and good position who have succumbed to some sudden or special temptation.

Such a man may have to undergo retributive or deterrent penalties when the offence has been serious enough or is fashionable. In other cases Binding Over is appropriate. In any case, to attempt to reform these men by education or probation would be absurd.

The third limitation to Reformation is that, even if the individual is suitable for reformative treatment, this treatment may not be deterrent, but even encouraging, to other similar potential offenders. Some years ago a boy at Sheffield, caught in the act of burglary, was found to have in his pocket a letter reading, "Dear Bill, I'm having a grand time at Borstal. Mind you do some burglaries at once and get sent here." I have reason to believe that a number of children offend with the clear conscious intent to get themselves sent to approved schools. Of course, practically all methods of reform adopted (or even suggested) by Courts involve some loss of liberty, and to that extent may be disliked in expectation by many offenders, but, as the Borstal boy's letter suggests, this is not so always. The other day an experienced Police Officer wrote, "It is very rare that the child (or parent) shows any emotion when what is supposed to be a severe punishment, that is, sending to an Approved School, is ordered, which is clear proof that it has neither a punitive nor a deterrent effect." (*Police Review*, 1/3/1946, p. 124.) (By "punitive" he means "retributive.")

If, therefore, all offenders of any particular type—whether all who commit any particular offence or all of a certain age or class or category—are invariably subjected to a particular method of reform, which is regarded as pleasant by many potential subjects of it, the result may be an actual increase of offences.

This is, by postulate, not desirable. It can perhaps be avoided by publicised use of the choice of penalty possessed by the Court. If potential offenders know that they may be subjected to the desired reform, or on the other hand may have to suffer penalties far less pleasant—the uncertainty thus created may act as sufficient deterrent.

It is with considerations such as these in mind, that where the Court actually helps an offender, this is done behind the scenes. For instance, one man who had been convicted and imprisoned on several occasions for stealing handcarts, being convicted once more of the same offence, committed to enable him to do a job of furniture removing, the Court publicly bound him over and in private, out of the poor-box, bought him a handcart for his own. This man's gratitude reformed him—but the procedure never got into the newspapers!

Speaking generally, Reformative procedure is limited by the fact that it must not be pleasant in prospect, so as to encourage the commission of further offences; yet, at the same time, it must be calculated to produce that change of heart which involves the feeling that the world is a decent place for decent people—to resolve this apparent contradiction is a practical problem.

The present procedure, whereby a youngster has to wait in prison or Remand Home before entering Borstal or Approved School, and the methods of education adopted, do go some way towards such solution, but that is all.

To sum up, as to Reformation. It is a fact that, with rare exceptions, all forms of reformation now used involve some restriction of liberty—both of practical necessity, and as theoretical desideratum —and from this, and usually from other aspects also, involve, or should involve, some measure of deterrence. I should add that, while at first the offender may resent what is done, that resentment must be overcome, either by authority or by the offender himself, and the offender must ultimately willingly cooperate with his would-be reformers, before the outcome can be satisfactory. This change of heart is always hopèd and often arrives, but can never be confidently predicted. (*See* "Redemption Island," by Evan John.)

An excellent picture of the modern reformative attitude (mainly toward children) is given in the following, written by an American judge. It will be noticed, however, that within reform he includes some forms of deterrence and of prevention:—

I conceive this whole vast field as being closely comparable to the field of public health. As a matter of fact, my every act is on a basis of pretence. I pretend that I am a doctor dealing with sick kids and sick parents. Delinquent children are those infected with the germ of bad conduct and bad thinking. The Court building is a conduct-health centre or clinic. Probation officers are its employees or staff doctors. Detention home is an emergency orthopedic hospital, and the attendants are nurses. The County Jail is my hospital where parents are given a rest cure to correct their diseased mental attitudes toward their parental responsibilities. Police officers are public health officers bringing in the afflicted who endanger the public health. Patrol cars are ambulances. Juvenile sections in jail are isolation wards. Training schools are hospitals for cases requiring more extended treatment. These are, of course, merely examples of my parallels of pretence.

But this concept must not be construed as being an emotional or sentimental approach to the problem. There is nothing very emotional or sentimental in a good doctor. A child afflicted with diphtheria or leprosy is indeed sick; but he is also dangerous to others and must be isolated. A gangrenous limb is also an illness; but it also may require amputation. Accordingly, if the child's condition requires isolation, we isolate; and if the condition requires amputation from the family, we just cut it off. Like the doctor, we try to ease the pain as much as possible; but, like the doctor, we must administer the treatment required. There is neither vengeance nor "sob-sister" sentimentality involved in the process.

On this basis of pretence, then, my conception of this law-enforcement problem is that we are all engaged in one vast enterprise of public health in the field of conduct. Each of us has a specialised part to perform. The problem of any one of us is, in part, a problem of all. The success of any one is, in part, the success of all. No one of us alone can bring about public well-being; but, all together, we can raise its level.

(WILLIAM J. LONG,
Judge of King County Superior Court, Seattle)
(Extracted from the *Police Journal*, October, 1945.)

General Observations

I have spoken so far of prison as if, whether it reformed or not, it were always either a deterrent or merely ineffective, but in at least three classes of cases it has the opposite effect to that of a deterrent: (*a*) the case of the incapable man who welcomes free board and lodging, e.g. the tramp, who throws a stone through a window in order to pass the winter in prison, and (*b*) the case of the petty sexual offender. For reasons which psychologists profess to understand and explain, imprisonment of such a man, particularly after his first conviction, makes him a great deal worse than before. The only hope for him is sympathetic medical treatment, either as a voluntary patient or under the supervision of a probation officer. (*c*) I have no doubt that all forms of painful punishment have the effect of stimulus and temptation to those (especially the young) who love risk, and lust after the excitement of danger—it may not be possible to climb Everest, to motor at 150 m.p.h. or to fly at 500 m.p.h.—but what a thrill to burgle a sleeping house in a city, or to drive past a policeman in a stolen car!

Where an offender can be neither reformed nor deterred, Courts tend to look towards prevention by lengthy imprisonment, but usually the most lengthy imprisonment practicable is merely temporary. At the end of his time the offender is set free with the certainty that he will resume his criminal activities. The question arises whether such temporary prevention is worth while. It may be said in its favour that it does to some extent vindicate the law and provide retribution, but this is unsatisfactory. One wonders whether the cost to the State is justified. Lawyers and reformers are notoriously bad financiers, but they are probably right in saying that Approved Schools and Borstal, and Probation Officers, when they succeed, are cheaper than perpetual recurrent imprisonment. But are they, when they fail? And is a prevention that prevents only for a while, a deterrence that does not deter, a reformation that does not reform, a retribution that is merely apparent—a satisfactory state of affairs? It would seem that other methods of dealing with some offenders should be developed. Would it not be worth while, both financially, and in order to achieve the basic social purpose of punishment, that of improving the harmony of society, if these other methods included Isolation Camps and Farms where offenders could be segregated and could lead moderately useful and moderately happy lives, and other methods of education and reform, such as those suggested by the Criminal Justice Bill?

I only hint at these matters because my main practical purpose in this paper has been to discuss how we should act now with our present powers, in the present state of society.

CONCLUSION

I HAVE SOUGHT to show that in imposing punishment the background is the vindication of the law, and the correlative social improvement of order and harmony. In the foreground, retribution can usually, though not always, look after itself, while prevention is seldom attainable, so that the choice is generally narrowed to deterrence and reformation.

Where the punishment is chosen as retributive, the emphasis is on the offence, elsewhere it is on the offender. Of course, it may be said with some offences, e.g. robbery with violence, the more atrocious the crime, the more atrocious is the criminal, so that he and his like need more severity for deterrence or longer training for reformation—and thus the purposes are blended—but this is not always true.

Again, as to deterrence and reformation; they are not necessarily contraries. A deterrent punishment, such as imprisonment, may be used to reform; and a reformative punishment, such as Borstal, may act as deterrent. Other punishments, such as a fine, may be almost purely deterrent, or such as dismissal plus help from the poor-box, may be reformative only.

It follows that the correct choice of punishment—punishment in its widest sense of "treatment," which may be unpleasant or may not—usually consists in a wise blending of the deterrent and reformative, with the retributive well in mind, and with a constant appreciation that the matter concerns not merely the Court and the offender, but also the Public and Society as a going concern. Punishment is therefore an art, a very difficult art, essentially practical and related to the existing state of Society. A punishment which is appropriate today might have been quite unacceptable a couple of hundred years ago, and probably would be absurd two centuries hence. It is, therefore, impossible to lay down hard and fast permanent rules, though the theoretical normæ should remain.

Of course, in this paper, I have concentrated only on the diminution of crime by the machinery of the Criminal Court. Actually crime is a disease of the community, and it may be reduced by many other means.

We can but hope that the general amelioration of manners and the improvement of standards of behaviour and of the protection of person and property, as Society evolves, may lead to less crime, and that crimes may become less atrocious, so that punishment may gradually diminish in barbarity and become more and more essentially reformative—but that happy time is not yet. Indeed, just now, the retrogression of general conduct has inevitably led to the increase of deterrent sentences. This I believe to be a passing phase.

Professor H. L. A. Hart

Prolegomenon to the Principles of Punishment

Introductory

THE MAIN OBJECT of this paper is to provide a framework for the discussion of the mounting perplexities which now surround the institution of criminal punishment, and to show that any morally tolerable account of this institution must exhibit it as a compromise between radically distinct and partly conflicting principles.

General interest in the topic of punishment has never been greater than it is at present and I doubt if the public discussion of it has ever been more confused. The interest and the confusion are both in part due to relatively modern scepticism about two elements which have figured as essential parts of the traditionally opposed "theories" of punishment. On the one hand, the old Benthamite confidence in fear of the penalties threatened by the law as a powerful deterrent, has waned with the growing realisation that the part played by calculation of any sort in anti-social behaviour has been exaggerated. On the other hand a cloud of doubt has settled over the keystone of "Retributive" theory. Its advocates can no longer speak with the old confidence that statements of the form "This man who has broken the law could have kept it" had a univocal or agreed meaning; or where scepticism does not attach to the *meaning* of this form of statement, it has shaken the confidence that we are generally able to distinguish the cases where this form of statement is true from those where it is not.[1]

From *Proceedings of the Aristotelian Society*, Vol. 60 (1959-60), 1-26, © 1960 by the Aristotelian Society. Reprinted by courtesy of the Editor of the Aristotelian Society.

Yet quite apart from the uncertainty engendered by these fundamental doubts, which seem to call in question the accounts given of the efficacy, and the morality of punishment by all the old competing theories, the public utterances of those who conceive themselves to be expounding, as plain men for other plain men, orthodox or common-sense principles, untouched by modern psychological doubts are uneasy. Their words often sound as if the authors had not fully grasped their meaning or did not intend the words to be taken quite literally. A glance at the parliamentary debates or the *Report of the Royal Commission on Capital Punishment* shows that many are now troubled by the suspicion that the view that there is just one supreme value or objective (*e.g.*, Deterrence, Retribution, or Reform) in terms of which *all* questions about the justification of punishment are to be answered, is somehow wrong: yet, from what is said on such occasions no clear account of what the different values or objectives are, or how they fit together in the justification of punishment, can be extracted.[2]

No one expects judges or statesmen occupied in the business of sending people to the gallows or prison, or in making (or unmaking) laws which enable this to be done, to have much time for philosophical discussion of the principles which make it morally tolerable to do these things. A judicial bench is not and should not be a professorial chair. Yet what is said in public debates about punishment by those specially concerned with it as judges or legislators is important. Few are likely to be more circumspect, and if what they say seems, as it often does, unclear, one-sided, and easily refutable by pointing to some aspect of things which they have overlooked, it is likely that in our inherited ways of talking or thinking about punishment there is some persistent drive towards an oversimplification of multiple issues which require separate consideration. To counter this drive what is most needed is *not* the simple admission that instead of a single value or aim (Deterrence, Retribution, Reform, or any other) a plurality of different values and aims should be given as a conjunctive answer to some *single* question concerning the justification of punishment. What is needed is the realisation that different principles (each of which may in a sense be called a "justification") are relevant at different points in any morally acceptable account of punishment. What we should look for are answers to a number of different questions such as: What justifies the general practice of punishment? To whom may punishment be applied? How severely may we punish? In dealing with these and other questions concerning punishment we should bear in mind that in this, as in most other social institutions, the pursuit of one aim may be qualified by or provide an opportunity, not to be missed, for the pursuit of others. Till we have developed this sense of the complexity of punishment (and this prolegomenon aims only to do this) we shall be in no fit state to assess the extent to which the whole institution has been eroded by or needs to be adapted to new beliefs about the human mind.

II

JUSTIFYING AIMS AND PRINCIPLES OF DISTRIBUTION

THERE IS, I THINK, an analogy worth considering between the concept of Punishment and that of Property. In both cases we have to do with a social institution of which the centrally important form is a structure of *legal* rules, though it would be dogmatic to deny the names of Punishment or Property to the similar though more rudimentary rule-regulated practices within groups such as a family, or a school, or in customary societies whose customs may lack some of the standard or salient features of law (*e.g.*, legislation, organised sanctions, courts). In both cases we are confronted by a complex institution presenting different inter-related features calling for separate explanation; or, if the morality of the institution is challenged, for separate justification. In both cases failure to distinguish separate questions or attempting to answer them all by reference to a single principle ends in confusion. Thus in the case of Property we should distinguish between the question of the *definition* of Property, the question why and in what circumstance it is a *good* institution to maintain, and the questions in what ways individuals may become *entitled* to property and *how much* they should be allowed to acquire. These we may call questions of *Definition, General Justifying Aim,* and *Distribution* with the last subdivided into questions of *Title* and *Amount*. It is salutary to take some classical exposition of the idea of Property, say Locke's Chapter "Of Property" in the *Second Treatise,*[3] and to observe how much darkness is spread by the use of a single notion (in this case "the labour of (a man's) body and the work of his hands") to answer all these different questions which press upon us when we reflect on the institution of Property. In the case of Punishment the beginning of wisdom (though by no means its end) is to distinguish similar questions and confront them separately.

(a) Definition

Here I shall simply draw upon the recent admirable work scattered through English philosophical[4] journals and add to it only an admonition of my own against the abuse of definition in the philosophical discussion of punishment. So with Mr. Benn and Professor Flew I shall define the standard or central case of 'punishment' in terms of five elements:

(i) It must involve pain or other consequences normally considered unpleasant.
(ii) It must be for an offence against legal rules.
(iii) It must be of an actual or supposed offender for his offence.
(iv) It must be intentionally administered by human beings other than the offender.
(v) It must be imposed and administered by an authority constituted by a legal system against which the offence is committed.

In calling this the standard or central case of punishment I shall relegate to the position of sub-standard or secondary cases the following among many other possibilities:

(a) Punishments for breaches of legal rules imposed or administered otherwise than by officials (decentralised sanctions).
(b) Punishments for breaches of non-legal rules or orders (punishments in a family or school).
(c) Vicarious or collective punishment of some member of a social group for actions done by others without the former's authorisation, encouragement, control, or permission.
(d) Punishment of persons (otherwise than under (c)) who are neither in fact nor supposed to be offenders.

The chief importance of listing these sub-standard cases is to prevent the use of what I shall call the "definitional stop" in discussions of punishment. This is an abuse of definition especially tempting when use is made of conditions (ii) and iii) of the standard case against the utilitarian claim that the practice of punishment is justified by the beneficial consequences resulting from the observance of the laws which it secures. Here the stock 'retributive' argument[5] is: If *this* is the justification of punishment, why not apply it when it pays to do so to those innocent of any crime chosen at random, or to the wife and children of the offender? And here the wrong reply is: That, by definition, would not be "punishment" and it is the justification of punishment which is in issue.[6] Not only will this definitional stop fail to satisfy the advocate of 'Retribution'; it would prevent us from investigating the very thing which modern scepticism most calls in question: namely the rational and moral status of our preference for a system of punishment under which measures painful to individuals are to be taken against them only when they have committed an offence. Why do we prefer this to other forms of social hygiene which we might employ instead to prevent anti-social behaviour and which we do employ in special circumstances sometimes with reluctance? No account of punishment can afford to dismiss this question with a definition.

(b) The nature of an offence

Before we reach any question of justification we must identify a preliminary question to which the answer is so simple that the question may not appear worth asking; yet it is clear that some curious "theories" of punishment gain their only plausibility from ignoring it, and others from confusing it with other questions. This question is: Why are certain kinds of action forbidden by law and so made crimes or offences? The answer is: To announce to society that these actions are not to be done and to secure that fewer of them are done. These are the common immediate aims of making any conduct a criminal offence and until we have laws made with these primary aims we shall lack the notion of a 'crime' and so of a 'criminal.' Without recourse to the simple idea that the criminal law sets up, in its rules, standards of behaviour to encourage certain types of conduct and discourage others we cannot distinguish a punishment in the form of a fine from a tax on a course of conduct.[7] This indeed is one grave objection to those theories of law which in the interests of simplicity or uniformity obscure the distinction between primary laws setting standards for behaviour and secondary laws specifying what officials must or may do when they are broken. Such theories insist that all legal rules are "really" directions to officials to exact "sanctions" under certain conditions, *e.g.*, if people kill.[8] Yet only if we keep alive the distinction (which such theories thus obscure) between the primary objective of the law in encouraging or discouraging certain kinds of behavior and its merely ancillary sanction or remedial steps, can we give sense to the notion of a crime or offence.

It is important however to stress the fact that in thus identifying the immediate aims of the criminal law we have not reached the stage of justification. There are indeed many forms of undesirable behaviour which it would be foolish because ineffective or too costly to attempt to inhibit by use of the law and some of these may be better left to educators, trades unions, churches, marriage guidance councils, or other non-legal agencies. Conversely there are some forms of conduct which we believe cannot be effectively inhibited without use of the law. But it is only too plain that in fact the law may make activities criminal which it is morally important to promote and the suppression of these may be quite unjustifiable. Yet confusion between the simple immediate aim of any criminal legislation and the justification of punishment seems to be the most charitable explanation of the claim that punishment is justified as an "emphatic denunciation by the community of a crime." Lord Denning's[9] dictum that this is the ultimate justification of punishment can be saved from Mr. Benn's criticism, noted above, only if it is treated as a blurred statement of the truth that the aim not of punishment, but of criminal legislation is indeed to denounce certain types of conduct as something not to be practised. Conversely the immediate aim of criminal legislation cannot be any of the things which are usually mentioned as justifying punishment: for until it is settled what conduct is to be legally denounced and discouraged we have not settled from what we are to *deter* people, or who are to be considered *criminals* from whom we are to exact *retribution*, or on whom we are to wreak *vengeance*, or whom we are to *reform*.

Even those who look upon human law as a mere instrument for enforcing "morality as such" (itself conceived as the law of God or Nature) and who at the stage of justifying punishment wish to appeal not to socially beneficial consequences but simply to the intrinsic value of inflicting suffering on wrongdoers who have disturbed by their offence the moral order, would not deny that the aim of criminal legislation is to set up types of behaviour (in this case conformity with a pre-existing moral law) as legal standards of behaviour and to secure conformity with them. No doubt in all communities certain moral offences, *e.g.*, killing, will always be selected for suppression as crimes and it is conceivable that this may be done not to protect human beings from being killed but to save the potential murderer from sin; but it would be paradoxical to look upon the law as designed not to prevent murder at all (even conceived as sin rather than harm) but simply to extract the penalty from the murderer.

(c) General Justifying Aim

I shall not here criticise the intelligibility or consistency or adequacy of these theories that are united in denying that the practice of a system of punishment is justified by its beneficial consequences and claim instead that the main justification of the practice lies in the fact that when breach of the law involves moral guilt the application to the offender of the pain of punishment is itself a thing of value. A great variety of claims of this character designating 'Retribution' or 'Expiation' or 'Reprobation' as the justifying aim, fall in spite of differences under this rough general description. Though in fact I agree with Mr. Benn[10] in thinking that these all either avoid the question of justification altogether or are in spite of their protestations disguised forms of Utilitarianism, I shall assume that Retribution, defined simply as the application of the pains of punishment to an offender who is morally guilty, may figure among the conceivable justifying aims of a system of punishment. Here I shall merely insist that it is one thing to use the word Retribution *at this point* in an account of the principle of punishment in order to designate the General Justifying Aim of the system, and quite another to use it to secure that to the question "To whom may punishment be applied?" (the question of Distribution) the answer given is "Only to an offender for an offence." Failure to distinguish Retribution as a General Justifying Aim from retribution as the simple insistence that only those who have broken the law—and voluntarily broken it—may be punished may be traced in many writers even perhaps in Mr. J. D. Mabbott's[11] otherwise most il-luminating essay. We shall distinguish the latter from Retribution in General Aim as "retribution in Distribution." Much confusing shadow-fighting between Utilitarians and their opponents may be avoided if it is recognized that it is perfectly consistent to assert *both* that the General Justifying Aim of the practice of punishment is its beneficial consequences and that the pursuit of this general aim should be qualified or restricted out of deference to principles of Distribution which require that punishment should be only of an offender for an offence. Conversely it does not in the least follow from the admission of the latter principle of retribution in Distribu-tion that the General Justifying Aim of punishment is Retribution though of course Retribution in General Aim entails retribution in Distribution.

We shall consider later the principles of justice lying at the root of retribution in Distribution. Meanwhile it is worth observing that both the most old fashioned Retributionist (in General Aim) and the most modern sceptic often make the same and, I think, wholly mistaken assumption that sense can only be made of the restrictive principle that punishment be applied only to an offender for an offence if the General Justifying Aim of the practice of punishment is Retribution. The sceptic consequently imputes to all systems of punishment (when they are restricted by the principle of retribu-tion in Distribution) all the irrationality he finds in the idea of Retri-bution as a General Justifying Aim; conversely the advocates of the latter think the admission of retribution in Distribution is a refuta-tion of the utilitarian claim that the social consequences of punish-ment are its Justifying Aim.

The most general lesson to be learnt from this extends beyond the topic of punishment. It is, that in relation to any social institu-tion, after stating what general aim or value its maintenance fosters we should enquire whether there are any and if so what principles limiting the unqualified pursuit of that aim or value. Just because the pursuit of any single social aim always has its restrictive qualifier our main social institutions always possess a plurality of features which can only be understood as a compromise between partly discrepant principles. This is true even of relatively minor legal in-stitutions like that of a contract. In general this is designed to enable individuals to give effect to their wishes to create structures of legal rights and duties and so to change, in certain ways their legal position. Yet at the same time there is need to protect those who in good faith understand a verbal offer made to them to mean what it would ordinarily mean, accept it, and then act on the footing that a valid contract has been concluded. As against them, it would be unfair to allow the other party to say that the words he used in his verbal offer or the interpretation put on them did not express his real wishes or intention. Hence principles of "estoppel" or doctrines of the "objective sense" of a contract are introduced to prevent this and to qualify the principle that the law enforces contracts in order to give effect to the joint wishes of the contracting parties.

(d) Distribution

This as in the case of property has two aspects (i) Liability (Who may be punished?) and (ii) Amount. In this section I shall chiefly be concerned with the first of these.[12]

From the foregoing discussions two things emerge. First, though we may be clear as to what value the practice of punishment is to promote we have still to answer as a question of Distribution "Who may be punished?" Secondly, if in answer to this question we say "only an offender for an offence" this admission of retribution in Distribution is not a principle from which anything follows as to the severity or amount of punishment; in particular it neither licenses nor requires as Retribution in General Aim does more severe punishments than deterrence or other utilitarian criteria would require.

The root question to be considered is however why we attach the moral importance which we do to retribution in Distribution. Here I shall consider the efforts made to show that restriction of punishment to offenders is a simple consequence of whatever principles (Retributive or Utilitarian) constitute the Justifying Aim of punishment.

The standard example used by philosophers to bring out the importance of retribution in Distribution is that of a wholly innocent person who has not even unintentionally done anything which the law punishes if done intentionally. It is supposed that in order to avert some social catastrophe officials of the system fabricate evidence on which he is charged, tried, convicted, and sent to prison or death. Or it is supposed that without resort to any fraud more persons may be deterred from crime if wives and children of offenders were punished vicariously for their crimes. In some forms this kind of thing may be ruled out by a consistent sufficiently comprehensive utilitarianism.[13] Certainly expedients involving fraud or faked charges might be very difficult to justify on utilitarian grounds. We can of course imagine that a negro might be sent to prison or executed on a false charge of rape in order to avoid widespread lynching of many others; but a *system* which openly empowered authorities to do this kind of thing, even if it succeeded in averting specific evils like lynching, would awaken such apprehension and insecurity that any gain from the exercise of these powers would by any utilitarian calculation be offset by the misery caused by their existence. But official resort to this kind of fraud on a particular occasion in breach of the rules and the subsequent indemnification of the officials responsible might save many lives and so be thought to yield a clear surplus of value. Certainly vicarious punishment of an offender's family might do so and legal systems have occasionally though exceptionally resorted to this. An example of it is the Roman *Lex Quisquis* providing for the punishment of the children of those guilty of *majestas*.[14] In extreme cases many might still think it right to resort to these expedients but we should do so with the sense of sacrificing an important principle. We should be conscious of choosing the lesser of two evils, and this would be inexplicable if the principle sacrificed to utility were itself only a requirement of utility.

Similarly the moral importance of the restriction of punishment to the offender cannot be explained as merely a consequence of the principle that the General Justifying Aim is Retribution for immorality involved in breaking the law. Retribution in the Distribution of punishment has a value quite independent of Retribution as Justifying Aim. This is shown by the fact that we attach importance to the restrictive principle that only offenders may be punished even where breach of this law might not be thought immoral: indeed even where the laws themselves are hideously immoral as in Nazi Germany, *e.g.*, forbidding activities (helping the sick or destitute of some racial group) which might be thought morally obligatory, the absence of the principle restricting punishment to the offender would be a further *special* iniquity; whereas admission of this principle would represent some residual respect for justice though in the administration of morally bad laws.

III

Justification, Excuse and Mitigation

WHAT IS MORALLY at stake in the restrictive principle of Distribution cannot, however, be made clear by these external examples of its violation by faked charges or vicarious punishment. To make it clear we must allot to their place the appeals to matters of Justification, Excuse, and Mitigation made in answer to the claim that someone should be punished. The first of these depends on the General Justifying Aim; the last two are different aspects of the principles of Distribution of punishment.

(a) Justification and Excuse

English lawyers once distinguished between 'excusable' homicide (*e.g.*, accidental non-negligent killing) and 'justifiable' homicide (*e.g.*, killing in self-defence or the arrest of a felon) and different legal consequences once attached to these two forms of homicide. To the modern lawyer this distinction has no longer any legal importance: he would simply consider both kinds of homicide to be cases where some element, negative or positive, required in the full definition of criminal homicide (murder or manslaughter) was lacking. But the distinction between these two different ways in which actions may fail to constitute a criminal offence is still of great moral importance. Killing in self-defence is an exception to a general rule making killing punishable; it is admitted because the policy or aims which in general justify the punishment of killing (*e.g.*, protection of human life) do not include cases such as this. In the case of 'justification' what is done is regarded as something which the law does not condemn or even welcomes.[15] But where killing (*e.g.*, accidental) is excused, criminal responsibility is excluded on a different footing. What has been done is something which is deplored, but the psychological state of the agent when he did it exemplified one or more of a variety of conditions which are held to rule out the public condemnation and punishment of individuals. This is a requirement of fairness or of justice to individuals independent of whatever the General Aim of punishment is, and remains a value whether the laws are good, morally indifferent, or iniquitous.

The most prominent of these excusing conditions are those forms of lack of knowledge which make action unintentional: lack of muscular control which make it involuntary, subjection to gross forms of coercion by threats, and types of mental abnormality, which are believed to render the agent incapable of choice or of carrying out what he has chosen to do. Not all these excusing conditions are admitted by all legal systems for all offenders. Nearly all penal systems make some compromise at this point as we shall see with other principles; but most of them are admitted to some considerable extent in the case of the most serious crimes. Actions done under these excusing conditions are in the misleading terminology of Anglo-American law done without "mens rea";[16] and most people would say of them that they were 'not voluntary' or 'not wholly voluntary.'

(b) Mitigation

Justification and Excuse though different from each other are alike in that if either is made out then conviction and punishment are excluded. In this they differ from the idea of Mitigation which presupposes that someone is convicted and liable to be punished and the question of the severity of his punishment is to be decided. It is therefore relevant to that aspect of Distribution which we have termed Amount. Certainly the severity of punishment is in part determined by the General Justifying Aim. A utilitarian will for example exclude in principle punishments the infliction of which is held to cause more suffering than the offence unchecked, and will hold that if one kind of crime causes greater suffering than another then a greater penalty may be used to repress it. He will also exclude degrees of severity which are useless in the sense that they do no more to secure or maintain a higher level of law-observance or any other valued result than less severe penalties. But in addition to restrictions on the severity of punishment which follow from the aim of punishing special limitations are imported by the idea of Mitigation. These, like the principle of Distribution restricting liability to punishment to offenders, have a status which is independent of the general Aim. The special features of Mitigation are that a good reason for administering a less severe penalty is made out if the situation or mental state of the convicted criminal is such that he was exposed to an unusual or specially great temptation, or his ability to control his actions is thought to have been impaired or weakened otherwise than by his own action, so that conformity to the law which he has broken was a matter of special difficulty for him as compared with normal persons normally placed.

The special features of the idea of Mitigation are however often concealed by the various legal techniques which make it necessary to distinguish between what may be termed 'informal' and 'formal' Mitigation. In the first case the law fixes a maximum penalty and leaves it to the judge to give such weight as he thinks proper in selecting the punishment to be applied to a particular offender to (among other considerations) mitigating factors. It is here that the barrister makes his 'plea in mitigation.' Sometimes however legal rules provide that the presence of a mitigating factor shall always remove the offence into a separate category carrying a lower maximum penalty. This is 'formal' mitigation and the most prominent example of it is Provocation which in English law is operative only in relation to homicide. It is not a matter of Justification or Excuse for it does not exclude conviction or punishment; but "reduces" the charges from murder to manslaughter and the possible maximum penalty from death to life imprisonment. It is worth stressing that not every provision reducing the maximum penalty can be thought of as "Mitigation": the very peculiar provisions of s. 5 of the Homicide Act 1957 which (*inter alia*) restricted the death penalty to types of murder not including, for example, murder by poisoning, did not in doing this recognise the use of poison as a "mitigating circumstance." Only a reduction of penalty made in view of the individual criminal's special difficulties in keeping the law which he has broken is so conceived.

Though the central cases are distinct enough the border lines between Justification, Excuse, and Mitigation are not. There are many features of conduct which can be and are thought of in more than one of these ways. Thus, though little is heard of it, duress (coercion by threat of serious harm) is in English law in relation to some crimes an Excuse excluding responsibility. Where it is so treated the conception is that since *B* has committed a crime only because *A* has threatened him with gross violence or other harm, *B*'s action is not the outcome of a 'free' or independent choice; *B* is merely an instrument of *A* who has 'made him do it.' Nonetheless *B* is not an instrument in the same sense that he would have been had he been pushed by *A* against a window and broken it: unless he is literally paralysed by fear of the threat, we may believe that *B* could have refused to comply. If he complies we may say *'coactus voluit'* and treat the situation not as one making it intolerable to punish at all, but as one calling for mitigation of the penalty as gross provocation does. On the other hand if the crime which *A* requires *B* to commit is a petty one compared with the serious harm threatened (*e.g.*, death) by *A* there would be no absurdity in treating *A*'s threat as a Justification for *B*'s conduct though few legal systems overtly do this. If this line is taken coercion merges into the idea of "Necessity"[17] which appears on the margin of most systems of criminal law as an exculpating factor.

In view of the character of modern sceptical doubts about criminal punishment it is worth observing that even in English law the relevance of mental disease to criminal punishment is not always as a matter of Excuse though exclusive concentration on the M'Naghten rules relating to the criminal responsibility of the mentally diseased encourages the belief that it is. Even before the Homicide Act 1957 a statute[18] provided that if a mother murdered her child under the age of 12 months "while the balance of her mind was disturbed" by the processes of birth or lactation she should be guilty only of the felony of infanticide carrying a maximum penalty of life imprisonment. This is to treat mental abnormality as a matter of (formal) Mitigation. Similarly in other cases of homicide the M'Naghten rules relating to certain types of insanity as an Excuse no longer stand alone; now such abnormality of mind as "substantially impaired the mental responsibility"[19] of the accused is a matter of formal mitigation, which like provocation reduces the homicide to the category of manslaughter which does not carry the death penalty.

IV

THE RATIONALE OF EXCUSES

THE ADMISSION OF excusing conditions as a feature of the Distribution of punishment is required by distinct principles of Justice which restrict the extent to which general social aims may be pursued at the cost of individuals. The moral importance attached to these in punishment distinguishes it from other measures which pursue similar aims (*e.g.*, the protection of life, wealth, or property) by methods which like punishment are also often unpleasant to the individuals to whom they are applied, *e.g.*, the detention of persons of hostile origin or association in war time, or of the insane, or the compulsory quarantine of persons suffering from infectious disease. To these we resort to avoid damage of a catastrophic character.

Every penal system in the name of some other social value compromises over the admission of excusing conditions and no system goes as far (particularly in cases of mental disease) as many would wish. But it is important (if we are to avoid a superficial but tempting answer to modern scepticism about the meaning or truth of the statement that a criminal could have kept the law which he has broken) to see that our moral preference for a system which does recognise such excuses cannot, any more than our reluctance to engage in the cruder business of false charges or vicarious punishment, be explained by reference to the General Aim which we take to justify the practice of punishment. Here, too, even where the laws appear to us morally iniquitous or where we are uncertain as to their moral character so that breach of law does not entail moral guilt, punishment of those who break the law unintentionally would be an added wrong and refusal to do this some sign of grace.

Retributionists (in General Aim) have not paid much attention to the rationale of this aspect of punishment; they have usually (wrongly) assumed that it has no status except as a corollary of Retribution in General Aim. But Utilitarians have made strenuous, detailed efforts to show that the restriction on the use of punishment to those who have voluntarily broken the law is explicable on purely utilitarian lines. Bentham's efforts are the most complete, and their failure is an instructive warning to contemporaries.

Bentham's argument was a reply to Blackstone who in expounding the main excusing conditions recognised in the criminal law of his day,[20] claimed that "all the several pleas and excuses which protect the committer of a forbidden act from punishment which is otherwise annexed thereunto reduce to this single consideration: the want or defect of will" .... [and to the principle] "that to constitute a crime .... there must be first a vitious will." In the Principles of Morals and Legislation[21] under the heading "Cases unmeet for punishment" Bentham sets out a list of the main excusing conditions similar to Blackstone's; he then undertakes to show that the infliction of punishment on those who have done what the law forbids while in any of these conditions "must be inefficacious: it cannot act so as to prevent the mischief." All Blackstone's talk about want or defect of will or lack of a "vitious" will is he says "nothing to the purpose," except so far as it implies the reason (inefficacy of punishment) which he himself gives for recognising these excuses.

Bentham's argument is in fact a spectacular *non-sequitur*. He sets out to prove that to *punish* the mad, the infant child, or those who break the law unintentionally or under duress or even under "necessity" must be inefficacious; but all that he proves (at the most) is the quite different proposition that the *threat* of punishment will be ineffective so far as the class of persons who suffer from these conditions are concerned. Plainly it is possible that the actual *infliction* of punishment on those persons, though (as Bentham says) the *threat* of punishment could not have operated on them, may secure a higher measure of conformity to law on the part of normal persons than is secured by the admission of excusing conditions. If this is so and if Utilitarian principles only were at stake, we should, without any sense that we were sacrificing any principle of value or were choosing the lesser of two evils, drop from the law the restriction on punishment entailed by the admission of excuses; unless, of course, we believed that the terror or insecurity or misery produced by the operation of laws so Draconic was worse than the lower measure of obedience to law secured by the law which admits excuses.

This objection to Bentham's rationale of excuses is not merely a fanciful one. Any increase in the number of conditions required to establish criminal liability increases the opportunity for deceiving courts or juries by the pretence that some condition is not satisfied. When the condition is a psychological factor the chances of such pretence succeeding are considerable. Quite apart from the provision made for mental disease, the cases where an accused person pleads that he killed in his sleep or accidentally or in some temporary abnormal state of unconsciousness show that deception is certainly feasible. From the Utilitarian point of view this may lead to two sorts of 'losses.' The belief that such deception is feasible may embolden persons who would not otherwise risk punishment to take their chance of deceiving a jury in this way. Secondly, a murderer who actually succeeds in this deception will be left at large, though belonging to the class which the law is concerned to incapacitate. Developments in Anglo-American law since Bentham's day have given more concrete form to the objection to this argument. There are now offences (known as offences of "strict liability") where it is not necessary for conviction to show that the accused either intentionally did what the law forbids or could have avoided doing it by use of care: selling liquor to an intoxicated person, possessing an altered passport, selling adulterated milk[22] are examples out of a range of 'strict liability' offences where it is no defence that the accused did not offend intentionally, or through negligence, e.g., that he was under some mistake against which he had no opportunity to guard. Two things should be noted about them. First, the justification of this form of criminal liability can only be that if proof of intention or lack of care were required guilty persons would escape. Secondly, 'strict liability' is generally viewed with great odium and admitted as an exception to the general rule with the sense that an important principle has been sacrificed to secure a higher measure of conformity and conviction of offenders. Thus Bentham's argument curiously ignores both the two possibilities which have been realised. First, actual punishment of those who act unintentionally or in some other normally excusing condition may have a utilitarian value in its effects on others; and secondly, that when because of this probability, strict liability is admitted and the normal excuses are excluded, this may be done with the sense that some other principle has been overridden.

On this issue modern extended forms of Utilitarianism fare no better than Bentham's whose main criterion here of 'effective' punishment was deterrence of the offender or of others by example. Sometimes the principle that punishment should be restricted to those who have voluntarily broken the law is defended not as a principle which is rational or morally important in itself but as something so engrained in popular conceptions of justice[23] in certain societies, including our own, that not to recognise it would lead to disturbances, or to the nullification of the criminal law since officials or juries might refuse to cooperate in such a system. Hence to punish in these circumstances would either be impracticable or would create more harm than could possibly be offset by any superior deterrent force gained by such a system. On this footing, a system should admit excuses much as, in order to prevent disorder or lynching, concessions might be made to popular demands for more savage punishment than could be defended on other grounds. Two objections confront this wider pragmatic form of Utilitarianism. The first is the factual observation that even if a system of strict liability for all or very serious crime would be unworkable, a system which admits it on its periphery for relatively minor offences is not only workable but an actuality which we have, though many object to it or admit it with reluctance. The second objection is simply that we do not disassociate ourselves from the principle that it is wrong to punish the hopelessly insane or those who act unintentionally, etc., by treating it as something merely embodied in popular *mores* to which concessions must be made sometimes. We condemn legal systems where they disregard this principle; whereas we try to educate people out of their preference for savage penalties even if we might in extreme cases of threatened disorder concede them.

It is therefore impossible to exhibit the principle by which punishment is excluded for those who act under the excusing conditions merely as a corollary of the general Aim—Retributive or Utilitarian —justifying the practice of punishment. Can anything positive be said about this principle except that it is one to which we attach moral importance as a restriction on the pursuit of any aim we have in punishing?

It is clear that like all principles of Justice it is concerned with the adjustment of claims between a multiplicity of persons. It incorporates the idea that each individual person is to be protected against the claim of the rest for the highest possible measure of

371

security, happiness, or welfare which could be got at his expense by condemning him for the breach of the rules and punishing him. For this a moral license is required in the form of proof that the person punished broke the law by an action which was the outcome of his free choice, and the recognition of excuses is the most we can do to ensure that the terms of the licence are observed. Here perhaps the elucidation of this restrictive principle should stop. Perhaps we (or I) ought simply to say that it is a requirement of Justice, and Justice simply consists of principles to be observed in adjusting the competing claims of human beings which (i) treat all alike as persons by attaching special significance to human voluntary action and (ii) forbid the use of one human being for the benefit of others except in return for his voluntary actions against them. I confess however to an itch to go further; though what I have to say may not add to these principles of Justice. There are, however, three points which even if they are restatements from different points of view of the principles already stated, may help us to identify what we now think of as values in the practice of punishment and what we may have to reconsider in the light of modern scepticism.

(*a*) We may look upon the principle that punishment must be reserved for voluntary offences from two different points of view. The first is that of the rest of society considered as *harmed* by the offence (either because one of its members has been injured or because the authority of the law essential to its existence has been challenged or both). The principle then appears as one securing that the suffering involved in punishment is a return for the harm done to others: this is valued, not as the Aim of punishment, but as the only fair terms on which the General Aim (protection of society, maintenance of respect for law, etc.) may be pursued.

(*b*) The second point of view is that of society concerned not as harmed by the crime but as *offering* individuals including the criminal the protection of the laws on terms which are fair, because they not only consist of a framework of reciprocal rights and duties, but because within their framework each individual is given a *fair* opportunity to choose between keeping the law required for society's protection or paying the penalty. From the first point of view the actual punishment of a criminal appears not merely as something useful to society (General Aim) but as justly extracted from the criminal as a return for harm done; from the second it appears as a price justly extracted because the criminal had a fair opportunity beforehand to avoid liability to pay.

(*c*) Criminal punishment as an attempt to secure desired behaviour differs from the manipulative techniques of the Brave New World (conditioning propaganda, etc.) or the simple incapacitation of those with anti-social tendencies by taking a risk. It defers action till harm has been done; its primary operation consists simply in announcing certain standards of behaviour and attaching penalties for deviation, making it less eligible, and then leaving individuals to choose. This is a method of social control which maximises individual freedom within the coercive framework of law in a number of different ways, or perhaps, different senses. First, the individual has an option between obeying or paying. The worse the laws are, the more valuable the possibility of exercising this choice becomes in enabling an individual to decide how he shall live. Secondly, this system not only enables individuals to exercise this choice but increases the power of individuals to identify beforehand periods when the law's punishments will not interfere with them and to plan their lives accordingly. This very obvious point is often overshadowed by the other merits of restricting punishment to offences voluntarily committed, but is worth separate attention. Where punishment is not so restricted individuals will be liable to have their plans frustrated by punishments for what they do unintentionally, in ignorance, by accident or mistake. Such a system of strict liability for all offences, it is logically possible,[24] would not only vastly increase the number of punishments, but would diminish the individual's power to identify beforehand particular periods during which he will be free from them. This is so because we can have very little grounds for confidence that during a particular period we will not do something unintentionally, accidentally, etc.; whereas from their own knowledge of themselves many can say with justified confidence that for some period ahead they are not likely to engage intentionally in crime and can plan their lives from point to point in confidence that they will be left free during that period. Of course the confidence justified does not amount to certainty though drawn from knowledge of ourselves. My confidence that I will not during the next twelve months intentionally engage in any crime and will be free from punishment, may turn out to be misplaced; but it is both greater and better justified than my belief that I will not do unintentionally any of the things which our system punishes if done intentionally.

V

REFORM AND THE INDIVIDUALIZATION OF PUNISHMENT

THE IDEA OF Mitigation incorporates the conviction that though the amount or severity of punishment is primarily to be determined by reference to the General Aim, yet Justice requires that those who have special difficulties to face in keeping the law which they have broken should be punished less. Principles of Justice however are also widely taken to bear on the amount of punishment in at least two further ways. The first is the somewhat hazy requirement that 'like cases be treated alike.' This is certainly felt to be infringed at least when the ground for different punishment for those guilty of the same crime is neither some personal characteristic of the offender connected with the commission of the crime nor the effect of punishment on him. If because at a given time a certain offence is specially prevalent a Judge passes a heavier sentence than on previous offenders ("as a warning") some sacrifice of justice to the safety of society is involved though it is often acceptable to many as the lesser of two evils.

The further principle that different kinds of offence of different gravity (however that is assessed) should not be punished with equal severity is one which like other principles of Distribution may qualify the pursuit of our General Aim and is not deducible from it. Long sentences of imprisonment might effectually stamp out car parking offences, yet we think it wrong to employ them; *not* because there is for each crime a penalty 'naturally' fitted to its degree of iniquity (as some Retributionists in General Aim might think); nor because we are convinced that the misery caused by such sentences (which might indeed be slight because they would need to be rarely applied) would be greater than that caused by the offences unchecked (as a Utilitarian might argue). The guiding principle is that of a proportion within a system of penalties between those imposed for different offences where these have a distinct place in a common-sense scale of gravity. This scale itself no doubt consists of

very broad judgments both of relative moral iniquity and harmfulness of different types of offence: it draws rough distinctions like
that between parking offences and homicide, or between 'mercy
killing' and murder for gain, but cannot cope with any precise assessment of an individual's wickedness in committing a crime. (Who
can?) Yet maintenance of proportion of this kind may be important: for where the legal gradation of crimes expressed in the relative severity of penalties diverges sharply from this rough scale,
there is a risk of either confusing common morality or flouting it
and bringing the law into contempt.

The ideals of Reform and Individualization of punishment
(*e.g.*, corrective training, preventive detention) which have been
increasingly accepted in English penal practice since 1900 plainly
run counter to the second if not to both of these principles of Justice or proportion. Some fear, and others hope, that the further in-
trusion of these ideals will end with the substitution of "treatment"
by experts for judicial punishment. It is, however, important to see
precisely what the relation of Reform to punishment is because its
advocates too often mis-state it. 'Reform' as an objective is no doubt
very vague; it now embraces any strengthening of the offender's
disposition and capacity to keep within the law which is intentionally brought about by human effort otherwise than through fear of
punishment. Reforming methods include the inducement of states
of repentance or recognition of moral guilt or greater awareness of
the character and demands of society, the provision of education in
a broad sense, vocational training, and psychological treatment.
Many seeing the futility and indeed harmful character of much traditional punishment speak as if Reform could and should be the
General Aim of the whole practice of punishment or the dominant
objective of the criminal law:

> The corrective theory based upon a conception of multiple causa-
> tion and curative rehabilitative treatment should clearly predominate
> in legislation and in judicial and administrative practices.[25]

Of course this is a possible ideal but is not an ideal for punishment. Reform can only have a place within a system of punishment
as an exploitation of the opportunities presented by the conviction
or compulsory detention of offenders. It is not an alternative General Justifying Aim of the practice of punishment but something the

pursuit of which within a system of punishment qualifies or displaces altogether recourse to principles of justice or proportion in determining the amount of punishment. This is where both Reform and individualized punishment have run counter to the customary morality of punishment.

There is indeed a paradox in asserting that Reform should "predominate" in a system of Criminal Law, as if the main purpose of providing punishment for murder was to reform the murderer not to prevent murder; and the paradox is greater where the legal offence is not a serious moral one: *e.g.*, infringing a state monopoly of transport. The objection to assigning to Reform this place in punishment is not merely that punishment entails suffering and Reform does not; but that Reform is essentially a remedial step for which *ex hypothesi* there is an opportunity only at the point where the criminal law has failed in its primary task of securing society from the evil which breach of the law involves. Society is divisible at any moment into two classes: (i) those who have actually broken a given law and (ii) those who have not yet broken it but may. To take Reform as the dominant objective would be to forgo the hope of influencing the second and—in relation to the more serious offences—numerically much greater class. We should thus subordinate the prevention of first offences to the prevention of recidivism.

Consideration of what conditions or beliefs would make this appear a reasonable policy brings us to the topic to which this paper is a mere prolegomenon: modern sceptical doubt about the whole institution of punishment. If we believed that nothing was achieved by announcing penalties or by the example of their infliction either because those who do not commit crimes would not commit them in any event or because the penalties announced or inflicted on others are not among the factors which influence them in keeping the law then some dramatic change concentrating wholly on actual offenders would be necessary. Just because at present we do not entirely believe this we have a dilemma and an uneasy compromise. Penalties which we believe are required as a threat to maintain conformity to law at its maximum may convert the offender to whom they are applied into a hardened enemy of society; while the use of measures of Reform may lower the efficacy and example of punishment on others. At present we compromise on this relatively new aspect of punishment as we do over its main elements. What makes this compromise seem tolerable is the belief that the influence which the threat and example of punishment exerts is often independent of the severity of the punishment and is due more to the disgrace attached to conviction for crime and to the deprivation of freedom which many reforming measures at present used, would in any case involve.

NOTES

———————————————————

1. See Barbara Wootton *Social Science and Social Pathology* for a clear and most comprehensive modern statement of these doubts.

2. In the Lords' debate in July 1956 the Lord Chancellor agreed with Lord Denning that "the ultimate justification of any punishment is not that it is a deterrent but that it is the emphatic denunciation of the committing of a crime" yet also said that "the real crux of the question at issue is whether capital punishment is a uniquely effective deterrent." See 198 *H. L. Deb* (5th July) 576, 577, 596 (1956). In his article "An Approach to the Problems of Punishment" (*Philosophy*, 1958) Mr. S. L. Benn rightly observes of Lord Denning's view that denunciation does not imply the deliberate imposition of suffering which is the feature needing justification (325 n.1).

3. Chapter IV.

4. K. Baier, "Is Punishment Retributive?" *Analysis*, March 16, p. 26 (1955). A. Flew, "The Justification of Punishment," *Philosophy*, 1954, pp. 291–307. S. I. Benn, *op. cit.* pp. 325–326.

5. Ewing, *The Morality of Punishment*, D. J. B. Hawkins, *Punishment and Moral Responsibility** (The Kings Good Servant, p. 92), J. D. Mabbott, "Punishment."* *Mind*, 1939, p. 153.

6. Mr. Benn seemed to succumb at times to the temptation to give "The short answer to the critics of utilitarian theories of punishment—that they are theories of *punishment* not of any sort of technique involving suffering" (*op. cit.* p. 322). He has since told me that he does not now rely on the definitional stop.

7. This generally clear distinction may be blurred. Taxes may be imposed to discourage the activities taxed though the law does not announce this as it does when it makes them criminal. Conversely fines payable for some criminal offences because of a depreciation of currency became so small that they are cheerfully paid and offences are frequent. They are then felt to be mere taxes because the sense is lost that the rule is meant to be taken seriously as a standard of behavior.

* Also reprinted in this volume.

8. Cf. Kelsen, *General Theory of Law and State*, 30–3, 33–34, 143–144 (1946). "Law is the primary norm which stipulates the sanction. . . . " (*id.* 61)

9. In evidence to the Royal Commission on Capital Punishment, Cmd. 8932. § 53 (1953). Supra, n.2.

10. *Op. cit.*, pp. 326–335.

11. *Op. cit.* It is not always quite clear what he considers a "retributive" theory to be.

12. Amount is considered below in Section III (in connexion with Mitigation) and Section V.

13. See J. Rawls, "Two Concepts of Rules," *Philosophical Review*, 1955, pp. 4–13.

14. Constitution of emperors Arcadius and Honorius.

15. In 1811 Mr. Purcell of Co. Cork, a septuagenarian, was knighted for killing four burglars with a carving knife. Kenny, *Outlines of Criminal Law*, 5th Ed., p. 103, n.3.

16. Misleading because it suggests moral guilt is a necessary condition of criminal responsibility.

17. *i.e.*, when breaking the law is held justified as the lesser of two evils.

18. Infanticide Act, 1938.

19. Homicide Act, 1957, sec. 2.

20. *Commentaries*, Book IV, Chap. 11.

21. Chap. XIII.

22. See Glanville Williams, *The Criminal Law*, Chap. 7, p. 238, for a discussion of and protest against strict liability.

23. Weschler and Michael, "A Rationale of the Law of Homicide," 37 *Columbia Law Review*, 701, esp. pp. 752–757, and Rawls, *op. cit.*

24. Some crimes, e.g., demanding money by menaces, cannot (logically) be committed unintentionally.

25. Hall and Glueck, *Cases on Criminal Law and its Enforcement*, 8 (1951).

Jerome Hall

The Purposes of a System for the Administration
of Criminal Justice

"Criminal law" in English-speaking countries refers primarily to the common law of crimes, and the fact that much of it has been enacted into legislation has not altered its paramount significance. This law, as is well known, has its roots in popular custom and belief and it extends rather definitely from the beginning of the thirteenth century to the present one. If the origin of the professional literature may be conveniently located in the work of Bracton, we also have an unbroken line of thoughtful analysis and scholarship in the criminal law from that brilliant century to our own times.

It is also clear that while many changes have been made, for example, by the invention of the offenses comprising "theft," changes in punishment, especially in the latter eighteenth and early nineteenth centuries,[1] and the rise in this century of probation, parole, presentence hearings and so on, there has also persisted a core of ethical principle in the criminal law which was progressively refined as knowledge advanced. It is expressed in an organized set of ideas; and this system of criminal law,[2] no less than that of the physical sciences, is evidence of a high order of imagination and rationality. Man is distinguished not only by such conceptual thought and reasoning but also by language, by a body of knowledge and the invention of instruments to apply it, by artistry and, last, though

This lecture, delivered at Georgetown University, Washington, D.C., October 9, 1963, inaugurated the Edward Douglas White Lecture Series given in the Law School in celebration of the 175th anniversary of the founding of Georgetown University, and is printed here with permission of the author and of the Georgetown University Law School.

far from least, by a sense of justice. Every one of these aptitudes and achievements is reflected in the law of crimes.

The values of the criminal law are specifically articulated in terms of certain disvalues classified as crimes and generally expressed as legal principles such as that of *mens rea*. The values of person, reputation, property, and political, economic, social and religious institutions are elucidated more precisely and realistically in the criminal law than in any other discipline including ethics as it is usually taught in universities. Only a narrow view of criminal law would find it merely an apparatus of compulsion or a set of prohibitions. The apparatus of compulsion is meaningful only in relation to actual harms which, in turn, are significant in relation to the voluntary conduct that produced them. And the theory that criminal law is a set of negative commands not only ignores the fact that the harms proscribed imply important values, it also ignores the fact that the restraint of penal law makes freedom possible. This is the meaning of "liberty under law," for unless potential criminals are restrained the law-abiding have no freedom.

How then are we to account for the fact that in a current mode of thought, "criminal law" summons an image of harsh reprisal against persons regarded as unfortunate deviants? It would require an intellectual history of the twentieth century to comprehend the events, motives, and movements of thought which have influenced many scholars to oppose punishment and to press for what they confidently believe would be a better day and way of dealing with deviants. They see themselves, and probably all of us, as sharing in the guilt of the criminal and believe that punishment is ineffective and degrading. They sense the tragic overtones of what existentialist philosophers and psychiatrists have discovered about the human situation and the deep recesses of human nature, and if they are religious, they feel all the more how much ought to be done to raise and rehabilitate those who have fallen by the wayside. Even if the criticism of criminal responsibility by some psychiatrists is only a strategy and rehabilitationism is, at best, less than half a penal policy, may they not help to bring about much needed reform?

I share the critics' doubts about many penal institutions and certainly do not wish to check compassion for unfortunates, including that for the victims of criminal attack; and I also think psychiatry, which occupies a central position in the reform movement, can help to soften rigorous moralistic attitudes towards many offenders even if it does not permit us to forgive the harms they inflicted not on us but on other persons. But the problem of crime cannot be solved or alleviated by the elimination of punishment, and I shall accordingly try to show why the movement to abolish punishment is a seriously mistaken one.

The dependence of punishment upon responsibility is widely recognized; those who would consign punishment to the lower depths of Madame Tussoud's museum, therefore, direct their criticism at its moral foundation. The most sweeping criticism takes the form of a "hard" all-pervasive determinism. One of the greatest trial lawyers of this century, Clarence Darrow, who was also a very compassionate man, put the case uncompromisingly: "Man," he said, "has no more power than any other machine to escape the law of cause and effect. He does as he must. Therefore, there is no such thing as moral responsibility. . . ."[3]

Darrow was much influenced by the philosophy of nineteenth century biology. But determinism in one form or another dates from the very dawn of Western history. It found dramatic expression in Greek tragedy centered in the omnipotence of the Fates, in whose grip even the gods were unable to change the course of destined events. In England, two centuries ago, Robert Owen, castigating what he regarded as theological and ethical nonsense concerning conscience, choice, and evil, viewed conduct as wholly determined by environment. Responsibility was, for him, merely a rationalization of social injustice and the prerogatives of the rich.[4] In this century, scientifically oriented psychiatry has added psychological determinism to the earlier varieties, and the implication is, again, the total elimination of responsibility.

One would not suspect from the unmitigated criticism of criminal responsibility by psychiatrists who profess to be disciples of Freud that Freud strongly supported legal institutions as essential to the preservation of civilization.[5] Some phases of his ethics are, of course, naturalistic, for example, the ego is described as making expedient compromises between instinctual demands and the inhibitions of a super-ego which represents not knowledge of morality but parental desire and control.[6] But the hypothesis of determinism was not employed by Freud when he shifted to a genetic perspective concerning the origin and successive stages of the conditions that culminated in the present illness. In this view, he could not help but think that what occurred was not inevitable. And in therapy, the deterministic hypothesis is obviously abandoned. The premise then is that the patient whose repressed traumatic experience has been discovered can help himself towards integration: "Where id was, there ego *shall* be."[7] Moreover, the Unconscious was not used by Freud as a substitute for explanation in terms of the conscious direction of conduct but as a theory to explain actions which could not be accounted for on rational grounds, such as lapses of memory and mistakes.[8] Much of the best current psychiatry is also opposed to the notion that repressed experiences inexorably determine human action, that men are puppets who dance to a tune played by a hidden orchestra.

Professional ethicists who espouse determinism in less implausible terms include a person's character among the principal causes of his action, which is thought to explain the sense of freedom. This does not alter the fact that being influenced by reasons, evidence, and criminal law must be distinguished from movements caused by observable phenomena which operate as their necessary and sufficient condition. More is involved, however, than so-called "determination by reason." For if a person's character determined his every action even in that more persuasive sense, there would be no such thing as turning over a new leaf, the lives of great men would be unintelligible, and the most interesting parts of history would be fairy tales. There would be no explanation of effort and the sense of effort which is experienced by persons who, avoiding the path of least resistance, rise above their present character to achieve a new level of moral insight. The criminal law expresses this ethics in imposing liability for homicide under great provocation, in excluding homicide from the scope of the doctrine of coercion, and in limiting the defense of necessity. Finally, if all actions were determined, including the decisions of judges and the imposition of sanctions as well as the behavior of criminals, talk about the *justification* of punishment would be meaningless.

The implausibility of the theory of pervasive determinism is reflected in the fact that critics of the criminal law are apt to concentrate on a narrower objective; they wish to eliminate criminal responsibility only to the extent that it is relied upon to support punishment. The relevant problems are raised in two interesting versions of this type of criticism of current criminal justice.

The first is the proposal for a treatment-board to determine the sentence and administer the treatment. As presented in 1954 by a psychiatrist on the staff of Sing-Sing prison, "the question of responsibility would not have to be raised, if the concept of management of the anti-social individual were changed from that of punishment . . . to a concept of the anti-social individual as a sick person, in need of treatment rather than punishment." He stated that the functions of the police and prosecutors "would remain essentially the same" as at present, namely, to collect "the data necessary for the proper determination of the guilt or innocence of individuals charged with these offenses. . . ." He also said:

> The function of the Courts would remain the same, with one notable exception. The problem of determining guilt or innocence, with all of the questions of proper procedure, adequate safeguards for the rights of the individual, proper presentation of evidence, etc. would continue unchanged. The major alteration in procedure would come in the handling of the guilty offender. Instead of meting out punishment . . . the court would order the offender to a treatment facility, for proper diagnosis and treatment. The length of time the offender would have to remain in such an institution would depend upon his psychological problems, and his response to treatment.[9]

In terms of this proposal, accidental, inadvertent, coerced or mistaken movements would still be distinguished from voluntary conduct, and the distinctive end-seeking or end-hazarding meaning of "cause" would also be retained as well as the principle of legality. These legal concepts imply responsibility, *i.e.*, capacity, authorship, and accountability, each of which is articulated in terms of certain rules, doctrines and principles of criminal law. The advocates of the above program thus assert (a) to the point of conviction, it is sound to proceed on the basis of a system built on the premise that responsibility and guilt are meaningful, and (b) this shall be ignored when the question of sanctions is faced.

Admittedly, the apparatus has performed the function it was designed to do, namely, to separate criminals from innocent persons. To maintain that this is a sound way of determining who needs non-punitive treatment is to ignore the fact that there is no significant correlation between the voluntary commission of harms or the gravity of the harms committed and the need for rehabilitation. The proposal therefore amounts to saying to accused persons: "we shall consider everything relevant to whether you are a responsible agent who in a moral-legal order should be held accountable for your actions," and then saying to them after conviction:

> . . . we shall completely ignore all that and consider only whether you require education and how to educate you, if we can. In a word, you are a convicted robber or murderer, a normal adult who has violated precious legally protected values of persons and personality. Regardless of that (or is it "therefore"?) we shall send you not to jail, but to Yale, our only regret being that attendance is compulsory.

It may be thought that such benevolence would out-weigh the value of justice, including that to the victims of criminal attack and the community, but one should consider the character of the benevolence actually envisaged. Then, too, there is the other extreme of the spectrum if the treatment-board decides that it will take twenty years or more to educate a petty thief.

We are therefore bound to ask: how far is it justifiable in a democratic society to impose coercive education based even on actual knowledge of rehabilitation, assuming it to be available? In addition, if murderers and robbers were confined for a relatively short time, what would be the effect of such individualized treatment on potential murderers and robbers; and if the old values somehow persisted, what would be the effect on the community of such an imbalance? Again, rehabilitation has limited applicability since some criminals are very superior persons, while many more are so fixed in their personality-structures that they cannot be rehabilitated. Are they to be exculpated because education is irrelevant or impossible? What would be the effect of all of this on the inmates of the institutions who, thinking fairness, equality, and loss of their freedom are important, find only discrimination in treatments that are wholly unrelated to the gravity of the harms committed? For these reasons rehabilitationism would be a very inadequate policy quite apart from the incompatability of the treatment-board reform with the ideas and law accepted to the point of conviction.

Much of the difficulty in current criticism of punishment is that, considered in isolation from the harm, the conduct, the causal connection, and legality, punishment can mean only the senseless infliction of suffering on a human being. But if there is a legal system which justifiably proscribes the commission of certain harms, this implies that the punishment of offenders is a *deserved* privation which, in addition, has or can have beneficial consequences. A legal system includes commands and sanctions; and the distinctive sanction of penal law is punishment—that sanction is the index of the kind of system or legal order that the criminal law is. Accordingly, since punishment cannot validly be isolated from the concepts that give it meaning and since they, in turn, have no other purpose than that of sustaining punishment, the actual issue raised in the proposal for a treatment-board is abandonment of the criminal law.

If that should ever happen, the questions now asked—what is criminal conduct or who are criminals, what harms must they have committed, what may be done to them?—would become literally "nonsense." But since men would not simultaneously be transformed into angels, the problems of harm-doing would persist. Social harms, however, are not labeled or perceptible entities, and what we now know as criminal harms is the achievement of a legal system representing centuries of thoughtful experience. The "natural crime" of the Italian positivists has long been abandoned in criminological research but, presumably, either that would be revived or an equivalent formula would need to be supplied. Someone would decide what is "natural crime" or anti-social conduct, who are dangerous persons or what conduct violates "the sound feelings of the people" or the attitudes of the treatment-board; and obviously, this would be done in the complete absence of *nulla poena sine lege*. Plato postponed his reform until a philosopher-king in Utopia would decide such questions with perfect justice. The proposal for a treatment-board has the advantage of simplicity. It simply abandons any quest for justice.

Based also on an optimistic appraisal of psychiatry and an equal distaste for retributive punishment is the discussion by Lady Barbara Wootton who, in her 1959 book, said that responsibility might be "by-passed" and later, in an article, she took a more definite position where only the time when responsibility would be allowed to "wither away,"[10] not the desirability of that, was left uncertain. Her position regarding responsibility was placed, however, on a very different foundation from that just considered. In her view, since "mental health and ill-health cannot be defined in objective scientific terms that are free of subjective moral judgments, it follows that we have no reliable criterion by which to distinguish the sick from the healthy mind."[11] This is devastating strategy, indeed, and if it is also sound, it is not only futile to raise the question of responsibility but one cannot even imagine the enormity of the injustice of the past trials of the issue of insanity.

The literature on "mental health"[12] and "mental disease" is voluminous, but since lack of conformity is not itself a valid ground for deciding that anyone is mentally ill (indeed it is said that rigid conformism may be symptomatic of illness), statistical definitions may be dismissed from consideration. So, too, operational definitions of "mental illness" in terms of the characteristics of persons being treated by psychiatrists or of persons in mental hospitals are based on the influence of mores, socio-economic status and motivation, accident and fraud;[13] moreover, this sort of definition puts the cart before the horse.

"Mental health," which is often used by psychiatrists as a synonym for "normality,"[14] has been defined as "full and free expression of . . . potentialities," "harmony" with our fellows, "good physical and mental constitution," "so well adjusted . . . that his emotional and intellectual balance cannot be disturbed by either internal conflicts or the vicissitudes of life," "able to fulfill the social role . . . in society," "optimum of growth and happiness," "confidence in himself," "accepts, works with, and enjoys other people," works and plays "with confidence and enthusiasm and with a minimum of conflict, fear and hostility," "adjustment . . . with a maximum of effectiveness and happiness," "able to love someone apart from himself," "ability to live . . . happily, productively, without being a nuisance," "happiness . . . but it should be lasting happiness . . . ,"[15] "flexibility," "capacity to learn," "maturity," "unity of personality," "cognitive adequacy," dominance of "conscious processes" and so on.[16] "Mental health" is usually regarded as only the absence of mental illness but sometimes "mental health" includes additional criteria, and a person is not regarded as "mentally healthy" even though he is not "mentally diseased."

In any case, "mental disease" has been defined as unhappiness, maladjustment, lacking in confidence, being a social nuisance, uncooperative, not integrated and in other terms that exclude the various specifications of "mental health." Inevitably, scholars who simply placed definitions of "mental health" and "mental disease" side by side on a common plane of equal significance and validity concluded that "mental disease" "means little more than deviation from some expected social behavior,"[17] that "the meaning of *mental disease* is personal to each practitioner,"[18] that it reflects each definer's *Weltanschauung*, the prevailing vision of the Good Life and so on.

In more radical appraisals, the concept of "mental disease" has been completely rejected because it is very misleading in suggesting that mental disease bears a close analogy to physical disease,[19] because the concept is unnecessary in the work of psychiatrists who only seek to help their patients solve personal problems,[20] or because it is merely a psychiatrist's convention shown, for example, in Freud's treatment of hysteria as a mental disease and not as mere malingering,[21] in a prison psychiatrist's statement that previously classified sexual psychopaths are psychotic,[22] and in that of others reversing their previous position and agreeing to testify that all psychopaths are mentally diseased.[23] When we add to all of this the fact that some psychiatrists say that everybody is mentally ill[24] and that others say that all criminals are mentally ill,[25] the confusion is compounded to the point of complete chaos.

Nevertheless, I suggest, with deference, that the thesis that responsibility must be "by-passed" and allowed to "wither away" is neither an implication nor a necessary consequence of the lack of an objective definition of "mental disease."[26] In the first place, it is necessary to distinguish the definition of "psychosis" from that of "mental disease." The boundless diversity of definitions of "mental disease" does not imply that there is equally wide disagreement regarding the definition of "psychosis."[27] In any case, it seems rather evident that most definitions of "mental health" and "mental disease" were not formulated with a view to distinguishing extreme mental illness from normal mentality but with that of distinguishing healthy persons from neurotic ones.

Second, the above thesis assumes that because psychiatrists are in hopeless disagreement in defining "mental disease," it is impossible soundly to separate those who are legally responsible from those who are legally incompetent. But the formulation of definitions is a philosophical, linguistic task, while particular decisions are a function of practical judgment. This is well illustrated with reference to the definition of such notions as "good" and "right," regarding which there is a large philosophical literature. But the lack of an adequate solution of this theoretical problem has not barred or invalidated innumerable daily decisions that certain conduct is good or bad. Again, able judges may be unable to articulate the meaning of "stare decisis" or "ratio decidendi," but this does not detract from their insight and skill in deciding specific cases. So, finally, the fact that there is no agreement among psychiatrists regarding the definition of "mental disease" does not imply that they do not agree that at least some persons are mentally diseased. The fact is that they not only do agree regarding that but some of them have said that laymen are equally able to recognize extreme cases of mental illness;[28] and the fact that they cannot give a satisfactory definition of "insanity," "know," "wrong" and so on does not invalidate their findings.

It should also be noted that in current discussions of the M'Naghten rule, the principal criticism of it is that the rule hinders the exculpation of some psychotic persons, not that the persons exculpated under it were not psychotic. If to this is added the opinions of psychiatrists who support the rule, the weight of expert opinion is very preponderantly that some mentally incompetent persons are very easily distinguished from normal persons; thus, the pertinent question is not the abandonment of criminal responsibility but whether a better rule can be formulated. In sum, even if the above argument for "by-passing" responsibility is taken to mean not only that there is no agreed definition of "mental disease," "psychosis" or any "syndrome" of either but also that in the actual recognition of psychotics, each psychiatrist and juror disagrees with every other psychiatrist or juror, what must be said is that the facts contradict that interpretation.[29]

Finally, even if psychiatrists were in complete disagreement about both the concepts of "mental disease" and "psychosis" and even if it were also true that no two psychiatrists agreed that any person was psychotic, it would still be a fact that for centuries laymen have recognized that some persons were psychotic. That is simply a fact of daily life, and the differences among psychiatrists regarding their interpretations or theories of those facts and their inability to agree that any person is psychotic (if that were the fact) would not invalidate the findings of juries any more than, to use the late Susan Stebbing's example, physicists' interpretation of desks as moving clusters of atoms invalidates either the ordinary use of the word "desk" or the meaning of the sense-data in the perspective of daily life.

It must be added that the agreement of psychiatrists as well as that of juries in the recognition of at least some psychotic persons cannot be explained by the laws of chance. There must be something about some persons which permits such common recognition of them as psychotic. I suggest that this is their extreme irrationality, and it is that which accounts for the common assessment regarding the M'Naghten rule, noted above. In sum, at least very irrational persons are easily recognized, and that alone makes it impossible to "by-pass" responsibility.

This is supported by other inferences that must be drawn from the above discussion. Once it is granted that some criminals, rebels, geniuses, and other deviants are not mentally diseased, neither definitions nor diagnoses of "mental disease" or "psychosis" can be based solely on behavior. Repeated acts of violence, robbery or stealing in themselves signify greater culpability, not illness. Accordingly, Lady Wootton suggested that the "irresistible impulse" thesis is fallacious because the argument is circular, reasoning from behavior to disease and from that to the behavior. She also recognizes that once the M'Naghten rule is abandoned, there is no defensible point to stop short of complete abandonment of criminal responsibility.[30] Unfortunately, she did not extend her inquiry to the point of discovering the weight of psychiatric opinion regarding the incidence of irrationality in serious mental disease.[31] But what has been made perfectly clear about definitions of "mental health" and "mental disease" is that they imply standards, and standards imply the cognition of standards. Accordingly, for many reasons I share Lady Wootton's view that the "irresistible impulse" hypothesis is fallacious. Moreover, since "the will" is regarded as a myth in current psychology and there is no way to measure the strength of impulses even if such evidence alone could be persuasive and since the notion that emotion surges forth in wholly unstructured ways is plainly untenable,[32] the only place to find independent criteria to support a diagnosis of extreme mental illness relevant to criminal responsibility is in impaired cognition or in a condition where that is included. For seriously impaired intelligence, of course, affects control of conduct and the other principal functions of the personality.

The next inference, which also allows one to introduce some degree of order into the vast literature on this subject, is that one must ask, by whom were "mental health" and "mental disease" defined and for what purpose?[33] The definitions have been provided by members of the mental health professions, lawyers, and a miscellaneous group interested in popular cultural concepts.[34] Many purposes were pursued, and there are also numerous sub-groups in each of the above classes—clinical psychiatrists, psychiatrists in hospitals, social psychiatric workers and many specialists such as psychoanalysts, organicists, psychobiologists as well as various schools of thought which intersect these groups such as Freudians, neo-Freudians, Jungians, Adlerites, Reichians, Rankians, existentialists and so on. So, too, there are legal definitions formulated in relation to whether the issue concerns capacity to make a will, consent to sexual intercourse, the conduct of a business, civil commitment, penal liability and so on. Obviously, there is no single correct definition of "mental disease" which will suffice for all purposes.

This leads to the final inference, namely, that the invalidity of an all-purpose definition does not exclude the possibility of specifying valid criteria with reference to a particular purpose. Some psychiatrists who treat patients suffering from abnormal fears, anxieties, sense of guilt, and so on seem to have been surprised in a criminal trial by questions concerning the defendant's capacity to know the rightness or wrongness of his conduct, although they were doubtlessly familiar with the other usual question, that concerning knowledge of the nature of his act, since the ego and "the reality principle" are involved. But does this indicate anything except that the purpose and perspective of the clinic are not apt or, at least, are not adequate to the social-legal purposes of a trial of criminal responsibility? This is the precise point emphasized in the criticism of their colleagues by forensic psychiatrists who are sensitive to the relevant social, moral and legal criteria. In sum, a perfectly impossible condition is created if everything said on some occasion or other by a variety of psychiatrists, psychologists of mental health, social workers and so on is pitched into a heap of theories, definitions, syndromes, and other opinions of "mental disease."

As has been indicated, the condition of solving any problem in this field is warranted selection, and if the problem is moral responsibility, that determines the basis of selection. It seems evident that, as stated by H. D. Lewis, "We must begin by noting an obvious condition of moral responsibility, namely that the agent should be aware of the distinction between right and wrong."[35] To this end, the M'Naghten rules do not purport to provide a definition of "insanity" but, in aid of recognition of insane persons, they specify certain criteria of extreme mental illness in terms of understanding everyday actions and values.

But, it will be asked, even after the question has been focused on what is relevant to the practical legal task of recognizing the seriously incompetent persons, does not one still confront the sharpest sort of disagreement among psychiatrists, for example, as regards the M'Naghten rules, the "irresistible impulse," "inability to conform" test, the product test, sociopathy and so on? The answer is obviously in the affirmative. But for the reasons stated above, this does not invalidate the current law or legal findings; it only requires that a defensible selection among contradictory opinions be made.

What we witness in this regard is not a "struggle between the rival empires of medicine and morality."[36] but only an attack on criminal responsibility by a small number of articulate forensic psychiatrists. Opposed to their opinion is that of other forensic psychiatrists and a very wide literature extending from some of Freud's writing to that by Heinz Hartmann and many others in the Freudian tradition, which strongly supports moral responsibility.[37] In addition, there are entire schools of psychiatry which place moral responsibility in the very center of psychiatric diagnosis and therapy.

If moral responsibility makes sense and there is very substantial psychiatric authority in the highest quarters which supports that, what more can be asked in dealing with this problem? Is one really expected to conjure up a solution which conforms both to the psychiatry that supports responsibility and also to the psychiatry which is either irrelevant or utterly negates it? Even less to be expected is that lawyers, laymen, and uncommitted psychiatrists should accept psychiatric opinions which are wholly incompatible with moral responsibility.

The validity and utility of the two principal classes required for the legal purposes—responsible and not responsible—do not, however, solve the problem of the borderline cases or that of so-called "diminished capacity." There is no way of eliminating the former problem although there is psychiatric support for the view that psychosis is a sharp breaking-off from neurosis, a marked difference in kind, not simply in degree; and on that premise, the class of "normal" or "normal neurotic" extends clearly to the point of the radical psychotic divergence. Even if the alternative theory is adopted, that there is no sharp break but, instead, a continuum from the core of normality to obvious psychosis, no evidence has been produced to establish the invalidity of the practical discharge of what may be called the primary function of the criminal law, to separate the innocent from the guilty. It must also be remembered that competent administration can attend to prisoners who become psychotic or are recognized as such in peno-correctional institutions. Finally, it can hardly be doubted that the problem of borderline cases would be greatly enlarged by the use of amorphous tests of insanity.

Despite the current agitation regarding the M'Naghten rules, the likelihood is that it is not the primary function of the criminal law that raises a serious problem but rather the equally important auxiliary function of management of the large number of convicted persons who suffer various degrees of impairment short of that warranting exculpation. The current concept of "diminished capacity" should effect sounder results than did the judgments in *Fisher* v. *United States* and *R.* v. *Ward*.[38] At present, however, "diminished responsibility" is only a rather awkward way of requiring that in trials of murder the defendant's actual, impaired state of mind be considered. What needs to be recognized is that the underlying principle is that of subjective guilt. There are other important areas of criminal law, especially other aspects of criminal homicide, where objective liability continues to reign supreme, and it is time that the feasibility of the admittedly more just subjective test should be investigated.

When the significance of "diminished responsibility" is generalized, it touches a large number of offenders, among them the seriously neurotic ones who are criminally responsible but entitled to mitigation and special treatment. This problem cannot be avoided by the supposition that there is no difference between some mental hospitals and some penitentiaries. Patients in hospitals sometimes suffer much pain but no one thinks of that as punishment since there is no question of their deserving the pain. Nor does the fact that sick persons are abused in some mental hospitals provide any reason to dissolve the difference, but only one for getting rid of a malevolent staff.

It is, instead, the difficulties in sentencing and the lack of proper institutions that raise serious questions in this regard. The extremely inadequate staffing of mental hospitals to the point where their complete abandonment was advocated in the 1958 presidential address to the American Psychiatric Association[39] reveals the unreality of current criticism of the criminal law based on the assumption that knowledge of rehabilitation as well as adequate staff and other facilities are available. There are very important additional problems in a democratic society which lacks colonies to which unruly persons may be transported, where unemployment is a constant problem, and where public works projects are regarded with disfavor. Any thorough program of crime prevention and management of vast numbers of impaired persons who cannot be rehabilitated is apt to meet constitutional prohibitions unless it is placed on a voluntary basis.

Within the limits of feasibility, what can be said of the "dilemma" raised by the fact that so far as an offender is culpable, he must be punished, but to the extent that he is lacking in normal capacity, he should be treated as a sick person? It is hardly possible or wise to require such persons to spend Mondays, Wednesdays and Fridays in a penitentiary and the rest of the week in a mental hospital or school; and although the European dual-track system of following punitive sanctions by corrective detention may be logical, it does not seem realistic and might easily be abused by the infliction of so-called "measures of social defense" which, in fact, are indistinguishable from the previous punishment.

A resolution of the dilemma is sought by some Utilitarians in the elimination of retributive punishment as a nasty business and of deterrence as ineffective, leaving only rehabilitation. Something was said previously about the inadequacy of a penal policy restricted to rehabilitation. Here we can only attend briefly to the validity of the current criticism of retributive punishment. In the first place it seems evident that the common law of crimes is a veritable monument to the success of human efforts to limit passionate retaliation and that the principle of legality is the only assured protection anyone has against the vengeance of his rulers. And although it is also obvious that it is impossible to impose sanctions that are identical with many criminal harms, who except Utilitarians has said that such literalism is a requirement of retributive justice? On the other hand, the problem of proportioning punishment to the culpability of the criminal is, indeed, a difficult one. But, again, the criminal law has made important contributions to the solution of this problem. There is a careful classification of objectively defined crimes, a system of precisely articulated ideas concerning degrees of guilt, the pre-sentence hearing and so on. Of course, it is impossible exactly to discover and evaluate all the conditions, temptations, resistance to temptation and so on which influenced any criminal action if "exactly" means "mathematically." But "precision" is a relative term, and not only criminal law but all other law, most of medicine and much else in practical life rest on comparisons and appraisals which physicists and engineers would regard as very crude; yet these disciplines serve important purposes to good effect. The fact that men are not omniscient is hardly a reason to abandon retributive punishment.

Questions about the precision of retributive punishment become significant only when comparison is made with the precision of alternative policies. A current assumption is that non-punitive treatment must be preferred on scientific grounds, that while any estimate of moral responsibility is bound to be mere guesswork and deterrence is almost equally uncertain, one is on firm ground when he treads the path of rehabilitationism. But if the desert of criminals is too difficult to ascertain even with the help of a highly articulated and carefully elucidated system of legal and moral ideas, how much less precise are measures of rehabilitation! What, indeed, is known about that?[40] Where is the evidence that psychiatrists rehabilitate criminals, or that they can determine with any degree of practical precision that a particular person is or is not socially dangerous? Where is the evidence that psychiatrists even do a better job than intelligent wardens who assume that criminals are responsible for their actions and who, therefore, treat them as moral agents?[41]

Nor is it correct to say that because retributive justice considers past action, it has nothing to do with the present and the future.

In an obvious sense, the past cannot be undone by anyone; it is irreversible, as Omar Khayyam said of "the moving finger." But the belief that the past is "done and finished" does not take account of the fact that in another sense, the past lives in the present and what men do may change their view of the past. In any case, the legally relevant question is, what should be done here and now? The just thing to do is to act in such a way that the wrong committed is condemned and the significance of that is expressed in an apt way. This means more, however, than saying that punishment is an expression of society's disapproval. Just as the harm committed was actual, not verbal, and as the criminal's guilt also exists or subsists in an intelligible sense, so, too, does punishment. Sensitivity to the subtle bonds upon which society depends is not compatible with the notion that retributive punishment is only "backward-looking." For when the breach in the moral fabric of society has been repaired or at least when all that can be done in that regard has been done, does not this affect us here and now? Does it not also influence the quality of future interpersonal relations? Accordingly, while retributive punishment is imposed because a criminal deserves it, the reason for such punishment must be distinguished from its effects.

If time permitted, it could also be shown that deterrence is not quite the ineffective policy that rehabilitationists would make of it,[42] even though retributive justice places sharp limitations on what may be done on deterrent grounds. And, of course, it is universally agreed that rehabilitation has an important place in any civilized system of criminal justice. A problem is raised by the conflict that sometimes arises between two or more of these phases of an inclusive policy, and if that problem cannot be solved simply by abandoning important aspects of that policy, we must look elsewhere for a solution.

What cannot be done arbitrarily and what is excluded by the logic that punishment is punishment while treatment is treatment, is as a matter of fact what the best peno-correctional administrators succeed in doing. Instead of perpetuating a logical dichotomy, they have discovered that there is a logic of the heart which, in practice, allows a combination of punishment and non-punitive treatment. They find that, consistently with the maintenance of discipline and the imposition of privations, it is possible to rehabilitate. If the administration of the institution is resourceful and humane, a con-

victed person can understand that he is deprived of his liberty because he voluntarily committed a harm proscribed by penal law,
that he must eat simple food and so on because he deserves that sort
of privation; and at the same time he can also understand that he was
not entirely at fault, that he has various impairments and that, in
any case, he is not subjected to abuse or indignity. Doctors, vocational guidance personnel, chaplains and others are employed in
eloquent testimony of public recognition of his human claims and
of the desire to assist him, not least by curing him, if possible, of
defects caused by lack of education, poor environment, traumatic
experience and the like.

Plato would have been startled by the current sharp dichotomy
of punishment and education since, for him, punishment was educational. For many other thoughtful persons, the notion that education must be pleasant from the outset even for cruel and unruly
persons seems a sadly mistaken pedagogy. One would avoid anything as dull or presumptious as a homily but perhaps a single question may be excused: If life is a bitter-sweet composite for the best
of men and if most human achievements require painful effort no
less than they are rewarded by gratification, why cannot this insight be employed in peno-correctional institutions by competent
administrators?

In the programs of some rehabilitationists, however, serious
dilemmas would be met because while the public and the offenders
would be concerned with law and justice, a treatment board could
ignore both of these values and decide, for example, that certain
petty harm-doers required long confinement while, at the opposite
extreme, that certain murderers or large-scale embezzlers did not
require any education. There are also cases where understanding
and remorse have followed the commission of a crime, and there is
no more to be done by anyone in the way of correction. In these
instances, there would certainly be a clash between the board's
theory on the one hand and retributive justice, the need for deterrence and public opinion. In the present law, however, this problem, while difficult, only requires the sort of decision which we
constantly make in daily life. Values conflict in countless situations,
and we follow certain guides, for example, that one value is "higher"
than others; we seek the maximum possible value. In recent years a
substantial consensus among students of penology has been reached

on this question, and the pertinent problem is: How can the various objectives of a democratic system of criminal justice be soundly fused?[43] This is certainly not an easy task, but current methods of carrying it out can be and are being improved; we are bound in any case to evaluate a penal policy and its administration only after comparison with proposed alternatives.

In the light of the above considerations, when we take another look at Lady Wootton's thesis that responsibility should be "by-passed" or allowed to "wither away," the image of this reification of responsibility is that of an obstruction in the road or of a noxious growth. We are here, and the obstacle or growth is out there, blocking the road to progress. But this is surely an unhappy metaphor not only because the "progress" seems to be towards an Erewhon in which human goals, like the spelling of words, would take very dubious directions, but also because the apt question is whether human beings are sometimes responsible for their actions. In this more realistic context, to speak of "by-passing" responsibility or allowing it to "wither away" means that we are to try to conceive of human nature and the criminal law in a very strange way.

Actually, it seems impossible even to visualize a world of human beings in which responsibility and punishment were non-existent. We can only infer that it would be a world in which no question was ever asked regarding the competence of anyone, where no distinction was made among the movements of a sleep-walker and end-seeking conduct. It would be a world where no one was ever blamed and, therefore, in which approval and reward had also disappeared. It would be a world without freedom, where no responsible psychiatrist could be found to discover its vague traumatic stirring in the unconscious racial mythology of a strange biped. In sum, it would not be a world of human beings.

In "by-passing" responsibility with evident reluctance, Lady Wootton takes comfort in the belief that social science will provide the knowledge required to deal with harm-doers scientifically. In this country the arrival of such science has been touted by trustful souls these past fifty years, echoing programs as old as those of Hume and Comte. But we are still, alas, without that sort of science; and we must carry on with what insight, experience, good-will and knowledge of criminal law we have, without illusions regarding human justice.

For the reasons discussed above, it is plain that the movement to restrict penal policy to rehabilitation rests largely on, and has probably been stimulated by, the fallacious assumption that punishment is always an evil. Since men can abuse their freedom and frequently do so, especially when they voluntarily harm human beings, punishment is necessary, as Freud and many other psychiatrists have recognized; and the only just punishment is retributive punishment.[44] It also gives meaning and vitality to the value of freedom. To speak of retributive punishment as a "necessary evil" is therefore inapt; one does not speak that way of modern surgery.

In immediate relation to the criminal law, responsibility is associated with punishment. But in the wide realm of freedom protected by the criminal law, responsibility connotes a way of life to be sought, maintained and enlarged. To be a responsible person in this sense is to be a mature participant in social life, sensitive to other persons' needs and potentialities as well as to one's own development. In this context, the principal purpose of a system of criminal justice is to preserve and improve the moral fabric of interpersonal relations upon which social life, freedom, and individual creativity depend. It is evident, I trust, from what was previously said about an inclusive penal policy, that those who have harmed their fellow men should be helped to participate in this value-cosmos.

The greatest teachers of the human race have opened our eyes and hearts to the beauty and poignancy of the moral life. As a student of criminal law, I have tried to add a footnote to the legacy they have bequeathed us. If we recognize and appreciate the ways of goodness and of right, we do that by virtue of the potency of human thought and feeling and the influence of their expression especially in the legal institution which protects our most precious values, not least our freedom for unbounded commitment and adventure.

NOTES

---

1. HALL, THEFT, LAW AND SOCIETY (2d ed. 1952).

2. HALL, GENERAL PRINCIPLES OF CRIMINAL LAW (2d ed. 1960); Hall, *The Scientific and Humane Study of Criminal Law*, 42 B.U.L. REV. 267, 269, 273 (1962).

3. Darrow, Crime—Its Cause and Treatment 274–275 (1922).
4. Owen, A New View of Society and Other Writings (1927).
5. Freud, Civilization and Its Discontents 59–60, 86, 87, 92 (1930). Freud, The Future of an Illusion 9, 11–13, 16, 19 (1928); See West, Conscience and Society 168–176 (1942). Cf. "Mental health cannot be defined without reference to processes of integration and we have emphasized before the integrative function of moral codes." Hartmann, Psychoanalysis and Moral Values 68–69 (1960).
6. Rieff, Freud, The Mind of the Moralist 275–277 (1959).
7. See the discussion of this Freudian epigram by MacIntyre, The Unconscious 93 (1958). (Emphasis added.)
8. The relevant distinction is between motive as "cause" in a factual or scientific sense, and motive as reason or ground of action. See Peters, The Concept of Motivation (1958).
9. Glueck, *Changing Concepts in Forensic Psychiatry*, 45 J. Crim. L., C. & P.S. 123, 127, 128, 128–29 (1954).
10. Wootton, Social Science and Social Pathology 248–49 (1959); Wootton, *Diminished Responsibility: A Layman's View*, 76 L.Q. Rev. 224, 239 (1960).
11. Wootton, Social Science and Social Pathology 227 (1959).
12. Jahoda, Current Concepts of Positive Mental Health (1958).
13. Swartz, *"Mental Disease": The Groundwork for Legal Analysis and Legislative Action*, 111 U. Pa. L. Rev. 389, 399–401 (1963). In the United States in 1948, in more than 10 percent of the admissions to mental hospitals, no mental disorder was reported. Eaton and Weil, Culture and Mental Disorders 232–33 (1955).
14. Redlich, *The Concept of Health in Psychiatry*, in Explorations in Social Psychiatry 142 (Leighton, Clausen, and Wilson, eds. 1957).
15. Wootton, supra note 11, at 211–14.
16. Redlich, supra note 14, at 152.
17. Wootton, supra note 11, at 223.
18. Swartz, supra note 13, at 391.
19. "[O]nly in the United States has psychoanalysis been defined as a medical specialty. Although physicians seem to be the preferred candidates everywhere, a significant proportion of European psychoanalysts are medically untrained." Szasz, The Myth of Mental Illness 95 (1961).
20. Marzolf, *The Disease Concept in Psychology*, 54 Psychological Rev. 211 (1947).
21. Szasz, supra note 19, at 77–84.
22. Glueck, supra note 9, at 125.
23. In re Rosenfield, 157 F. Supp. 18, 21 (D.D.C. 1957); see Campbell v. U.S., 307 F.2d 597, 598 and opinion by Burger, J., at 608–10 (D.C. Cir. 1962).
24. Karpman, *Criminal Psychodynamics: A Platform*, 1 Arch. Cr. Psychodynamics 96 (1955); Menninger, The Human Mind 460 (3d ed. 1946). Cf. "It is hardly necessary to dwell on the emptiness of an ideal notion of

mental health, perfect and unattainable." Lewis, *Health as a Social Concept*, 4 BRIT. J. Soc'y 113 (1953).

25. For references to studies showing that "no series of traits can distinguish deviants from nondeviants," see CLINARD, SOCIOLOGY OF DEVIANT BEHAVIOR 138–39 (rev. ed. 1963).

26. WOOTTON, supra note 11, at 227.

27. "The concept of mental disease is well-defined and beyond controversial interpretation only in a central core of the concept, i.e., with regard to such conditions in which the sense of reality is crudely impaired, and inaccessible to the corrective influence of experience—for example, when people are confused or disoriented or suffer from hallucinations or delusions." Waelder, *Psychiatry and the Problem of Criminal Responsibility*, 101 U. PA. L. REV. 384 (1952). See note 29 infra.

28. Redlich, *Definition of a Case for Purposes of Research in Social Psychiatry*, in INTERRELATIONS BETWEEN THE SOCIAL ENVIRONMENT AND PSYCHIATRIC DISORDERS 120 (Milbank Memorial Fund 1953); Redlich, *The Concept of Normality*, 6 AM. J. PSYCHOTHERAPY 551, 564 (1952).

29. "Although we do not possess any general definition of normality, either from a statistical or from a normative viewpoint, we, experts and public, are in reasonable agreement about extreme abnormality. But even extremely abnormal behavior has not been described in a fashion which will lend itself to an unequivocal definition." Redlich, *The Concept of Normality*, 6 AM. J. PSYCHOTHERAPY 551, 562–63 (1952).

30. WOOTTON, supra note 11, at 249.

31. "We take for granted the positive value of rational thinking and action for the individual's adjustment to the environment." Hartmann, *Rational and Irrational Action*, in 1 PSYCHOANALYSIS AND THE SOCIAL SCIENCES 379 Roheim ed. 1948).

32. Leeper, *A Motivational Theory of Emotion to Replace "Emotion as a Disorganized Response,"* 55 PSYCHOLOGICAL REV. 5 (1948); ARNOLD, EMOTION AND PERSONALITY (1960).

33. Redlich, supra note 14, at 139.

34. Gruenberg and Bellin, *The Impact of Mental Disease on Society*, in EXPLORATIONS IN SOCIAL PSYCHIATRY 346 (Leighton, Clausen, and Wilson eds. 1957).

35. LEWIS, MORALS AND REVELATION 47 (1951).

36. WOOTTON, supra note 11, at 339.

37. See, e.g., HARTMANN, supra note 5; Szasz, *Psychiatry as a Social Institution*, in PSYCHIATRY AND RESPONSIBILITY 13, 17 (Schoeck and Wiggins eds. 1962); Wertham, *The Psychiatry of Criminal Guilt*, in SOCIAL MEANING OF LEGAL CONCEPTS—CRIMINAL GUILT 167 (1950); Waelder, *Psychic Determinism and the Possibility of Predictions*, 32 PSYCHOANALYSIS Q. 15 (1963).

38. 328 U.S. 463 (1946); [1956] 1 All E.R. 565 (Crim. App.).

39. "The large mental hospital is antiquated, outmoded, and rapidly becoming obsolete. We can still build them but we cannot staff them; and

therefore we cannot make true hospitals of them. . . . I do not see how any reasonably objective view of our mental hospitals today can fail to conclude that they are bankrupt beyond remedy." Solomon, *The American Psychiatric Association in Relation to American Psychiatry*, 115 Am. J. Psychiatry 7 (1958).

40. "Clear evidence that reformative measures do in fact reform would be very welcome." Wootton, supra note 11, at 335.

41. "But on principle to divorce the idea of punishment by the state from moral considerations has, in the long run, proved a fatal error. Only on a moral basis is it possible to argue with the law-breaker." Mannheim, Dilemma of Penal Reform 21 (1939).

42. "In face of extremist claims about the futility of punishment it is well to remember such facts as: of 81,012 people committed to prison between 1930 and 1939 in the U.K. 65,147 (80.4 percent) had not returned there by 1941." Flew *Crime or Disease*, 5 Brit. J. Soc'y 50 (1954).

43. "[N]o penal philosophy can today be based upon one single idea. . . ." Mannheim, *Some Aspects of Judicial Sentencing Policy*, 67 Yale L. J. 971 (1958).

44. Hall, General Principles of Criminal Law, ch. 9 (2d ed. 1960).